SOCIAL STRUCTURE IN TWENTY-FIRST CENTURY

Social Structure
in
Twenty-First Century

By
Anil Saxena

ANMOL PUBLICATIONS PVT. LTD.
NEW DELHI - 110 002 (INDIA)

ANMOL PUBLICATIONS PVT. LTD.
4374/4B, Ansari Road, Daryaganj
New Delhi - 110 002
Ph.: 23261597, 23278000
Visit us at: www.anmolpublications.com

Social Structure in Twenty-first Century

First Published, 2005

ISBN 81-261-2137-8

PRINTED IN INDIA

Published by J.L. Kumar for Anmol Publications Pvt. Ltd., New Delhi - 110 002 and Printed at Mehra Offset Press, Delhi.

Contents

Preface

Social Structure is the formative setup of a Society or Social System. It evolves from history tradition, norms, culture and heritage. It is the basis of any society. In our country, the Social Structure is based on an age-old legacy, which we have inherited from our ancestors.

Indian society is one of the oldest in the world. A sort of social system was framed by wise people in ancient times. During medieval period, this structure was reformed and polished by the contemporary sociologists and scholars. No doubt, it was influenced by the ruling class and other forces at work.

Later, in modern times, the impact of the Westrerners changed the social conceptions altogether. The British, not only gave this country a new system of governance, but they also influenced it with their cultural, civilizational and academic advances. In fact, it was a new avtar of society in India, which emerged after the confluence of traditional Indian and modern western cultures .

After independence, Indian society evolved and cultivated itself further.

Growing urbanisation and social mobility changed the Social Structure further. Now, the present society in India is a cosmopolitan society, a mixture of many a regional culture, capped by western trends.

Recently, our society has become greatly exposed to American culture, way of life and the materialistic approach in particular, which has shaped it into an ultra-modern social, fabric. Ironically, our new social standards, are deprived of morality and spirituality. Our education system is going the European way at a fast pace, which is not a good sign.

This situation alarms the sociologists, social workers and of course all those concerned with the new threatening trends. The same concern has motivated the undersigned to accomplish the task, resulting in this comprehensive book on Social Structure. It covers all the factors at work, in details and provides a pleasant, but, awakening reading to all those, who may prefer to go through this modest work.

Editor

1

Introduction

Era of Change

In India, impact of modern Western-culture gave birth to a new awakening in India. The 18th and 19th centuries witnessed a great ferment of new ideas throughout Europe which influenced the British outlook towards India to a great extent. It was the age of the French illumination when the spirit of rationalism and individualism dominated European thought. It proclaimed supremacy of reason over faith. The great French Revolution of 1789 with its message of liberty, equality and fraternity generated powerful democratic sentiments and unleashed, the force of modern nationalism. The most important characteristics of the new thought were rationalism or faith in reason, and humanism or love of man. A new ideology burst forth upon the static life, moulded for centuries by a fixed set of religious ideas and social conventions. It gave birth to a critical attitude towards religion and a spirit of inquiry into the origin of state and society. Indian civilization was condemned as static, it was looked down upon with contempt. Indian customs were considered uncivilized, Indian institutions corrupt and decadent, and Indian thought narrow and unscientific. The doctrine of humanism led them (the English) to desire the improvement of Indian people. The humanism of these men was aroused by the social injustice of such institutions as the caste system and untouchability, such customs as Sati, and the low status of women in general and of widows in particular. Their scientific minds were also outraged by the many superstitions that gripped the minds of the Indian people. The answer to India's ill, appeared to lie in the introduction of modern Western sciences, philosophy, literature, in all-out rapid modernization. The. period following the Governor-Generalship of Lord Corn-wallis was the seed time for new India. During the Governor-Generalship of Lord William Bentinck, Indian began to assert themselves for their rights. Then commenced the protestant movement in the realm in religion, and new trend in the field of literature. These Indians of new breed drew their inspiration from the West. It was the lovely dawn of a new era the commencement of new India. India passed from the medieval to modern age. The close contact with the West, effected through the advent of the British, the exertions of the well-known educationists like David Hare, missionaries like Carey, and administrators like Macaulay brought about a radical change in political, social and religious outlook of the Indians. The Christian missionaries who never failed to point their fingers of scorn at ancient Hindu religious and social institutions were educators as well as crusaders in India. They supported a programme of Westernization. The British were more successful in helping to revolutionize the intellectual life of India through the introduction of modern education. English education broke the intellectual isolation of the Indian. A new world of ideas revealed itself to the wondering gaze of the young Indian students in education and social institutions. In the struggle against medievalism, it laid the foundation of modern democratic, scientific and rationalist culture. In its struggle against the religious obscurantist ideology of the middle ages, it forged the weapon of modern rationalism. Britain produced giants of thought in every sphere of social endeavour. It produced a galaxy of thinkers such as Darwin, the discoverer of one of the most valuable scientific theories, the theory of evolution of organic life, spencer the profound sociologist, Locke, the great philosopher, J.S. Mill, an exponent of individual liberty, Adam Smith, the father of modern economic sciences, Newton, the brilliant mathematician, physicist, Carlyle, critics of social injustices, B. Shaw, the master of social satire and a host of others. These giants of thought have contri-buted to the building up of the rich modern world culture. The study of the

English language provided on opportunity to the Indians to study the social libertarian, natural scientific and rationalist philosophical literature in that language. This study helped to build up a democratic and rationalist outlook. The intelligentsia exercises great ideological influence on the people. The most important impact of Western culture on India was the replacement of blind faith on current traditions, beliefs and conventions, by a spirit of rationalism which seeks to inquire and argue before accepting anything. The English education brought about a great change in social and religious outlook.

The impact of Western education and intellectual interchange was a critical long-term force in the making of the new, modern Indian culture as it emerged in the 19th century. The new mentality was conspicuously different from that of the Mughal twilight. The notions of justice and reason received wider currency as contemporary intellectuals and ideologies advocated a more just, rational and critical reordering of the universe. The gamut of experiences which is after collectively described as the awakening started in Bengal at the beginning of the 19th century. A degraded Indian society was modernized by the civilizing mission of the West. Western impact on the Indian mind was propelling force that drove dominant currents within Indian society to the surface, starting a critical spirit of self-enquiry. Western impact was largely channelled through agencies such as the educational system, law courts, missionary enterprise and the press. In Bengal, the rationalizing effect of English education at first manifested itself more in religious and social ideas, but it was not long before it profoundly affected also the political consciousness of the people. The Brahma Samaj was the outcome of the first, and it has often been claimed that it had contributed to the ideals of political freedom'. This is, however, not to suggest that it was Western impact alone that changed Indian society. It was only an element that accelerated changes that were affecting both Hindus and Muslims of India. Ranade pointed out, No more foreign grafting can ever thrive and flourish unless the tender plant on which the grafting is to be made first germinates and sends its roots deep into its own indigenous soil. When the living tree is thus nourished and watered, the foreign manure may add flavour and beauty to it.

The Portuguese were the first Europeans power to expand into India. Their activities were essentially an extension of the Christian crusade against Islam, and in search for trade, while the 17th century marked the Zenith of India's medieval glory, the 18th century was a spectacle of corruption, misery and chaos. The glory of the Mughals had vanished, life had become insecure, and intellectual curiosity had given way to superstitious beliefs. In this atmosphere, literature, art and culture could barely survive. On the other hand, this was the age of enlightenment, and Europeans had gone through a process of rebirth. Thus, the impact of the Western culture on India was that of a dynamic society on a static one. The West provided India with the necessary impetus to for a real stock taking and reform. The introduction of Western education, culture, and scientific technique gave traditional Indian life a Jolt, shocking Indians into a new awareness and vitality in thought and action. Long dormant intellectual impulses emerged and a new Indian spirit was born. Western influences became effective in India mainly through the British, who were the pioneers of a new technological and industrial civilization. On the other hand, the earliest stirrings of the Indian cultural renaissance appeared under the leadership of Raja Ram Mohan Roy, who made the first organized efforts to adopt Hinduism to the new situation. A devout Hindu Ram Mohan Roy inspired by the vedantic philosophy, he was also deeply influenced by Sufism and was an admirer of Christianity and Western thought, especially the writings of Montesquieu, Blackstone, and Bentham. Raja Ram Mohan Roy challenged the current religious beliefs and social practices of the Hindus as not being in consonance with their own scriptures. The standard of revolt he thus raised against the medieval tyranny of dogmas unleashed forces which created what may be called Modern India and makes him worthy to rank by the side of Bacon and Luther. According to Buch:

> "The first assumption of Raja Ram Mohan Roy is that there is a universal reason at work in nature and in society, and that religions in their pure and pristine form are the expression of that reason in man. The task of reason today is to disentangle the elements of permanent and universal truth in each faith from the

> mass of accretions which has gathered round them and to return to them as the basis of our religious life."

He opposed the worship of images of Gods and Goddesses, denounced Sati, Polygamy, and abuses of caste system, favoured remarriage of Hindu widows. He tried to reconcile individual reason with ancient scriptures and individual conscience with social authority.

The new spirit of humanism and rationalism stimulated Indian thought and literature enormously. No longer was Indian writing appended to theology, mythology, and scholasticism. No Gods and Goddesses descended from heaven and played a part in human life. Man now occupied the foremost place, starting this course of life without divine help. Soon new ideas began to fill old patterns and Indian thinkers were inspired not only by the renewed spirit of humanism but also by the French revolutionary spirit of liberty and equality. The emerging ethos of enlightened rationalism assumed in Bengal in institutional shape for the first time in the Hindu College of Calcutta. But the inherent and incipient radicalism of the liberal Bengali youth could hardly be restrained as they rallied round the college teacher Henry-Louis-Vivian-Derozio. The subsequent expulsion of Derozio did not restrain the rising tide or of rationalism which continued to prevail with increasing strength. The establishment of the Hindu College was followed by the founding of the "School Book Society" and "the school society" which played a key role in improving school education in Calcutta. The choice of subjects of study and their emphasis was new English, Mathematics, Geography and natural sciences. The establishment of other higher institutions of learning and the Indian newspapers contributed considerably to the creation of a new and more critical public opinion. In Bombay a similar function was performed by the Elphinestone College which in many respect was the counterpart of Calcutta's Presidency College. The college was instrumental in creating an intelligentsia in Bombay which sustained modern social and political movements in Western India. In Madras city the Presidency College became an important centre. In North India after having lagged behind for more than half a century, the Muslims led by Syed Ahmed Khan joined forces to design and establish at Aligarh the Mohammedan Anglo-Oriental College. The implication of the new educational system were far reaching. This imbibing of world culture helped the educated Indian not only to reinforce his knowledge but also to develop a world outlook and perspective. They were able to get rid of the isolationist conception. Besides, the intelligentsia exercises great ideological influence on the people. In India, advanced intellectuals who imbibed modern scientific world knowledge through their study of English began to transmit it to their people. The educated Indians, who studied English/democratic literature and imbibed its democratic principles, felt inspired to rebel against the reactionary social institutions and world outlook of a bygone era, such as caste and authoritarian social philosophies which sought to enslave the individual and suppress his free initiative. The study of the English provided an opportunities to study the social libertarian, natural scientific and rationalist philosophical literature and this helped to build up a rationalist outlook. The rationalist philosophy became an instrument to liberate the mind from dark superstition. The reawakening provided a strong stimulus to the vernacular literature to progress. Bengal took the lead in this sphere. The first great distinguished writers in Bengali were Ram Mohan Roy, A.K. Dutta, Madhusudan Dutta, Rajnarain Bose, Iswar Chandra Vidyasagar, Debendra Nath Tagore, Bankim Chandra. Various aspects of vernacular literature were improved considerably. The influence of Europe had also enriched Indian literature by deve-loping a keen interest and deep regard for the historic past of India. The songs of Bharati, Tagore, works of famous Hindi poets Bharatendu Harischandra and Maithilisharan Gupta, the songs of Urdu poet Iqbal were intensely nationalist. Through the English language the Western literatures were thrown upon to Indians and a flood of ideas was let loose. Through translation, the Indian could study the philosophical system of Democritus, Plato, Aristotle, Descarts, Kant, Compte, Hegal, Karl Marx. He could also assimilate the social theories of Plato, Holbach, Helvetius, Diderot, Voltaire, St. Simon, Marx and Engles, anarchist Bakunin, Syndicalist proudhon and others. Indians could enrich their scientific knowledge by studying the works of Mathematicians, Physicists, and Philosophers of world fame. They could also enjoy the artistic creations of such non-English literary artists of the first rank as

Chekhov, Dostoevski, Turgenev, Gogol, M. Gorky, Emile Zola, Anatole France, Victor Hugo, Gpethe, Isben and others.

After the death of Rammohan Roy, the Brahmo Samaj remained the focus of the Hindus renaissance. Debendranath Tagore, continued the monotheistic tradition. He proclaimed the supremacy of human reason, which was in its original intuitions really the eternal light of God reflected through the mind of man, over all scriptures and hallowed injunctions. He founded the Tattvabodhian Sabha, which played a significant role in the cultural revival of India. Keshab Chandra Sen, who followed him, carried this protest still further and proclaimed the absolute supremacy of individual conscience over every form of outside authority in the determination of human conduct. He widely read in Western philosophy he was especially attached by Carlyle and Emerson. He believed that many Hindu rituals and usages could be reinterpreted and restored with new symbolic meaning to suit the Brahmo Samaj. He was a relentless opponent of hypocrisy, insisted on social purity and upright individual conduct. He was the first Brahamo Samaj leader to advocate the welfare and rights of men, to attempt a new interpretation of history, and to evolve a modern prose style in Bengali. According to L.S.S.O' Malley:

> "The spread of Western education and ideals stimulated movements within Hinduism designed to preserve its essential principles and at the same time to remove excrescences which were opposed not only the spirit of Hinduism but also to the ideals spread by Western culture. What is the spirit of Hinduism? What are its essential principles? The spirit of science is not dogmatic certainly, but the disinterested pursuit of truth, and Hinduism is infused by the same spirit. Fixed intellectual beliefs mark off one religion from another, but Hinduism sets itself no such limits. It is comprehensive and synthetic, seeking unity not in a common creed but in a common quest for truth. Hinduism is more a way of life than a form of thought. It insists not on religious conformity but on a spiritual and ethical outlook in life. It is fellowship of all who accept the law of right and earnestly seek for the truth".

In the 19th century Bengal the most important persons were Bankim Chandra Chatterjee, the great novelist, and Madusudan Datta, the first epic writer of Bengal. In subsequent years, the field of fiction was dominated by R.N. Tagore, and Sarat Chandra Chatterjee. Regarding Hindi, it was under the impact of the West that Hindi prose literature came into existence, although the language had its prose writers in Goraknath and Jyotiswar in the 14th century, and in Sadasukhlal and Inshaha Allah Khan in the 18th century. In Maharashtra Vishnu Shastri laid the foundations of Marathi drama. In Gujarat, Dayaram composed love lyrics. Both Gujarat and Marathi literatures profited appreciably by the models set up by the Bengal literary revival. Regarding Urdu, its poetry was as its height of popularity. Also, the growth of Urdu prose was a marked feature very famous poets flourished during this period, the most important being Ghalib. In the field of philosophy and science also, the contributions were great. In the realm of philosophy India received from the West philosophies of materialism, realism and idealism and it created intellectual ferment in the educated classes. Modern Indian literature are the products of Western impact. Contact with the European spirit through English literature, gave a new course to the literatures in modern India. This contact with the Europeans mind first began in Bengal and by the middle of the 19th century, the modernization of the mind of Bengal and of Bengali literature had already begun. European methods of literary approach were eagerly adopted. The European type of blank verse, and verse from like the Italian sonnet were introduced. There was hardly any aspect of life and society which was not deeply affected by the West. The ideals and method of education underwent a revolutionary change. Besides, under the influence of the West many Indian vernacular printing presses were setup and many newspapers in Indian languages were started. In 1780, Hicky commenced the publication of the Bengal Gazette in English. It was followed by the first Indian vernacular newspaper Bengal Samachar in 1816. The news papers and periodicals of the Indian languages brought the Indians into close contact with the various countries of the world. In the words of L.S.S. O' Malley:

> "With the growth of the British power the old order weakened... Many were dazzled by the civilization of

> West. A few were so enchanted by it they took to Western culture. Proclaiming the futility of India's social and religious institutions, they wished to rebuild the structure of national life on new foundations. The newly educated classes used Western learning for improving their own culture and adapting it to the new impulse created by contact with the West."

Social Dimensions

Rationalism means the type of philosophy that regards reason as the chief instrument and test of knowledge. Rationalism in philosophy is primarily a theory of knowledge, as opposed to empiricism, which holds that all knowledge, comes from perception, it maintains that the most important part of knowledge comes from intellectual insight. At the same time rationalism is that system of philosophy which assets that human reason unaided is competent to attain objective truth. Rationalism have stressed the superiority of the deductive over all other methods in point of certainty. Further, rationalism is a comprehensive expression applied to various theoretical and practical tendencies which aim to interpret the universe purely in terms of thought or which aim to regulate individual and social life in accordance with principles of reason. In individual and social life rationalism seeks to establish universal principle for the regulation of human behaviour. The man of the middle classes learned to shape life rationally on the basis of his own foresight. Rationalism come to play a new role in political and social life.

According to the extreme rationalist doctrine all the truth of physical science and history could in principle be discovered by pure thinking. Rationalism came to signify a skeptical or anti-religious attitude. Rationalism is conceived as the ally of liberalism in the struggle against religious intolerance. It was first explicitly formulated by Plato and it reached its highest development in the 17th century. It is the rationalist spirit which urges us to approach nature as masters rather than as pupils. Ethical rationalism was also first developed by Plato under the inspiration of Socratic dictum, virtue is knowledge. By the end of 19th century rationalism had become an anti-religious movement, after combined with empiricism and materialism and identified with practically atheistic forms of agnosticism. On the other hand, Humanism is the attitude of mind which attaches primary importance to man and to his facilities, affairs, temporal aspirations and well-being. The humanists of renaissance asserted the intrinsic value of man's life before death and the greatness of his potentialities. It is basically a philosophical outlook centred on the autonomy of man as a dignified rational beings, possessing within, himself the sources of truth and right. Its goal is man's greatest good in this finite existences. Its spirit is secular, liberal and tolerant. Humanism controlled man, stresses his essential worth and dignity, expressed invincible faith in his tremendous creative potential, and proclaimed freedom of the individual and his inalienable rights. It was centred on a notion of man that did not reject earthly joy, recognized the dignity and beauty of the human body, opposed religious asceticism, and defended man's right to pleasure and satisfaction of earthly desires and requirements. The humanists rejected religious mortification of the flash and withdraw from the world. They urged man to seek joy on this earth rather than, an after life which the Church advocated. According to protogaras man is the measure of all the things. The renaissance humanists developed the new learning, whose essence was the revival of the true classical spirit. It has been antagonistic to positive and authoritative religious beliefs. Revolt against injustice, cruelty and unnecessary hardship was to be a sure mark of humanistic spirit. Scientific humanism aims to supplant religion and make scientific knowledge the instrument of freeing man and enhancing his life.

Humanism had its roots in the earlier period but became dominate in the renaissance. With the growth of urban society the ecclesiastical leadership of intellectual, aristocratic and even religious life declined. A literate found the values of monastic culture to restrictive, scholasticism was a theology that did not speak of the human conditions, education was the preserve of clerics and humanism was a revolt against all this. The humanists is more interested in the material world around, in the contents of the physical universe then in Gods, angles or demons, whereas the medieval man were more interested in Gods, angels or demons. The medieval man regarded life as a painful preparation for a happier life which, they thought, would come after death, whereas the humanist is concerned to make the most of his brief life happier. This transformation which the renaissance inaugurated may be termed as making the passage from religion to secularism. The new learning also promoted individualism, that is a satisfaction with oneself and a glorying in one's achievement. This is quality of individualism, as practised by humanists, was in sharp contrast with the self-abnegation of the medieval ages. This particular perception of man was reflected in the age's 'hardy explorer's and colonists, daring pirates and freebooters, gambling middlemen, all leading to a total repudiation of established traditional authority. we can trace the origin of individual in the social contract theories of Locke and Rousseau. But it is in the 19th century that the individualist thought flowered in its proper shape. It was J.S. Mill and H,. Spencer who developed individualism as a social and political theory. They were great advocates of individual freedom and happiness. Another group that attracted intellectuals was Deism. The deists believed in a God as the creator but not as the redeemer. The essence of religion is awe and reverence before the rationality and perfection of the universe. Voltair was the epitome of the new enlightment. To him all priests were imposters, all miracles were illusions and all revelation were human inventions. Empiricism arose as a reaction to scholasticism. It may be defined as an approach which holds that the sensory experience is the only source of knowledge. It affirms that all knowledge is founded on experience. Francis Bacon, one of pioneers of empiricism emphasized the inductive method. This method relied for knowledge on observation, experimentation, collection of data and their classification for their discovery of general laws. It paved the way for the advancement of modern science. At the same time, liberalism arose as a reaction against the authority of the feudal barons, the Govt. by aristocrats, and the power of the clergy. Broadly speaking liberalism in its classical sense stood for the liberty of the individuals, democratic institution and free enterprise. Liberalism came into existence as a consequence of the struggle of the middle classes against feudalism and the power of the clergy. The economic theory of liberal thought was mainly derived from Adam Smith's wealth of Nations, which was a theory of free trade, free market etc. The wave of liberalism passed through England affected even her distant administration of India. Various 'ism' and Western thought like rationalism, individualism, Humanism etc. had a deep impact in the mind of the Indian intellectuals. The educated Indians who studied democratic principles, felt inspired to rebel against the reactionary social institutions, such as caste and authoritarian social philosophies which sought to enslave the individual and suppress his free initiative. The study of the English language provided an opportunity to study the social libertarian, natural scientific and rationalist philosophical literature in that language. This helped to build up a democratic and rationalist out look. The study of the English language unfolded the treasure of democratic thought crystalized in precious scientific works.

Raja Ram Mohan Roy was essentially a democrat and a humanist. He was deeply influenced by the monotheism and anti-idolatry of Deism of Sufism, the ethical teachings of Christianity and the liberal doctrines of the West. He began to take a keen interest in Europeans politics, specially in the course of the French Revolution. He tried to interpret and assimilate into himself the highest elements of Christianity, and modern rationalism and Humanism. He stood for a rational approach to religion. He wanted his countrymen to accept the rational and scientific approach and the principle of human dignity and social equality of all men and women. His plea for state support to Western education seeking and enlightened system of instruction, freedom of the press etc. were inspired by a faith in reason and rational argument. The Brahmo Samaj, under his leadership launched an offensive against the caste system branding it as undemocratic and inhuman. Ram Mohan Roy was an admirer of the liberal democratic culture of the West. He relied on the power of human reason which was in his view was the final touch stone of any doctrine, Eastern or Western. The best example of his life-long crusade against social evils was the historic agitation he organized against the inhuman custom of women becoming Sati. He was a stout champion of Women's right. He opposed the rigidities of the caste system. Infact he inaugurated the modern age in India. Derozio, and Anglo-Indian teacher inspired his students to think rationally and freely, to question all authority and to love liberty, equality and freedom. Akshay Kumar Dutta, editor of the Tatva Bodhini Patrika wrote several didactic works, where, without denying the existences of God, he sought arguments in its favour in the grand book of nature itself. His subsequent work on Indian religions was a critical sociological examination of religious sects in a spirit of rational and enlightened enquiry. In all these deliberations compete's positivism and utilitarian doctrines constituted important influences. Tompain's "age of reason" and "rights of man", Macaulay's "essays" were widely read. From these were derived new nations of reason, Justice and utilitarian concerns of welfare. Educated Indians came to appreciated that Europe had conquered the world of knowledge. Europe thus infected India with the curiosity to discover the inner working of all phenomena by observations and experiment. Reason had therefore to be empirical and scientific for it was reason alone that showed the way to progress. The development of social protest was evident in the proliferation of plays after the mutiny—Nil Darpan, Zamindar Darpan etc. Iswar Chandra Vidyasagar was a great humanist who possessed immense sympathy for the poor, and the oppressed. His humanism was aroused to the full by the suffering of the Hindu widows. He also protested against child marriage and campaigned against polygamy. The Bethun school founded in Calcutta was the first fruit of the powerful movement for women's education. Conscientious protest evolved eventually into political nationalism. Bankim too educated from national enquiry to a profoundly emotional patriotism, note the passion for the motherland in Anandmath. Meanwhile several educated youngmen in Maharashtra formed the students literary and scientific society. The society organized lectures on popular science and social questions. Gopal Hari Deshmukh advocated the reorganization of Indian society on rational principles and modern humanistic and secular values. K.T. Telang wrote on political and social issues drawing inspiration from Western ideologues like Spencer and J.S. Mill. Similarly one of the greatest rationalist thinkers of Modern India, Gopal Ganesh Agarkar, was an advocate of the power of reason. He criticize any blind dependence on tradition. A significant feature of humanism was expressed in a new humanitarian morality which included the motion that humanity can progress and has progressed and that moral values are those which favour human progress. At the same time, the popularity and accessibility of Western literature influenced indigenous literary enterprise. Rise of proseform, fiction, drama, biography and history, essays and articism were the most important by-product of the time. Bankim's first novel Durgeshnandini had striking similarities to Scott's Ivanhoe. R.C. Dutt's Rajput Jivana Sandhya also testified to the new spirit of the age. So there is a growth of critical consciousness among the Indians was a process that absorbed new elements adopted itself to new needs and restated itself in new terms.

2

Unit of Society

There is poetic justice in sociologists' writing on the concept of man. Did not sociology in several ways attempt to abolish man from its theoretic constructs? The exhortation for 'bringing man back-in' (Homans, 1964), the nostalgia for the 'lost science of man' (Becker, 1971), and the research of the 'images of man' in the traditions of sociological theorizing (Mills, 1960) represent both, a feeling of guilt among sociologists as well as the deepening crises in the paradigms of sociology. Central to this is the debate in sociology on the ontological and ethical nature of man. The crisis is both epistemic and historical. Epistemologically, the emergence of sociology as a discipline marked a degree of obsolescence of the traditional cognitive categories, philosophical premises and worldviews for the understanding of human condition. Historically, the process of this obsolescence was immanent in the material conditions and social forces generated by the western society, which gave birth to sociology following industrial revolution. Sociology to this extent assumed the role of a demystifying discipline for which it was a matter of course to call into doubt or even to reject many traditional categories and value premises about the nature of society and man. But paradoxically, sociology could not, despite this radicalism of its premises and categories, disburden itself from its past.

Man being Important

The past of sociology, as of most other social sciences, lies in meta-physical-philosophical traditions of the Graeco-Roman origin, theological metaphysics of the middle ages and the social philosophical contributions of the periods of Renaissance and the Enlightenment. It is indeed a highly burdensome heritage of paradigms. In many ways sociological concept of man was a deliberate refutation of the notion of man as projected through purely rationalistic theory of man in metaphysics and the hierarchical theory of man in theology. Nevertheless, many critical tensions in the notion of man in sociology did survive because sociology's meta-theoretical separation either from philosophy or theology has never been complete. On the contrary, during the past few decades, one could discern tendencies of differentiation in sociological paradigms which are indeed rooted directly in philosophy. There has particularly been a revival of interest in neo-Platonic ideas in sociological constructions in the writings of sociologists like Max Horkheimer and Theodore Adorno (1973) and a resurgence of linguistic philosophical approach in sociology (cf. Gellner, 1965; Winch, 1951; Cicourel, 1973, etc.).

The reason behind these developments bears close connection with the concept of man in sociology which in course of its classical commitment to positivistic theory and emphasis on raw empiricism fragmented and intrumentalized the notion of man. It also led to a refraction in the vision on man and society with the loss of the critical (moral) perspective. This perspective existent in ethics and philosophy had thus to be reinstated. Horkheimer and Adorno write:

> Thus, the fundamental difference between what since Comte we have become accustomed to call 'sociology' and the philosophic doctrine of society of Plato—as well as that of Aristotle or even Hegel—is no longer merely one of subject matter, but a profound difference of conception and method. The great philosophy had as its ideal the development of a doctrine of society derived from the absolute principles of Being. Socio-logy, however, ever since it bore that name, prided itself on precisely the opposite: like the natural sciences it wanted to emancipate itself from any sort of teleology and to be satisfied solely with causal relations formula-

> ble by laws ... From the very beginning of the new science the joy in progress was muted: its thought on society took pride in not transcending that which was. The impulse of philosophy, to transform the Ought into the Is readily gave way to the sober acceptance of the Is as the Ought. And so it has remained from the days of Comte down to most famed teachers who founded the schools of the new sociology, Max Weber, Emile Durkheim, Vilfredo Pareto. Whenever the voice of this science is raised in the greatest pathos, one can be sure that it is proscribing something for itself, and precisely that essential for the sake of which men reflect about society. Equivocation often has very sound reasons: sociology has remained 'positive' not only because it desires to keep to the given and wants to extirpate the wish as the father of thought, but also because it takes a positive stance towards that which exists. It has enjoined itself to refrain from treating that which exists critically (Horkheimer & Adorno, 1973: 7).

Sociology in its voyage of self-discovery from the time of Comte to this day has not succeeded into realizing a unity of its paradigms. Its strength lies on the other hand in projecting a worldview which sets into perspective the vital relationships between man and society. This worldview is characterized by a dual quality: it is *synthetic* and *substitutive*. These two aspects of sociological worldview pull this discipline into two different creative directions. The synthetic element in sociology tends to infuse in its worldview values and categories with roots in multiplicity of paradigms on man, nature and society. This explains the pulls and creative tensions that are continually generated in sociology towards other sciences. It is also explicated by the facts that writings of the few of the founders of sociology contained a singularity of paradigms. Comte, Pareto, Marx, Weber and Durkheim, all of them show tensions of competing paradigms in the structure of their ideas, and project a synthetic worldview of sociology. The substitutive character of sociological worldview sets it apart, sharpens its self-awareness, draws conceptual and methodological boundaries that separate it from other sciences. More often, it is based on the elaboration of a single paradigm and its operationalization.

That sociological worldview is synthetic as well as substitutive adds a dialectical quality to its cognitive structure. It lends a critical attribute to its formulations on man and society, and more specifically endows sociology with qualities of objectivity and apperception to understand the reality and problem of man. The question, however, considering the great variety of paradigms in sociology and the synthetic yet substitutive character of its worldview is how to review the concept of man so that the two major contributions made by sociologists in the understanding of man, first, the social structural bases of human problematic and secondly, innovation of conceptual theoretical categories and systems to diagnose and explain this problematic, are adequately explicated.

Treatment of the concept of man in sociology should proceed in two directions: it should explicate the theoretic contingencies in sociology to the concept of man. In addition to this, it should highlight contributions made by sociology to the understanding of existential dilemmas and problems of man in changing social structure, its historical dialectic and direction. History and theory should thus offer two complementary frames of reference for treatment of man in sociology. Its significance rests also on the fact that sociology as it emerged as a discipline in the west, it carried with it the imprints of western civilizational ethos, its ideational patterns and its social structure. Sociological worldview, even its cognitive categories, thus tend to be culturally relative rather than universal. In treatment of concept of man in sociology, it would be, therefore, not possible to detach the issue of historical particularities of social structure and culture from theoretic cons-tructs for the understanding of the problem.

Ideological Basis

There are two meta-theoretical assumptions in sociological theories which bear directly on the concept of man. The first set of these assumptions relates to the conception of the relationship between man and society and the place of man in society. There are sociologists who construct a model of society in order to derive from it the sociological model of man. Contrariwise, the step is reversed by other sociologists who first construct a model of man in order to understand societal reality. Society as a category indeed occupies central place in thinking and investigation in both frames of reference. Philosophically, the two positions correspond closely to 'realism' and 'nominalism' in meta-theory. The ground for debate on the abolition of man as an active concept in sociology was primarily a reaction against certain radical theories based on sociological realism. The second meta-theoretic component in sociological theory has its anchorage in the dichotomy between positivism and idealism. Indeed, it is rare to find sociologists taking radical stances in respect of positivistic or idealistic positions but all forms of sociological theories bear the imprint either of the one or the other in their meta-theoretic orientation. Realism-nominalism and positivism-idealism thus constitute ideal typical meta-theoretic dimensions in the matrix of sociological categories. Within each meta-theoretic position there have emerged variations and sub-variations but broadly these two frames of reference do have a place in all varieties of socio-logical theories, and the concept of man that each theory posits is influenced by the nature of these assumptions.

Theoretical Basis

Comte and Spencer whose names are associated with the origin of sociology were both staunch positivists. Positivism, in fact, represented the ethos of Enlightenment period which also dominated the sociological theory. It was normal at this time to borrow models from the natural sciences, physics, biology and chemistry and to employ them analogically as it were for the understanding of sociological realities. Spencer borrowed his model from biology and Comte from physics. Spencer also took a clearly 'realist' position in regard to the relationship between man and society. In *his Principles of Sociology* (1898) he wrote:

> Carrying the controversy between nominalism and realism into another sphere, a nominalist might affirm that just as there exist only the members of a species, while the species considered apart from them has no

> existence; so the units of a society alone exist, while the existence of society is but verbal... But without disputing the other steps of his argument, the last step may be denied. The arrangement temporary in the one case, is permanent in the other, and it is the permanence of the relations among component parts which constitutes the individuality of a whole as distinguished from the individualities of its parts. A mass broken into fragments ceases to be a thing; while conversely, the stones, bricks and wood, previously separate, become the thing called a house if connected in fixed ways. Thus, we consistently regard a society as an entity, because, though formed of discrete units, a certain concreteness in the aggregate of them is implied by general persistence of the arrangements among them throughout the area occupied. And it is this trait which yields our idea of a society (pp. 447-48).

Spencer's concept of man, following the rational utilitarian tradition of positivism, is that of an abstraction and not an existential reality. He formulates his idea of man when he begins to describe 'social types' in his *Principles of Sociology.* Here, he develops both a quasi-racial theory of man and differentiation of personality types in types of societies—militaristic and industrial. In his distinction between these two societal types and their processes of 'metamorphoses' he posits the concept of man through analyzing the relationship between the state and citizen and through his formulation how the idea of voluntary cooperation and civil ties, rights and duties only develops in an industrial society. He writes: "The regions whence changes towards greater political liberty have come, are the leading industrial regions ... Where industrial activities and structures evolve, this branch of the regulating system, no longer as in the militant type, a rigid hierarchy, little by little loses strength, while there grows up one of a different kind: *sentiments* and institutions both relaxing. Right of private judgement in religious matters gradually establishes itself along with establishment of political rights. In place of uniform belief imperatively enforced, there come multiform beliefs voluntarily accepted" (ibid.: 567). The will of the citizens is thus possible only at the stage of industrial society.

In August Comte's sociology we find another expression of the positivistic approach to the concept of man, once again very dimly visible to perception. In his *Philosophie Positive and Polity* (cf. Barnes, 1961), one would find formulations of the relationship between the individual and society and individual and the state respectively which very closely forerun that of Spencer. In *Polity* he particularly establishes the similarity between individual and social organism. "The difference between the individual and the social organism in Comte's opinion are only that the latter is essentially immutable while the social organism is capable of immense improvement. Similarly, the individual is capable of lesser degree of differentiation of functions than the social organism. Society is governed by the law of scientific progress which to individual is denied. This position completes what has been described as Comte's sociologistic positivism.

More dynamic conception of societal processes and implicitly also that of the concept of man, however, one may find in Comte's theory of social progress, particularly in his theory of positive religion. Unit of society to Comte is not individual but the family which is based on the feeling of affection; on this rest the superstructures of state, or city and church, the state representing the principle of action, and the church synthesizing all the action processes of the former two. These institutions evolve slowly with the evolution of *cerebral system* (based essentially on Gall's phrenological principle of psychology). The church has thus to enforce universal surveillance. Comte's concept of man is reflected in the postulate of cerebral system from which the essentials of personality system can be derived. The cerebral system comprises of feeling, action and intellect; feeling is the basis of morality which passes according to Comte into three stages in which man's nature finds its expression: the family, the state and finally the race. Man's highest moral height, altruism, finds its origin in family; during the Middle Ages it took the shape of civic culture, and in the 'positivistic' period morality should become universal. These three stages also represent advancement in sympathetic capacities of man, of attachment, of veneration, and finally of benevolence. These emotional stages in the evolution of the dominant drives of man also coincide with periods of religious institutionalizations; fetishism which is linked with the origin of family is dominated with attachment; polytheism, which is at the root of the origin of state is based on veneration principle and finally, monotheism, with its universality favours the sentiment of benevolence.

Comte builds into his theory of positive religion also his scheme of positive social reconstruction. Its philosophy also rests on three-fold division of human personality: action, intelligence and feeling. Material forces, wealth and social classes are based on the principle of action. Intellectual force, founded on speculation, is considered in idealistic and aesthetic expressions and moral force based on affection is expressed in command, prompted by character and obedience, and inspired by the heart. Women represent the principle of heart, also they symbolize the highest feeling of affection and tend to be the embodiment of moral principle compared to classes which affect action and represent materialistic forces or leaders who direct our activities. The principle of social hierarchy should be based on this hierarchy of affection intellect and feeling in which the new priests of the positive religion of humanity—sociologists—would occupy the highest position without an iota of temporal power. Their function would be directive, moral and universalistic based on the principles of positive science.

Comte's conception of man could be deduced from his formulation of structure of human nature and its derivative expressions both societal and cultural. One would also notice a faint resemblance in his formulation of human nature with later-day postulates of personality system in the functional theories of sociology, especially Parsonian three-fold modes of orientation. Only, Comte's postulates are not logically exclusive, have no roots in dynamic psychology and his sociology is completely devoid of concept of man as a unit of actors in the social system. What exists is mere social category and not man. Only a faint shadow of man, if not his ghost, houers over Comte's sociology.

Pareto is another classical positivist in sociology who pushed man far back into the dark corner in sociology. This is so despite two major innovations in Paretian sociology which distinguish it from that of Comte and Spencer: a theory of social action as component of social system and a theory of the structure of sentiments. Since sentiments occupy an infrastructural place in Pareto's sociology, and provide the building blocks for his sociology of action, it needs explanation. Unlike Comte, Pareto's formulation of sentiment does not have a psychological connotation at all. It is an abstract hypothetical notion, which in itself is neither true nor false, but assumes a form only through social acts. The social act has reality but the sentiment has none. Thus, Pareto's famous distinction between the 'residue and derivatives' which lay the foundation for his social system and action frame of reference is mechanistic rather than normative or existential (cf. Henderson, 1937: 63-64). Pareto's concept of social system is more formal than sociological. A 'residue' is the manifestation of a sentiment. A 'derivate' is non-logical argument, explanation, assertation, appeal to authority, or association of ideas or sentiments in words. Of about fifty residues, the important ones are: residues of combination, of persistence of aggregates, of manifestation of sentiments through overt acts, of sociability, of integrity of individual and finally of sexuality. Among the important 'derivations' are: affirmation, authority, accord with sentiment or principles and verbal proofs.

The concept of man in Pareto's sociology is linked with his theory of elite to which the notions of residues and derivatives are organically linked. He divides population into the categories of elites and masses based on the predominance of residues of combination, action and integrity of individual in the former and of persistence of aggregate, sentiment and sexuality and sociability in the latter. He further divides the elites into two categories, viz., governmental and non-governmental, based on the same two types of dominant residual tendencies, of persistence among the governmental elites and combination among the non-governmental elites which in course of time leads to the petrification of the elan of the governmental elites and their eventual replacement by the non-governmental. History thus to Pareto is not only a cemetery of aristocracies but also of the governing elites.

The concept of man that emerges from these formulations of

Pareto is not existential but categorial, a characteristic of all positivist sociologists of the 19th century. Man, as a being, remains in the background, and in the forefront of their treatment is man as a member of class or mass. Inferentially, notion of man is non-dialogical (cf. Casslerer, 1948) and is based on a typification which renders man into a form of abstraction. Pareto's own deductive logic in the formulation of the 'abstract man' emerges sharply when seen negatively, in contrast to that of Marx than when seen positively, in terms of his own constructions. Unlike Marx, whose notion of man we shall discuss later, Pareto denudes man completely of his existential being as well as his structural being or species being. His distinction of human action into the categories of the logical, where means are commensurate with ends and the non-logical, where means are not commensurate with ends, and his justification of these by 'derivatives' of various sorts, does introduce a partial dynamic element in the existential component of man; these also introduce an element of demystification of man, a challenge to the positivistic progress ideologies rampant at his time. His notion of elite as a foxy, brutish and opportunist being, out always to use 'ideologies' of various sorts to beguile the gullible masses, his faith in the susceptibility of masses to fall victims to such vulpine tactics are indeed counterpoints to Marx's notion of 'proletariat' basically revolutionary, praxeological and humistically transcendent. It is in this contradistinction between Marx and Pareto that one can get, though negatively, a glimpse of Pareto's notion of man.

The positivistic sociology slowly undergoes critical tensions from within its cognitive structure. The writings of Emile Durkheim symbolize this turning point. In his writings, utilitarian positivism of Spencer and Pareto is replaced by a sociologistic positivism, which later imbibes many attributes of symbolic interactionism. Sociology, as a truly mature and systematic discipline, owes much to the contribution of Durkheim. He also makes far more significant contributions to the concept of man.

Durkheim's concept of man emanates from his concept of society. Through his notions of societal structure, function, its differentiation and evolution, Durkheim develops theories of knowledge, ethics and education, normal and pathological modes of behaviour, crime, suicide and religion. His concept of alienation and alienative forms of division of labour are also organically linked with his treatment of society, and social facts. Defining social facts as 'things' having attributes of exteriority and constraint, slowly Durkheim builds a theory of society which is essentially symbolic and immanent in nature. Society is defined as a reality *sui generis;* it renders man a product of societal processes and his freedom a resultant of progressive differentiation, of societal roles, forms and institutions. In his *The Division of Labour in Society* (1933), Durkheim states his conception of man as he develops his theory of social differentiation. He posits two states of societal evolution through changes in the structure of its solidarities: the mechanical and organic. Visible symbol of social solidarity is law: with repressive sanction in mechanical solidarity and restitutive sanction in organic solidarity. Man does not have a personality of his own in a society in the state of mechanical solidarity, as it is a solidarity through likeness. Personal or civil rights, contractual obligations do not exist at this stage. Man as a person is only endowed with psychic images of the collective and not of their representations or symbolic forms. The latter does not have a differentiated structure in mechanical solidarity. With organic solidarity coming into being owing to the growth of population, clustering populations in townships, etc., there is increase in the volume of social interaction as the 'dynamic density' of society increases. Correspondingly, there is increase in the 'moral density' of society.

At this stage of societal development from the chrysalis of the solidarity emerges the individual representation; collective representation is thus differentiated, functional specialization follows not because of man's inherent rationalism, his hedonistic urge or heredity but because of the fundamental fact that societal structure itself has undergone a basic transformation. Durkheim writes:

> Collective life is not born from individual life, but it is, on the contrary, the second which is born from the first. It is on this condition alone that one can explain how the personal individuality of social units has been able to be formed and enlarged without disintegrating society. It is not the absolute personality of the monad,

which is sufficient unto itself, and could do without the rest of the world, but that of an organ or part of an organ having its determined function, but which cannot, without risking dissolution, separate itself from the rest of the organism. Under these conditions, cooperation becomes not only possible but necessary. Utilitarians thus reverse the natural order of facts, and nothing is more deceiving than this inversion. It is a particular illustration of the general truth that what is first in knowledge is last in reality. Precisely because cooperation is the most recent fact, it strikes sight first (ibid.: 279-80).

Increasing division of labour in society, its role structures and functions not only bring into being the notion of man as a separate existential reality but it also leads us to diagnose the sociological problematic of man in modern industrial society. Alienation of man from society as a result of the progressive complexity and specialization of functions is a theme which Durkheim for the first time introduces in sociology. He has in this respect been a forerunner among sociologists on the concept and the problematic of man.

Alienation of man in societies with progressive organic solidarities results, according to Durkheim, for two reasons: first, due to the state of anomie in society, a condition in which the differentiated elements of social structure cease to be at the requisite level of interaction essential in organic solidarity, and secondly, because of the normative erosion in society following anomie. When components of social system that require continual interaction of higher intensity and coordination, as the parts now have attained autonomy, are not able to do so, as 'opaque environments' interpose between them, the solidarity of the whole is transformed into the alienation of the parts. This also results from the rapid rate of changes that follow the industrial revolution in society; this introduces realms of autonomy in social structures much faster than the generation of the sociological and moral forces in society to coordinate the level of interaction.

Under these circumstances, man is caught in a moral vicious circle, because to Durkheim, the source of morality also lies in the self-same societal processes which give birth to anomie and alienation of societal forms. He writes:

> "Society is not then, as has been thought, a stranger to the moral world, or something which has only secondary condition of its existence. It is not a simple juxtaposition of individuals who bring an intrinsic morality with them, but rather man is a moral being only because he lives in society, since morality consists being in solidary with a group and varying with this solidarity. Let all social life disappear, and moral life will disappear with it, since it would no longer have any objective" (ibid.: 399).

Linked with questions of anomie and morality is the notion of the normal and pathological social facts and behaviours that assume significance in Durkheim's formulation of the concept of man. In his *The Rules of Sociological Method* (1950) and *The Suicide* (1951), he has developed the notion of man to a new existential level, a forerunner of contemporary cognitive sociology (cf. Cicourel, 1973). Traditionally, the idea of human responsibility and free will had dominated the notion of man both in utilitarian philosophy and medieval Christianity. The distinction between normal and pathological was made on the grounds of man's choice of his deeds and his consequent responsibility; the normative judgement by society of the human deed was not put into question at all, Durkheim has almost radicalized the notion of human responsibility and free will by rendering them obsolescent. He postulates that normal action cannot be judged on the basis of *normative* frame of reference of a particular society which would elude detection without a scientific indicator. Normal behaviour would itself prove the reality of the existence of a particular form of normative structure; this behaviour can be judged only through the generality of the forms of social actions. This generality would further be specific to societies, and normal and pathological cannot be formulated for all societies for all times to come.

In terms of human condition, it revolutionizes the relationship between the judge and the judged. Men commit suicide not because of a monomania—a taint of free will or personal sin—but because of interposition of socially 'opaque structures' between their individual representations and images and that of society, and between their definition of the reality resulting from this interposition and that of the society. So, suicide is sometimes reflection of man's over-conformity to societal ideals, it is altruistic; sometimes it results from under-conformity, it is egoistic; and at other times it is because the norm of conformity is itself in a flux, in the processes of rapid social change, then suicide is anomic. Hence, pathological and normal are not categories to be defined by a transcendental normative principle but through essential reflexivity of human situation in society and its social processes. It has a deeper significance to the concept of man; it gives man a moral reprieve not available to him in the past.

These ideas of Durkheim on the concept of man find their final expression in his later work *The Elementary Forms of the Religious Life* (1961) and his famous essay on "The Dualism of Human Nature and Social Condition" (1914). He uses the theme of religion to explicate his sociology of knowledge, but in the centre of this problem is the concept of man. Religion has its basis in the bipartite division of all phenomena "which embraces all that exists, but which radically excludes each other. Sacred things are those that interdictions protect and isolate; profane things, those to which these interdictions are applied and which must remain at a distance from the first. Religious beliefs are representations which express the nature of sacred things and the relations which they sustain, either with each other, or with profane things" (ibid.: 56). This realm of the sacred is further divided into the personal and collective, which in two opposite forms manifest the same reality. Man as mere body is profane; he ascends in status as he imbibes more and more of the sacred through his proximity to religious symbols or gods. Yet, gods also need man to sustain them. Durkheim writes: "If it is true that man depends upon his gods, this dependence is reciprocal. The gods also have need of man; without offerings and sacrifices they would die" (ibid.: 53).

Durkheim now treats the concept of man in extension of, as well as, in contradistinction with the concept of god. The separation between soul and body, the basis of animistic beliefs in primitive religions, he maintains, is not born of irrationality but a quantum jump of human consciousness to conceptualization and self-objectification from the levels of mere sensate awareness. He says:

> The fact is that man is not merely an animal with certain additional qualities: he is something else. Human nature is the result of a sort of recasting of the animal nature, and in the course of the various complex operations which have brought about this recasting, there have been losses as well as gains. How many instincts have we not lost? The reason is that men are not only in relation with the physical environment, but also with a social environment infinitely more extended, more stable and more active than the one whose influence animals undergo. To live, they must adapt themselves to this. Now, in order to maintain itself, society frequently finds it necessary that we should see things from a certain angle and feel them in a certain way; consequently, it modifies in ideas which we would be inclined if we listened only to our animal nature; it alters them, even going so far as to put the contrary sentiments in their place. Does it not even go so far as to regard our own individual lives as something of little value, while for the animal this is the greatest thing? (ibid.: 83).

Religion is thus a symbolic externalization of societal reality through human consciousness, which in the first instance had subjectively internalized it through societal interaction. It is the source of formation of conceptual world, its universal as well as specific manifestation. Man attains his human qualities, his selfhood and identity through the mediation of his psyche with society; in the process societal objective reality gets internalized into his psyche, qualitatively transforming it and endowing with new capacity for its symbolization and externalization. It is this form of societal self-externalization through man that offers us the objective reality of social phenomena. Universal categories, therefore, for ever remain in the realm of the ideal possibilities since the very process of mediation through which the symbolic universe of man projects societal self-awareness is never fully complete; it is always partial, dialectical and critical. Durkheim writes:

> ...it is rather at the school of collective life that the individual has learned to idealize. It is in assimilating the ideals elaborated by society that he has become capable of conceiving the ideal. It is society which, by leading him within its sphere of action, has made him acquire the need of raising himself above the world of experience and has at the same time furnished him with the means of conceiving another. For society has constructed this new world in constructing itself, since it is society which this expresses. Thus both with the individual and in the group, the faculty of idealizing has nothing mysterious about it. It is not a sort of luxury which a man could get along without, but a condition of his very existence" (ibid.: 470-71).

In his essay following the *Elementary Forms of the Religious Life,* Durkheim further crystallized his views on man and nature of man. He now clearly formulated the concept of man as *homo-duplex*. Man, at the same time, he said, is both I and We. There is a dialectical relationship between these two dimensions of human nature which grows constantly with growth in societal self-awareness. Summarizing the ideas on Durkheim's notion of homo-duplex, Tiryakian writes:

> Durkheim states that the body-soul dichotomy is echoed in the human psyche itself. The mind is a composite of sensation and feelings, as well as intellectual and moral activity. Our bodily appetites are self-centred but our mental activity very often seeks impersonal ends or disinterested pursuits. Physical sensation cannot be transferred to others; nobody can perceive or have the same sensory experiences of the same phenomenon as I do. On the contrary, concepts are always common to a plurality of men and can always be shared, even if they are initially the product of one person; our intellect functions by means of impersonal concepts which are by nature universal. According to Durkheim, these considerations verify the old notion of *homo-duplex*.

> Our inner life has what might be called a double centre of gravity: there is an awareness of our own proper individuality, which is grounded in our biological nature, and there is also an awareness of an extra-individual component of the self. I perceive and react to the world in terms of both my own personal experiences, localized by my body in space and time, and also in terms of a much greater, impersonal sort of knowledge about the world. In man, then there is a being which sees everything in the light of its own self and which in its activity has no other end but itself; but there is also another being which knows things *sub specia aeterni-tatis,* as if it participated in a mental activity other than its own, and which tends in its actions to realize extrapersonal ends. Between these two aspects of man there is a fundamental and irreconcilable opposition. How could we belong, asks Durkheim, completely to ourselves as well as completely to others? The ego (the conscious self) cannot be completely something other than itself, for then it would dissolve (as in ecstasy). In order to think, one must be, one must have an individuality. But from another perspective, the self cannot be wholly or exclusively itself, for then it would become void of all content. If being is necessary for thought, thought is equally necessary for being (1962: 47-48).

Durkheim thus not only consolidates the position of sociology as a discipline in its own right, beyond an analogical extension of the other social sciences, but he laid down the foundation of most ideas and issues on the concept of man which remain live and valid even today. It is indeed significant that in his conception of man one can easily see the mirror image of the contemporary sociological conceptions of man—be it the symbolic-interactionist, phenomenological, structural or ethno-methodological. Even a similarity between the Marxist or neo-Marxist conception of man and the one constructed by Durkheim in his later works can be discerned, especially in the context of structural dialectics (as distinct from historical dialectics).

Practical Aspects

From utilitarian positivism of Spencer's sociology, mechanistic positivism of Pareto and sociologistic positivism of Comte, Durkheim's sociological positivism was of a highly transient and critical character; it was, as we have observed, imbued with internal tensions. Sociology following the works of these classicists branched off in two major directions both having a neo-positivistic hue. While the Paretian tradition was extended by Henderson and Homans, the Durkheimian tradition, especially in its early positivistic form, emerged as a new functional theory in social anthropology of Malinowski and Radcliffe-Brown and sociology of Parsons, Merton, Davis and other sociologists, mostly in the United States. It is interesting that the symbolic-interactionist and phenomenological aspects of Durkheimian sociology did not at first develop in the United States, but in the Continent itself, especially in interaction with the immanent interpretive tradition of the German sociology. To this we shall return later.

The metamorphosis of positivism into functional sociology took place under historical circumstances, such as the emergence of Freudian theory of man and society, disillusionment of the west with the negative consequences of industrialization, the two world wars which left an indelible scar on the conscience of European man and the emergence of Marxism not merely as an alternative ideology of science but also as a new state craft in the Soviet Union. All these developments deeply influenced sociology following its classical origin. Functionalism as an approach in sociology has imbibed an empirical orientation, a systemic perspective on structure and function of social entities, mainly role structures or action systems, and an overt or covert psycholo-gical dimension depending upon whether the psychological frame is Freudian or behaviouristic.

The concept of man in functional sociology emerges in various forms and at several levels of analysis: personality formation and the role of primary institutions in child-rearing, social structure and characterological forms of men, and alienation of man in the context of structural complexity and contradictions. These are some of the major themes in functional sociology around which the concept of man is postulated. This would be evident from the works of prominent functional sociologists such as Parsons, Merton and Homans.

Parsons has formulated his concept of man synthesizing three major theoretical orientations, viz., sociological, Freudian-psychological and behaviouristic-psychological. In his *Social System* (1972), he treats man as a *plastic* and *sensitive* being; both plasticity and sensitiveness constitute together the sociological nature of man. He defines plasticity as the capacity of the human organism to adapt to infinite variations of the eco-cultures and social situations and sensitivity as capacity of man to learn and internalize values and to institutionalize them into roles and functional skills. The two important dimensions of sensitivity in man are motivational structure and value structure: the former is rooted into the phylogenetic and ontogenetic organic characteristics of man through which Parsons establishes the link between Freudian approach and his own; the value structure, on the other, is primarily sociogenic and its foundation lies in the processes of institutionalization and legitimation at the societal level and socialization at the personality level. Socialization and institutionalization are thus two mutually reinforcing processes.

These processes reflect themselves through system states, socialization in the personality system, institutionalization through the societal and cultural systems, but the linking process between the two are the roles or action orientations of men in society. This action frame of reference at the level of human personality emerges primarily from the critical tensions of motivational structure and not the cultural structure. Parsons, on the basis of the postulates of primacy of 'motivational integration' in the personality system and of the 'cultural integration' in the social system, distinguishes between two problematics of sociology: alienation and anomie. Alienation, according to him, is a state of disorientation in the role structure at the personality level resulting from the internal dislocation of relationships within the components of motivational structure e.g. cathection, cognition and evaluation; it results from imperfections in the introjection and internalization of value orientations through the mechanism of socialization. The malintegration in the value orientation structure of society, Parsons would define as a state of anomie. Though heuristically or even substantively distinct both alienation and anomie have an interactive character.

In his collaborative work *Toward a General Theory of Action* (1951), as different from his *Social System,* Parsons takes a more overtly psychological approach to personality system. He more explicitly elaborates the structure of human need dispositions, dynamics of motivational orientations and their organization through different psychological mechanisms.

The distinguishing feature of concept of man in Parsons sociology, however, remains the effacement of man as an existential historical being. His, like most other functional approaches in sociology, is a conception not of man but of a personality, not of a being but of an abstract psycho-organic system. He does raise some interesting issues on man in his *Social System* but their significance lies in demonstrating the impact of societal and cultural systems on the role integration of man in society. The most significant notion that Parsons develops in this context is that of 'basic personality structure' which he borrows approvingly from Kardiner and Linton. It represents a form of modal personality through a fit between the dominant cultural values enshrined in primary institutions of a society and the personality systems of the members of that society. Through this notion, Parsons endorses two important trends in social sciences: first, the theory of ontogenetic growth of personality, a neo-Freudian innovation, and secondly, the need to study the variations in modal personality of men in specific techno-ecological and cultural systems through child-rearing and socialization processes. This latter trend in the analysis and diagnosis of human personality, its characterological contours and its processes have since occupied a great deal of attention of functional sociologists (see works of Parsons and Bales, Whiting, Kardiner and Linton, etc.) As the emphasis shifted from man to the concept of personality, the historical and philosophical issues on man and his future were lost to operational and empirical diagnostic concerns.

The main weakness of studying man through mechanisms of personality formation or its characterological variations is that in this perspective the more significant problems of man and his relationship with society, such as his autonomy to reflect critically about societal reality as an object external to him, his power not only to empathize but also to apperceive, and his reflexivity, are lost sight of. It also neglects other existential problems such as man's alienation not merely as a role deviance, the sense in which Parsons uses this term, but as historical evolutionary dialectics of society, as immanently given to it. Paradoxically, Parsons who embarked upon the heroic task of synthesizing and improving upon the theoretical contributions of the classicists, in his zeal for the construction of logically closed and coherent system-categories, emasculated sociology of its more fundamental concerns existent in the works of Marx, Weber and Durkheim upon whose works he tried to build his system theory.

Merton is another important innovator in functional sociology. His impact on contemporary sociology has been as great as that of Parsons even though his contributions are not that architectonic. He is less historical than Parsons, more realistic about theorizing, more lucid in style but essentially in regard to his contribution to the concept of man, he has little more to offer than Parsons. Despite his raising the problem of man in modern society in a changing paradigmatic context, his focus in the study of man is confined to the analysis of deviant modes of adaptation of a person. Merton writes:

> Until recently, and all the more so before then, one could speak of a marked tendency in psychological and sociological theory to attribute the faulty operation of social structure to failures of social control over man's biological drives. The imagery of the relations between man and society implied by this doctrine is as clear as it is questionable. In the beginning, there are man's biological impulses which seek full expression. And then, there is the social order, essentially an apparatus for the management of impulses, for the social processing of tensions, for the 'renunciation of

> instinctual gratification' of Freud. Non-conformity with the demands of a social structure is thus assumed to be anchored in original nature. It is the biologically rooted impulses which from time to time break through social control. And by implication, conformity is the result of a utilitarian calculus of unreasoned conditioning.
>
> With the more recent advancement of social sciences, this set of conceptions has undergone basic modification. For one thing, it no longer appears so obvious that man is set against society in an unceasing war between biological impulse and social restraint. The image of man as an untamed bundle of impulses begins to look more like a caricature than a portrait. For another, sociological perspectives have increasingly entered into the analysis of behaviour deviating from prescribed patterns of conduct. For whatever the role of biological impulses, there still remains the further question of why it is that the frequency of deviant behaviour varies within different social structures and how it happens that deviations have different shapes and patterns in different social structures (1968: 185).

Consequently, the concrete outcome of Merton's study of man does not go beyond a "systematic approach to the analysis of social and cultural sources of deviant behaviour". His aim is to "discover how some social structures exert a definite pressure upon certain persons in the society to engage in non-conforming rather than conforming conduct" (ibid.: 186), which he explains through incongruence-congruence between legitimate cultural goals and institutionalized means that individuals adopt in their role performance especially with regard to major areas of choices of goals and means for realization of social objectives. On this basis he formulates two types of adaptations of behaviour, viz., conformity, where there exists a congruence between cultural goals of society and means legitimized by it for their achievement and deviance where this congruence does not exist. On the basis of the variations in deviance either in respect of culturally defined goals, its legitimate or institutionalized means or both, Merton postulates four model adaptations of deviant behaviour: *innovation,* where new means are introduced for realizing culturally defined goals; *ritualism,* where means themselves become all too important to the neglect of culturally defined goals; *retreatism,* where actor is indifferent both to culturally defined goals as well as the means; and finally, the *rebellion,* where both culturally defined goals as well as the means are thrown overboard to be substituted by new ones. Merton views conformity as the trait of persons in stable societies, although he does not rule out over-conformity as a deviant form of adaptation homologous to retreatism in the reverse.

All forms of deviant modes of adaptation in behaviour emerge in more endemic form in a state of anomie in a society. Social structures give way to anomie following increase in the deviant modes of personal adaptation as well as they might also generate it. To Merton, anomie is a state of societal malintegration of role structures and their institutionalization and not a state of mind as held by other social psychologists and sociologists (he specially criticizes McIver's definition of anomie as a state of mind (cf. McIver, 1950).

We would notice that Merton like Parsons identifies the concept of man with that of personality system as an integrated system of role structures and role performances. He too concentrates on deviance as the most relevant parameter for analyzing the man-society relationships and more than Parsons he schematizes the notion of man by rendering it an outcome of a 'property-space model' generating logical sets of categories. Similarly, like Parsons, Merton too develops the concept of 'modal personality' or 'status personality' in his treatment of bureaucratic structure and personality. Specialized roles, according to him, expose persons to norms of over-conformity, the case in instance being bureaucracy; this generates 'trained incapacities' on the one hand and ritualism on the other. The more a person due to this reason over-conforms to his specialized roles, the more he is rendered marginal to the rest of the roles he has to perform and is also thereby exposed to maladjustments.

Both Parsons and Merton, in their treatment of personality and role-specific problems of integration of man in modern society, especially industrial society, raise indirectly questions of alienation, anomie, deviance, over-conformity, etc., which do tend, to be significant issues on the concept of man in sociology. They anticipate problems of man in modern society such as those of 'organization man' (cf. Whyte, 1956; Galbraith, 1967), 'industrial man' (cf. Burns, 1969), 'other-directed man' (cf. Reisman, 1950) and 'one-dimensional man' (cf. Marcuse, 1964) etc., but they do still fail to project a proper concept of man since they look at man primarily as a system of role structures; it is endowed, of course, with socio-organismic dynamics but is devoid of historical-biographic dynamics.

George C. Homans, in this context, raises a pertinent question in his exposure of the limitations of 'functional theory' which led to the exile of man from sociological analysis. He says the functionalist's fundamental unit, the role, was a social fact in Durkheim's sense. And their theoretical programme assumed, as he did, that sociology should be an independent science, in the same sense that its propositions should not be derivable from some other social science, such as psychology. This meant, in effect, that the general propositions of sociology were not to be propositions about the behaviour of individual consciousnesses—or, as I should say, about men—but propositions about the characteristics of societies or other social groups as such (cf. Homans, 1964: 810). This led to the neglect of the concept of man from functional sociological theory (as different from functional analysis which does not imply prepositional format for explanations). This critique is indeed symptomatic. One might, therefore, ask about the concept of man that Homans postulates in his sociological theory: Is it the one that restores man really back to his substantive status in sociological analysis? Does it restore back to him his historical and biographical self-awareness?

Indeed, one is disappointed when he takes a close look at the notion of man that Homans develops in his sociology. Despite his plea for 'bringing man back-in' his notion of man is mechanistic; man's all activities result, according to him, from a set of fundamental psychological dispositions or processes. These dispositions can be converted into universal psychological propositions which according to him are at the root of all forms of human activities, social interactions and modes of institutionalization in society. Amongst these, four propositions are crucial: the success proposition, the stimulus proposition, the deprivation-statiation proposition, and the frustration-aggression proposition. Human interaction situation directed by these psycho-behaviouristic propositions is a game of exchange of gratifications and values and it determines its own dynamics. Man operates in society following his personal matrix of exchange with others of gratification-deprivation though rooted these may be in social institutions and contexts (Homans, 1961: 30-78). Obviously, the theoretical framework of Homans' notion of man is in the behaviouristic psychology, particularly in the Skinnerian form. It is psychological, reductionistic and completely ahistorical as well as non-biographical. It also does not recognize human problems of alienation and over-conformity in modern societies since all such modes of human conditions can always be explained by interposing one or another set of psychological propositions. Its orientation on the concept of man thus remains empirical and operational in a mechanistic sense.

It would thus appear that functional sociology both in its systematic postulates such as those of Parsons and Merton or in its micro-systematic form as in Homans has rendered man a peripheral concept. Man is treated not in the fullness of his existential being, but as an abstraction or as a process; in the former sense it is equated with role or constellations of value patterns in the personality system and in the latter merely as a by-product of imputed psychological dispositions. It is indeed paradoxical that functional sociology which claims its development from Durkheim failed completely to develop the concept of man as postulated in his notion *of homo-duplex*. It thus failed to notice the most creative as well as critical aspects of the concept of man, the substantive issues of man's growing self-estrangement and his growing self-awareness as dialectical processes in contemporary industrial and post-industrial societies.

The loss of this critical perspective on man has been primarily due to a certain scientific notions of sociology which these socio-logists wanted to develop. Consequently, we find more wholesome treatment of man in those sociologists, even though they have some orientation of functional variety (in Kingsley Davis' sense; cf. Davis, 1955), who were less overwhelmed in establishing a homologous relationship between science and sociology. David Reisman, Lewis Mumford, Daniel Bell, Wilbert Moore and several other sociologists who fall under this category; were not so self-conscious about the nomological aspect of sociology, but have contributed deeply to the understanding of the relationship between modern industrial society and man. Reisman and Glazer in *The Lonely Crowd* (1950) make a characterological assessment of man's changing nature, motivational orientation and value syndromes from the traditional to modern society. It passes through three stages: 'tradition-directed' in traditional societies to 'inner-directed' in transitional societies to 'other-directed' in the modern societies. In the inner-directed syndrome, the dominance is of the "drive to live upto an ideal"—a phenomenon which according to Reisman and Glazer was pervasive in the 19th century-United States, whereas in the other-directed type, the dominant value syndrome is of "making good through making friends"—a tendency which reflects the problem of alienation of man in modern societies. Lewis Mumford in his *Condition of Man* (1944), Wilbert E. Moore in *Man, Time and Society* (1963) and Daniel Bell in *The Coming of the Post-industrial Society* (1914) have analyzed the implications of the modern technological, media-explosive post-industrial society to the being and consciousness of man. If Mumford analyzes it from diagnostic and prescriptive points of view, Moore and Bell delve deeper into the mystery of fundamental structural revolution that modern society is under-going today—a change which basically alters man-society, man-nature relationships by introducing the imperatives of re-scheduling and re-synchronization of 'time' in ordering human activities (Moore, 1963). This need gets acute since post-industrial society also introduces contradiction of *New Societies* amidst plenitude or affluence that it generates.

Daniel Bell postulates that post-industrial society is primarily an information society; the industrial society is goods-producing society. The primacy of information creates new problems. These are: inadequacy and hypertechnicality of information, new problems of coordination, marginality of participation and feeling of powerlessness, constriction of social interaction, and social 'diremption of time'. It creates new cultural dilemmas for society which introduce new elements in the definition of man. Bell writes:

I have attempted to suggest the agenda of issues which

emerge with the onset of post-industrial society: the new hierarchies of technical elites and the bureaucratization of science; meritocracy and equality; the antino-mian thrust of an adversary culture, the communal society and the difficulty of consensus. These run the gamut from ethos and value to politics and social organization. Yet, in an intangible way, there may be more—a change in consciousness and cosmology, the dark tinge of which has always been present at the edge of man's conception of himself and the world, which now moves to the phenomenological centre.

In existentialist terminology, man is 'thrown' into the world confronting alien and hostile powers which he seeks to understand and master. The first confrontation was with nature, and for most of the thousand years of man's existence, life has been a fight against nature to find shelter. Man as *homo faber* sought to make things and in making things he dreamt of remaking nature. To rework nature, to make fabricated things, was to enhance man's power. In the industrial society, the cosmological vision was the game against fabricated nature. The post-industrial society turns its back on both. In the salient experience of work, men live more and more outside nature, and less and less with machi-nery and things; they live with and encounter one another. In the daily round of work men no longer confront nature, as either alien or beneficent, and fewer now handle artifacts and things. The post-industrial society is essentially a game between persons. Will this changed experience create a change in consciousness and sensibility?

For most of human history, *reality was nature* and in poetry and imagination men sought to relate the self to the natural world. Then *reality became technics,* tools and things made by men yet given an independent existence outside himself, the reified world. Now *reality*

> *is primarily the social world*—neither nature nor things, only men experienced through reciprocal consciousness of self and other. Society itself becomes a web of consciousness, a form of imagination to be realized as a social construction. Inevitably, a post-industrial society gives rise to new utopianism, both engineering and psychedelic. Man can be re-made or released, their behaviour conditioned or their consciousness altered. The constraints of the past vanish with the end of nature and things. But what does not vanish is the duplex of man himself—the murderous aggression, the primal impulse to tear apart and destroy; the search for order, in art, and life as the bending of will to harmonious shape. It is this ineradicable tension which defined the social world and which permits a view of Utopia that is perhaps more realistic than the here-and-now millennium on earth that modern man has sought. Men in their imagination will always seek to make society a work of art; that remains an ideal. Given the tasks that have to be solved, it is enough to engage in the sober construction of social reality (1974: 481-88).

This reflection on man in post-industrial society represents the peak of maturity in line with the tradition of Durkheim we analyzed above. It is also noteworthy that it raises more fundamental phenomenological issues on man in modern society than could be possible within the framework of functional theory of Parsons, Merton or Homans.

Different Views

Dialectical sociological theory owes its origin to a tradition altogether different from that of positivism or functionalism. It is rooted in philosophy and history and has always been skeptical of the varieties of raw empiricism. Its emphasis is on immanent law and meaningful relations in social systems rather than on external causal relationships. Karl Marx represents a tradition of sociology with focus primarily on the immanent laws and on social dialectics.

Max Weber, responding indirectly to Marx, shifted the emphasis from immanent laws to meaningful systemic understanding of social reality. Both drew their inspiration from philosophy—Marx from Hegel and Weber from Kant. Both as they developed their ideas, transformed the philosophical constructs of their predecessors. Marx not only inverted but also transformed the tenets of Hegelian philosophy. Weber rejected the Kantian dissociation between phenomenon and noumenon and tried to synthesize it through sociology.

But the most distinctive mark of the dialectical and interpretive theories in sociology has been their recognition of the problematic of man in modern society. It constitutes the central problem of their sociological theory.

Alienation of man is central concern in Marx's sociology; to this end his analysis of stages of revolutionary social transformation provides answer to the puzzle of human condition. Similarly, for Weber, modern capitalist society, its rational bureaucratic organization and legal rational forms of authority assume relevance as these inaugurate new concept of man and new sets of relationships between man and society.

Marx develops his concept of man in his *Economic and Philosophic Manuscripts of 1844* (1974) on which the impress of Hegelian philosophy though in an inverted form is at its highest. He locates the critical element of human destiny in the species character of man; man is a body and also a member of a collectivity which is carrier of his accumulated historical endowments, his past and his future potential. The uniting link between the organic and species levels of his being is *labour*—a typically human attribute. It is human attribute because man alone is capable of confronting through mastery over nature the objectified product of his labour, labour *estranged* from him as a product of history. Man makes history through progressive stages of estrangement of his labour and by giving it species form. It is an immanent law of social life but its validity lies not in the *principles* but in the material conditions, modes of production of concrete men in concrete societies. Since man alone is capable of self-reflection on the product of his estranged labour, that represents most of the societal phenomena that surround him, he alone is a candidate for freedom.

The notion of freedom which Marx develops in his later works through his emphasis on revolutionary praxis marks the culmination in his concept of man. In his manuscripts, however, he deals primarily with the historical conditions of human estrangement. Marx writes:

> What then constitutes alienation of labour? First, the fact that labour is *external* to the worker, i.e., it does not belong to his intrinsic nature. Its alien character emerges clearly in the fact that as soon as no physical or other compulsion exists, labour is shunned like the plague. We have considered the act of estranging practical human activity, labour, in two of its aspects: (1) The relation of the worker to the *product of labour* as an alien object exercising power over him. This relation is at the same time the relation to the sensuous external world, to the objects of nature, as an alien world inimically opposed to him. (2) The relation of labour to the *act of production* within the *labour* process. This relation is the relation of the worker to his own activity as an alien activity not belonging to him; it is activity as suffering, strength as weakness, begetting as emasculating, the worker's own physical and mental energy, his personal life—for what is life but activity?—as an activity which is turned against him. Here we have self-estrangement, as previously we had the estrangement of the thing (1974: 66-67).

Apart from these two levels of estrangement, Marx also visualizes a third form of estrangement of man, at the level of his species being, and it is in this context that he raises the concept of freedom and alienation. He writes: "Man is a species being, not only because in practice and in theory he adopts the species (his own as well as those of other things) as his object, but—and this is only another way of expressing it—also because he treats himself as the actual, living species; because he treats himself as a *universal* and therefore a free being" (ibid.: 67). Man proves his species character through his work which is objectification of man's species life, "for he duplicates himself not only, as in consciousness, intellectually, but also actively in reality, and therefore, he sees himself in a world that he has created" (ibid.: 69). Man's physical existence is thus rooted in his degradation of spontaneous free activity and its enthrallment "in such a-way that species (life) becomes for him a means; estranged labour is thus turned through man's species-being, both nature and his spiritual species-property, into a being alien to him, into a *means* for his *individual existence.* It estranges from man his own body, as well as external nature and his spiritual aspect, his *human* aspect. An immediate consequence of the fact that man is estranged from the product of his labour, from his life activity, from his species-being is the *estrangement of man from man"* (ibid.: 69).

The notion of man in the *Economic and Philosophic Manuscripts* is essentially phenomenological, the emphasis being on existential problems of man. Marx in his later works moves from this position to overwhelmingly praxeological concept of man. It is indeed not absent from his early works, but later on it becomes paramount in his treatment of man. In *The German Ideology* (1968), Marx and Engels give a much fuller treatment to the concept of man from this perspective. Emphasis now is on socio-logical analysis of structural differentiation of human society, its historical basis and its impact on the consciousness of man. Interestingly, in this aspect of sociological analysis, one could discern some faint resemblances between Marx and Engels and Durkheim. The statement that "as individuals express their life, so they are. What they are, therefore, coincides with their production, both with *what* they produce and with *how* they produce. The nature of individuals thus depends on the material conditions determining their production. This production only makes its appearance with the increase of population. In its turn this pre-supposes the intercourse (Verkehr) of individuals with one another. The form of intercourse is again determined by production" (1968: 32, italics added). Increase in population as a causal factor in social differentiation was also emphasized by Durkheim; he called it the increase in the dynamic density of society, but unlike Marx and Engels he did not attribute this change directly to the existential and historical nature of man. Marx and Engels attribute growth in population through a chain of sequential developments on the basis of which lies the being of man. They write:

> The first promise of all human history is, of course, the existence of living human individuals.The writing of history must always set out from these natural bases and their modification in the course of history through men. Men can be distinguished from animals by consciousness, by religion or anything else you like. They themselves begin to distinguish themselves from animals as soon as they *produce* their means of subsistence, a step which is conditioned by their physical organization. By producing their means of subsistence men are indirectly producing their actual material life (ibid.: 31-32). Men thus construct their own social reality; they produce their ideas, concepts and cons-ciousness through their material intercourse with men, 'real, active men'. Consciousness can never be anything else than conscious existence, and the existence of men is their actual life-process. If in all ideology men and their circumstances appear upside-down as in a *camera obscuro,* this phenomenon arises just as much from their historical life-process as the inversion of objects on the retina does from their physical life-process (ibid.: 37).

Evidently, now, emphasis shifts from existence to consciousness and on history as mediating process for man. History is not given to man, but man makes history. He makes it by his first historical act of production and reproduction to satisfy his needs. "The production of life, both of one's own in labour and of fresh life in procreation, now appears as a double relationship: on the one hand, as a natural, and on the other, as a social relationship. By social, we understand, Marx and Engels say, the cooperation of several individuals, no matter under what conditions, in what manner and to what end.Thus, it is quite obvious from the start that there exists a material connection of men with one another, which is determined by their needs and their mode of production, and which is as old as men themselves" (ibid.: 41). Marx and Engels draw a sharp distinction on this basis between man and animal: the animal does not enter into 'relationship' with anything, it does not enter into any relation at all; relationship as also consciousness are entirely human attributes. "Consciousness is from the very beginning a social product, and remains so as long as men exist at all. Consciousness is at first, of course, merely consciousness concerning the *immediate* sensuous environment and consciousness of the limited connection with other persons and things outside the individual who is growing self-conscious. At the same time, it is consciousness of nature, which first appears to men as completely alien, all powerful and unassailable force, with which men's relations are purely animal and by which they are overawed like beasts. It is thus purely animal consciousness of nature (natural religion)" (ibid.: 142). Nature at this stage of growth of consciousness is hardly modified historically; man is less advanced praxiologically and herd consciousness prevails. This consciousness grows further with division of labour following increase in population. "From this moment onward consciousness can really flatter itself that it is something other than consciousness of existing practice, that it *really* represents something without representing something real; from now on consciousness is in a position to emancipate itself from the world and to proceed to the formation of 'pure' theory, theology, philosophy and ethics, etc. But even if this theory, theology, philosophy, ethics, etc., comes into contradiction with existing relations, this can only occur because existing social relations have come into contradiction with existing forces of production" (ibid.: 43).

This linkage between history (mode of production and its relationships) and consciousness immanently inheres contradictions so long as the resulting division of labour is governed by moments of forces of production, the state of society and consciousness in a manner that "intellectual and material activity—enjoyment and labour, production and consumption—devolve on different individuals and that only possibility of their not coming into contradiction lies in the negation in its turn of the division of labour". Indeed, "division of labour offers us first example of how, as long as man remains in natural society, that is, as long as a cleavage exists between the particular and the common interest, as long, therefore, as activity is not voluntarily, but naturally, divided, man's own deed becomes an alien power opposed to him, which enslaves him instead of being controlled by him". This structural contradiction is result of assignment of exclusive sphere of activity for each individual which he cannot escape. This could only be abolished in a communist society which according to Marx and Engels will resolve the contradictions of division of labour and consequent fragmentation of human consciousness by abolishing the exclusive sphere of activity to each individual, rendering possible the emergence of a whole man. They write: "In communist society, where nobody has one exclusive sphere of activity but each can become accomplished in any branch he wishes, society regulates the general production and thus makes it possible for me to do one thing today another tomorrow, to hunt in the morning, fish in the afternoon, rear cattle in the evening, criticize after dinner just as I have a mind, without ever becoming hunter, fisherman, shepherd or critic" (ibid.: 45). Achievement of this ideal is possible only through revolutionary praxis. Two conditions are necessary for this according to Marx and Engels: first, great mass of humanity must be rendered propertyless accompanied by great increase in productive power of society, and secondly, a universal intercourse between men in their *world-historical* rather than local being (rendered possible only through increase in productive power and universal propertylessness) which brings about the universal individual into being.

It is at this level that Marx combines in his notion of universal man or whole man (cf. Fischer, 1973: 15-30) the theory of revolutionary praxis. He also in the same process postulates his theory of human nature. The *universal man* emerges through the evolutionary dialectics of the *historical man* and the *natural man.* The natural man is a sensuous man, a passionate man who enjoys interpersonal relationships. Erich Fromm equates Marx's emphasis on passion in human relationship with Freud's libido and treats it as the elemental factor in his theory of human nature (Fromm, 1973: 80-81) but he does also see a progressive evolution in his concept of man. He writes: "Speaking of psychology as a 'a natural science of man' (identical with 'a human natural science"). Marx starts out with a concept of human nature that runs through his whole work until the last pages of *Capital,* where in the third volume he speaks of working conditions—'most adequate to their human nature and most worthy of it'. While in the *Economic and Philosophic Manuscripts* of 1844 Marx speaks of 'essence of man' or the 'species life' of man, in *German Ideology,* he qualifies the use of essence by stating that this essence is 'no abstraction' and in *Capital* he replaces the concept of 'essence' with that of 'human nature in general', to be distinguished from 'human nature as modified in each historical period' (ibid.: 70). These variations in the concept of Marx also represent the progressive growth in his paradigm as it changes from philosophical to sociological orientations. His sociology of man emanates logically from his critique of the modern industrial society and its series of transformations over the primordial form.

Max Weber postulates the concept of man from the same structural perspective but with a contradistinct paradigm. He rejects positivism and treats social phenomena as meaningful symbolic realities, but his approach to sociological analysis is formal and schematic and not dialectical. He uses history but for comparative schematization and not as an instrument of social transformation. His value judgement, however, on industrial society as well as on capitalism does give a ring of resemblance with that of Marx. The concept of man in Weber's sociology can be constructed from his analysis *of The Protestant Ethic and the Spirit of Capitalism* (1965), his *Sociology of Religion* (1966) and his *Essays in Sociology* (1952). His theory of division of labour as formulated in *The Theory of Social and Economic Organization* (1964) is an indirect reflection on the forms of rationality in social action; it implicitly touches upon the notion of man.

In the *Protestant Ethic and the Spirit of Capitalism,* Weber develops his concept of man through his analysis of ethical transformation in society resulting from Protestant reformation. Traditionally, man did not have autonomy of choice in action or freedom of initiative to alter his life situation in this world or the other world. Even redemption of man could not be individual but only collective. Emphasis was on other-worldly asceticism, negation of self, and conformity to collective ethical norms. Man as a free actor did not exist at this stage of religious belief. Even in Lutherian reformation and the notion of 'calling' that he introduced, Weber says, the individuality of man was circumscribed: "the individual should remain once and for all in the station and calling in which God had placed him, and should restrain his worldly activity within the limits imposed by his established station in life. Thus, for Luther, the concept of calling remained traditionalistic" (Weber, 1965: 85). Man's liberation from this Providential bondage was possible only through ethical revolution of Protestantism which shifted the emphasis from other-worldly asceticism to this worldly asceticism. The idea of collective redemption was now replaced by individual piety and ethical responsibility. This brought into being a new spirit, the spirit of capitalism, as also the notion of man as an ethically responsible being.

This new ethic imposed on man a moral imperative to "establish kingdom of God on earth", to practise frugality, self-denial and productively use time towards progressive accumulation and investment of material and intellectual resources. This led to the productive rationality of man in the capitalist society. Thus, man as a responsible being comes into existence. Weber is, however, skeptical whether this creative responsibility goes always with rationality of man. He postulates that man's rationality is only partial, since its critical boundary lies within the influence of traditional 'affect' and transcendental 'charisma'. The interplay of tradition and charisma renders man's rationality always problematic. This also happens to the capitalist society and its ethic of this-worldly asceticism. He evaluates the capitalist ethic in these words:

> In fact the *summum bonum* of this ethic, the earning of more and more money, combined with the strict avoidance of all spontaneous enjoyment of life, is above all completely devoid of any eudaemonistic, not to say hedonistic, admixture. It is thought of so purely as an end in itself, that from the point of view of the happiness of, or utility to, the single individual, it appears entirely transcendental and absolutely irrational. Man is dominated by the making of money, by acquisition as the ultimate purpose of his life. Economic acquisition is

> no longer subordinated to man as the means for satisfaction of his material needs. This reversal of what we should call the natural relationship, so irrational from a naive point of view, evidently as definitely a leading principle of capitalism, as it is foreign to all peoples not under capitalist influence (ibid.: 53).

Another dimension of Weber's concept of man can be found in his treatment of 'legitimate order' and its exemplification in his sociology of religion. He particularly makes use of the concept of 'charisma' to add a creative transcendental element in the existential character of man. In his sociology of religion the manifestation of charisma is located in the prophet or prophecy. Even Protestant reformation had its share of prophets. Social systems 'change only through prophecy either of the 'exemplary' character or of 'imitative' character. Charisma endows a legitimacy to prophecy in society which sets into motion a new wave of reform and change. In course of time charisma is routinized and rationalized. Man, to Weber, is thus simultaneously an 'affective being,' a 'rational being' and above all, he is a 'charismatic being'. Charisma effaces traditional interpretation and adds innovative elements to rationality and affectivity. "The charismatic quality of an individual as perceived by others, or himself, lies in what is thought to be his connection with (including possession by or embodiment of) some *very central* features of man's existence and the cosmos in which he lives. The centrality, coupled with intensity, makes it extraordinary. The centrality is constituted by its formative power in initiating, creating, governing, transforming, maintaining or destroying what is vital in man's life" (Shils, 1966: 201). This charismatic quality of man though not equally available to all human beings is yet a universal qualitative resource in man, because charisma involves intensity of contact to the followers as it means intensity of cognitive upsurge to the prophet.

Weber is a systematic sociologist. He proceeds in his formulation of the concept of man also of other sociological categories through a scheme of typifications. The components of tradition, rationality and charisma are principles on the basis of which man's existential character and his sociological roles are typified. The extent of freedom and unfreedom that a man may enjoy would depend upon as much the growth of social structure as on his individual typification. This links Weber's concept of man on the one hand with phenomenology and on the other with symbolic interactionism.

Distinct Views

Sociology, both of the Marxist and Weberian theoretic traditions, underwent major changes and syntheses following the holocaust of the Second World War. Critical theory and neo-Marxist theory in sociology emerged as a direct consequence of this. Max Horkheimer, Jurgen Habermas, Theodore Adorno, Erich Fromm and Herbert Marcuse initiated theoretical and empirical studies from a new synthetic framework on the basic existential character of man. One finds a creative mix of neo-Platonism, Marxism, neo-Freudianism and phenomenological ideas of Edmund Husserl, Max Schiller and Mannheim in the paradigms of critical theory. The aim is to bring back the essential dialogical and dialectical character of man's existential being. It is clearly evident in the writings of Horkheimer and Adorno. They observe:

> The most important consequence to be drawn from insights into the interaction of the individual and society—and, to be sure, just that which positivistic sociology avoids—is that the human being is capable of realizing himself as an individual only within a just and humane society. This insight is already contained in the Platonic theme, that functional social coherence is the precondition for the actualization of the idea implanted in every human being. Only the just society will permit the human being to realize his idea. *The more concrete his thought becomes, the more it becomes one that is critical of society* (italics added) (1973: 46-47).

It is in this critical perspective that Horkheimer and Adorno see inherent instability in the 'bourgeoise man' who is tyrannized by oppositions, such as between the bourgeoise particular existence and politically general existence, as well as between the private and professional spheres.

Critical theory combines empirical understanding with theoretical constructions that lead to praxis. *The Dynamics of Prejudice* (1950) by Bettelheim and Janowitz, *The Authoritarian Personality* by Adorno and his associates (1950), *Prophet of Deceit* (1919) by Lowenthal and Guterman, etc. have gone into the analysis of the pathology of man, his ideological self-rationalization and negative projections in modern industrial society. The central theme of the *Authoritarian Personality* is a relatively new concept the rise of an 'anthropological' species which Adorno would call the authoritarian type of man. "In contrast to the bigot of the older style he seems to combine the ideas and skills which are typical of a highly industrialized society with irrational and anti-rational beliefs. He is at the same time enlightened and superstitious, proud to be an individualist and in constant fear of not being like all the others, jealous of his independence and inclined to submit blindly to power and authority" (Adorno et al, 1950: ix). The portrayal of the authori-tarian personality based on intensive empirical investigations and clinical analysis proceeds on the logic of 'character typology' which Adorno's theory of negative dialects refutes. In his work *Negative Dialectics* (1973) Adorno writes:

> Contradiction is not what Hegel's absolute idealism was bound to transfigure it into: it is not of essence in a Heraclitean sense. It indicates the untruth of identity, the fact that the concept does not exhaust the thing conceived. Yet the appearance of identity is inherent in thought itself, in its pure form. To think is to identify.
>
> Conceptual order is content to screen what thinking seeks to comprehend. The semblance and the truth of thought entwine. The semblance cannot be decreed away, as by avowal of a being-in-itself outside the totality of cognitive definitions.
>
> Contradiction is non-identity under the aspect of identity; the dialectical primacy of the principle of contradiction make the thought of unity the measure of

> heterogeneity. As the heterogeneous collides with its limit it exceeds itself. Dialectic is the consistent sense of non-identity. It does not begin by taking a standpoint. My thought is driven to it by its own inevitable insufficiency, by my guilt of what I am thinking (1973: 5).

Critical theory, in its epistemological postulate, was, according to Adorno, negative dialectical in nature. It rendered norms of validity of concepts inherently dissoluble and problematic. In his empirical study of the authoritarian personality, the use of character typology introduces thus a logical contradiction. The non-identical element of the identity of authoritarianism get neglected. Adorno anticipates this criticism. He writes:

> The reason for the persistent plausibility or the typological approach, however, is not a static biological one, but just the opposite: dynamic and social. The marks of social repression are left within the individual soul. Individualism, opposed to human pigeonholing, may ultimately become a mere ideological veil in a society which actually is inhuman. Thus typification is linked with the theory of negative dialectics (1950: 747).

Adorno's concept of man is both phenomenological and clinical. Where phenomenology sharpens the understanding of human situation, the clinical analysis, its negative dialectics offers scope for praxis. It is this constant tension between theory and praxis that informs critical theory.

Erich Fromm and Herbert Marcdse have, though in a less epistemologically sharp manner, used a similar problematic for the understanding of man. There is, however, a difference. The attempt in the works both of Fromm and Marcuse to integrate Freudian notion of man and society with the Marxist one is central and direct. Fromm deliberately breaks away from the meta-psychology (death and life instinct and primal consciousness) of Freud and builds primarily on his theory of instinctual drives, which he finds has ciose resemblance with Marx's emphasis on man as a sensuous being. He also rejects Freudian theory of phylogenesis, especially his universal Oedipal complex. He, on the contrary, postulates that each society governed by its socio-economic and material conditions develops its own pattern of libidinal structure which shapes man's character structure—a basically ontogenetic process. Indeed, this led to his differences with Adorno, Horkheimer and Marcuse.

In his *Man for Himself* (1964) Fromm develops a dialectical concept of man, linked with his species-nature. It is endowed with internal dichotomies, both existential and historical. Man is different from animal rather negatively, by "the relative absence in man of instinctive regulation in the process of adaptation of the surrounding world"; "self-awareness, reason and imagination have disrupted the 'harmony' which characterized animal existence. Their emergence has made man into an anomaly, into the freak of the universe. He is part of nature, subject to her physical law and unable to change them, yet he transcends the rest of nature" (ibid.: 40). Man has no innate drive for progress, says Fromm; it is the contradictions of his existence that goad him to proceed onwards. The fundamental existential contradictions of man are life and death. Death is an unalterable destiny for man, hence he puts all he has for life. With this is also related another contradiction: man is alone, he is alone as much as he is unique, not identical with anyone else. His lifespan being short, his capacity to bear loneliness being susceptible, he seeks compensation in social solidarity. Man is a social being. But this also leads to contradictions—historical contradictions in individual and social life "which are not necessary part of human existence but are man-made and soluble, soluble either at the time they occur or at a later period of human history"(ibid.: 43). Man can annul historical contradictions by his own action, but he cannot annul existential contradictions. He may try to sublimate it by pursuit of pleasure or business but the tension in human life remains.

Man can resolve this dilemma, according to Fromm, only through commitment to ideals. He says: "Man is not free to choose between having or not having ideals, but he is free to choose between different kinds of ideals, between being devoted to the worship of power and destruction and being devoted to reason and love" (ibid.: 49). This is the basis of his 'humanistic ethic', its basis in contradistinction to authoritarian ethics lies in the affirmation of life, the unfolding of man's power, (where) virtue is responsibility towards his own existence.

In *Escape from Freedom* (1942), Fromm deals with the general problems of man's existential conditions. "The main theme of this book is that man, the more he gains freedom in the sense of emerging from the original oneness with man and nature and the more he becomes an 'individual', has no choice but to unite himself with the world in the spontaneity of love and productive work, or else to seek a kind of security by such ties with the world as destroy his freedom and the integrity of his individual self" (ibid.: 18). Alienation of man is a result of his feeling of isolation and powerlessness which can be resolved only through enrichment of interpersonal relationships; to realize this, the negative condition of man through his atomization or isolation as 'freedom from' should be transformed into the positive activity of the integrated total personality or 'freedom to'. This would entail structural as well as ethical changes in society.

In *The Sane Society* (1955) Fromm again reiterates his humanism, now called 'normative humanism' as a solution of the problem of man's self-alienation and its societal concomitants. Theoretically, he covers almost the same ground he explored in *Escape from Freedom,* but he now shifts his emphasis to the needs of man, both material and psychic. The impress of Marx is now more prominent, as he says, "the species man can be defined not only in anatomical and physiological terms: its members share basic psychic qualities" (ibid.: 121). He also analyzes the structure of the capitalist society and the state of human situation, anonymous authority, anonymous institutions and progressive alienation of man from his own objective reality and the progressive schism in his psyche. The 'road to sanity' that he suggests is once again the reiteration of his normative humanism which implies societal structural changes to reinforce this value system.

Marcuse's position basically differs from Fromm's. First, Marcuse does not reject Freudian presuppositions of meta-psychology. He retains the postulate of Thanatos—the death instinct and reiterates the Freudian hypothesis of intensification of destructive activity in the wake of civilizations. In his *Eros and Civilization* (1955) he gives a positive interpretation to Thanatos whose aim was not aggression only but also end of tension in life—the *'Nirvana* principle'. Civilization no doubt enslaves and alienates man owing to its 'performance principle' and Marcuse approvingly quotes Schiller that in such a society "...enjoyment is separated from labour, the means from the end, exertion from recompense. Eternally fettered only to a single little fragment of the whole, man fashions himself as a fragment; ever hearing only the monotonous whirl of the wheel which he turns, he never develops the harmony of his being, and, instead of shaping the humanity that lies in his nature, he becomes a mere imprint of his occupation, his science (Schiller in Marcuse, 1955: 135).

How could man redeem himself from this fate that modern industrial society imposes upon him? Marcuse's answer is that since it "was civilization itself that 'dealt modern man this wound', only a new mode of civilization can heal it. The wound is caused by two polar dimensions of the human existence...sensuousness and reason, matter and form (spirit), nature and freedom, the particular and universal". To overcome this contradiction it would be necessary that the 'play impulse' of man is reinvigorated through creating in him mental faculty to exercise his freedom through *imagination*. "Once it has gained ascendancy as a principle of civilization, the play impulse would literally transform the reality. Nature, the objective world would then be experienced primarily neither as dominating man (as in primitive society), nor as being dominated by man (as in the established civilization), but rather as an object of contemplation" (ibid.: 137). Very much like Marx, Marcuse reiterates that realm of freedom and non-repression lies in abundance, "freedom is not within but outside the struggle for existence". The realm of necessity is the realm of unfreedom. This state of man's liberation from alienated labour (non-aesthetic work imagination) is the state of *Nirvana*.

At this level of analysis Marcuse's *Eros and Civilization,* which starts primarily as a neo-Freudian construction, takes on a purely sociological dimension. It is this idea that he further develops in his *One-Dimensional Man* (1964). In this work, his diagnosis of modern industrial society remains more or less unchanged but his agenda for social change undergoes some basic changes. It moves towards social nihilism of a kind. One-dimensionality is a characteristic of the over-conformist industrial society. He writes:

> *One-dimensional Man* will vacillate throughout between two contradictory hypotheses: (1) the advanced industrial society is capable of containing qualitative change for the foreseeable future; (2) that forces and tendencies exist which may break this containment and explode the society (ibid.: 13).

Marcuse diagnoses the problem of one-dimensionality in modern society in such processes as complete information and media control and its standardization, closing of the political universe through anonymity of relationship between the rulers and the ruled, containment of change and conquest of the unhappy consciousness through 'repressive desublimation'. This last element Marcuse defines as, "flattening out of the antagonism between culture and social reality through the obliteration of the oppositional, alien and transcendent elements in higher culture by virtue of which it constituted another dimension of reality". This liquidation of two-dimensional culture, he says, takes place not through the denial and rejection of the 'cultural values' but through their wholesale incorporation into the established order through their reproduction and display on a massive scale" (ibid.: 57). The result of all this is the emergence of one-dimensional thought, the triumph of positive thinking.

Marcuse is hopeful to resolve this contradiction in social life and the life of man through the abolition of reified nature of institutions and human relationships that one-dimensionality introduces. It would call for release of repression both in conceptual and experiential realms. Emphasis should shift from abstract general categories, mass production of culture to specific experien-ces and meanings. He says, "the philosophic concept 'man' aims at the fully developed human faculties which are his distinguishing faculties which appear as possibilities of the conditions in which men actually live. The concept articulates the qualities which are considered 'typically human'. The vague phrase may serve to elucidate the ambiguity in such philosophic definition—namely, they assemble the qualities that pertain to all men as contrasted with other living beings, and, at the same time, are claimed as the most adequate or higher realization of man" (ibid.: 169). The alternative that Marcuse suggests for the solution of this dilemma of modern man goes beyond the aesthetic and becomes revolutionary nihilism, especially in his *Reason and Revolution* (1960) and other essays, Marcuse even pleads for a violent revolution to throw away the one-dimensionality of the society and man. He justifies it on the basis of his construction on the Freudian theory combined with Marxism.

Phenomenological sociology which emerged as a reaction to the idealistic epistemology and social philosophy has contributed richly to the concept of man. Its roots could be found both in classical phenomenologists like Edmund Husserl and Max Schiller (whose concept of man we have already discussed) as well as in classical sociologists like Marx, Weber and Durkheim. Its concept of man also overlaps the works of C.H. Cooley and George Mead—the symbolic interactionists. Among the prominent phenomenological sociologists who have synthesized the paradigms of Husserl with Weber is Alfred Schutz. Husserl wanted to create presuppositionless philosophy by rejection of assumptions about the generality of categories and by founding them on experiences of conscious human beings who live and act in the 'world' and apperceive and interpret it. To him, forms of consciousness are tied to experience, which is man's attention directed on objects both real and imaginary, material or ideal and which constitutes object of his 'intentionality'. This reality can be grasped only after elimination of all preconceived notions concerning reality and through initial suspension of beliefs in the 'outer world'. Reality of the outer world is neither confirmed nor denied; it is 'bracketed' in an act of phenomenological reduction. What is left after elimination of all ontological assumptions is "inner world of conscious individual", the concern of phenomenology.

Husserl also formulated a theory of transcendental phenomenology where one could 'bracket' not only outer world but also individual consciousness! Much of Husserl's formulations thus relate to problems of inter-subjectivity and individual consciousness in the life-world. It does not grapple directly with the problems of social structure and the situation of man. Alfred Schutz, has, therefore, rightly criticized Husserl for his lack of social science concern and in his own phenomenological formulations drawn heavily from Weber, especially his interpretive paradigm and emphasis on typification as a process of social construction and management of meanings and experiences. He formulates his concept of man through his treatment of the 'cognitive setting of the life-world' where he states that each individual constructs his own 'world'. The life-world is a social world which one finds pre-structured but the essence of human identity or self lies in mediating between the pre-structured life-world that he inherits through existent typifications and the exercise of his own intentionality. He particularly deals with this problem in the context of the 'stranger' who being raised in his community finds himself in an outside culture; the stranger has to reconstruct the reality of the host community piece-by-piece through *rules* of the community (Schutz, 1970). Schutz constructs the existential structure of man combining the perspective of social psychology; he treats man's motivation as anchored in two-fold directions: first, future-oriented, goal-directed motives which constitute 'in-order-to' motives; and secondly, motives concerned with reasons of their action, based on past experiences; these constitute 'because motives'. The problem of relevance in human action, the problematic of man is rooted into the structuration of human motives in the life-world. Man makes dramatical rehearsal of future action, he is capable of 'motivated phantasying' which serve both as cushions and crises in the being of man. Borrowing from Weber, he also classifies social action as rational and non-rational, but he treats rational action as a mere ideal not realizable in everyday life conduct. Schutz emphasizes the role of symbols in synchronization of the 'shocks' of human experiences of everyday life; man proceeds through manipulating symbolic universe and takes 'leaps' in his consciousness with their help. This ability of symbolic leaps in man is the basis of his humanity.

It is true that Schutz, like most phenomenologists, deals primarily with the structural inquiries; these alone provide the context for the problematic of man. But, in contemporary phenomenological sociology, one may find efforts to grapple directly with the existential problems of man, not to the exclusion of the context of social structure but as its interactive dimension. Berger and Luckmann in *The Social Construction of Reality* (1966) and Berger in *The Sacred Canopy* (1969) and Berger and others in *The Homeless Mind* (1974) portray phenomenologically this aspect of the concept of man. In *The Social Construction of Reality* emphasis is more on man's comprehension and construction of social reality. Sociology of knowledge is not treated as a separate branch of sociology but the very medium through which social reality externalizes from man's subjective experiences. Man is treated both as a body, a phenomenon of 'here', and as existent in time, a 'now'; all social reality is thus here-and-now reality in which man first subjectively internalizes the social reality through his intentionality and then externalizes the same through symbolic typification. "Consciousness is always intentional; it always intends or is directed towards objects." This consciousness progressively expands through hierarchies of typification from the face-to-face experience to remoter levels of interactions and their symbolization. Internalization of objective reality of society through socialization process and its institutionalization later in the form of objective social reality determines the dialectic of social reality. It is mediated through symbols; man constructs social reality both through his personal symbolic manipulation as well as through universal symbolic language which Berger and Luckmann call the 'canopy'. The symbolic universe provides the order and meaning to human life and is the aid to solve the many continual puzzles of human existence. Problems that man faces arise both out of contradictions in the symbolic universe (its malintegration, lack of legitimation or institutionalization) as also through contradiction in the subjective experience of man.

This problem is dealt with more concretely by Berger in his *The Sacred Canopy,* which is a treatment of religion and its existential moorings from a phenomenological perspective. The explication of the phenomenology of man and the dialectic between man and society through religious symbolic universe is its main theme. Berger writes: "Society is a product of man. It has no other being except that which is bestowed upon it by human activity and consciousness. There can be no social reality apart from man. Yet it may also be stated that man is product of society." There is a dialectical relationship between man and society. "The fundamental dialectical process of society consists of three moments, or steps. These are externalization, objectivation, and internalization. Externalization is the ongoing outpouring of human being into the world, both in the physical and the mental activity of men. Objectivation is the attainment by the product of this activity (again both physical and mental) of a reality that confronts its original producers. Internalization is the re-appropriation by men of the same reality transforming it once again from the structures of the objective world into structures of subjective consciousness" (ibid.: 4). Also, "man does not have a given relationship to the world. He must ongoingly establish relationship with it. The same instability marks man's relationship to his own body. In a curious way, man is "out of balance with himself. He cannot rest within himself, but must continuously come to terms with himself by expressing himself in activity" (ibid.: 5). Formulated in this term, sociological concepts of man, according to Berger, is essentially humanizing, it refers back the imposing structure of social reality to the living human beings. Man also produces values and "discovers that he feels guilt when he contravenes them". Alienation of man emerges as a result of conflict between identity as socially assigned and the identity as subjectively appropriated by man; there is internal confrontation that man faces between the socialized and non-socialized self and external confrontation on account of maladjustment between society and individual. When consciousness is alienated, it ceases to be dialectical. To resolve it, man depends upon 'recipes' of symbolic systems, religion is one such system, but even secularization keeps the problematic intact.

The theme of secularization and human situation is discussed by Berger and his colleagues in *The Homeless Mind* which is a critique of modern society and man. Modern society introduces the phenomenon of 'componentiality'—a process in which man's life experiences are fragmented and he is alienated from himself. This happens through the very institutions that modernization is supposed to bring about, modern technology, bureaucracy (which lead to multi-relationality), pluralization of interactions and emphasis on taxonomic order. The solution of this problem lies in the creation of adequate symbolic system or value systems and not in taking recourse to a 'counter culture', as the ideology of modernization. Without adequacy of values none of these structural changes would solve the problem of man.

Berger has formulated his phenomenology after duly synthesizing in his work the postulates of Durkheim, Schutz and also Mannheim. Specially Mannheim's diagnosis of our time as a phenomenon of contemporaneity of non-contemporaneous', or the lack of it between values, psychological orientations and structural changes in society, especially the changes in the elite structure. In his Man and Society in *An Age of Reconstruction* (1940) Mannheim suggests the need for creation of a psychological response to structural changes of modern time commensurate with the new challenges. It should neither be bourgeois-oriented in ideology nor should it be total planning-oriented. It should follow a middle path between the two based on pragmatism. Freedom of man should be combined with new planned social order. Only this type of social construction will be able to transform man equal to the challenges of the contemporary society.

Closely related to the phenomenological approach to the concept of man is that of symbolic interactionism in sociology, led by George H. Mead, elaborated by Herbert Blumer and given a new form by Erving Goffman. Mead, in his *Mind, Self and Society* (1934), formulated a dynamic interactional theory of the relationship between self and society. Self develops in society from the ego principle T, with the help of social interaction in family setting. The human child internalizes society in his self-objectivation into 'me', through 'conversation of gesture', in play and in primary group interaction. His consciousness is also formed in the same process. Mind, self and society are thus products of the same interactional process and bear a dynamic relationship. Man's self and his consciousness are thus creators as well as products of society. This defines the contingency of human problem. The notion of *praxis* in Mead is that hand mediates both with nature as well as in relation with other men. Labour has played a great role in evolution of man from the ape; speech and hand go together to shape the history of human evolution.

In his *The Philosophy of the Present* (1932), Mead says that "the past (or the meaningful structure of the past) is as hypothetical as future", the past is involved in the present, hence successful policy on man should recognize this truth and evolve conscious responses to be able to deal with "several things at once". He is a relativist through and through since he believes in the capacity of man to be at home with two or more exclusive systems. His dialectical approach to self, and society, bears close resemblance to Martin Buber's approach in *I and Thou,* his philosophical anthropology that sociality results only from social interaction. Only Buber's approach to man's existential problems is ethical whereas Mead's is relativistic rational.

Herbert Blumer states the premise of his theory as: "Human society is made up of individuals who have selves (that is, make indications to themselves); the individual action is a construction and release, being built up by the individual through noting and interpreting features of the situations in which he acts; that group or collective action consists of the aligning of individual actions, brought about by the individual's interpreting or taking into account each other's action" (quoted in Zeitlin, 1973). Blumer, in his emphasis on the interactional dimension, neglects completely the role of social forces in defining the role of men in society.

From the viewpoint of the concept of man in sociology the contribution of Erving Goffman is really original. His is not only a dramaturgical but also a debunking notion of man. Man as actor, he postulates in his *Presentation of Self in Everyday Life,* presents a front; his real self is never in judgement because we infer meaning from others, action based on the impressions that we register about him. Men, therefore, try consciously to manage impressions. There is thus a discrepancy between the human self and social self. Man deliberately creates 'front regions' to project those aspects of his self which he wants to be noticed and 'back regions' for those that he wants to conceal. Apart from these two regions is the 'outside' sphere, the goings on of the establishment outside the walls. Groups in which actors act have their secrets, 'dark' and 'strategic', and in each of them gets introduced what Goffman calls 'discrepant roles', the role of informer, posing as a member of the team. Each organization creates its social world and its inmates experience this world subjectively through slow formation. In *Asylums,* the study of hospital inmates, Goffman makes this analysis of subjective structure of the inmates and its dynamics. Hospitals which are based on professional knowledge "present a partisan view" of themselves to the non-professional inmates. This is the demand of the impression management.

Through these and various other studies on the role structure and subjectivity of members in small groups, Goffman brings to bear upon us the tension inherent in human interaction and social actions. He also in this process projects a concept of man which is totally demystifying and marks the end of an illusion.

Roots of the Problem

In what way does a sociologist distinguish himself from other social scientists when he talks of man or of concept of man? Answer to this question would lie primarily in the worldview that sociology has been able to project as its own. This worldview, a product of structural transformation in society following industrial revolution, was basically of positive humanism—a humanism which sometimes blended with rationalism as in Comte and Pareto and sometimes transcended it to reach a new apperceptive level of empathy and critical view of societal processes as in Marx and Schiller. It was also a demystifying worldview, a perpetual challenge to the conceptual superstructure of the establishment and its ideology. Peter Berger remarks that "sociology is essentially a debunking discipline. It directs, uncovers only rarely inspires. Its genius is very deeply negative, like that of Goethe's Mephistopheles who describes himself as a 'spirit that ever says no'. To try to change this character is to destroy whatever usefulness sociology may have— especially its moral and political usefulness, which comes from being held in balance, simultaneously and within the mind of the same person, with the affirmation of moral passion and humane engagement. Therefore, we offer no apology for the negative tone to our argument" (Berger et al., 1974: 207).

It is indeed true that sociological concept of man in most of its treatment is diagnostic, tends to focus upon problems such as alienation, anomie, deviance, diremption and contradictions of human life. As we found in the treatment of Goffman it also tends to be highly cynical and truly debunking. Berger has, therefore, a point when he caricatures the role of sociology in the interpretation of human condition. But he pays little attention to yet another dimension of sociological concept of man—its substitutive normative structure. Sociology is not merely an art of apperception to demystify and debunk, but it also offers an alternative worldview. As C. Wright Mills postulates, sociologist observes, empathizes and portrays with understanding every 'worry' of man in private and public situations when it becomes 'trouble'. He does so by linking biography of man with his history. This effort indeed belongs to the truly constructive contribution to the understanding of the problem of man. Once sociology was deeply involved with this type of understanding. The lament of Ernest Becker for the *Lost Science of Man* refers particularly to this creative period of sociology, when it was less cynical more humanistic and purposive. It is true that Spencer's sociology was a "a perfect compliment to the narrow classical economics", but even though classicists like Ward and Small treated sociology as a "science of purposive mind, not passive matter. Sociology is a 'telic' science, a science in the service of human well-being and progressive development" (Becker, 1971: 16). Critical and humanistic concern was predominant in Karl Marx; praxeological orientation was his main contribution not only to sociology but also to the concept of man; Durkheim was not morally neutral, he had not only a substitutive ethic but also its commensurate epistemology.

Negativism in sociology is indeed a phase in its development when the western society faced peculiar problems of a post-industrial society. The obsolescence of the liberal capitalistic worldview and ideology, disenchantment of youth from the establishment culture and their search for a 'counter culture', and distrust in formal methodology were at its root. Most cynical expression of this pressure in sociology one could find curiously among those who still believe in an alternative. John O'Neill writes: "Sociology owes its fortune to the fact that nothing occupies man like himself. We are amazed by the misfortune of others as by our own good fortune... Sociology is a study of people. It is a human pastime with pretensions to science", but despite this extreme cynicism, O'Neill does not loose hope, he believes in redemption and exhorts: "In calling sociology a skin trade, I want to restore its symbiotic connection with the body politic and to situate it in relation to the exchange of organic needs and Utopian celebration of the libidinal community which surpasses all understanding. This means that the rhetoric of scientism in sociology as well as its humanism must be tested against commonsense relevance of everyday life" (1972: 10). The alternative in this case is reflexive sociology.

The proponents of reflexive sociology, however, omit the fact that what they call reflexivity of sociology, the quality of cognitive and emotive rapport between the sociologist and the subject of his study was for ever the basic theme of phenomenological sociology; it epitomized Schiller's thesis on the nature of sympathy and Husserl's transcendental phenome-nology. What it really represents today is symptomatic. It is not a crisis of universe of discourse or method of sociology but of the value system of society which has been rendered obsolete. This indirectly reflects the responsive nature of sociological paradigms to social issues and social change.

There is yet another level—the moral level—in which sociology's contribution to the concept of man has been indeed revolutionary. It emanates from its analysis of deviant behaviour and 'deviant roles'. Sociology by locating the source both of the cognitive categories and moral structure of society in the society itself and in its dynamic processes has abolished at least in moral sense the dichotomy between the normal and pathological, the deviant and the conformist, the retreatist and the revolutionary. This development is not new since the beginning of the wave of 'cognitive sociology' as Cicourel thinks but its roots lie in Durkheim's theory of ethic and epistemology. Cicourel, while portraying the approach of cognitive sociology, writes: "Our description of social structure, therefore, must always incorporate the ways in which normative accounts presuppose an unstated reliance on thought processes, socially organized memory, selective attention, and several sensory modalities. Rather than viewing the blind or the deaf as social problem, we can reconceptualize our feelings and treatment of such persons by recognizing that they develop special strategies for dealing with their lack of modality (italics added; Cicourel, 1973: 9).

This reiterates in another form the humanistic and substitutive worldview of sociology and its continual reassertion in different forms in its treatment of man and the problematic of man in society.

3

Significant Elements

The aim of the state (and the society) in India is to transform itself from a traditional agricultural to a modern industrial society, It has also been seen that the Indian Constitution, in its chapters on Fundamental Rights and Directive Principles of State Policy, has clearly laid down that the society should be inspired by the ideals of social justice, equality of opportunity and secular outlook. Thus, the goal is to remove social inequalities arising out of caste system, promote universal literacy and education and liquidate poverty so that each individual in the rural as well as in the urban areas can become educated and have the means to earn his livelihood so that he can provide the minimum necessities to his family, namely, nourishing foods, adequate clothing and housing and see that his children enjoy good health, upbringing and education and are well-equipped to achieve their rightful place in society. This goal is to be achieved by the state providing "a minimum level of social consumption for the different areas and sections of the community" as the Fifth Five-Year Plan document puts it. The objective of the "national programme of minimum needs" is to provide education and health services, supply of drinking water, all-weather roads, sites to the landless people for building their homes and electricity for lighting and to meet the agricultural and industrial needs in the rural areas.

In the Foreword to the Seventh Five Year Plan, the Prime Minister and Chairman of the Planning Commission Rajiv Gandhi stated that "Planning has given us a strong base for building a modern, self-reliant industrial economy. Indian industry today is highly diversified, producing a wide range of products, many embodying a high level of technology. The public sector has a commanding presence and has played a pioneering role in many areas. We have a broad entrepreneurial base and ample technological and managerial manpower. But some weaknesses have also become evident. Much of our industry suffers from high cost. There is inadequate attention to quality. In many areas, we are working with technology that is obsolete. We have reached a watershed in our industrial development, and in the next phase we must focus on overcoming these problems. Our emphasis must be on greater efficiency, reduction of cost and improvement of quality. This calls for absorption of new technology, greater attention to economies of scale and greater competition.

In the final analysis, development is not just about factories, dams and roads. Development is basically about people. The goal is the people's material, cultural and spiritual fulfilment. The human factor, the human context, is of supreme value. We must pay much greater attention to these questions in future. The Seventh Plan proposes bold initiatives in these areas. Outlays for human resource development have been substantially increased. Policies and programmes in education, health and welfare must also be restructured to provide a fuller life for our people.

The ultimate aim of the society is economic development with social justice. Without economic development poverty cannot be reduced. Without adequate investment in the social sectors, particularly with respect to the backward areas in the country and the backward sections of the population, real economic development cannot take place. Economic growth is possible only when there are fundamental changes in the social structure as well as in the personality structure. The social structure should be flexible giving scope for social mobility and for increase in the size of the middle class; there must also be alterations in the personality structure to enable an individual to use the opportunity provided by the flexibility of the social structure; the individual must be rational, time conscious, future-oriented; he must have strong motivation to make the full use of his ability and the opportunity; he must have a sense of responsibility and commitment to work; he must utilize his leisure to improve his education and training. It is only when there is a change in the social structure and the personality structure that there can be real economic growth. Each individual will be able to contribute to the economic growth to the full extent that he is capable of by his ability, aptitude and training. This involves the abandonment of the traditional method of upbringing children to fit them to the roles of their parents and the inculcation of ideals which enable them to take their legitimate place, based on their education and training in a society with expanding opportunities and new occupations.

The experience in the last quarter of a century has shown that mere economic development without any change in social structure or in personality structure, without any change in child upbringing and education has not affected either poverty or illiteracy; real urbanization in the country has not been brought about.

In all the various spheres like agricultural production, industrial production, transportation, communication, construction of multi-storeyed buildings, the record of achievement is impressive indeed compared with the 1950 base. But compared with requirements of the population in the rural as well as urban areas, the achievement is terribly inadequate. Higher GNP does not ensure higher per capita income; higher per capita income does not ensure that the members of the backward sections, whether living in forward areas or in backward areas, have a fair deal. The proportion of those living below the poverty line continues to be around 40 per cent despite the doubling of agricultural production and even more of the industrial production. Besides the contribution of income from the agricultural sector to GNP continues to be around one half. Also the proportion of the population engaged in the industrial sector continues to be around ten per cent.

Social structure continues to be hierarchic based on birth with the members of the backward classes continuing to suffer social handicaps in the rural as well as urban areas. There has been hardly any change in the personality structure either of the hundreds of millions of the backward classes or of the millions who form the advanced classes; the members of the backward classes continue to be submissive and the members of the forward classes continue to be dominant, despite solemn affirmations of social justice and social equality. The right of exercising the vote according to adult franchise has not really affected the outlook or the aspirations of the backward classes as a whole.

From this, it is clear that while economic development is necessary, it is not sufficient to ensure structural changes in the society. It is also clear that democratic constitution, adult franchise and periodical elections do not ensure that structural changes will take place in the society. Experience has also shown that pro-viding school services at the doors of the people does not ensure literacy. All these provisions *enable* the individual and the group to change; but experience of the last four and a half decades, that is two generations, shows that they do not guarantee the utilization of the amenities provided. This shows how important is the factor of social mobilization.

As Deutch wrote, social mobilization is a summary term for the process by which the major clusters of old social and economic commitments are broken and people are socialized along new patterns, and are being exposed to education and mass media so that they are ready to move out of the place of their birth, if necessary, to new areas where, diverse occupational opportunities are available.

Important Factors

Our analysis has shown that the cultural factors are very significant. Old, values have to be modified in view of the changed conditions and new values have to be incorporated in the personality structure and in child upbringing. The population explosion in the sixties has clearly shown that the old values regarding the need for a large family are continuing to operate in spite of the altered rates in mortality and the increasing longevity. The small family norm has to be accepted by the families in the villages and in the urban slums in order to bring down the birth rate deli-berately.

Technological adoption as well as innovation also depend on the cultural factors. Still the belief persists that the best was in the past and that the present is the very worst (with great truth because of the unprecedented rise in cost of living); there is no pervasive faith in the present or in the future. Nor is there faith in rational solutions to problems. Tradition and emotionality prevail when one is confronted by new situations; there is mob violence instead of rational and constitutional procedures; truth and non-violence are conspicuous by their absence.

Cultural factors appear to be strongly operating both at the production and at.the consumption levels. The main problem in the economic situation is the need to break up the vicious circle of poverty with low production, low consumption and low savings. Production of luxury goods has increased considerably; the signals of the producers are fixed on the satisfaction of the needs of the affluent sections. The aim of the economy must be not only to increase production but also to increase the consumption of the manufactured goods by the masses, particularly in the rural areas; this increased consumption is possible only when there are increased employment opportunities and an increase in wages so that the landless agricultural labourers can purchase goods which improve the standard of living of their families.

The central problem of the social, economic and political situation is the persistence of caste hierarchy, in spite of the constitutional and legal changes emphasising equality of opportunity and social justice. Legislation cannot bring about cultural change. Our analysis has shown how in the present social context it is necessary to emphasise *sadharana dharma,* the practice of truth, non-violence, compassion and other humanistic virtues, and *svadharma* in the sense of commitment to one's work rather than *varna dharma* or *jati dharma.* It is true that this cultural outlook can emerge only when there is a change in the living copditions, personal habits, education and training of the backward classes, who constitute more than half of the population. But it must be realised that this is not a mere economic problem. It is essentially a cultural problem. The cultural inheri-tance since the days of the *Dharma Sutras* and Manu in *Dharma-shastra* made the Vedic *class system* into a rigid *caste system.* It is necessary that the forward classes practice the *sadharana dharmas* and abandon *jati dharma* in their dealings with people at large, particularly in the rural areas where 80 per cent of the population live.

Education and economic development are the means to improve the level of living and thinking of the vast masses in rural and urban areas. The main obstacle to educational and economic development in the recent decades appears to arise not so much from the Brahmin as from the advanced non- Brahmin castes who look upon the improvement in the quality of life and the aspirations of the backward classes as a threat to their social prestige.

Similarly, the mere removal of the legal disabilities in the path of the women has not affected the social status of the women. This is again a cultural problem. The rural parents and the parents in the backward classes do not want their girls to go to school and become educated. The lower middle class families are against their women folk working to earn money. Women who work come either from the lowest class or from the upper middle class.

The importance of the cultural factors, the beliefs and value systems come out very clearly in the analysis of the educational situation. Premi (1972) has shown that the figures published by the Director of Public Instruction of Madras State for 1960-61 give the distribution of pupils on the basis of the occupation and income of parents. The figures show a definite trend of reduction in the proportion of pupils from the officials and professionals to tradesmen, agriculturists, and unskilled workers. While 234 children period persons designated as officials went to school only 57 children per 100 traders, 34 children per 100 agriculturists went to school. The backward classes do not have any faith in education. The problems of wastage and stagnation have been there right from the twenties of this century as far as published data is concerned. The resistance to adult literacy can be traced even earlier. The backward classes do not want to become literate; they do not want their children to become literate. The agriculturist as well as the artisan have tradition and experience to support this resistance. So long as occupational aspirations are based on tradition, the need for education is totally irrelevant. Apathy has its own role to play. The desire for immediate returns makes the parents to prevent the children from continuing their schooling even if they are persuaded to get them enrolled. The teachers, who generally come from the forward classes, are not sympathetic to the slow learners. These children are slow learners not because they they lack in ability but because they lack the experience and guidance at home to profit by the schooling. The language as well as the themes of the textbooks are heavily loaded in favour of the forward classes. Thus, the child of the backward class, who is able to rise above all these obstacles, is indeed a hero. If he becomes frustrated when he continues to be treated as a 'low caste' fellow in spite of his education, the social system is certainly to be blamed.

He cannot be expected to be docile and submissive. Among the various factors which lead to student unrest like large enrolment in the liberal arts courses which do not prepare the youth fora job, the prospects of unemployment which confronts them, the rising cost of living, etc., the arrogant behaviour of the forward classes may also be an important factor.

Modernisation is closely related to universal literacy , technical training and liberal education. Any proposal to modernize and industrialize the country is idle when secondary education is not geared to meet the needs of industry. The great barrier is the cultural attitude against manual and skilled labour and in favour of white-collar jobs. These attitudes prevent the success of all attempts to modernize the society.

Our analysis has further shown that there is a great amount of over- urbanization. The populations in the towns and cities are not truly urban. One-fifth of the urban population live in slums. Most of those who live in the cities are only physically in the city; socially they are rural; they live together in one area as caste groups, creedal groups and linguistic groups. The solidarities are 'mechanical' and particularistic, based on kinship and not 'organic' and universalistic.

The influence of cultural values is also very clear in the area of social mobility. It is the traditionally advanced groups that are making use of the opportunities to move up in status. The traditionally backward continue to be inhibited by their own limited self-images. Adult franchise has not liberated them. They are unable to view themselves as the citizens of this great nation and inheritors of this great culture. Their kinship ties and upbringing bind them to their traditional identities.

All these trends clearly show that the mass media have not been able to affect the lives of the vast majority. The messages from the mass media do not help in building up new mobile personalities. The traditional messages are more in prominence than messages which can modernize their outlook, attitudes and aspirations. They reinforce the old outlooks and attitudes.

Secular outlook is yet to be built up among the elite themselves, let alone the masses. Rituals have a firm hold on the classes as well as masses; rationalism, empiricism and readiness to change are yet distant.

Particularistic outlook with respect to caste, creed and language inhibit the development of universalistic outlook which is necessary to promote national integration.

Hierarchic outlook based on birth, and education, and wealth associated with birth prevails, particularly in the rural areas where 80 per cent of the people continue to live. While during election campaigns equality is emphasised, between elections inequality is practised. One outstanding feature is the plight of the 'converted' Harijans. They get themselves converted to Christianity, Islam, Sikhism or Buddhism to escape the religious, social and economic inequalities to which they are subjected to as Hindus. But they find that their social disabilities do not end with conversion. They continue to be treated as Harijans both by this new co-religionists and the Hindus; they lose the facilities provided for the "Hindu Harijans". So they plead in a pathetic way that they should be treated as *Harijans* and not as Christians, Muslims or Buddhists. They can escape the caste barrier only by education and migration.

The Dimensions

The aim of planned change is to attain the goals which have been framed. It must be remembered that the primary aim of the first four Five-Year Plans was to increase the GNP and to diversify the economic structure so that the economy can be self-sufficient to meet the internal needs and to export manufactured articles in order to raise the economic potential of the country. Any social goals contemplated were only secondary. Bearing this in mind, it is necessary to develop a set of indicators which will help us to find out whether the society is moving in the direction indicated above, namely, towards a flexible social structure providing scope for social mobility, towards the requisite change in personality structure of the citizens so that illiteracy and poverty could be minimized if not eliminated by the development of the necessary skills. Such indicators will enable us to find out whether the society is moving in the direction envisaged and the rate at which it is likely to bring satisfaction to large sections of the people; they will also enable us to detect the discrepancies in the various aspects so that appropriate remedial steps could be taken. They can give us a measure of social mobilization.

In spite of the importance of developing indicators of social change, particularly when technical planning is used to bring about social change, it is unfortunate that investigations in this direction have not proceeded beyond the state of description. Attention may be drawn to the work of the Organization for Economic Cooperation and Development (OECD) which has tried to develop a set of indicators for basic physical needs and for basic cultural needs. One of the urgent needs is to make State comparisons within the country and district comparisons within each state, and taluk comparisons within each district, in order to find out the way in which the physical as well as the cultural needs of the community are being satisfied by the planned effort so that deficiency in the programme and achievement can be rectified early. An attempt may be made to develop a set of indicators for socio- economic change which will be helpful in the evaluation of the attempts to bring about change in a society, particularly with respect to the developing societies.

Nutrition. Work in nutrition has now established measures to determine whether a group is getting adequate nutritional requirements so that an individual could live in a healthy way and work vigorously to produce goods and services for the society and enjoy the recreational facilities. In this respect there are two indicators, namely, the food consumption in terms of calories per head and in terms of protein consumption.

Clothing. It is very difficult to determine an index for clothing because of variations in temperature. Still one of the ways in which we can reduce clothing to a basic denominator is by calculating kilos of clothing consumed per head per year. However, the available figures relate only to the length of cloth consumed.

Housing. It is even more difficult to determine an indicator regarding this basic need of housing. An independent house is absolutely necessary for the proper socialization of the children and to develop healthy interrelation between parents and children which is basic for social development. From this point of view it may be laid down that each family should have an independent house or an independent self-contained apartment. In a rough way, it may be said that there should be at least per cent of independent houses or apartments in relation to the total population. Probably, the ideal would be 20 per cent of independent houses or apartments, so that a family of five persons can have a house or apartment.

Health Service. In a country like India with thousands of villages, the goal should be at least one well for drinking water in each village. It is impossible to provide protected water supply unless probably the population of the village or town is more than 5,000. So, we can have two sets of indicators. One for the small villages in terms of wells for drinking water and another for the bigger habitations in terms of protected water supply.

Another important indicator that has been accepted is the provision of health service in terms of the number of hospital beds per 10,000 population and the number of doctors and nurses per 10,000 population.

Education. Studies have now shown that enrolment in the school is not the real indicator of progress in education. There are so many absentees among them and there is the problem of withdrawal of students after a short period of enrolment. So it would be fruitful and realistic to take into account the proportion of the children of the school-going age of 11-14 who are in schools as an indicator. Even more significant in this respect is the propor-tion of girls between 11-14 who are in the schools.

Another very important indicator is the literacy in general population particularly among the women. A third important indicator of educational development in terms of social develop-ment is the proportion of technical schools. Provision of facilities for general education, paiticularly at the secondary school level, is absolutely useless because studies have shown that there are only about 20-25 per cent of the children who have the adequate educational aptitudes to make use of these facilities. Further, the progress of the society depends not upon mere general education; it is the training in technical skills which enable the production of goods and services which is most critical.

Mass Media. The number of radio receivers for 10,000 population is a very good index of the extent to which the people whether literate or illiterate are exposed to new information, etc. Similarly, the cinema seats available per 10,000 population is also a good index of the exposure to mass media. As regards newspapers, they are useful only when the people at large become literate enough to purchase and read newspapers. Among the various types of indices possible, the newsprint consumption per head per year is good index.

Communication and Transportation. As regards the roads and the railways, the absolute length is really no index since it depends upon the area of the country on the one hand and the population of the country on the other. As regards railways, it is now generally computed in terms of kilometer length of railway per 10,000 population. Probably, a similar calculation regarding the length of the black-top roads may be useful. A third index used is the tonne-kilometre road and rail freight per head. The number of motor vehicles for 10,000 population is another index.•This will include motor cycles, cars, vans, lorries, etc. The number of telephones per 10,000 population is another useful index. As regards the post offices, there is again the problem of the two variables-area and population. Probably we could depend on one index as far as rural people are concerned, namely, the number of villages with post offices within one mile.

Energy Consumption. Economic as well as social development depend upon the utilization of non-muscular energy. So the total installed capacity of generating plants by oil, steam and electricity in relation to population will be a useful index. Another index is the percentage of towns and villages with electricity. Here again, the domestic consumption of electricity is a very useful indicator of social development Finally, the number of electric pump sets in relation to cultivated area is an indicator of economic as well as social development.

Proportion of Industrial Workers. Any real social change depends upon proportion of people engaged in production of goods. One of the chief reasons for frustration in the Indian situation today may be attributed to the fact that in spite of all the industrial advancement during the last seventy-five years as a result of the two World Wars and the seven national Five-Year Plans, there is hardly any change in the proportion of working population in the secondary sector. It looks as if a mere increase in the magnitude or in diversity of industrial proportion is really no index of social development if only a small proportion of people are working in this sector. It is when this proportion increases significantly that there may be social change because of the new opportunities available to the people.

The Birth and Death Rates. The reason for the apparent stagnation in the social situation in India is the increase in population due to the birth rate remaining at 27 per thousand while the death rate has declined substantially. The aim of the family planning programme is to see that the birth rate comes down to 25 or even 20 per thousand so that the population is stable with very little increase. So a substantial decrease in the birth rate which matches the decrease in death rate is a good indicator of social development

Urbanisation. Finally, urbanization may be taken as a very good index of social development. As noted above there has been no substantial impact of the first four Plans on urbanization; though in actual magnitude there is a tremendous increase in urban population, the population as a whole has also increased. As noted above, mere urban population not a good indicator since one-ftfth of the population at present love in urban slums. So there is need for two indices: proportion of population having in urban areas and proportion of urban population living in slums.

It is a great pity that there have not been significant studies in India either with respect to the country as a whole or with respect to the individual States using the various indices which could help us to assess social development. In particular, district studies within each State would be very valuable to help in planning for social development. Beginning was made by the census authority in 1961 to classify the district according to some of the indices. In spite of these limitations in the availability of figures, an attempt may now be made to study the progress or lack of it in the last nearly three decades. The following lable gives the figures for 1951,1961,1969,1971,1979,1980 and 1990.

The main problem of the Indian social situation is demographic, the steep increase in population from 361 million in 1951 to 844 million in 1991 due to a fall in death rate from 27 per thousand in 1951 to 10 or less in 1991. As a result the age structure shows an increase in the proportion of those between 15-59 years from 55.5 per cent in 1985 to 57.5 per cent in 1990. Further, there is an increase in the size of the ill-treat group from 301 million in 1951 to 324 million in 1991, though the illitracy rate has gone up from 16.6 per cent to nearly 52.11 per cent in the same period. The figures regarding nutrition and clothing show a stagnant situation. This clearly indicates that the vast majority continue to be living in poverty in spite of the economic development generated by the Seven Five- Year Plans. There is, however, very impressive increase in health services which is clearly reflected in the decrease in death rate and infant mortality rate. The mass media facilities have greatly increased, though doubts are there regarding the relevance of the messages communicated. There is a great, increase in communication and transportation facilities and in energy generation. However, there is no significant increase in the proportion of industrial workers; in other words, there is no significant increase in the proportion of those producing manufactured goods.

Different Fields

The indicators of social and economic development clearly show the areas in which success has been achieved and the areas in which there has been utter failure. Poverty and illiteracy continue to be the outstanding features of the Indian society even after seven Five-Year Plans. Divisive forces, violence and destruction of public property which have become endemic clearly show that the plans have failed to change the social situation. The multiplicity of political parties and the infighting in each party, particularly in the ruling party, have brought the country to a desperate situation. The events of 1967 showed that the State Governments formed by the United Fronts were weak and could not last even a few months. But the events of 1973 and 1974 have shown that even a single party with comfortable majority cannot give a stable government in several states. Infighting within the majority party leads practically to civil war conditions as in Uttar Pradesh in 1973, Gujarat in 1974 and in Bihar in 1974-75, when civil order could be restored only by calling up the military assistance.

The instability of the State Governments is an index of the frustration among the people which the opposition political parties and the opposition factions within the party in power are exploiting for their own end;. While the bank nationalization policy of 1969 and the "garibi hatao" slogan of 1971 appeared to consolidate the party in power, the unprecedented rise in the cost of essential commodities have heightened the sense of frustration and despair in all sections of the people in the whole country. A stable and efficient government is the prerequisite condition both for social stability and peaceful social change. This has become an impossibility with increasing corruption and increasing cost of living. The Governments are apathetic to grievances of the people. Action is taken only when there is rebellion. The Cabinet members and legislators are preoccupied with their own problems and meet only their admirers; they are out of touch with the citizens.

Our analysis above has clearly shown that conflicts at the cultural level and between social norms have been responsible for the large scale sense of frustration in the country. Democracy, socialism and secularism are preached but hierarchy, inequality, emotionalism and particularism are extensively practised at home and in all sectors of the society.

The pattern variable of *particularism* and *universalism* have been clearly brought out in ancient Indian thought in Yogavasishtha: *Ayam bandhuhu ayam neti ganana laghu cheeasam udaracharitanam tu Vasudhaivabtwn- bakhtism.* "He is my friend, he is not my friend, so thinks the narrow-minded person. For a large-hearted person, the whole humanity is his family." The immediate and urgent task of education and communication is to counteract the influences at once which emphasise particularism (familism, casteism, lingoism, etc.) and promote universalism by making people "large-hearted" *(udaracharitanam)* and look upon the people of all states, languages, creeds and castes as members of one Indian nation.

Failure to implement the constitutional requirement of universal elementary education even after forty five years since independence is a glaring failure. Education and communication can be helpful in changing the attitudes and values of the people. As Dube (1974) has shown the major failures with respect to education and communication are that they have not projected a positive image of new India: they have not promoted the attitudes and values conducive to modernisation, they have not imaginatively handled the new system of rewards and sanctions necessary for economic development. Of course these are failures in the utilization of education and communication as means to attain the ends proclaimed. Today both education and communication are being utilized to promote the traditional values more than to promote the values associated with modernisation. The various media are promoting false values of aggrandizement and affluence through advertisements of air-conditioners, frigidaires, etc. rather than the new values of the work ethic; education has become the "highway to elite status", instead of equipping the individual with the attitudes and skills necessary for rational and empirical outlook and promoting his ability to solve problems with objectivity and detachment.

One thing is clear, Indian experience of the last nearly four decades has shown that investment in heavy industry without proper planning and efficient direction in the fields of education and communication to promote the values associated with social and economic development, and the values of human dignity and work, fail to bring about both economic and social development. Economic change, instead of being looked upon as a means to bring about social change, must be looked upon as a consequence of social change.

To use Gandhian terminology *sarvodaya* is the means for individual as well as social development, for economic growth as well as political stability.

In a brief way some of the implications of the concept of *sarvodaya* may be described. It involves the consciousness of common good, an awareness of the dignity of man. It involves a faith in the essential goodness of man, the goodness of even the criminal: it involves a faith in the possibility of the regeneration of each human being. It emphasises the duty of each man to contribute actively to the well-being of every individual as well as the society as a whole. It is based on "bread-labour", that is, no one who does not work has no right to eat, except the children, the disabled and the aged. It promotes the sense of self-dependence and condemns dependence on others, including the state. *Sarvodaya* recognizes the social diversity on the basis of function, merit and work and negates the diversities based on caste, creed, colour, race, etc. Finally, it promotes the right of an individual to disown and fight against an social norms as wen as legal norms which promote discrimination and' which stand for social injustice. In other words, the concept of *sarvodaya* is based on the universal concept of *ṣadharan dharma* and repudiates the particularistic and ascriptive concepts of *varna dharma* and *jati dharma*.

To conclude, social change in Indian society is possible only through the establishment of an open society which gives full scope to each individual to develop his full potentialities so that he can work for his own development and for the well-being of the whole society, *lokasangraha* as the author of the *Gita* puts.

4

Social Institutions

Like most other social sciences in India, Indian Sociology has grown through an encounter with the western philosophical and social scientific traditions. Its specificity in matters both of the choice of concepts and theories and the substantive coverage of the problems for study bears an imprint of this historicity. Nevertheless, sociology in India has also been deeply influenced by the numerous internal processes which signify the passage of India from a colony of the British to the status of an independent republic. Indian sociology, in various measures, embodies in its theoretic orientations and choice of themes for observation and analysis these historical forces which have constituted its 'social conditioning' (see, Singh, 1986). A sociology of knowledge perspective is, therefore, necessary to constitute and to comprehend the many trends and orientations with which the Indian sociology began its growth in India during the colonial period, the new theoretic, methodological and substantive concerns which emerged following independence, the internal differentiation that sociology has undergone during the past fifty years and the challenges and opportunities that sociology faces in the future in response to the changing 'social conditions' in India and abroad.

Initial Trends

Sociology, before it took its place as a teaching discipline in the academic institutions in India, had emerged as a generalized social ideology which viewed the social institutions of the societies from a scientific evolutionary viewpoint at a global level. This was particularly so in the case of the societies with a history of past civilization. In the colonial context in which many such societies were ensnared, sociology became for the many intellectuals from these countries an ideology of revolutionary social and political movement for emancipation from the foreign rule. In the Indian case, this is illustrated by the publication of a journal, *Indian* Sociologist by Shyamji Krishna Verma, a non-resident Indian political and social revolutionary in Britain, in 1905. In London, Verma came into contact with Herbert Spencer, the founder of the British sociology. He was so deeply influenced by Spencer's sociological ideas that he established six fellowships for Indian students to study in Britain on the conditions that they would go back to India after completing their studies, would not undertake government job in India and would dedicate themselves to the social services in their country. He also instituted a lectureship in the name of Spencer for which he donated a thousand pounds (see, Chaturvedi, n.d.). The *Indian* Sociologist continued to be published from 1905 until the beginning of the First World War. Despite Verma's closer contacts with Herbert Spencer, it was not a professional journal. It published articles and commentaries on social, political and cultural issues which were of contemporary relevance and which articulated the reformist and democratic revolutionary ideologies. The printer of this journal was sentenced in July 1909 and the journal had to migrate to Paris for its publication. Shyamji Krishna Verma was himself a scholar of distinction in Sanskrit and an established Indologist who was appointed as a teacher of Sanskrit, Marathi and Gujarati at the Oxford University. Even though Verma was deeply influenced by the contributions of Herbert Spencer, his own journal did not focus upon sociology either as a discipline as enunciated by Spencer, nor did it focus primarily on social and cultural issues within the frame of reference of sociological categories, strictly speaking. The emphasis on social and political issues was rather generalized and issues discussed had a mix of the orientations of social reformism and political activism.

This orientation in sociological contributions in India continued during the first two to three decades of the nineties. Many

Indian academics, trained in the universities of England, France and Germany, contributed to sociology directly and indirectly through their commentaries and exegeses on the writings of the European sociologists and social anthropologists, particularly with reference to their views on Indian society and culture. In a way, this tradition had its basis in the cultural and intellectual renaissance in India during the middle of the 19th century. We may refer in this context to the contributions of Rammohun Roy (1772-1833), Ishwar Chandra Vidyasagar (1863-1902), Swami Vivekananda (1863-1902), Swami Dayananda Saraswati (1834-1883), Swami Sradhananda (1856-1928), Dadabhai Naoroji (1825-1917), Lala Lajpat Rai (1865-1928), J.G. Phooley (1827-1888) and M.G. Ranade (1824-1901) and several others who through their writings and social movements created intellectual and social self-awareness in the country about India's cultural and civilizational strengths and yet pleaded for radical reforms in society in order to encounter the challenges of the western civilization and its colonial expansionism. This period of Indian history is a precursor to the many forms of cultural and political social movements, and it also coincides with the beginning of the institutionalization of the university and college systems in India based on the western pattern. The disciplinary foundations of the many social sciences including sociology and social anthropology were established during this period.

This period followed the inauguration of the early sociological writings by scholars in India either as a sequel to or in response to the writings by the western sociologists on India or in response to the issues of epistemology and history. Most of this type of writing tends to be dialectical and exegetic. The contributions of B.N. Seal and B.K. Sarkar could be mentioned in this context. In case of former, one witnesses critical and discursive response to the comparative evolutionary treatment of various societies and cultures, including that of India, by the British social anthropologists and sociologists, which often reflected not only the wrong premises in their treatment of other cultures or societies but also carried unjustifiable value loads. Seal refuted attempts to interpret the Indian social and cultural reality from a reductionist evolutionary frame of reference, so common in the early 20th century contributions of the western sociologists and social anthropologists. He maintained that institutions could only be compared if they were historically co-existent. Sarkar wrote extensively in response to the writings of the German Indologists and sociologists in whose writings one could clearly discern biases of the 'orientalist frame of reference'. Particularly, the contributions of Max Weber on Hinduism and the culture and social structure of Indian society came under his very critical analysis (see, Singh, 1983; Mukherjee, 1979). Similarly, many other social scientists such, A.R. Wadia, B.N. Dutta, K.P Chattopadhyaya and S.V Ketkar etc., created academic ambience through their writings for the teaching and research in sociology either directly or indirectly. One common stream of consciousness, however, in all these writings was that of historicity of the Indian civilization and its distinct cultural and social identity which was denied the centrality it deserved in most western social science or sociological writings on India. These contributions were not strictly in the domain of systemic sociological analysis of the Indian social and cultural realities but indeed, these had a very high degree of sensitizing effect on the Indian academic scene to provide legitimacy to the teaching and research in Indian sociology.

The teaching of sociology as an academic discipline, though still imbued with deeper humanistic and civilizational orientations, started at the Bombay University with Patrick Geddes joining as professor of civics and sociology in 1919 where he served upto 1924 (see, Mairet, 1957). Formalization of sociology in terms of methods and conceptual framework began with his contributions, but in a much diffuse and generalized form. Geddes' major focus was upon viewing social reality from a moral, communitarian, global and multidisciplinary perspective. He maintained that, "our great need today is to grasp life as a whole, to see its many sides in their proper relations; but we must have a practical as well as a philosophical interest in such an integrated view of life" (Mairet, 1957: xii). Geddes had exposure to various disciplines in sciences and humanities ranging from botany, zoology, mining, engineering to sociology. He was influenced by the works of the biologist Thomas Huxley and through him that of Herbert Spencer, the sociologist. He admired Huxley but disagreed with him on his emphasis to look at science from a purely amoral perspective. For this reason, he also admired the French sociologist August Comte, his positive philosophy and religion of humanity. He used to frequently attend the Comtean

Church though it was laughed at by Huxley as 'catholicism without Christianity'. On this issue, Geddes differed from his teacher. Later, he moved to Paris from England and was deeply impressed by the French university tradition; its centrality on the pursuit of what Geddes calls the 'morality of truth', 'morality of action', and the 'spirit of immeasurable literary, scientific and constructive endeavour'. Here, he was influenced by Fredric Le Play's writings on regional and ecological aspects of civilization. Le Play's triadic categories of 'work, place and family' have deeply influenced Geddes' own schematization of conceptual categories for the growth of regional cultures of societies, particularly his schema of 'work, place and folk'. Similarly, one could also witness the impact of Comte in Geddes' formulation of the diagrammatic hierarchy of the sciences, with mathematics and logic being at the base, physics, chemistry and biology in the middle and sociology (not social physics as Comte adumbrated) at the top. Geddes had also schematically worked out the boundary conditions in which sociology could closely interact with other sciences. In this case, he listed anthropology, ecology and statistics as the major disciplines for interactive integration with sociology.

Geddes extensively used the technique of constructing 'property space' (in diagrammatic boxes) for generation of concepts and methods for sociological investigation. He emphasized the need for ethical, regional and communitarian sensitivity in sociological studies, but his primary emphasis was upon practical outcome and social engineering. To this end, we find him in the role of a moral architect along with his focus upon the physical architecture of town planning; he consistently laid emphasis upon the regeneration of city life and ecological self-awareness in the planning of the social and cultural habitats at regional and global levels.

Unfortunately, Geddes' entry into the Bombay University's teaching department was of a very short duration and his sociological approach which had a strong blend of empirical methods with philosophical orientations could not get time enough to be institutionalized. Nevertheless, he was instrumental in his successor G.S. Ghurye going to Cambridge for research in anthropology and taking the charge of the department on his return. Ghurye, a Sanskritist and Indologist of great eminence, brought to bear this scholarship together with that of anthropology in developing the pedagogy of sociological teaching at the Bombay University. This is reflected in the curricula for the teaching of sociology. It is also reflected in the researches that Ghurye himself did or directed his students to undertake. In his own writings we witness a creative blend of historicity with Indology, particularly where studies of social structure such as caste, occupation and race are concerned. One can also easily see his emphasis on comparative historical treatment of the formations of social structure and culture with a unique sensitivity to the notion of civilization. Ghurye contributed to sociological writings over several decades and his works cover a vast range of themes relating to the study of concrete structures such as rural and urban communities, social stratification, comparative cultural behaviours, processes of social change and social conflict, cultural styles (dress and fashion), and traditional social formations and sects such as the *sadhus* and *sampradayas*. He also made use of a multiplex of methodologies in these studies, ranging from diachronic historical observations of rural changes to empirical surveys and uses of historical materials and traditional Indological texts. Even though empirical studies of micro-social systems do find a place in his sociology, his main focus has always remained on macro-historical and comparative studies. This tradition has been continued by his successors at the Bombay University.

Apart from his individual researches, Ghurye's larger contribution to the Indian sociology lies in the training of a whole generation of very distinguished sociologists who gave leadership to the profession in the country, and contributed to its institutionalization and modernization as a social science discipline. These sociologists led the direction of research and teaching in the field of sociology during the decade of the 1950's which witnessed a massive expansion in the number of universities and colleges in the country.

Another equally important centre for the early growth of teaching and research in sociology has been the Lucknow University, where the pioneering role was played by Radha Kamal Mukherjee and his two distinguished colleagues, D.P Mukherji and D.N. Majumdar. Radha Kamal Mukherjee established the Department of Economics at the University of Lucknow in early 1930's and introduced the teaching of sociology as a part of economics at the

M.A. level. It is of interest to note that both at the universities of Bombay and Lucknow, the teaching of sociology was not imparted exclusively; it was integrated with civics and political science at Bombay and with economics at Lucknow University. This is understandable considering the fact that during the first two to three decades of the 20th century teaching of sociology as an independent discipline was confined to very few universities in England, Germany and France, and its curricular structure had a broad multidisciplinary social science perspective. Some of the major universities in England, such as Cambridge and Oxford, started departments of sociology much later during the1960's.

The contributions of Radha Kamal Mukherjee like that of Ghurye are stupendous and multidimensional. Radha Kamal, unlike Ghurye, however, showed greater sensitivity to issues of sociological theory and methodology. Indeed, he is one of the earliest sociologist-economists in India to not only integrate the western theoretical and methodological paradigms in the studies of social and economic problems and issues in India but also the one who clearly lays down the foundation of a distinctive Indian sociological paradigm and theoretic structure. His contributions range from the study of slums and industrial labour problems, regional economic structures, problems of peasantry and agrarian economy, study of social stratification and caste (particularly using scalar methodology to measure social distance), study of the 'social structure' values and social ecology to a comparative philosophical treatment of civilizations. He undertook a critical and philosophical diagnosis of the emerging crises of human condition in the industrial societies and its civilization. The reach of his sociological and economic concerns and his treatment of these problems is indeed unique among the Indian social scientists. His sociology reflects not only the endogenous consciousness and the Indian civilizational anchorage, rather he continually responds creatively to most of the contemporary philosophical, theoretical and methodological orientations and shifts in the paradigms of the western social sciences and sociology. His lecture tour of the universities in America in 1930's brought him closer to many significant American social science orientations of that time such as the focus on social ecology, problems of urbanization and its morphological character, the importance of regional and institu-tional economics (such as in the writings of Commons, Veblen and Mitchell etc.) and the utility of empirical survey designs of research etc.

But one of the most significant contributions that Radha Kamal Mukherjee has made to sociology, and the debate on which has since continued in one form or another, relates to his formulation of a general theoretical paradigm of social science and sociology from the perspective of the Indian philosophical traditions. It is a paradigm which attempts to generate a universal general theory for the study of social and cultural phenomena as an alternative to the western theoretical approaches in sociology. He offers an alternative worldview of sociology and social science drawn from the philosophical traditions of the Vedanta, Buddhism and Taoism. These traditions, according to him, are embedded in the values of universal humanism and ethical piety rather than in materialistic rationalism or positivism. Mukherjee is perhaps the only sociologist of his times in India who attempted this ambitious alternative philosophical paradigm for generating a universal theory of sociology and social science both as a corrective and as an alternative to the western traditions of social science theory.

In his presidential address delivered at the Third All India Sociological Conference in 1958, on the theme A *Philosophy of Social Sciences,* he postulates an integral and interdisciplinary view of social sciences (including sociology and social anthropology) and diagnoses the dilemma of the western social science in its one-dimensional focus upon the analysis of human condition and social phenomena from the perspective of rationalistic utilitarianism (product of the Enlightenment period) treating humans as 'homo faber' rather than 'homo symbolicus'. He accepts the relevance of the dialectical method in social science reasoning but refuses to confine it to 'dialectical materialism'. He locates the roots of the dialectical methods in the Indian traditions of Buddhism and Vedanta philosophies. He finds their formulations to be more holistically embedded in logic for the scientific exploration of human realities. He also finds in this context the Taoist conception of being and self-identity to be integrally relevant. He writes:

> "The philosophy of dialectical materialism today promotes the universal notion of an inevitable pattern of development through struggles and conflicts of global revolution and war and subsumes all human progress

> within the dialectic of the economic movement. Modern evolutionary naturalism, Spencerian, Marxian or Bergsonian, reduces man's mind and values as passive entities manipulated mechanically by a vast process that he cannot intelligently direct or control. Evolution as revealed to modern thought has its many levels and dimensions in which persons, values and societies develop in nature. Values are creative and not merely means of adaptation to the environment. The environment also changes, acted upon by human goals, values and ideals" (Mukherjee, 1960: 118, quoted in Singh, 1986).

Mukherjee says that "man thinks and lives dialectically. All social relations and behaviour and values that lie deep seated in them embody polar principles and tendencies" but also that "through the dialectic of the Vedantic *neyti neyti,* Buddhist *sunyat* and Taoist namelessness, the self identifies itself in the reality and the supreme value" (ibid.: 4). Mukherjee thus refutes the logic of reductionism implicit in the western social science formulations of the human actor and social institutions. He postulates, on the other hand, a view of human actor as an eternal negotiator between the existential (deterministic) the transcendent. This he achieves through "the immanence in himself of the not-self, the neighbour, the whole universe" (ibid.: S). This ability alone justifies the status of human actor as 'homo symbolicus', as value-creating being rather than one involved in mere innovation of technologies to resolve the daily problems of existential survival and development.

In his later contributions, Mukherjee, like P Sorokin in the U.S.A., began to focus more on the study of comparative civilizations and his treatment of values and cultural traditions became more diagnostic rather than analytical. But his central concern for rendering the western social sciences free from their positivistic and utilitarian anchorage through integrating in their paradigms correctives from the Oriental, particularly the Indian philosophical and civilizational perspectives, remained intact.

D.P. Mukherji and D.N. Majumdar, both colleagues of Radha Kamal Mukherjee, contributed richly to the teaching and research in sociology and social anthropology. Their approach in some ways could be termed as supplemental to the established orientation. For instance, D.P Mukherji, like Radha Kamal Mukherjee, acknowledges the relevance of the Indian tradition and philosophy for arriving at valid theoretical and conceptual schemes for the study of the Indian society. He, despite being sympathetic to Marxian method and logic, disputed its categories and conceptual structures which, he thought, were largely western-centric. He could see no relevance for many of its categories, for instance, the notions of class and modes of production as formulated in classical Marxism. Innovations were required in this regard for studying the Indian social realities. Such categories for studying the Indian society, according to him, should be derived from the Indian tradition and history, for instance, the traditional notions of community or *sangha* may be more appropriate to understand the social situation of the rural and urban structures in India rather than the notion of class. We see in this orientation a degree of similarity with Radha Kamal Mukherjee's propositions. But there is a degree of difference, D.P. Mukherji does not totally reject the Marxian contributions, particularly its dialectical logic enunciating the centrality of the processes of conflict and contradiction in the social processes of the society. Similarly, D.N. Majumdar supplements Radha Kamal Mukherjee's contributions to the development of the empirical tradition of research. But, beyond this, we may not find many similarities. Majumdar was a trained social anthropologist, a student of B. Malinowski and an avid field observer of the tribes and tribal cultures in India. His concern was more towards capturing the realities of the tribal cultures and social structure through ethnography and to observe its institutional linkages with the rest of the Indian society. His contribution to the ethnography of the Indian tribes is monumental indeed but his theoretical interests hardly go beyond ethnographic comparisons.

D.P. Mukherji, on the other hand, does reflect analytical theoretical orientation in his writings, particularly when he uses the dialectical-historical perspective of 'Marxology' as he preferred to describe his approach, for the study of the middle class structure and formation in India. He also examines the processes of social change and planning in the country and demonstrates the relationship between the Indian tradition and the western conceptual frames of analysis. But he does not show the same degree of interest, as Radha Kamal Mukherjee did, about offering a general theoretical paradigm of sociology rooted in the Indian philosophy, history and traditions as a counterpoint to the western theoretical approaches. Trained in economics and history, and being a literary writer and novelist, D.P. Mukherji's approach to the teaching and research in sociology was more innovative and non-conventional. This led him to write on many themes of sociology, such as music, art and culture which were not conventionally popular during his days but assumed greater significance later as sociology began to grow through institutional expansion and disciplinary specialization.

The generation of sociologists from Ghurye to D.P. Mukherji, who led its teaching and research from the 1920's to the middle of the 1950's, laid a very solid foundation of the profession in India. In their own writings this generation was more encyclopaedic and macro-analytic in approach. The period of specialization has yet to begin. But we may have to remember that even in the west, disciplinary specialization and methodological sophistication in researches began to gain momentum following the end of the Second World War. These early beginners of the Indian sociology pioneered the vision of sociology and social science as having a historical-civilizational anchorage; they felt acutely uneasy in accepting the positivistic, utilitarian and the general evolutionary constructions and premises of the western sociology; they consistently introduced the perspectives of historicity, culture and values in the formulation of sociological concepts and their theoretical underpinnings; their sensitivity to the methodological aspect of sociological research was open-ended and broadly inclusive of all available techniques and methods as found appropriate. Research methodology or technique was supposed to be a matter of preference for the individual researcher, who, it was felt, should have maximum flexibility in devising and using tools for the observation, documentation and construction of the social reality.

Organisational Setup

A new phase for the growth of the Indian sociology was ushered in following independence. Its main attributes were: first, the professionalization of sociology; secondly, the emergence of the new institutional supports for its teaching and research (with the expansion of universities and colleges and funding agencies); thirdly, with such growth a beginning in the specialization in sociological researches in terms of the choices of themes and methods began to take place; fourthly, there was unprecedented growth in methodological consciousness in the discipline, and the teaching of methodology began as a specialized course at most places; fifthly, the emphasis upon the social relevance of the discipline particularly in the areas of development planning and social reconstruction of the society gained greater ascendancy; and finally, a debate on 'a sociology for India' began in a systematic manner. It began to be increasingly felt that the Indian sociology should reflect not only the philosophical, historical and cultural specificities of the Indian society but also it should accordingly improvise and innovate upon the existing sociological çoncepts and categories largely drawn from the western sociology.

Independence in 1947 released new historical forces and aspirations in the country. The country's political leadership, intellectuals and people were acutely conscious of the challenges of nation-building, development and reconstruction of the Indian society. A constitution reflecting the future vision of India as a republic was adopted. Within the framework of a mixed economy, a strategy for the planned development of the Indian economy and society was worked out. The Planning Commission was set up to formulate the priorities and plans for national development. Within its framework, organizations and institutions were set up for the expansion of higher education in the fields of sciences, technology, management, engineering, medicine, social sciences and humanities. Several research councils were set up to augment its growth. A large number of national laboratories in various fields of science were established; agricultural universities were opened; several institutes of technology came up in different parts of the country and there was an unprecedented growth in university and college education.

The teaching of sociology began to expand as new universities and colleges were set up contributing to the increase in the number of teachers and researchers. In order to provide funds and regulate the standards of teaching and research in the universities and colleges, the University Grants Commission (UGC) was created.

Funds for conducting researches on policy related problems were also made available by the Planning Commission. The momentum among the sociologists and social scientists to conduct researches in the areas of greater social and economic relevance was accelerated. The new focus upon researches differed from those of the colonial times. The Planning Commission sponsored a series of studies in the areas of urban sociology, rural and agricultural development, the nature of poverty, the social and economic conditions of the weaker sections, the scheduled tribes and scheduled castes etc. Most of these studies were prioritized on the basis of their relevance for planning and development and in many cases based on the need to generate benchmark data required for development projects.

These processes, together with other developments in the field of education, contributed to the professionalization of sociology and social sciences. Sociology was now taught in various universities and colleges as an independent subject and full-fledged sociology departments were set up in the colleges and universities. Its teaching was no longer clubbed with either economics as at the Lucknow University or with civics and political science as at the University of Bombay in the past. The Indian Sociological Society, which for a number of years had confined its membership to the sociologists of the western India, became an all-India association of the Indian sociologists towards the end of the 1950's. The regional associations of sociology, particularly the one from the northern India, sponsored by the sociologists of the Lucknow University, merged with the Indian Sociological Society. The Society meets regularly and provides a national forum to the teachers and researchers of sociology in the country. It regularly publishes a journal, *Sociological Bulletin,* which is internationally recognized. It networks with the International Sociological Association of which it is an organizational member. These institutional processes of growth have broadened and deepened the national and international concerns of the Indian sociologists towards many sociological issues which may range from the theoretical and methodological to those of choices of themes of relevance in teaching and research.

The professional growth of sociology has contributed to the modernization and standardization of its curricular structure. This has been supported by the UGC which set up subject-wise national panels of professors to periodically review, upgrade and modernize the syllabi in consultation with its teachers. The UGC national panel of sociology undertakes and sponsors research projects, seminars, workshops, etc., to evaluate the state of the discipline and its profession to help in formulation of policies for the upgradation and modernization of the curricular structure of sociology. With the higher degree of the regional diversities in terms of institutional standards and linguistic policies in teaching, effort based is made to evolve consensus on the modernization of curricula by the participation of the teachers of sociology from all regions of the country in the work of the national panel. The empirical researches on the state of teaching of sociology and its profession in the country also help in formulating the issues that deserve discussion at the national level, and where the comparative international level of upgradation of sociology teaching and research is required. So far, the recommendations and suggestions made by the national panels have been widely appreciated and incorporated in the syllabi of sociology in the universities and colleges within the country. This has kept the curricula of sociology in India at comparable international standards.

The UGC's efforts towards modernization of the syllabi in sociology and improvement in the quality of teaching, teaching materials and aids cater mainly to the college and university levels of education. After independence, sociology was also introduced at the secondary level of school education. Even otherwise, the education at the primary and secondary levels of education in various subjects required institutional support for continual modernization of the quality and standard of teaching. The National Council of Educational Research and Training (NCERT) was set up to perform this task. NCERT has significantly contributed to the quality of sociology teaching at the secondary level in India through production of textbooks, training of teachers and conducting workshops and seminars from time to time in the country. The fact that sociology is being taught in India right from the secondary to higher degree levels is a testimony to its professional growth and institutionalization.

Impetus to the growth of sociology, particularly in the field of research, gained new momentum when towards the end of the 1960's the Indian Council of Social Science Research (ICSSR) was established. Its objective is to improve and promote the quality of research in social sciences in the country and to make funds and grants available for this purpose. It is also responsible for setting up research institutes of social sciences in the Indian states and provide them funds to undertake researches. It offers fellowships and grants to the teachers and students of sociology to conduct their own researches. It supplements the efforts of the UGC which mainly looks after the universities and colleges. The ICSSR has made a great impact upon the professional and disciplinary growth of the researches in sociology and social anthropology. So far, it has published three decennial surveys of researches done in India in the fields of sociology and social anthropology.

A significant aspect of the contribution made both by the UGC and the ICSSR to the teaching and research in sociology is that their efforts sharpened the concern for relevance in the evaluation and structuring of the pedagogy of the discipline (see, Singh, 1984). Theoretical researches apart, the focus on relevance tends to be a common value frame promoted both by the UGC and the ICSSR, the former seeks it in the curricula and the choice of the research projects and the latter focuses primarily on the selection of the research themes and methods. This is evident from the reports of the national panels of the UGC in sociology, social anthropology, economics, political science and geography.

We witness in these reports the sense of commitment of the profession of sociology and social sciences to reach higher level of achievement in quality of teaching and research. But we also observe that in matters of defining relevance, most members of the profession show unanimity about the indegenization of concepts and theories. Without erecting walls of separation between social sciences in India and abroad, it is felt that along with creative adaptation of concepts, methods and substantive discoveries made by social sciences in the west and in other countries abroad, the Indian sociologists and social scientists should aim at evolving concepts and methods in tune with Indian historicity, its social and cultural specificity and its goals of social and economic development. For instance, the report of the economics panel says: "the standard economics is supposed to explain the *modus operandi* of an idealized capitalist economy. The Indian economy being anything but that, the orthodox paradigms must perforce collapse"; further, "most of the theoretical concepts evolved in the context of the developed industrial societies of the west are mechanically doled out to unsuspecting batches of students in this country. Not unnaturally we find these rarefied tools of analysis to be of little avail in comprehending their own situation" (see, Singh, 1979). A similar emphasis on indegenization of concepts and methods in the teaching and research is found in the reports of the panels in sociology and political science. Evidently, the notion of relevance as postulated by the sociologists and other social scientists goes beyond mere indigenization of the concepts or methods. It also covers the choice of problems undertaken for research and enunciation of their research methodology. It is evident from the policies both of the UGC and the ICSSR which aim at promoting researches in priority areas which are of national concern for social and economic development. The ICSSR constituted a standing committee of sociologists to promote studies on the educational backwardness of the scheduled caste and scheduled tribe students in various states of India empowering the committee to commission sociologists from these states to undertake research on this problem. The need for this arose because fewer sociologists were observed to be undertaking research projects of their own choice in this area of national concern. From time to time, the ICSSR in consultation with the social scientists evolves the priority list of the areas of research which are funded on a preferential basis. In this category we may refer to sociology of law, gender sociology, problems of the peasantry, minorities and deprived sections of society., The researches on the problems of health, poverty and malnutrition and of the problems of people in remote and more backward areas of the country also receive priority. These priority areas are continually revised and updated.

The Distinctions

The processes of institutional recognition and professionalization of sociology contributed to the enlargement of the range of research interests of sociologists in India. Its linkage with the policy planning and social and economic development reinforced this process. Historically, the end of the Second World War had shifted the gravity of influence in the world of social sciences from Europe to the United States of America where social sciences and sociology had made unprecedented strides in the applied areas of sociological researches and brought about a myriad of innovations in research methodology. Even otherwise, the American sociological traditions had always had a relatively greater applied and policy oriented direction of growth in comparison to the European sociological tradition. This process of growth in the American sociology logically resulted in the differentiation and specialization in sociology. In fact, America had played a leadership role in this direction.

Thus, we witness a convergence of two types of influences of the American sociology upon the Indian sociology soon after independence. The first relates to the emergence of the American sociology as a domineering influence upon the European or even the global sociology following the Second World War, and secondly, its rich and unparalleled advances in policy-oriented research methodologies and techniques accorded it a leadership role in sociology and social sciences. As a consequence of these developments and also because in India the process of planned development had just started, the influence of the American sociology and social anthropology began to grow. Indian sociology increasingly came under the influence of the American sociological and social anthropological conceptual and theoretical orientations.

The process of differentiation in the Indian sociology at this juncture can be seen growing in two directions: first, in the expansion and diversification of the nature of the social, cultural and developmental problems which sociologists began to study and secondly, in the diversification and differentiation of methodologies and tools of research which were now available to sociologists and which sociologists and social anthropologists used increasingly. It may, however, be also pointed out that the emerging national concern for planned development of the Indian society and economy which ranged from rural development, urban planning, empowerment of the scheduled tribes and scheduled castes, weaker sections and minorities to the industrialization of the economy etc. had opened up a vast vista of researchable problems for sociologists and social scientists. The most urgent concerns in the early 1950's were, however, in the areas of rural development and agricultural modernization to overcome the acute problem of food scarcity.

In thematic terms, therefore, the first major differentiation in sociological studies in India was between rural and urban sociology. The decade of the 1950's witnessed a proliferation in the studies of the Indian villages. The pioneering work in this field was done by S.C. Dube, M.N. Srinivas, Ramkrishna Mukherjee, A.R. Desai and several other Indian sociologists. A large number of American and a few British and French social anthropologists also contributed to the village studies in various parts of the country. The American social anthropologist, Oscar Lewis who studied a north Indian village (and had formerly studied a Mexican village) was also associated with the Indian Planning Commission as an advisor. These village studies overwhelmingly had an anthropological orientation. Most were observational, descriptive and holistic in terms of coverage. They attempted a reconstruction of village social structure, culture and customs, its economy and polity etc. from an ethnographic perspective. Very few of them were analytical.

There were few exceptions; however, M.N. Srinivas, while portraying the caste profile of the village did make analytical use of a set of indicators of the caste status, such as ritual status, economic status, political status and status due to numerical strength to arrive at the concepts of 'dominance' and 'dominant caste'. The dominant caste was defined as the one which enjoyed a high status on all these or a maximum number of these status indicators. Similarly, he used the cultural attribute of the lower castes imitating the ideology and way of life of the upper castes to formulate the concept of 'sanskritization'. The attribute of the upper castes who imitated the lifestyle and values of the western civilization, on the other hand, he termed as 'westernization'. The concepts of sanskritization and westernization were extensively made use of by him and a whole generation of sociologists and social anthropologists to explain the processes of social change in India. Similarly, McKim Marriott used the terms 'universalization' and 'parochialization' to explain the dynamics of cultural values and practices in the 'folk-elite' traditions in villages and towns. This conceptual distinction is based on the Chicago university anthropologists, Robert Redfield and Milton Singer's schematic distinction between folk and elite cultures based respectively on the 'little tradition' of the former based on oral culture and the written or the textual tradition of the elite, called the 'great tradition' of culture. Marriott maintained that continually the elements from the folk cultural tradition were lifted up from its local oral ritual or cultural context and were generalized or 'universalized' in the textual (scriptural) great tradition of India. This process he reported from his observation of the cultural institutions and practices in India. Several studies of the folk cultural traditions soon followed.

Ramkrishna Mukherjee's *Dynamics of a Rural Society* and A.R. Desai's (edited volume) *Rural Sociology in India* could be quoted as studies of the rural society which departed both methodologically and analytically from the above social anthropological treatment of the village studies. The former makes use of statistical data from various sources to generate conceptual categories of the class structure in villages and analytically posits them to unravel the problem of rural social structure and development from a quasi-Marxist perspective. The use of the statistical data makes this study comparable to those in other regions and states of India, although Mukherjee confines his attention to West Bengal. A.R. Desai, in his book-length introduction to the *Rural Sociology in India,* explicitly makes use of the historical-systematic and Marxist methods of analysis for the understanding of rural society and its problems; of course, he also refers to the contribution of a few American sociologists who contributed to the systematic methodology for the study of the rural and urban phenomena.

Quite a few rural studies during this period were also conducted with the direct purpose of reinforcing the policies of rural development; this particularly related to the studies focusing upon the community development and extension services and the local panchayat institutions which were introduced by the government. Many American social anthropologists took part in such studies and in several studies, rural leadership, local political institutions and their historical role in rural self-governance were analyzed. In this venture, a number of political scientists also joined, and in course of time these and related studies contributed to the development of the behavioural school of political analysis and political sociology in India. S.C. Dube made a comprehensive study of the impact of the community development institutions on the rural society in India; among the political scientists the contributions of Rajni Kothari and Iqbal Narain are quite noteworthy.

A differentiation process within rural sociology emerged by the end of 1950's. It was first on methodological lines, between those who used anthropological and holistic method for the study of a single village and those who used statistical-survey data for the study of several villages using selected number of analytical variables. Between these two approaches were also studies of the rural phenomena from a folk-elite cultural perspective. Indra Deva and S.L. Srivastava have made in-depth study of the folk culture of villages not only holistically or within a single village but using a regional comparative perspective. A distinction thus between micro-systematic and macro-systematic studies of rural realities has emerged. Differentiation also seems to have emerged between those who study villages directly with the purpose of impact analysis of rural development schemes launched by the state and those who undertake village studies for understanding its institutional structure and its processes.

A large number of urban studies were also conducted during this period although their scale and coverage could not be comparable to the rural studies. The Research Programme Committee of the Planning Commission sponsored more than a dozen and a half studies of cities in India; these studies with a few exceptions were based on a survey design standardized by the experts in the Planning Commission in order to generate comparable data which could be used for urban planning and development. Not only sociologists or social anthropologists but economists, geographers and other social scientists were also involved. These urban studies did help in generating data about the nature of urban social structure, its institutional organization, the nature of urban services, land use pattern and urban demographic features etc. and only few of them such as the Calcutta survey by N.K. Bose contributed to our understanding of the cultural and sociological profile of the urban life. These studies, apart from contributing to urban policy planning, helped in generating interest among sociologists to study urban phenomena in India from its specific historical, institutional and cultural background. It also led to a number of studies of small towns and their socio-economic structure and processes. The studies which followed began to focus more on the rural-urban linkages in historical, institutional and structural-economic domains rather than studying villages or cities individually as social isolates. G.S. Ghurye's study of the 'urban community' and M.S.A. Rao's study of 'fringe villages' belong to this tradition. The study of the structure and formation of the urban life also underwent change as sociologists began to explore the specific rather than the general features of the urban social structure. A number of urban studies have concentrated upon the nature of the entrepreneurial classes in the cities. Satish Saberwal studied a town in Punjab to explore the structure and social mobility among the entrepreneurs whom he describes as the 'mobile men' and Milton Singer made a study of entrepreneurs in Madras. A number of studies of specific communities of traditional entrepreneurial classes have followed since then. These could be classified both in the categories of the industrial as well as urban sociology.

There is a logical relationship between differentiation and specialization in the growth of the social science disciplines. Of course, scholars also opine that the social sciences follow a cycle of differentiation and synthesis; each period of differentiation is in course of time followed by efforts to synthesize the ideas and substantive findings of the diversified social science contributions into an integrated or general theoretical framework. We find that during the decades of 1960's and 1970's in India pressure did begin to build up towards a need for synthesis particularly in uses of conceptual schemes and methods and also in some measure in the operationalization of the choice of substantive themes for study. Yogendra Singh's *Modernization of the Indian Tradition* (1973) represents an attempt to view sociological studies in India through a paradigm to demonstrate the logical linkages and integrative relevance of various isolated conceptual schemes and categories used by sociologists to analyse social change and modernization in the Indian society.

The differentiation in sociological researches now grew in several directions. One could now talk of sociologies in India rather than a single or synthetic sociology. For example, we begin to find research studies in the fields of sociology of rural and urban life, social stratification, industrial sociology, family sociology, sociology of religion, sociology of caste, scheduled caste/scheduled tribe, sociology of medicine, sociology of profession etc. Without being exhaustive, one could now visualize the theoretical and methodological diversities and tensions of differentiation and synthesis in the conceptual schemes and theoretical orientations of the sociological studies. It increasingly became difficult to have an objective view of social change in India without taking into perspective the various dimensions of the findings of the specialized studies of social phenomena. Their evaluation from a schematic and comparative perspective became necessary both in conceptual terms as well as substantively.

New Developments

The process of differentiation and professionalization that we witness during the 1950's-1960's period owed its growth to the institutional expansion of sociology and the increasing contact and interaction of Indian sociologists with the researchers from the west, particularly America. By the decade of 1970's major changes took place both within and outside the country which began to impact upon the paradigms of sociology. The involvement of America in the Vietnam war had created a global disillusionment about that country which began to delegitimize its role and leadership; this process also reverberated in the world of social sciences and sociology. The focus on method and technique in sociological studies, identified singularly with the American influence in sociology, came increasingly under criticism for its emphasis on the premise about social systems being essentially consensual and self-integrative or self-maintaining. Functional theory in sociology, a counterpart of such methods, began to be treated as inadequate in diagnosing or analyzing the significant processes within the social system because it neglected the role of conflict and contradictions in the structure and process of social realities. Consequently, not only in Europe or the developing world, but also in America, many alternate theoretical paradigms, particularly those related to conflict theory, Marxist historical materialism or dialectical materialism, phenomenology, ethno-methodology and critical theories, began to gain acceptance. These developments were not *sui generis* but product of emerging global social situation; they exemplify the close relationship that has always existed between theory and social conditions that influence its orientation and growth.

In India, the results of the planned efforts towards social and economic development during the decades of 1950's-1970's were now visible in many directions. In rural India, green revolution had begun to take root, food self-sufficiency was within reach; the welfare policy of reservation had energized the scheduled castes, scheduled tribes and weaker sections to give impetus to new social movements and a 'limited elite' had arisen amongst them to provide leadership; the expansion of industries, government institutions, educational institutions, expansion of the governing and developmental bureaucracy, technocracy and professional services, law and order agencies, para-military and military forces etc. contributed to the expansion of the middle classes in urban areas; and green revolution, even though it was confined to a limited section of the rural peasantry, brought into existence a powerful rural middle class. These changes in society signified 'success' but also triggered many new dimensions of conflict and contradiction in the society indicating 'failures'. The incidence of inter-caste, inter-class violence in the villages increased; the marginalization of the weaker sections, the dalits, women, landless labourers, minorities, etc., was sharpened creating disillusionment and anxiety.

The impact of these changes in society upon Indian sociology during the 1970's onwards can be very clearly observed. The rural studies now increasingly began to use Marxist categories for sociological analysis; the community development projects and extension services came under severe criticism for their status guoism on policies of land reform and support to rich peasantry to the exclusion of the weaker sections. The contributions of A.R. Desai and K. Gough primarily exemplify this orientation. More than sociologists, a large number of economists conducted studies (if the agrarian social structure and its processes of change using the categories and methods of Marxism; they operationalized several 'indicators drawn from the rural economy and society to measure its socio-economic formations; for example, 'feudalism', 'semi-feudalism', 'pre-capitalism', etc. The debate among the Marxist Economists; in which a few sociologists also joined, issues raged as to which type of the above social formation the agrarian social and economic structures (region-wise) could be attributed to belong). But a more significant development in Indian sociology during this period was the recognition of the relevance of the studies of social movements.

From 1970's onwards, disenchantment from the functional explanation of social processes and structures had begun. It was noticed that societies underwent changes not merely through internal differentiation of roles and institutions as they underwent differentiation and growth, a postulate supported by the functional theory, but significant and sudden changes took place in societies through mass mobilization and movements of the people or concerned sections of society. This phenomenon was also recognized by Indian sociologists as they witnessed such changes happening in their own society. Moreover, the cumulative effect of the policies of planned development in India had by this time energized several sections and interest groups to mobilize protest movement to realize their demands which ranged from economic, social to political domains. The approach to the study of social change in India from the paradigm of social movement implied application of the theory of 'collective behaviour' in which the significant variables were: the existing state of disenchantment among the concerned people on a set of issues, construction of new identities, the ideological rationalization of the issues into specific goals, the emergence of a leadership, formation of an organizational base and its institutional networks and formulation of the strategies for articulation of demands through the movement in which not only protest but also its withdrawal or reconciliation played an important role.

Thus, a vigorous tradition of a sociology of social movements started in India. Since the studies of social movements were so far confined only to the historians and political scientists, the contributions by sociologists which introduced several sociological concepts and methods in the studies, particularly in the contemporary times, enriched the nature of the movement studies and also brought about an interdisciplinary orientation in sociology. M.S.A. Rao studied the SNDP reform movement in Kerala and published his findings in a systematic form. He also brought together in several volumes contribution of a large number of sociologists to the study of a variety of social movements in India. Peasant movements in various regions of the country were studied by A.R. Desai, T.K. Oommen, D.N. Dhanagare and Rajendra Singh. P.N. Mukherji made a systemic study of the Naxalbari movement in West Bengal which had a unique place in social movement as its strategy was based on class struggle and violence. He made conceptual contributions to the study of violent social movements. Similarly, T.K. Oommen's study of the *Sarvodaya* and *Gramadana* movement in Rajasthan makes use of the conceptual-theoretical paradigm of 'charisma' and its sociological dimensions to explain the processes within a movement. Dipankar Gupta has studied the Siva Sena movement in Maharashtra and farmers movement in western Uttar

Pradesh. The studies of women's movement through sociology of gender have gained momentum. Among several others, contributions in this field have been made by Neera Desai, Veena Majumdar, Gail Omvedt, Maitrayee Chaudhari, Lindsey Barnes, etc. A large number of studies on the dalits, backward classes, tribes and minorities have been completed. The contributions of Gail Omvedt and M.S. Gore can be noted as being rich both in terms of substantive analysis and theoretical contextualization. The second and the third survey reports in sociology and social anthropology published by the ICSSR outline in detail most of these studies as also give full account of the advances made and diversification or differen-tiation achieved by the Indian sociology.

Apart from the study of social movements, the study of structural and cultural aspects of the society gained momentum. L.P. Desai's study of the family system in Gujarat used a diachronic multigeneration perspective for the study of the family structure. This study has provided empirical evidence to support the theory of cyclical structural changes in the family system (joint-single-joint family structures) in place of the prevailing theory of continuum (change from joint to single family system) based on the western experiences. A.M. Shah made a systematic study of the family system in India using the concept of 'household' as the operational unit of the family. He also contributed to the tradition of historical sociology making use of geneology and local history.

Many studies on the sociology of social stratification in India were made which attempted to synthetically conceptualize the role of caste, class and power and other conceptual schemes to explain the structure and processes of status determination, ranking and differentiation in the Indian society. A major contribution to this field came from Andre Beteille. He used the categories of caste, class and power to analyze the changing principles of social stratification in a village in south India. This study has significant analytical value for general understanding of the changes in the system of social stratification. Notable contributions to this theme have been made by K.L. Sharma, Victor D'Souza, Dipankar Gupta and Yogendra Singh. Sociology of profession has emerged as a separate specialization and many studies of the professions and professionalization processes in India have been made. Lawyers, doctors, nurses, managers, civil servants, academics, etc., have formed the subject of such studies. Subs-tantial contributions have been made by studies related to these new social structural phenomena; among the many sociologists who have contributed to such studies, we may refer to T.N. Madan's study of the medical profession, T.K. Oommen's study of nurses, N.K. Singhi's study of civil servants, J.S. Gandhi's study of lawyers and Yogendra Singh's study of university academics. Contributions have also been made towards the study of culture, leisure, communication and media etc. from the systematic sociological perspective. Yogendra Singh, T.K.N. Unnithan and Indra Deva attempted to evolve a theoretical approach to the study of culture and its changes in India from the perspective of the 'sociology of culture'. Communication system which was earlier studied by Y.B. Damle has now been studied more exhaustively. A systemic and critical study has been done by K. Sondhi. I.P. Modi has contributed to a sociological study of leisure and its changing patterns in one of the cities of Rajasthan.

As these new directions of study in sociology have gained strength, the studies in the conventional areas such as that of religion, caste and rural-urban structures etc. have also continued. Of course, these studies now imbibe new methodological and conceptual sensitivity which was absent during the past.

The decades 1980's-2000's have witnessed further differen-tiation in the Indian sociology. These refer to the choice of subs-tantive areas of study as well as the theoretical concerns. During these decades, the global developments in sociology have already thrown up and crystallized new theoretic perspectives and greatly enlarged the substantive concerns in sociology. This has coincided once again with the new forms and directions of the structural and cultural changes, particularly in the developed societies of the west, such as Europe and America. These changes have had a bearing upon ideology, theory and issues for sociological explorations. The transition from the industrial to post-industrial phase of development in the western societies, poised as they seem to be on the verge of growing into a full-fledged 'information society', has exposed them to challenges and crises which manifest themselves at the levels of social structure, demography, culture, ideology, economy and polity. The process of globalization which these societies have sponsored worldwide through their techno-logical and economic achievements is a synthetic expression of their successes as well as failures.

The decline in population and the ageing of society in Europe has necessitated the reliance on more and more migrant workers (skilled and unskilled) from the less developed countries. This results into inter-cultural conflicts and challenges of multiculturalism. The technological advancements in the production system make it possible to have economic growth without generating employment; resulting in the end of tenure jobs, job-security and institutions of trade unions and factory mode of production. The production process has moved from the pre-eminence of the commodity sector to that of services. The community and family structures have suffered a great erosion of roles. Computers, telephony and internet have abolished the community's social space which has now been filled up with the individual actor whose sense of freedom may have increased but the resultant individualism breeds subjective alienation and emotional anxieties. The processes of decision-making in the polity and economy have become too complex and faceless to be comprehended by common citizens. Hence, representative democracy, celebrated so far as being a major achievement is seen to be flawed requiring 're-invention'. The political party system is in disarray. Increasingly, the demand is made to move from representative democracy, which in practice is considered to be less accountable, than expected, to a form of participatory democracy through networking of the voluntary associations and decentralization at the grass roots. The industrial production system is also under challenge from the environmentalist movements, and governments are under pressure from the civil rights and human rights organizations. The weakening of the bonds of community and family and the perception that state is too faceless and unaccountable have strengthened these movements which support the causes of the migrants, refugees, women, children, marginalized sections of population and the ever new varieties of the underclass.

These changes in the structure of the societies of the developed world have not only led sociology to study new areas of substantive social concerns, such as the role of communication and media, ecology and environment, human rights, civil rights, multiculturalism and cultural identities, the structure of leisure and lifestyles and the future shape of the civil society etc., but theoretically, sociology has tended to become more reflexive, cognitive and interpretive. The empirical methods of observation and analysis have not been forsaken but the treatment of social realities using tools of empiricism and objectivity have been made responsive to the demands of empathy and reflexivity in the construction of social realities. This has resulted into a large-scale creative inter-mixing and synthesization of theories hitherto considered to be contradistinct.

Indian sociology following the decade of the 1990's has been deeply influenced by these developments in the western societies. Also, it has been influenced by many new processes of change within the Indian society, particularly those which reflect upon the social structure and political processes, issues of sustainability in economic growth, problems of ecological and environmental protection in the process of industrialization, displacement of population, particularly from the weaker sections due to urbanization, setting up of mega-industrial projects of irrigation dams, power units and atomic centres etc. The problems of corruption in public life, the protection of civil rights, reforms in the judicial system and public interest litigation, etc., have emerged as new issues of social concern. Social pathologies of homicide, suicide, dowry deaths, and social depravities and exploitation related to women, senior citizens and weaker sections tend to increase during the new processes of social change. The focus on these and several new social problems gains urgency as the country enters into a phase of change which is characterized by an anomalous growth in which the number of the middle classes and those below the poverty line is equalized. This may trigger many unanticipated social and cultural conflicts. It strengthens the legitimacy of the new social movements for the empowerment of the scheduled castes, scheduled tribes, backward classes, minorities, women and other deprived sections of the society. The third survey of research in sociology and social anthropology is indicative of the type of sociological studies which were conducted during the past two decades. The survey reveals that during this period major areas of research in sociology were science, technology and development, problems of the scheduled castes and protective discrimination, studies of old age, women's studies and women's development, sociology of youth in India, culture communication and development, political sociology and political anthropology, crime, delinquency and correctional methods, social movements: old and new, sociology of religion and rural development (see, The Third Survey of Research in Sociology and Social Anthropology, Vols. I and II, 2000). We may notice that there has been a continuity in certain areas of research from the past, and at the same time new areas of emerging sociological concerns have begun to be investigated. The reports also reveal that even though the areas of study in some instances remain conventional, the analysis and theoretical treatment of the data now invites fresh conceptual and methodological explorations.

An important feature of the sociological researches during the period 1980-2000 is that the institutional context in which these researches are being carried out has differentiated. Formerly, universities, institutes and colleges etc. comprised the institutions from where most sociological researches originated. Now, the country has seen a stupendous expansion of the 'non-govern-mental organizations' which not only conduct but also fund sociological researches. Most of these researches are in the applied sociological area and cover themes which conventional sociologists are bound to neglect. The studies of human rights, environment and ecology, empowerment of women and children, studies of displaced communities, social forestry, etc., are a host of new areas in which these voluntary organizations have been instru-mental in sponsoring or conducting researches.

Indegenous Experiment

An important area of sociological debate in India which has persisted relates to the quest for a particularistic Indian sociology. As we have noted in the writings of Radha Kamal Mukerjee and D.P. Mukherji, the emphasis on the development of a paradigm of sociology drawn entirely from the Indian philosophical traditions was visualized, but its focus was not on a particularistic Indian sociology. Its aim was to sensitize sociology in general to the perils of gross applications of the methods of positivism and scientism. But, the new debate, initiated by Louis Dumont, suggested that Indian sociology could be confined to the study of ideology of the Indian society. He identified 'hierarchy' or caste as the central ideological principle on which the social structure of the Indian society was anchored. He distinguished this ideology from the western ideology of 'equality' as a measure of contradistinction between the sociology of India and the western sociology. According to him, the Indian sociology is to be founded upon Indology and anthropological observations. The journal *Contributions to Indian Sociology* which was jointly edited by L. Dumont and D. Pocock published the debate between him and Pocock on this premise in the numbers issued in 1957 and 1960. Pocock disagreed with Dumont's proposition as according to him sociology studies not merely structures of society constructed ideologically but also as empirical observable facts. Hence, Pocock felt one could not confine sociology to any particularistic domain. Its findings had inter-societal comparability.

This debate, however, has generated substantial sociological articles and books in which the implications of a sociology for India as a particularistic discipline have been examined. Starting from 1957 the debate has continued in the columns of the *Contributions to Indian Sociology* (new series edited by T.N. Madan et al) well upto the 1980's and continues to simmer. In these debates, the Indian sociologists recognize the need for indigenization of concepts and tools of sociological investigation. The premise of L. Dumont, however, has been overwhelmingly rejected. Even if the centrality of caste system in the social structure of India is accepted, the historical and empirical data on caste in India do not support the hypothesis of its being entirely an ideological system. Caste has many other features rooted in the Indian economy, power structure and instruments of control and exploitation. Indian sociologists tend to accept the need of indigenization of concepts in sociology but at the same time also hold that these may have to be logically integrated with other comparable principles of ranking and social differentiation to offer general explanation. For example, caste could be an indigenous cultural principle of social ranking but its more universal meaning located it in the principle of status determination which may vary from society to society.

Over the years, particularly following the period between

1990 and 2000, the debate on the sociology for India has rather become less resonant. The Indian sociology has gained a very substantial identity of its own which is evident from the size of sociological researches conducted in India. The three consecutive surveys conducted of the researches done in sociology and social anthropology during this period by the ICSSR bear testimony to this fact. In these researches we witness a creative degree of intermix between the uses of the indigenous categories with the application of universal sociological concepts. As the Indian sociologists have expanded the scope of their interests, they have also thrown up methodological and theoretical insights which have been made use of by the sociologists from other societies. Indian sociology is moving fast from the earlier position of self-consciousness to a mature self-confidence, readily interacting and establishing partnership with sociologists at the global level.

New Trends

It is hazardous to talk of the future. In the case of the researches in Indian sociology and its future directions of growth, surmises can be reasonably attempted based on two parameters: first, on the basis of the trends in sociological researches conducted so far; and secondly, on the basis of the new challenges that processes of social change and transformation may throw up deserving sociological attention. The trends of researches in sociology so far have indicated that sociology responds closely to examine the new emergent problems arising out of social changes. The researches tend to be both diagnostic or policy-oriented as well as analytical. The future changes in India will result both from the cumulative effects of the previous changes in society and from the new and the predictable as well as unanticipated changes on account of the impact of the globalization and liberalization of economy, and also on account of the revolution in the technology of information and mass media (Singh, 2000). These changes will have deeper impact on culture, style of life, occupational structure, processes of urbanization and the nature of the family and community life. Indian sociological researches will have to focus upon these problems. The analytical and theoretical approaches will have to be creatively adapted to meet with the demands of the researches in the new areas. Already, the involvement of the non-governmental organizations in conducting social researches has highlighted the need for participatory researches. A greater degree of innovativeness and reflexivity would be required in the sociological researches as new issues and problems of social change are encountered. But, the direction of movement in these researches is bound to remain cumulative rather than show unexpected leaps and bounds.

5

Philosophical Orientation

In India, a review of the growth of sociology from the perspective of dominant theoretical innovations, changes in methodology and technique, its interactions with other social sciences, its own infrastructure as a profession, and the contribution that all these tendencies have made to the 'universalization' of this discipline during the period of a quarter of a century—1952-77—cannot be undertaken meaningfully without a framework of analysis that would be of a sociology of knowledge (cf. Singh, 1973; Mukherjee, 1965; Joshi, 1975) within the context of history. Colonialism, and its impact on the intellectual and cultural traditions in India, of which sociology and other social sciences are at a certain level manifestations, provides an important historical backdrop for its theoretic, ideological and professional evaluation. The cognitive and paradigmatic tensions of Indian sociology during 1953-77 bear deep imprints of the socio-historical forces released during the freedom struggle which shaped the responses of Indian intellectuals to the categories and structures of ideas in social sciences and sociology.

The first two decades of the 20th century which mark the beginning of sociology in India set out several of its orientations, such as descriptive and evolutionary studies of caste, social customs, folklore, land systems and the village community; and their comparison with similar institutions in the west (cf. Singh, 1967; Mukherjee, 1965). Its most important meta-theoretic contribution was in engendering an ethno-sociological awareness about Indian sociology which has continued to persist. It needs to be highlighted as the quest for 'universalization' of sociological categories. Indian sociology has significantly been refracted by this cognitive orientation. Whether sociology is a science with accompanying universalistic package of categories and techniques of research or it is a specific cognitive style marked by a mode of apperception or reflexivity in observation and comparison of structures of social relationships and ideas, are questions which have been debated right from the inception of sociology in India.

Sociology was in the beginning less professionalized, most of its patrons came from outside this discipline and were not initiated into its logic or methodology. Most of them treated sociology as a style of cultural critique or reformative ratiocination. Its character was thus defined by its responsive yet critical note on the western interpretations of Indian society, its institutions and cultural patterns. Radha Kamal Mukherjee, B.N. Seal and B.N. Sarkar constantly refuted the efforts of western Indologists and social anthropologists to try to interpret Indian reality in the evolutionary reductionist matrix. Seal thought institutions could only be compared when they were historically coexistent and parallel, and Mukherjee thought Indian social institutions to be unique. He found the sociological categories of the west inadequate for the interpretation (cf. Mukherjee in Barnes and Backer, 1961) of the Indian reality.

From 1920 onwards, sociology slowly became a teaching discipline in universities and its professional character began to emerge. The impact of the British and Continental sociology and social anthropology was very significant in shaping the sociological orientations of researchers and teachers of this time. The teaching of methodology as a separate discipline was still not prevalent; anthropological fieldwork tradition on the British pattern or historical research methods were the two skills which sociologists were generally initiated into for their researches. If they used other empirical devices, these were to be individually fabricated based on the nature of research problem. This trend changed during the Second World War period as sociology declined in the Continent through large-scale migration of scholars. Its centre of gravity shifted to the United States of America where sociology evolved a strong empirical-positivistic orientation, and led to phenomenal innovations of methods and techniques of 'scientific sociology'. At the beginning of the fifties in India, it was this dominant tradition of sociology, with its theoretic package and empirical style, which had made a headway in the tradition of Indian sociology. It also harmonized with the objectives that the national government had for systematic planning and investment of resources for social and economic growth. The need for developmental planning in the villages, cities and tribal areas initiated a series of empirical studies. This became a dominant tradition in sociology, but some philosophical orientations that pre-existed, continued to persist.

The theoretic directions in Indian sociology can be analyzed through the basic tensions which have existed in this discipline since its inception. These tensions are theoretical as well as ideological. Theoretically, the important tension in sociology exists, on the one hand, between the 'master theory' or 'general theory' and 'conceptual schemes' and on the other, between 'universalism' of concepts and propositions and their 'particularism' or contextuality. It would seem that sociologists' commitment to one or the other standpoint about 'theory' in sociology have fluctuated not only because of the nature of its discoveries or successes or failures in theory construction, but also in the light of the changing historical circumstances of the 'calling' of sociology (cf. Gouldner, 1970). This brings sociology face-to-face with another critical tension within its cognitive structure—that of the role of ideology in theory construction. The significance of universalization or particularization of concepts and categories in sociology is derived from the bases of these tensions.

Sociology in India has been experiencing these cognitive tensions from the very beginning of this discipline, but during 1952-77 these tensions have fluctuated significantly in response to the force of history and existential coordinates of knowledge. To review its theoretic directions and its changing structure of ideas, it would be useful to review sociology in four periods: 1952 to 1960, which primarily was a period of adaptive changes and innovations: 1960 to 1965, which was a period of significant shifts in theoretic priorities and the beginning of some critical tensions in theory and ideology of Indian sociology; 1965 to 1970, which was a period of marked sociological self-awareness and growth of new directions in theoretical and substantive contributions; and finally 1970 to 1977, a period when Indian sociology moved towards a new maturity and explored both theoretically and substantively new horizons of knowledge.

The four-fold periodization of Indian sociology, from 1952 to 1977, could probably be identified with certain predominant theoretic and ideological systems for each period, but Indian sociology during this period, like sociology in general, does not show succession of paradigms as we move from one period to another. What obtains is the co-existence of competing paradigms and theoretic orientations. Indian sociologists throughout this period have been less concerned with constructing 'master theories' or general theories, but more prone to using conceptual scheme for analysis of social problems. With the exception of Radha Kamal Mukherjee, who in his *The Philosophy of Social Science* (1960) and his presidential address to the third Indian Sociological Conference in 1958, proposes a general integrated social science model for explanation and understanding of social realities (cf. Singh in Unnithan et al., 1967: 22-23), no other systematic theoretical formulations have been made. Most socio-logists have remained satisfied with using conceptual schemes or where they have used general theoretic systems such as in dialec-tical or Marxist sociology, their writings do not show its awareness, as the emphasis throughout remains on the comprehensiveness of substantive analysis from an ideological position, rather than on the relative power of theoretical systems.

Some of the major theoretic orientations in Indian sociology which have shown varying degrees of ups and downs during the quarter of a century are philosophical, culturological, structural and dialectical-historical approaches. On the formalization criteria of theory none of these orientations has existed in a systematic form. Most of them have operated as styles of analysis or have been evolved into quasi-formal systems of conceptual schemes. All the four theoretic orientations, however, have existed in Indian sociology from 1952 or even before, and have continued to operate in varying forms. Only the philosophical orientation seems to have weakened because it did not have its organic linkages with the substantive problems as domains of sociological enquiry. We shall review, however, the changes in the theoretic structure of Indian sociology during each of the four periods outlined above in terms of innovation and universalization of concepts and categories, particularistic tensions in their formulation and the related interface of ideology, with specific reference to each of these four major theoretic orientations.

Ideological Basis

The philosophical orientation in Indian sociology is associated with Lucknow School of Sociology, in the contributions of Radha Kamal Mukherjee, D.P. Mukherji and A.K. Saran. Most of its contributions belong to the 1952-60 period, as in the subsequent years only A.K. Saran remains its proponent. It does not seem to have made a major impact on the theoretical nature of Indian sociology. The reason probably lies in the lack of an integrated or unified perspective in the philosophical theoretic contributions of these sociologists. The theoretic tensions in their writings are not homologous. Radha Kamal Mukherjee finds it possible to talk of universal series of concepts and general categories, which not only integrate sociology internationally, but also include other disciplines both in the natural and the social sciences. D.P. Mukherji, on the other hand, is ambivalent about the question of the 'universal' and 'particular' nature of the sociological categories. He is affectively oriented towards Marxism, but leans heavily on the 'particularistic' model of Indian sociology with emphasis on tradition and history. His writings bear deep influence of Dilthey as well as of Marx—the two rather contradictory orientations in meta-theory. Hence, his notion of dialectics, which he recommends as an important analytic device, never takes on the universalistic meaning which it has in popular interpretations of Marxist theory. A.K. Saran, on the other hand, takes a more logically rigorous and consistent stand on the philosophical and ideological nature of the social sciences and sociology. He propounds an approach to Indian sociology which tends to render it entirely particularistic. Hence, one may find that ideologically the three sociologists can be placed on a continuum where Radha Kamal Mukherjee would represent the extreme of universalistic orientation, A.K. Saran the extreme of particularism in sociology, and D.P. Mukherji would fall somewhere in the middle of the two positions.

Radha Kamal Mukherjee's systematic statement about philosophical foundations of sociology and other social sciences is contained in his *The Philosophy of Social Science* (1960). He postulates for each order of reality, from physical to metaphysical, a unified triadic principle of dialectical interaction which links one level of reality with other, and which also renders one level of concepts or categories significant and meaningful to other levels. Hence, his plea for non-compartmentalization of knowledge into the narrow grooves of disciplines. Dialectics, which is a funda-mental process linking one level with another and also endowing it with quality and power of self-transcendence, which Mukherjee treats as the essential feature of man as *homo symbolicus,* is not merely a process of conflict and encapsulation but more prominently of harmony and freedom. It is here that he differs from Marxist uses of the notion of dialectics. He writes:

> The philosophy of dialectical materialism today promotes the universal notion of an inevitable pattern of social development through struggles and conflicts of global revolution and war and subsumes all human progress within the dialectic of the economic movement. Modern evolutionary naturalism, Spencerian, Marxian or Bergsonian, reduces man's mind and values as passive entities manipulated mechanically by a vast process that he cannot intelligently direct or control. Evolution as revealed to modern thought has its many levels or dimensions in which persons, values and societies develop in nature. Values are creative and not merely means of adaptation to the environment. The environment also changes, acted upon by human goals, values and ideals (cf. Mukherjee, 1960: 118).

Mukherjee draws from Hegel, Vedanta, Buddhism and Taoism to formulate his notion of dialectics. Not only he says that "man thinks and lives dialectically. All social relations and behaviour and the values that lie deep seated in them embody polar principles and tendencies" but also that "through the dialectic of the Vedantic *neti-neti* Buddhist *sunyata* and Taoist namelessness, the self identifies itself with the reality and the supreme value" (ibid.: 4). He is opposed to all varieties of reductionist logic about human behaviour and values, be it biological, psychological or economic (materialistic). Dialectic means to him capacity of man to transcend through interplay of opposite forces to higher and higher planes of ethical and cognitive awareness. This transcendence is mediated through society. "Man's transcendence is mediated through society which is a constant tension inside", says Mukherjee. He adds: "It is the nature of man to transcend himself because of the immanence in himself of the not-self, the neighbour, the whole universe" (ibid.: 5). In terms of social models of solidarity, Mukherjee finds both the western liberal democratic pattern and the Marxist models inadequate. He suggests the alternative of the 'third way' or the 'middle way'. This imbibes the principles of individual freedom and dignity of common man from the liberal ideology and access to and sharing of societal resources by the working classes, as advocated by Marxism.

The alternative 'middle way' that Mukherjee proposes as a solution for the planning of the future social systems is supported by his postulate for an integrated social science model which will be united at a 'meta-scientific' and 'meta-anthropological' level. It would resolve the conflict between the philosophy of science and philosophy of values, would integrate into one system the diverse formulations in social sciences on the nature of man, values and society and would lead to the construction of a "human general theory of relativity" which "comprises a compre-hensive system of universal norms that belong to the nature of existence or reality or eternal goals of the cosmic process, including human history and civilization" (ibid.: 175). Mukherjee's philo-sophy of social science thus derives its frame of analysis from a notion of dialectics that is metaphysical. As contribution to sociological theory, its place remains very much at the level of axiomatic meta-theory. It is based on a system of deductive reasoning which is exegetic and speculative, hence different kinds of operationalizations of this meta-theory are possible for sociological studies. Attempts to undertake empirical studies on this model have not been made, although Mukherjee has to his credit several empirical studies in the fields of economics and sociology (cf. Bottomore, 1962: 102).

D.P. Mukherji, on the other hand, does not attempt to construct a general system theory or moral philosophy for global social transformation. He uses a notion of dialectics which is Marxist in formulation (he calls it 'Marxological') but still leaves it to individual social scientists to innovate upon its categories commensurate with their own cultural traditions. In his *Diversities* (1958) which contains most of his theoretical papers, Mukherji strongly pleads for the uses of history in social analysis. For Indian sociological practice the notion of 'tradition' occupies an important analytic place according to Mukherji, because the dialectics of class formation, class conflict and the structural tensions in Indian society bear the stamp of the historical contexts of its traditions and symbols. The sociological model that D.P. Mukherji puts forward is a synthesis between Dilthey and Marx: for him history matters in sociological analysis, the modes of production and related social relationships constitute essentials of historical forces, but its outcome is tempered also by tradition which provides these processes a specific contextuality. To this extent history also does not repeat itself.

D.P. Mukherji prefers historical-dialectical mode of sociological analysis rather than empirical-positivistic one. He rejects the atomism as a relevant notion for sociological analysis on which empiricism is anchored. He specially refutes the values of empirical methods such as surveys and quantitative-mathematical models as they essentially violate the phenomenology of Indian social reality which is devoid of the notion of individual, and has as its unit-category the collectivity or the *sangha*. This renders most models originating from the west, with the exception of an adapted and Indianized version of Marxism irrelevant for Indian sociology. This has a direct implication to the question of the universalism or particularism of categories in sociology. D.P. Mukherji does not rule out the possibility of comparison between historically distinct societal forms or systems or the relevance of objectivity in social sciences, but he strongly pleads for an awareness in formulation and uses of sociological categories which are derived from the native tradition. This introduces a notion of levels in the concept formation in sociology from the contextual to the comparative, from the particular to the universal and from the historical to the general, which has not been systema-tically dealt with by Mukherji, but is implicit in his sociological formulations.

A.K. Saran, who was Mukherji's student, and later his colleague, though inspired by his writings, takes on a logically more extreme standpoint on the theoretic formulation of sociology and its meta-theory. In his writings (cf. Saran, 1956, 1957, 1961) he proceeds to examine the meta-theory and underlying premises of sociology as a fundamentally western cultural and cognitive response to meet the historical challenges of its own disintegrating worldview, following the industrial revolution and eclipse of its traditional society. Weak and inadequate as is sociology as a cultural alternative, according to Saran, even for the west, to save it from the formidable challenges in the wake of the disintegration of its past traditional sacred worldview, its borrowing by non-western nations, particularly India, amounts to a double self-deception. It first lies in the neo-colonial roots of sociology. Sociology essentially inheres an ideological package which is of the western origin and alien to Indian ethos. Secondly, it is a bad alternative as a worldview to replace the traditional Indian worldview. The solution according to Saran lies in total rejection of sociology. Its concepts and categories, whether formulated in Marxian terms or in positivistic terms (of methodological indivi-dualism or social organicism), amount willy-nilly to safeguarding a false proposition—a proposition of naturalistic reductionism and evolutionism.

In critique of D.P. Mukherji's *Diversities,* Saran evaluates the notion of 'planned social order' implicitly equating it with the foundation of sociological theory of knowledge. He writes:

> The historic roots of the idea of a planned social order go back to the breakup of the worldview founded, among others, on the idea of the Great Chain of Being. The immediate positive reaction to the traditional worldview was to substitute the transcendental intuition of order by an immanentist conception of the social system. This was the logic-philosophical basis of the competitive, individualistic society which supplanted the traditional order in the West. The implicit auto-apotheosis (of Man) which characterizes modern thought on planned socio-economic systems is the result of this effort. With the addition of the idea of a collective secular Providence to the competitive worldview, there arises an inner tension between the notion of self-adjustment and the notion of planning (Saran, 1965: 129-30).

Saran has continued to develop his ideas in this direction of meta-sociological reasoning since early fifties. In an essay on "Sociology in India", he rejects Radha Kamal Mukherjee's effort towards sublimating social sciences through a dialectical reasoning on to the plane of moral freedom for man in a social system based on the alternative 'middle path'. He characterizes it as logically inconsistent. He also critically assesses D.P. Mukherji and says: "If the implications of his (Mukherji's) largest views are seriously followed up, they will lead us far beyond Professor Mukherji's present position, for its direction is towards *traditional sociology* not far removed from that of Coomarswamy and Schuon" (Saran, 1957). In his writings of the sixties and the seventies Saran has continued to build upon his earlier ideas in two directions. Firstly, he has refuted most western alternative constructions for sociology in India, particularly of Louis Dumont and David Pocock, and secondly, he has more sharply tried to expose the neo-colonial elements in the ties of Indian sociology with that of the West. His contribution of sociological reasoning thus leads directly not only to rejection of universalization of sociological categories but also of sociology.

Saran, along with D.N. Majumdar and other colleagues at the Lucknow University, had come out in the sixties with warning statements about American projects in India to study Indian society as harmful for national security (Saran, 1957). In the mid-seventies, he refuted Edward Shil's 'centre' and 'periphery' thesis on the growth of social sciences, calling it 'magisterial' in style. But his yet sharper comments on Indian sociology can be seen in his observations on Dumont's essay on the "World Renunciation in Indian Religions" (1957: 33-62) where an effort is made by Dumont to show the comparability of fundamental notions of Hinduism, such as *dharma, artha* and *kama* with principles of duty, profit and pleasure respectively, each coinciding with the notion of *varna* hierarchy. The particular passage to which Saran takes objection is as follows:

> The analogy with the hierarchy of *varna* is apparent: *dharma* corresponds to be Brahman or priest, *artha* to the king or Kshatriya, the temporal power, and *kama* to the others. This is not all, and one can go further with the help of Talcott Parsons' method of structural analysis. First, *kama* is opposed to the two others as an action flowing immediately from affective impulses is opposed to an action submitted to intellectual and moral considerations. Then, while *dharma* is moral universalism, *artha* is calculating egoism, something after the manner of 'rational action' in our economic theory—but extended to politics, since wealth here is

> little more than an attribute of power. While *artha* is opposed to *kama* as deferred satisfaction to immediate, *dharma* is opposed to both as ultimate ends to particular ends, as the sacred to the profane. In the language of Parsons, *kama* is expressive action, *artha* instrumental action, and *dharma* moral action. The triology gives an exhaustive classification of the types of action and is based upon a system of oppositions (Dumont, 1966: 41).

Saran in his review of Dumont objects particularly to his attempt to interpret the notions of Hinduism, viz., *dharma, artha* and *kama* through western categories, especially through the Parsonian transformation, overlooking the antinomy between the two distinctive value systems and worldviews. Dumont defends his effort to compare through outsider's point of view which he postulates, is an essential methodology of social anthropology and is based on the assumption "that man is not a mere word, although men are such through their belonging to one or other particular society or culture" (Dumont, 1966: 23). Saran is basically skeptical of this position when he writes: "...social reality *qua* reality has no 'outside' ... the only outside is its interpretation in terms of an alien culture ..." (Saran, 1962: 68). He further criticizes Dumont for "taking in the name of science, modernity or objectivity, a firmly provincial standpoint for the study of traditional or tradition-haunted societies". Saran has constantly been criticizing western sociology and social science for its 'positivistic' fallacy (cf. Saran, 1962); he finds Dumont too being involved in the same 'positivistic hybris'.

The commentary of Saran has provoked Dumont to write an angry note clarifying his position (Dumont, 1966). He attacks Saran for taking a position which logically forecloses the possibility of a universal language of sociology and leads to a position of cultural solipsism. This controversy has not evoked response from Indian sociologists on a scale that it deserves. Indeed, Dumont-Pocock publication of the series *Contributions to Indian Sociology* (1957, 1960, 1961, 1962, 1964, 1965 and 1966) have evoked rather a self-consciousness among Indian sociologists which has not entirely been in turie with the 'universalistic' postulates they have intended to project. Its main impact has been one of retroactiveness rather than of approval or acceptance. Dumont's *Homo Hierarchicus* (1970) falls also in the same category. Although *Contributions to Indian Sociology: New Series* organized a high level review symposium on this book, it failed to make an impact on Indian sociology.

On the Saran-Dumont controversy, T.N. Madan, editor of the *Contributions to Indian Sociology: New Series* has this to write:

> But I am not wholly satisfied with the Dumont-Pocock argument regarding the external point of view which they say the sociologist shares with the natural scientist. I am not convinced that such a point of view exists. (If we accept that it exists, then their and Bailey's positions are not opposed to one another). If it did, it should have been possible for us to study social life through observation by communication with the observed people... I want to go further and question if an observer can acquire any understanding of an alien culture, of the context, purpose and meaning of human action, without communicating with the actors through, their, his, or some other language, directly or through intermediaries. Once this happens, the external observer ceases to occupy the position of an outsider (Madan, 1966: 12).

The issues raised through this debate which is still going on in Indian sociology have both ideological and theoretic significance. Ever since the issue of the *Contributions to Indian Sociology*— 1957, where Dumont-Pocock first formulated the problem of what they called 'For a Sociology of India', through the seventies the debate on this question has been going on. Since its implications are wider and deeper related to several types of theoretic orientations of Indian sociology, we shall examine it at the end of our treatment of various theoretic orientations in sociology.

Logic and Culture

The most important landmark in the beginning of what we have heuristically called the 'culturological orientation' in the theoretic nature of sociology is Srinivas' work, *Religion and Society among the Coorgs of South India* (1952). This work led him to formulate the concept of 'Brahmanization' to represent the process of the imitation of life-ways and ritual practices of Brahamanas by the lower-caste Hindus. The concept was used as an explanatory device to interpret changes observed in the ritual practices and life-ways of the lower castes through intensive and careful field study. The notion of Brahmanization, however, had implicit possibilities of further abstraction into a higher level concept, sanskritization which Srinivas introduced because his own field data and those of many others indicated limitations of using only Brahamanic model as frame of reference (see Shahand and Shroff, 1959; Cohn, 1955; Pocock, 1957, etc.). Sanskritization as a concept thus replaced Brahmanization at a more abstract level.

Srinivas achieved this through enlarging the meaning of sanskritization and by distinguishing it from another concept, westernization, using both terms in a systematic manner to explain the processes of social change in India. This conceptual scheme, though referring mainly to the processes of cultural imitation, has a built-in structural notion, that of hierarchy and inequality of privilege and power, since the imitation is always by the castes or categories placed lower in social hierarchy and of castes and categories placed higher up in social and economic status. The concepts sanskritization-westernization soon became a matter of lively debate and exegesis in sociological circles and also of a series of minor innovations by field workers in different parts of the country, as also by historians, political scientists and Indologists.

Though introduced as a heuristic device, the two concepts also implied a systematic logic. Sanskritization characterized a change within the framework of the Indian tradition, while westernization was a change resulting from the contact with the British socio-economic and cultural innovations. Both processes, nevertheless, form a continuous series in terms of relative power of the groups, castes or categories placed within the traditions concerned. The low castes imitate the ritual styles and customs of the upper (twice-born) castes, and sanskritize; the upper castes imitate the cultural styles and institutions of the British or other western traditions, which leads to westernization. We find a systematic formulation of the two concepts in Srinivas' *Social Change in Modern India* (1966) where he defines sanskritization as "the process by which a 'low' caste or tribe or other group takes over the custom, ritual, beliefs, ideology and style of life of a high and, in particular, a 'twice-born' *(dwija)* caste. The sanskritization of a group has usually the effect of improving its position in the local caste hierarchy. It normally presupposes either an improvement in the economic or political position of the group concerned or a higher group self-consciousness resulting from its contact with a source of the 'Great Tradition' of Hinduism such as pilgrim centre or monastery or proselytizing sect" (1966: 67-68).

Along with the concepts of sanskritization and westernization, Srinivas has used the term 'secularization' to denote the processes of institutional innovations, and ideological formulation after independence to deal with questions of religious groups and minorities in India. Secularization is a process which as normatively stated in the Constitution of India and codified through various types of legislations, attempts to stabilize the foundations of religious tolerance and ideological co-existence among sects and communities in India. This, as a national ideology, was given a formal shape after independence.

The conceptual schemes that Srinivas has formulated to analyze the phenomenon of social and cultural change have made the outstanding impact on Indian sociology. It offered an analytic frame to many village studies conducted from 1952 to 1968 particularly (cf. Srinivas, 1955; Marriott, 1955; Majumdar, 1955, 1958; Chauhan, 1974) and later on in the discursive treatment of Indian sociology. It inspired historians and Indologists to re-evaluate their perceptions and premises on the processes in Indian society and culture (see, Raghavan, 1959; Chanana, 1961; Harper, 1959; Staal, 1963) and to critically examine the merits of this concept in the analysis of social and cultural change (Thapar, 1975). It also led some sociologists to study its latent merits which could throw light also on structural changes in India society (see, Gould, 1968; Singh, 1970, 1973) and others to compare it with 'reference group theory' in sociology (see, Damle, 1968; Lynch, 1966). Debate was also generated on Srinivas' concept of 'dominant caste', which, according to him, in most cases, served as reference model for the castes lower in position to borrow or imitate its customs and practices through sanskritization (Dube, 1965; Oommen, 1970). Finally, sanskritization also generated through examination by some sociologists of the structure of traditions in Hinduism which were claimed to be multiple and not unitary in character.

Sanskritization and westernization as concepts and theoretic orientations stirred Indian sociology more deeply than any other conceptual scheme so far. "Here was a concept which had an equal appeal for the Indologists, historians of Indian culture and sociologists and social anthropologists. It also satisfied those who had a special fondness for developing Indian concepts for analyzing national social cultural phenomena" (Singh, 1977: 99). These concepts have been debated in Indian sociology both for their viability as well as limitations to interpret social changes in society. Some debate has also ranged on the possibility of linking these with more abstract concepts such as 'reference group' and 'social mobility' in order to universalize them (Singh, 1973).

Another attempt to analyze the cultural processes of change in India has been made by Milton Singer and McKim Marriott following Redfield's model of 'social organization of traditions and civilizations' based on the dichotomy of the little and great traditions (see, Singer, 1959, 1970, 1972 and Marriott, 1955). The great tradition is that of the elite, urban centres and has a formal character, whereas the little tradition belongs to those of the folk in the villages and the unlettered many. Each tradition has its social organization, and there is a continual flow of themes, ideas or symbols from one to the other level, universalizing some and parochializing other traits of the tradition. This process is triggered both through orthogenetic and heterogenetic factors. Sanskritization as a process could also be incorporated in this process as well as westernization or modernization. Some field studies in villages and cities have been conducted by Singer, Marriott and their colleagues following this model, but it has not made a wide impact on Indian sociology as Srinivas' concepts of sanskritization and westernization. The reason is that except for some advantages of formalization and abstraction this model does not add much to the analytic advantages in studies with uses of its categories. Moreover, sanskritization and westernization can also lend historical and structural-analytic insights whereas the concepts of Singer and Redfield are devoid of possibilities of observing structural tensions in social processes both of modernization and traditionalization.

The major emphasis in study of social change through concepts of sanskritization-westernization and of the levels of traditions is on the changes in cultural styles, customs and ritual practices. There are, however, some presuppositions in the processes both of sanskritization and westernization which do imply precedent or concomitant structural changes, such as improvement in economic position of the sanskritizing caste, superiority and dominance of the caste being emulated and psychological disenchantment among the low castes from their own position in the caste hierarchy. Effort has been made to spell out the presuppositions contained in both the Srinivas and the Singer models and to integrate them on a logical paradigmatic principle (see, Singh, 1973). The two essential coordinates implicit in Srinivas' and Singer's formulations are that of the sources of change—heterogenetic and orthogenetic and the substantive domains of change—cultural structure, comprising the 'little' and 'great' traditions and social structure, comprising of 'micro-structure' and 'macro-structure'. Placed in a schematic form (of property-space) these lend us typologies of operational concepts in which notions of sanskritization and westernization cannot only be subsumed but also extended to explain also the structural change through generating logically related set of structural concepts of change, such as role differentiation, emergence of new structural forms, bureaucracy and elites through heterogenetic changes and pattern-recurrence, migration, internal social movement, circulation of elites and rise and fall of urban centres and dynasties, etc., through orthogenetic sources. Attempt has been made to analyze processes both of modernization and traditionalization through these conceptual categories based on sociological and historical data.

Study of Structure

The culturological orientation of Indian sociology whose theoretic tendencies we have examined has also been related primarily to studies of the village communities, caste structure, its institutional correlates and family, kinship and religious ideology of the people in villages. Most such studies being conducted through social anthropological and observational techniques had a holistic character. The social structure was studied at the village level, but it was more descriptive and sociographic than from a theoretical explanatory point of view. The structural orientation differs from culturological because, as Bailey says in structural studies, "we ought not to confine ourselves to the raw material provided by the 'principles that people themselves give', our only task is not to make sense of the flagrant contradictions in popular thought by abstracting out consistent elements that culturological study attempts. A valid sociological understanding can be achieved, given certain problems, by making abstractions imme-diately from behaviour or from other non-verbal information, and by using our own concepts (Bailey, 1959: 88-101). The pre-eminence of concepts or models is one characteristic of the structural studies. Its other important attributes are related to the nature of problems it undertakes for observation and analysis, such as the processes of structural cleavages and differentiation in societies, problems of equality and inequality, study of power structure, social stratification, social mobility, urbanization-industrialization, changes in the demographic and family structure, etc. Such studies also have a macro-structural and historical perspective.

In the structural studies, one important trend is the focus on comparative categorial relationship, such as caste and class relationship in India and its implication on the nature of the society. This trend has continued since late sixties. In such studies the analysis of social structure is undertaken with the help of two or more conceptual categories. This introduces the element of comparison and generalization in their theoretic power. Bailey's (1960) analysis of structural changes in India with the set of comparative categories like 'tribe', 'caste' and 'nation', Beteille's (1965) study of social structure of a village with analytic categories 'caste', 'class' and 'power' have been forerunners of a whole new series of structural studies. Additional sets of categories that have been used by sociologists for comparative study of social structure are, caste, religion and power (Aggarwal, 1971), caste, race and politics (Verba, Ahmed and Bhatt, 1971) tribe, caste and class (Aurora, 1972), mind, body and wealth (Pocock, 1974) to study the structure of beliefs rather than social relationship caste, class and politics (Bhatt, 1975) and language, religion and politics (Brass, 1975). Several other studies using such comparative sets of categories for analysis of social structure, beliefs, ideologies or cultural systems have been made during the past fifteen years (Thapar, 1977; Fox, 1971). The use of a set of more than two conceptual categories for analysis of social phenomena renders the theoretic elements in these studies not only comparative but also increases their power of generalization. This was not usually a characteristic of holistic studies of villages and tribal social structures conducted in the fifties and early sixties in India.

This tendency of comparison has also coincided with the use of theoretic and conceptual schemes not only to analyze but also explain changes in the social structure. The uses of the terms 'closed' and 'open' stratification (Bailey, 1963; Beteille, 1969; Singh, 1970) and 'harmonic' and 'disharmonic' systems (Beteille, 1971) do constitute attempts towards a new explanatory dimension in sociological analysis. The explanation of course does not reach the level of formal theory, but is a definite advancement from earlier descriptive studies of social structures in India.

The structural theoretic orientation of sociology during the seventies is also reflected in the spurt of urban surveys which were completed from 1957 to 1969 (D'Souza, 1974: 117). These urban surveys, sponsored mostly by the Research Programmes Committee of the Planning Commission, have been analyzed integratedly by Bulsara (1964) for nine cities, though in all more than two scores of surveys have been published. These surveys have dealt with items such as population, language, literacy, occupation and industry, internal migration, income, employment, housing conditions and social life, etc., in the cities. The surveys have used a statistical model for study with the help of schedules and questionnaires on a selected sample fraction. They have mainly generated benchmark data for planners and have occasionally contributed to innovations in methodology through standardization of the tools of research. They have also contributed to the training of a whole batch of researchers in survey type study, who today reinforce many social research organizations in the government and private industry. Cities have also been studied using the culturological model, especially the notion of 'sacred complex' (Vidyarthi, 1961, 1969) or 'cultural configuration'. Some conceptual evaluations of categories used in urban studies have also been undertaken from the criteria of logical adequacy, and principles of verification and validation (Mukherjee, 1965; Berreman, 1972). Studies of urban elite entrepreneurs and other specific structures and categories have been undertaken by several sociologists (Jones, 1975; Rosenthal, 1970; Berna, 1960; Hazlehurst, 1966; Saberwal, 1974). Sociologists have also studied slums in cities from a diagnostic as well as theoretical perspective (Desai and Pillai, 1972). Most of these studies have observed the levels of structural changes and accompanying contradictions in the process of urban growth. Some of them have also innovated upon conceptual schemes, as Saberwal's study of entrepreneurial structure in a Punjab township, which improves upon E. Hagen's thesis on the theory of innovations in developing societies and analyzes the structural notions related to economic and social risk-taking, its absence in the lower classes and its relationship with social mobility.

In the structural theoretic orientation, not only the number of conceptual schemes for comparative studies increases, but also the relationship between concepts and social reality undergoes a new formulation. This is evident in the replacement of studies of villages, so dominant in the sixties, by those of 'agrarian structure' and 'peasantry' in the seventies and eighties. The focus on the study of agrarian structure, and not the village, takes sociology into the macro-analytic domain. It introduces a theoretical rather than a territorial orientation in sociological thinking and also brings the Marxist and functionalist formulations of sociological theory face-to-face challenging each to test and verify their relative theoretic power. It also introduces a new dimension in the study of change, through emphasis on sociology of social movement and revolution. These innovations in concepts and theory have also led to a new methodological awareness in sociology. Sociologists now increasingly use historical method and archival and documentary data to formulate their propositions. This has brought history and sociology closer and there is a possibility of one reinforcing the other.

The interest in agrarian sociology is derived from interest in the study of basic changes in the rural social structure initiated through land reforms after independence. It covers studies of new class formations, social mobility and contradictions arising from these processes, with inter-regional and comparative perspective (cf. Joshi, 1971, 1975; Singh, 1974; Beteille, 1974; Oommen, 1972; Bhalla, 1976).There have also been studies of changes in agrarian relations resulting from 'green revolution' or agricultural prosperity in some regions (see, Ladejinsky, 1973; Oommen, 1977; Mencher, 1974). Many studies on the social movement among the peasantry have also been conducted to analyze historically, as well as in contemporary setting, the contradictions emergent in the agrarian social structure (Dhanagare, 1975; Gough, 1975). Social movements which have their origin either in tribal agrarian problems, or those sponsored by socio-economic reform movements like the Sarvodaya or by the radical movements as those of the Naxalities, have also been studied by sociologists (Oommen, 1977; Desai, 1975; Shah, 1974; Dasgupta, 1974; Mukherjee, 1977). The study of the historical bases of some regional movements like the Siva Sena and the caste movements such as neo-Buddhism have been explored (Gupta, 1977; Rao, 1975; Singh and Singh, 1977; Singh, 1977). The study of social movements has not only added a new methodological orientation but has also led to innovations in conceptualization and formulation of contexts and categories of social change. It makes a significant break from the functional notion of a creative and adaptive change and focuses on those processes of change which have the capacity to bring about a structural transformation in society.

The structural orientation in theory during the seventies has also led to new focus on kinship studies and family sociology (see, Shah, 1964, 1973, 1974; Dube, 1974; Gough, 1975); the emphasis on the diachronic process of changes in family structure, from jointness to nuclearity, has been replaced by that on family cycle studies (Desai, 1964; Nicholas, 1961; Gould, 1968, etc.). Historical studies of family structure and differentiation of its form have been followed by studies in the area of sociology of disputes (Srinivas, 1959) combining in-depth observations with historical social anthropology of villages. Cohn has applied it for macro-analytical study of the Indian civilization (Cohn, 1971). The studies of factional differentiation and conflict in social and political networks have also been conducted to reveal the bases of cleavages in Indian rural and urban society (Nicholas, 1968; Kothari, 1970; Brass, 1965; Weiner and Kothari, 1965, etc.). This has led to historical study of the rise of new elites and changes in their composition and social background (Leach and Mukherjee, 1970; Broomfield, 1969; Rosenthal, 1976). Studies of social mobility and changes in the caste and class structures, both from sociological and historical perspectives, have been particularly emphasized (see, Silverberg, 1968; Bose, 1968; Kothari, 1970; Srinivas, 1968).

An important theoretical insight which dominates the orientation in formulating categories is what may be called, preference for the notion of 'levels' rather than continuum in sociology and social sciences. The conceptual dichotomies through which changes in structure were observed proved too static and inadequate when seen in historical perspective. This was true specially for concepts like rural and urban, caste and class and 'nuclear' and 'joint family'. It also applied in the case of culturological concepts such as 'little' and 'great' tradition and the processes of traditionalization and modernization. Kothari writes: "The prevailing dichotomy between tradition and modernity has created a curious cognitive hiatus—in ideological thinking as well as in much of social science theorizing—between society on the one hand and polity on the other. The former is conceived as if by definition, as 'traditional', the latter as 'modern' and 'developmental'. In reality, however, this is a false approach to the phenomenon of modernization" (Kothari, 1970: 3).

The structural theoretic orientation has not only contributed to deeper insight in the understanding of the basic process in the Indian society but has also led to innovations in conceptual categories, paradigms of analysis and in addition to this brought sociology closer to the work of the historians, political scientists and economists. This has increased the viability of sociological studies and raised new significant professional implications.

View from History

The dialectical theoretic orientation is related primarily to Marxist methods and propositions for the analysis of social reality. We have used the terms dialectical and not Marxist because in Indian sociology, Marxist approaches comprise several adaptive models; many innovations have been made on classical Marxist formulations for the study of Indian society. Also, among Indian sociologists, there is growing awareness that Marxist categories and paradigms will have to be reformulated and tested against societal realities of various historical origins to validate them as universal or particular categories in sociology. In this perspective, when we look at the growth of dialectical-historical orientation in theory, we find that comparatively it is a less developed branch of Indian sociology. Most basic Marxist thinking in India was done in the forties and fifties by non-sociologists (see, Singh, 1973, 1977). Among the early sociologists who emphasized the significance of dialectical model were D.P. Mukherji and Ramkrishna Mukherjee.

D.P. Mukherji, whose contribution to sociological theory we have already examined, continually used the categories of structure, class conflict and the model of socialist society in his analysis of historical social processes in India. Both historical framework and dialectical orientation are essential, according to him, in sociological thinking. He did not conduct any empirical studies using this frame of reference. Ramkrishna Mukherjee made systematic historical as well as empirical studies using dialectical model. His *The Rise and Fall of the East Indian Company* (1958) is a contribution to economic and social history of the institutionalization of colonialism in India through stabilization of economic policies, disintegration of feudalism and aristocratic despotism, and the rise of new middle classes. In his *The Dynamics of a Rural Society* (1957), Mukherjee studies social and economic changes in a set of villages through changes in the structure of classes. He emphasizes the necessity to grasp the systematic and organic character of Indian society for understanding of its social processes. In his later works, Ramkrishna Mukherjee has changed from dialectical historical to a 'probabilistic nomological' approach for the study of social reality. He calls his approach 'inductive inferential' which is neutral to the type of propositions, Marxist or non-Marxist, that one chooses to test and verify. The role of history and dialectics in the sociological thinking and research, according to Mukherjee, stops at the level of formulation of propositions; these may help in even a taxonomic formulation of categories (see, Mukherjee, 1970, 1975) or social indicators, but beyond this the logical principles of test and verification would have to operate independently.

Among Indian sociologists one who has consistently advocated and applied dialectical-historical model in his sociological studies is A.R. Desai. In his studies of nationalism, analysis of rural social structure, the nature of economic and social policies of change in India and the structure of state and society, he has consistently tried to expose the contradictions and anomalies in policies and process of change resulting from the capitalistic-bourgeoisie interlocking of interest in the Indian society (see, Desai, 1959, 1966, 1975). According to Desai, the polarization of class interests, especially of the bourgeoisie in India, is the foundation of modern society in India. It has thus inherent in it the class contradictions and the logic of its dialectics. This has been thoroughly exposed by Desai in his several writings.

The dialectical theoretic orientation has subsequently increased in the studies of political structure, agrarian formations and social movements. The contradictions in Indian political, economic and social structure, and in its development pro-grammes, etc., have been highlighted by Bettelheim, who has concluded that although Indian case is one of mounting contradictions, the Indian bourgeoisie has relatively been more responsive to elimination of these contradictions, at least from some of the structures than bourgeoisie in other nations (see, Bettelheim, 1968).The judgement of several other Marxists within India also, however, coincides with these observations. But there is a significant difference of opinion as to the intensity and rate of expansion of contradictions in Indian society that may trigger off revolutionary movements (see, Desai, 1975). The agrarian studies conducted from the Marxist frame of reference have used 'feudalism', 'capitalistic' and 'pre-capitalistic' categories and mode of production frame of reference in the study of the social structures (see, Sau, 1973 Chattopadhyaya, 1972; Bhaduri, 1973; Saith and Tankha, 1972; Patnaik, 1972). Because of the uses of theoretic categories of feudalism, pre-capitalistic structures and capitalism, with accompanying variations in the modes of production and modes of social relationships, these empirical studies assume significance. Theoretically, the contribution of these studies is two-fold: first, these enrich our sociological understanding of the structural tensions or contradictions in the agrarian society and link them with its macro-structures; and secondly, these also lead to innovations in the Marxist sociological categories themselves, as these are put to test in a different socio-cultural and historical context. The need for such innovations in Marxist dialectical paradigm in India has been emphasized both by Indian and foreign sociologists (see, Joshi, 1974 and Thorner, 1973).

In addition to the uses for the analysis of agrarian relations and class structure, the dialectical theory has also been applied to the study of macro-structural social and economic processes in India. Here, the framework of capitalism is further informed by that of 'imperialism' and 'neo-colonialism' for the understanding of the forces of change (see, Patnaik, 1975; Frank, 1970) in society. There have also been some contributions on the exegesis of writings of Karl Marx on India by both Indian and non-Indian sociologists (see, Thorner, 1966 and Joshi, and Damodaran, 1975).

The dialectical-historical theoretic orientation in Indian sociology has grown rapidly in the seventies, when in addition to macro-structural studies of social, economic and political institutions, micro-structural realities at the empirical level have also been submitted to closer observation. This development has also coincided with more analytic sophistication in the study of macro-social problems. In August 1975, a journal *Social Scientist* was also started from Kerala which publishes Marxist-oriented writings by social scientists and political workers on various problems of theory and substantive realities in India. Evidently, studies with dialectical theoretical and methodological orientation have been on an increase in India with innovations in concepts, methods and categories.

Indegenous Philosophy

Having reviewed the main theoretical orientations in Indian sociology it may be useful to assess its impact on the process of universalization or particularization of categories and theory. This issue is both ideological and theoretical. Since Dumont and Pocock initiated the debate on "For a Sociology of India" in 1957, this issue has been debated in response to their and Bailey's writings and also independently. Dumont's emphasis in the study of Indian sociology is on its fundamental ideo-structural categories from an 'external point of view'. He would formulate his sociology from the language of the sources as it were, from the sentiments and ideas of the people themselves. Bailey finds fault with this model for its indifference towards study of 'relations', which is the main sociological category. With this frame of reference, sociology gets reduced to what Bailey calls 'culturology'. In his statement on "For a Sociology of India" in the final issue of *Contributions,* however, Dumont clarifies that he does not see the possibility of a particularistic sociology even though the substantive reality he would prefer the sociologist to deal with would be ideas and sentiments and not relations. Thus, without taking a structural position as that of Bailey, Dumont sees the possibility of a general sociology as the only way-out.

The debate between Dumont and Bailey led Indian sociologists to think on this problem from an Indian perspective, where the issue was not of two varieties of general sociology, of which the Indian sociology would be a part, but it was mainly whether Indian sociology could be universal or has to be particularistic. A seminar was organized on this problem in 1966 and its delibera-tions have been published (Unnithan et al., 1967). The conclusion of this seminar was that Indian sociology would have to operate at both levels, the particularistic and the universal. Some concepts or categories as Srinivas' sanskritization-westernization, would be of primarily particularistic and ethno-sociological relevance, but these could be further abstracted for cross-cultural comparisons (see, Singh, in Unnithan et al., 1967).

The debate on this issue has not subsided. It was given a sharper edge by linking the problem both of creativity and categories in Indian sociology to the colonial situation. J.P.S. Uberoi, in his "Science and Swaraj" concluded: "Every Swarajist should recognize what are the essential pre-conditions, under this system (structural asymmetries like rich-poor, international-national, white-black), for the advancement of universal science in our environment. Until we can concentrate on decolonization, learn to nationalize our problems and take our poverty seriously, we shall continue to be both colonial and unoriginal" (Uberoi, 1968: 123). This observation of Uberoi has echoed in many quarters. As we mentioned, Saran is its strong exponent. Many others who support it with qualifications, do not see contradictions in methods and categories of the ethnosociology and general sociology. The problem is ideological, and as such it pervades through all levels of sociological thinking in India where normative questions and not merely technology of research are involved.

Even the universality of methods and tools of research is questioned. Most of these involve translation of cultural idioms and symbols from one culture into another. What is more seriously questioned, however, is the choice of problems and research priorities that sociologists undertake for investigation. In a recent debate on this problem which is contained in *Social Sciences and Social Realities: Role of Social Sciences in Contemporary India* (Dube, 1976), such issues have been reopened for a variety of social sciences. The distortions in sociological thinking and practice are created by alienation of the professional sociologist from the other sections of elites and people of the society. This leads to the distantiation of sociologist from the major issues of national concern or with national identity. His uncritical acceptance of models of theory and research tools imported from abroad have come in for thorough examination (see, Singh, in Dube, 1976).

The question of universalization or particularism of sociological categories in Indian sociology or social science as such remains open. A more enduring solution to this issue would probably come from accumulation of empirical knowledge through the findings of Indian sociologists and social scientists from studies conducted with self-awareness and scientific objectivity within their own ideological setting.

Practical Strategies

Methodology comprises logic of enquiry and philosophy of science, techniques of operationalization of concepts and tools of research, problems of measurement, verification and validation, and finally questions of universality and particularity in tools of research that use symbolic-linguistic categories for measurement and observation. These components of methodology, therefore, at another level raise similar ideological issues that we discussed in the context of theoretical orientations of Indian sociology. Methodological problems also get entangled in the web of ethical questions, of communication of values, preservation of the confidence of respondents or its exploitation. Since social science research implies social interaction, between the researcher and his respondents, the observer and the people he observes, and also the act of cultural interpretation, the likelihood of asymmetry developing in the relationship of researcher and the human subjects of his inquiry is high and also ethically vital. Indeed, the movement of ethnomethodological ideology in research is a result of the dilemmas created by such ethical and structural problems in social research.

The methodological trends and its problems in Indian sociology have been reviewed earlier (see, Madan, 1973). The ethical questions posed by research methodology have also been discussed at philosophical and political levels. Much of the critique of sociology by Saran mentioned in the philosophical orientation belongs to this level of discussion. We could, however, examine the methodological contributions made by Indian sociology at two points of operation. First, with reference to the types of methods and techniques of research that have been used in sociology and the degree of their innovativeness. Secondly, we could also examine the types of reflections that sociologists have made on their own methodological craft, looking at it from a new context of *post-facto* objectivity.

Indeed, in the sixties, Indian sociology underwent a strong change in its orientation towards the tools and techniques of research. The two most common tools used by sociologists during this period were participant observation by social anthropologists and survey research design for urban studies or studies of social categories. Some social anthropologists also used historical methods in their study, but its vogue was muted only to revive more strongly in the sixties and seventies. Sociology teaching by this time invariably included courses in research methodology. Compared to other social sciences, with the exception of economics and psychology, methodological awareness has been higher in Indian sociology. Whereas survey design using statistical model of investigation has been quite common, the use of mathematical models has been rare. The application of cybernetic model, set theory, matrix algebra, etc., in sociological researches have been made only recently and by few sociologists (see, Rastogi, 1976, 1975; D'Souza, 1972, Mukherjee, 1976). As compared to the sociological practice in India during 1952-60, the trend in 1960-70 and 1970-71 has been more towards structural analysis from a historical and comparative perspective. This type of study did use simple quantitative techniques, but relied more on observational, case historical and documentary data. Only the Marxists studies on agrarian structure, we reviewed, conducted mostly by economists than sociologists have used higher mathematical techniques in survey design of research.

With few exceptions, the sophistication of quantitative methods of research in sociology is yet to be a popular movement. Instead, there is some evidence in recent sociological studies of social movements, historical life cycle of institutions that there is reaction against uses of quantitative techniques of research. Srinivas, in a recent article on this problem takes economists and others who devalue documentary and to task observational facts and insights in researches, and attributes this neglect to the many failings of the explanatory models of these sciences (see, Srinivas, 1975). Similar views have been expressed by other sociologists (Singh, 1976). This reasoning is strengthened by studies on the problems of conducting survey researches in India. It is revealed that many tools which take individual respondent's autonomy of views and opinions for granted (as in the west) do not apply in India, because of the different nature of relationship between individual and society in India (Rudolph and Rudolph, 1958). On the other hand, the emphasis on methods and scientific techniques is most pronounced in the writings of Ramkrishna Mukherjee, who insists that explanation of phenomena through research is not possible without the uses of experimental and inductive inferential models in sociology.

The second important development in Indian sociology is in respect of self-reflection by sociologists who have completed studies or major researches on the methodology they have employed in a post-facto exercise of self-critique and self-assessment. Also, there is a tendency to objectively examine some of the subjective and ideological issues which influenced their research strategy and choice of tools and techniques. We have an interesting account of social anthropologists on their own 'encounters and experiences' doing fieldwork in India (Beteille and Madan, 1975). A similar study on the craft of Indian sociology by sociologists, political scientists and psychologists who have conducted major studies in their field in India has been prepared where each social scientist reflects retrospectively on the problems he faced in his field study, the ideological leads that he now thinks had been implicit in his design of research and concepts and categories he has used (Singh and Oommen, 1977).

These reflections on tendencies in methodology and uses of techniques in Indian sociology and social sciences highlight certain common problems. Sociologists have now acknowledged the role of ideology in operationalization of concepts and theories in research designs and its techniques. They at the same time do not reject norms of scientific method or the statistical model in social researching favour of ethno-methodology. About the uses of techniques, however, their values and preferences are tempered by caution and circumspection. Uses of history, documentary data and reflexive insights are preferred in more recent sociological researches to simplistic attempts at quantification ad statistical reasoning. More important areas where such insights have been adequately found useful and innovative are that of family sociology, study of social movements, analysis of problems of inter-group relations and mobility of classes and categories. The utility of survey design and quantitative models has been found to be extremely high in studies with a bearing on applied problems or where generation of benchmark data is essential for implementing public policy.

Theoretically challenging uses of mathematical models have, however, not been in evidence in Indian sociology on any significant scale.

The Correlations

Indian sociology has interacted closely with other social sciences. The teaching of sociology has indeed differentiated from political science in Bombay University and from economics in Lucknow University—the two centres where its teaching made early impact on the profession of sociology in India. Its conceptual categories have also been influenced by discoveries in other social sciences and have in turn influenced their orientation. Historians have influenced deeply the wider uses of the notions of sanskritization and westernization, the study of middle classes and socio-economic formations in India. They have deeply contributed to the validation of propositions of Marxist and dialectical theoretical orientations in sociology as also offered refutation of some of its hypotheses. Political scientists' contributions through studies of political elites, power structure and political communication and studies of ideology have influenced similar studies in sociology. Rajni Kothari has contri-buted to the theory of political socialization in India which has enriched studies on the formation of cognitive and value systems in personality. Similarly, studies in political participation, political culture and its systemic treatment have offered new insight to sociologists working in this field (Kothari, 1970). The study of leadership by political scientists has enriched insights of sociologists in their own studies of leadership in rural and urban societies.

The influence of sociology and social anthropology has been considerable in India both on history and political science. History has not only influenced sociology but has been influenced by it, especially in the recent formulations of historical problems, where formation of structures, modes of production and other infrastructural realities of society deeply inform historical analysis (see, Thapar, 1975). Indian history bears the imprint of sociology as it moves from narrative history to problem history. It is evident in economic historical studies, analysis of social movements and agrarian structure by Indian historians. A.M. Shah writes: "During the last fifteen years or so, historians have become increasingly receptive to sociology and social anthropology. This is seen in the works of several historians such as Tapan Roy Chaudhuri, Dharma Kumar, Donald Smith, Robert Frykenberg, Eugene Irschic, Burton Stein, Morris D. Morris, Robert Crane, R. Hardgrave, S.C. Misra, Romila Thapar and A.L. Basham, among others. The new journal *Indian Economic and Social History Review,* founded by Tapan Roychaudhuri, has served to bring history and social sciences, including sociology and social anthropology, in closer relationship. Roychaudhuri has devoted almost the whole of the long preface to the second edition of his book, *Bengal under Akbar and jahangir* to sociology and social anthropology and their usefulness in history" (Shah, 1974: 453).

While the interaction between history and sociology, and political science and sociology, has been mutually reinforcing and has proved beneficial, the same type of interaction between sociology and economics has not taken place during the past one and half decades. Earlier, sociologists and economists used to interact more purposefully in uses of categories and in substantive studies. The reason for this lag lies in high mathematicalization of economics during the past one and a half decades which on the one hand endows economists with a sense of technical superiority in their researches, and on the other alienates sociologists, who often not trained in mathematical logic, tend to be mystified by economists' works without, however, being impressed by them. On the contrary, sociologists often consider such technological skill of economists rather misplaced and inadequate in capturing the essences of the social and cultural correlates of economic behaviour and its system (Srinivas, 1975) in India. It is hoped that as economists' study of social structures, such as the agrarian and industrial social formations, using their own frames of reference, becomes mature, they would also in the process generate insights other than mathematical which could be meaningful to sociologists.

6

Basic Problems

The globalization process has generated universal discontent and disenchantment. Those who applaud its arrival are fewer. Disenchantment prevails not only in the developing but also in the developed world. It needs to be analyzed as to what lies at the root of such discontentment. Also, globalization almost everywhere has given rise to a newer and sharper self-consciousness of identity. Such consciousness tends to be pervasive; it is not confined to the cultural minorities, local cultures, ethnic groups, tribes or weaker sections. The surge of identity consciousness and anxiety about preservation of cultural identity extends also in the relationships between nations. The nation or the set of nations which plays the dominant role in controlling the financial resources or the institutional instruments of globalization is perceived to have an unchallenged monopoly on the extension of its 'symbolic power' through marketing of its cultural products, practices, styles and symbolic forms. Amongst nations or communities which feel culturally subordinated, the sense of resentment generates forces leading to cultural nationalism or even fundamentalism. Can we treat these twin processes as contemporary pathology of globalization? The issue needs to be examined in all its dimensions. Moreover, we notice that despite massive literature being generated on the treatment of the specific dimensions of globalization such as its social, structural, economic, cultural and political correlates and consequences, a very substantial degree of ambiguity persists about its historicity, ideology and epistemological or conceptual status as a factor in the integrated social and economic development of the contemporary societies. This problem is global.

Globalization is a composite process. It results from the convergence of a series of developments in society which are qualitatively new. These include: contemporary revolution in science and technology of communication, high velocity move-ments of finance, capital and market, increased social mobility, migration of personnel and the emergence of a global diaspora. Its associated contributory processes are: intensification of cultural interaction among diverse groups through media exposure, increased incidence of leisure-time activities, growth in tourism, infrastructures of entertainment and marketing of cultural products, personnel and styles. These developments have an evolutionary character, as they are generally irreversible despite societies going through the cycles of growth and depression in economy, polity and social system. This attribute of globalization has social structural and political consequences which are often overlooked as most treatment of this process has focused upon a segmental rather than a holistic analysis of its nature and consequences. In a segmental approach, analysts have studied 'financial or capital globalization', 'telecommunication or media globalization' and 'cultural globalization' as separate developments, and then tried to view the impact of the one, for instance, 'financial or capital' globalization upon other segments such as the 'media', 'communication' or 'culture'. This approach has two weaknesses: first, it fails to help us in comprehending the role of the residual social structural realities and their emergent properties and the way they interact with any one of these three aspects of globalization, be it capital, communication or culture. Conse-quently, such treatment is unable to explain why some societies, communities or groups resist globalization and reject its institutions and ideology, whereas others accept it and celebrate its arrival. It is necessary to take note of this reality since it determines the historicity of globalization in specific societies, cultures and nationalities and takes into consideration the 'initial' historical and social-cultural realities of each society as it encounters the pressure for globalization. Secondly, the segmental approach does not give enough weight to a holistic treatment of the process of globalization. Particularly, it misses the point that globalization plays a vital contributory role in the evolution of a 'new' society, variously described as an 'information society' or a 'post-modern society'. The emergence of such a society inheres a basic structural transformation of economy, polity and culture, and the potential to go beyond the systemic features of a capitalist or a post-capitalist social order. Its unfolding may eventually contribute to the birth of a new social order.

This new social order, variously described as the "information society or the post-modern society" is yet to come into being; it does not exist as yet in a systemic form in any part of the globe. We see today only a selected set of institutional, structural and cultural attributes of such a society, which is probably in the process of being born. For instance, we witness substantial growth of homogenized occupational workforce of skilled manpower, such as in the professions, technology and services; there is growing global mobility and interdependency among societies in need of such skilled workforce. It contributes to the emergence of social and cultural diaspora with huge influence upon the economy and culture both of the nation of its origin as well as that of its settlement.

The increased social mobility and cross-cultural interactions release the forces of change in each society. In the developed world, it has released intense feeling of cultural identity leading to the growth in the ideology of the 'right' on the one hand and on the dissatisfaction with that existing form of political participation in democracy on the other. Focus now is on the movement from 'representative' democracy to 'participatory' democracy; from state sponsorship of social and economic agenda of societies to its formulation and management by the civil society and voluntary associations. The new slogan is to 're-invent democracy'. The revolutionary changes brought about in the communication technology, such as telephony, internet and new mass media, make it possible to envisage the possibilities of political, social and cultural interaction within and between societies and interest groups which are truly participatory and which bring about self-governing civil society into existence.

In this process, we witness radical changes at the economic level. The basic organs of economy, such as capital, market, modes of production and trade, are getting increasingly entwined into a web of global interdependence. This interdependence is not merely geographical or of capital and market, but it increasingly draws its synergy from new technological advances in the fields of communication through satellites, internet, television, telephony, etc. These technologies are helping not only the educated and the professional sections but also the fishermen, farmers, horti-culturists, floriculturists and people engaged in many other occupa-tions. These extend the scope of their operations such as techno-logy uses, marketing and capitalization. Similarly, branding of commodities is increasingly transforming production processes in an idiom which is cultural, communicative. It universalizes that which was once considered to be local.

To deal with its implications for a specific national society, institutional innovations within and at the international level are required. The contemporary institutions such as the World Bank, International Monetary Fund (IMF), World Trade Organization (WTO), etc., are some of the responses, but these do not yet inspire the level of consensus and confidence that could make the acceptance of the goals of globalization smooth. This fact, combined with the reality of the existing social inequalities among societies and its varying levels of intensity within each individual society, do not inspire confidence about the final outcome of globalization. Many questions are posed and many challenges are faced by societies yet in the process of new transformation. The recent experiences of near-economic breakdown in Indonesia, Malaysia and Thailand, once lauded as 'little tigers' due to the flight of capital, has left memories in the developing world which evokes disenchantment rather than reassurance from the processes of globalization.

Philosophical Basis

These operational contradictions of globalization have generated several ideological nuances in its contemporary conceptual and substantive evaluation. A range of ideologies, such as neo-Marxism-Leninism, post-modernism, critical theories of development, particularly those related to the impact of globalization on ecology, human rights of the weaker sections such as women, minorities, working classes and other marginalized groups, have generated a strident debate on the social, cultural and economic consequences of globalization. The fact that globalization has not yet resolved some of the basic contradictions in the realms of culture, economy and human relationships and in some cases it is supposed to have contributed to internal social conflicts goes only to lend credence to such ideologies. According to the contemporary Marxist-Leninist critique, globalization is only other manifestation of cosmopolitan capitalism with its classic imperialistic orientation remaining intact. Instead of contributing to trans-nationalism, it exposes societies and nations to endemic 'disasters' such as the recent food crisis in Africa and the onset of fundamentalism and communalism, both at the global and national levels. The acute social distresses, cultural conflicts and alienation (see, Patnaik, 1996) of the weaker and marginalized communities contribute to this process. No doubt, globalization with its emphasis on the supremacy of the market, quest for optimization of profits by the multinational corporations, continual unemployment due to the fluctuations in economy and capitalism-friendly labour laws and control over the management or gover-nance of globalization by the Bretton Wood inspired institutions of the rich capitalist nations who set the agenda, policies and practices of globalization lends credence to this critique. In fact, the Human Development Report (2002) echoes this despair and calls for reforms within the international institutions of development such as the WTO, World Bank, IMF, etc., by making them more accountable and representative.

It is said that, "nearly half the voting power in the World Bank and International Monetary Fund rests in the hands of seven countries. And though all countries have a seat and a vote in the WTO, in practice, decisions are taken in small group meetings and heavily influenced by Canada, the European Union, Japan and U.S. In 2000, 15 African countries did not have a single trade representative stationed at the WTO" (The *Hindu, July* 25, 2002). This political domination contributes to the acute differences in the perception as to the extent that globalization decrease or increase the levels of economic and social inequalities within a society.

The Marxist-Leninist critique of globalization is anchored into a theoretical paradigm which recognizes the role of the historical forces, systems of political economy and social structure. Yet another ideology, the post-modernist criticism of globalization, is essentially cultural. It derives sustenance from an epistemology which rejects the idea of a system or structure, and posits human social and cultural realities in a perpetual state of symbolic transience or flux, continually in the process of making and unmaking. "It challenges the postulate of rationality (the foundation of market economy) on which most social science categories such as, 'structure', 'system' and 'change' are anchored; it also attempts to invalidate the notions of the 'actor' or the 'subject' from the social science discourse or their moorings in the structure of social values. The French sociologist, J. Baudrillard articulates this view when he says that in matters of social discourse, "the things have never functioned socially, but symbolically, magically, irrationally". Social systems, according to the post-modern reckoning, are illusionary facades characterized by "micro-orders of domination" (Singh, 1998: 1). Thus, in the logic of its analysis, history has no role or significance. It treats the conjuncture of events and processes largely in terms of space as 'co-happenings' and not in order of temporal succession. The diversity of existence of identities is recognized but the causality of the same is rejected.

We also witness yet another ideology about globalization which emanates from the assorted movement of the NGOs. These NGOs represent a variety of 'interest groups' and many institutionalized forms of activism. The issues of their concern are as diverse as human rights, ecology and sustainable development, rights of the minorities, women, tribes, working classes, etc., which seem to converge upon their opposition to globalization for reasons some of which have a common basis, and others which are contradictory. Their ideology in some parts may seem eclectic with the underpinnings of Marxism, post-modernism, ecological and developmental humanism and focus on human rights etc., which are articulated in a generalized form.

In my view, globalization is a unique process. It is a product of such developments in the field of science and technology which are entirely new to human history. And, these offer new opportunities to humankind as also pose many challenges. It is a fact, however, that several of its features taken individually did indeed exist in the past, such as international trade by sea and land routes, capitalism and imperialism, market and capital mobility and transfer of workforce from one country to another. But, devoid as these processes in the past were of the advantages of the modern technologies, their total impact upon society and its direction of change was qualitatively different. Therefore, the nature of challenges was also different. Hence, to understand its fuller implications, a new ideological paradigm is necessary. It must be of an interdisciplinary nature, because globalization is a multidimensional and multidirectional process. Its implications have to be understood and analyzed from a holistic perspective. The particularistic perspective, either on the basis of political economy as we find in Marxist-Leninist critique or that of culture, symbols or images as we find in the discourse on post-modernism, remain inadequate. While highlighting some of the aspects of globalization, each one of them leaves a much larger segment of globalization, its nature and consequences etc., unaccounted for Sociology, to my mind, could be one such discipline which has a broad enough integrative theoretical perspective to offer a paradigm for the analysis of globalization. It focuses upon the study of the 'specific' or local in the perspective of the 'total' and the historical. Its methodology and epistemology offer both variety and flexibility of an approach to deal with social realities that may be 'normal' or 'enigmatic' or paradoxical. Globalization is a good candidate to merit its attention.

The Difficulties

Any revolutionary transformation in society brings in its wake both challenges and opportunities. This is true also for globalization. Not that these challenges are confined only to a developing society like India. The developed world is also not immune from them, as it too faces the challenges of globalization; only its character is different. In the developing societies, the tensions and anxieties on account of globalization are primarily economic which spill over to the anxieties about culture and identity. In the developed world, culture seems to top over all other anxieties on account of globalization. In Europe, we witness this in the crescendo of debate on multiculturalism and in the revival of the ideology of the 'right and the racial-cultural exclusiveness'. In India, however, the cultural and ethnic aspects of the challenges of globalization do exist, but these are in most cases derivatives of the anticipated unpredictable consequences to the economy, polity and social structure.

In terms of social structure, India remains essentially a rural-agrarian society. Only about 30 percent of our population is urban and the pace of urbanization remains slow. The addition to our urban population comes mainly from the rural poor, who migrate in search of employment. They remain marginalized in the urban economy and hold the lowest position in the urban social structure. Thus, a major challenge that globalization is likely to pose to our social structure is related to the nature of inequalities in the society. We witness these inequalities at several levels, such as between the village and town, between the middle classes and the working classes, between males and females, between marginalized ethnicities and the dominant castes or communities and between the mobile metropolitan diaspora and the illiterate masses in the villages, urban slums and at the periphery of the tribal lands. How is globalization going to affect these sections of our society? Its pace at present is no doubt measured and slow due to choice of policies and also because of the limitations that our social structure itself imposes upon the pace of globalization, but the challenges are likely to grow and pose serious problems in the future.

The impact of globalization on the structural changes in the society comes generally through the changes in the economic policies. India, since independence, has been following a policy of import-substitution and inward-looking market economy. This policy handicapped the economy in global competitiveness, in the manufacturing sector and in exportable commodity production. But its focus upon higher education in science and technology and agricultural infrastructures did compensate the loss. It is evident in 'green revolution' in agriculture, in our growing strength in the sectors of information technology, the professions, the rising middle classes and in the space research which has added edge to our growth in telephony, television and mass communi-cation. Also, the investment in the capital-intensive sectors, such as steel, petrochemicals, power, etc., have generated an economic and technological potential strong enough to cope up with the exposure to the contemporary challenges of globalization. The existing economic, social and cultural resilience of our society is to a large measure influenced by the rising middle class. It is estimated that by 2020 the half of the Indian population would comprise the middle classes even at the contemporary rate of the economic growth. Despite this, the challenges of globalization felt by India in early 1990's made it inevitable to change these policies. Of course, the difference (see, Herzog, 1999; Malhautra, 2001; Panchamukhi in Chadha, 2001) of opinion on matters related to economic liberalization continues to persist.

The Indian economic policies on globalization have rightly tended to be cautious. This does not rule out the need for faster movement in several areas. To some extent, our political-structural reality, our democratic path of development imposes restraints to our speed. This is inevitable, as the structural reality of our democracy is still deeply embedded in our social and economic inequalities. Besides, democracy is not merely an instrument of social and political development. It constitutes a fundamental ideal or normative principle of human development. It is an irony that globalization of economy does not by itself translate into the growth of a democratic society. The Human Development Report (2002) recognizes this fact and laments about it.

In our appraisal of the inward-looking economic policies of the past or in our overenthusiasm for the quick embrace of full economic globalization, we should not neglect our developmental goal of growing as a strong democracy and civil society. This goal, when posited against many policy objectives of economic globalization, calls for caution and graduated response. Our membership of the WTO and IMF etc. has devolved upon us the responsibilities for moving towards an open market economy. It exposes our farmers, consumer good industries, small-scale sector industries and those employed in the unorganized sectors to unequal competition from strong economies, which may increase unemployment or lead to many forms of economic and social displacement.

To take these factors into account and yet to encounter the challenges of globalization, an integrated policy is required. Increased export earnings and foreign trade on the one hand, and the need for massive foreign capital investment on the other depend upon how fast we move in this direction both at the federal and the state levels. In foreign trade and export earnings, we have a temporary advantage of low wages and human resources, but economies of scale and technological modernization of the production process are required. Reforms in management, governance, labour legislation and fiscal and monetary policies are required. Capital investment on a massive scale is needed to develop the infrastructures in tile sectors of power, roadways, railways, airports and ports etc. India has lagged behind in foreign capital investment, apart from other reasons also because of our weak infrastructure. Its inadequacy hampers the growth of our trade and modernization of agriculture. No doubt, globalization does create a "mismatch between growth of trade, growth of output and growth of employment" (Panchamukhi in Chadha, 2001: 11), but its negative consequences can certainly be avoided if our infrastructure is modern and our policies with regard to various sectors of economy are adequately synchronized. We may need to reinforce our legal expertise, laws about the intellectual property rights, banking and insurance policies and measures to protect our economy from unfair trade policies from abroad.

Modernization of agriculture is an urgent requirement as 70 percent of our population depends upon it. About 90 percent of employment in our country is offered by the unorganized sector, of which agriculture is a primary component. Studies reveal that during 1990-98 nearly 7 million Indian workers, of which about 4 million in the rural and 3 million in the urban sectors, lost their jobs. Also, the quality of workforce in the rural areas is poor; during 1993-94, 44 percent of rural males and 80 percent of rural females were found to be illiterate (see, Chadha, 2001). Hence, the urgent need for the improvement of the rural human resource base of our country. This would reduce the crisis of inequalities in the social and political structure and also strengthen the pace of our economic modernization. The farming sector in our economy has chronically suffered from underdevelopment due to lack of investment and adverse terms of trade and tariff policies. Despite this, globalization has so far not caused any massive dislocation, may be only because of its slow pace in our country or because of our policies. But, eventually, agriculture would have to become commercial and oriented to value added production. This is slowly taking place as some studies reveal (see, Panini, 1999), but its scale is still miniscule due to lack of investment and poverty of infrastructure and human resources.

These challenges of economic globalization have indeed created a social structural crisis of change in our society. The social inequalities have increased in relative terms. But to call it structural dualism may be an oversimplification. The studies on the consumption data indicate that the rural areas constitute about 80-90 percent of the market for the factory-made consumer goods. There exists a strategic linkage between the rural economy and the industrial sector producing consumer goods. A middle class has emerged in the villages and it continues to grow in size.

In bringing about these changes the expansion of the mass media has played an important role. The incidence of telephony, access to radio and television and in some areas even the uses of the internet are linking the rural social structure and economy with the outside world as never before. It reinforces inter-regional and inter-state linkages, alters the character of the social mobility of skilled and unskilled labour and in some measures it also creates inter-regional or inter-state inequalities. These changes have the potential in the long run to influence the nature of social inequalities in our society and also the pattern of political and cultural interactions among groups and regions within and across the states.

Significance of Individual

These developments do impinge upon the issues of identity. The social and economic developments augment the societal self-awareness within every society. The larger question of identity is related to the growth of social, economic, political and cultural self-awareness among groups and communities. Identity has its subjective root in the person, but it manifests itself objectively as a social product through the mobilization of collective self-consciousness. This consciousness is forged by a chemistry of several factors, such as history, mythology and instrumental rationality. The sense of identity is created by one's realization of the presence of the 'other'. For this, a historical context is necessary. The past and present experiences of social and cultural interaction with other cultures give shape to people's consciousness of their own identity. What form the identity consciousness will take, whether it would promote adaptive, assimilative, alienative or hostile attitude towards the other culture depends upon a variety of factors. Among them are included the presence or absence of a tradition of pluralism, the nature of the civilization and its past historical experiences of cultural contacts with the outside world. For instance, exposure to colonial control and its impact upon local culture and economy play a material role in the perception of cultural globalization in India.

Most discussions on the impact of globalization on the cultural and social identity of people relate to questions such as: Will globalization eventually bring about a cultural homogenization among societies which today enjoy cultural diversity? Which culture would dominate in this process? What would be the fate of local cultures? Will they face a total loss of identity? What about the cultural minority groups, religious groups and ethnicities? Will they face extinction through homogenization? Finally, is globalization of culture a new incarnation of westernization-a mark of cultural imperialism? I will like to briefly address some of these issues in the context of our own society.

India has been exposed to cultural contacts with other civilization since millennia. It has been continually making adaptive changes in its cultural styles, traits and forms as it encountered other cultures. It has a history of accommodating identities. The cultural impact of globalization on the identity of this civilization or its impact upon the identities of local cultures, therefore, is bound to be mediated by this resilience. There are several reasons for this observation. In the first instance, the initial historical conditions of the Indian social structure have been unique. It is characterized by immense plurality of communities, languages, cultural diacritical symbols and ethnic styles. A variety of cultural traits and cultural styles have over centuries given identity to communities but not in total isolation. Cultural interaction among regions and communities has persisted in a mode of co-sharing and mutual accommodation. This commonality has existed beyond the religious and ethnic divides. A recent study by the Anthropological Survey of India illustrates this fact. It observes that the sharing of cultural traits among communities in India, in all about 4,635 in number, shows "high correlation of traits among states within macro-regions such as those in the south, north-western India, central and western India and so on. There is very high correlation of traits between the Scheduled Castes and the Scheduled Tribes, between Scheduled Tribes and Hindus, between Hindus and Sikhs, between Hindus and Muslims (which is very high indeed) and between Hindus and Jains. The high correlation between Hindus and Buddhists may also be explained in the same way. This fact that these communities interact across space or states is important" (Singh, 1992: 99). Thus, we notice that despite the plurality of identities, a macro-linkage of cultural bonds has existed in India throughout history. It continues to subsist even today, and constitutes the cultural unity of India despite plurality of local identities.

The cultural impact of globalization gets enmeshed within this process of internal dynamics and resilience of the local cultures. The perception that globalization threatens local culture is being increasingly invalidated. It is observed that in the process of globalization local cultures are reinforced and also globalized. Ronald Robertson has called this process globalization. It indicates how local cultures get increasingly enmeshed with the global culture through selective adaptation of symbolic forms and styles in their products through micro-marketing. Based on the Japanese experience, this process affirms how local cultures begin to occupy a global space by constructing differentiation of consumers. Its examples are witnesses in the field of tourism and the popularity of ethnic supermarkets (see, Robertson, 1994). In India, we witness how our local cultural traditions are also making adaptive responses in the forms and styles of cultural products in tune with the inter-regional and global requirements. For instance, regional languages are being creolized across regions or even in global terms. The incidence of bilingualism has increased in our country from about 13.4 percent in 1971 to 64.2 percent in 1991. The culinary styles, the pattern of dress, local ethnic cultural objects, rituals, religious icons and local customs, etc., are now increasingly becoming pan-Indian and even global due to the increasing size of the Indian diaspora. The process of micro-marketing is penetrating deep into this sphere. The momentum for this is, of course, provided by the emergent forces of economic development. It has triggered a new wave of internal and external migration, and establishes a linkage between culture and market. It also extends the space for cultural interaction as never before. No doubt, it generates a threat perception about cultural identity, but correspondingly it also reinforces the identity consciousness. This ambivalence notwithstanding, the Indian response towards the 'other' cultures has throughout remained selective and adaptive. Globalization is, therefore, leading increasingly towards hybridization or fusion of cultural styles and forms rather than their total displacement. This only shows the strength of cultural resilience of the Indian society.

Contradiction in Ideas

This resilience, however, is not without tensions, both social structural and cultural. It is a global phenomenon. India, since independence, has been making conscious efforts through its democratic institutions, policies of welfare and devolution of power to the regional, ethnic and cultural minorities to establish a synergy between local identities and national development. The linguistic reorganization of states, the policies of protective discrimination, the continual effort to bring about better and more effective federal structure of governance by improving the centre-state relationship, the policy of offering protection to the ethnic-regional and cultural entities etc., have been continually implemented and updated to accommodate cultural, social and political identities. We have largely succeeded, but not in all cases, and not without conflict and violence. Globalization, to the extent that it generates new inequalities or sharpens the consciousness of inequalities, does contain within it the seeds of social and cultural conflicts in society. It makes the intensity of symbolic transmission across lands more effective and easier, and it also sharpens in people's mind the sense of social, economic and cultural deprivations. It has a regional, national and global dimension. The premise that globalization generates conflict in societies which sometimes have disastrous consequences is based upon the possibility of extreme mismatch between globalization and removal of poverty or deprivation of classes, communities and ethnicities. It is true that organized violence such as terrorism and insurgency erupts in societies where people feel that they are being subordinated culturally, politically or economically, where dominant powers are perceived to be totally unresponsive to democratic protest, and where basic human rights are denied. Does globalization increase poverty in a society or reduce it? Does it enhance the ability of some nations to structurally dominate the weaker ones? Ideological debate on these issues goes on but the result remains inconclusive. The evidence available so far suggests that globalization reduces the absolute level of poverty but does enhance the incidence of relative inequalities among people:

If we observe the pattern of social mobility and incidence of poverty since independence in our country, we find that measures of social welfare, education and economic development have contributed to the reduction of poverty, but the relative social inequalities have increased. In absolute terms, the standard of consumption has qualitatively improved in villages and towns; the reservation policy together with focus upon education has created a 'limited' middle class among the weaker sections, minorities and ethnic groups; the quality and extent of participation in politics and power sharing by the backward classes, tribes and scheduled castes etc. has radically changed. A substantial degree of empowerment of these groups has taken place in the political realm, but in the economic and educational fields the gap between them and the dominant classes or castes persists. In my view, globalization does pose challenges on several fronts, foremost of which may be economic. For reasons of history, pluralistic social structure and culture and the democratic path of development that we have adopted, we enjoy tremendous resilience to meet with the challenges of globalization. Notwithstanding this, a cautious fine-tuning and synergy in our economic policies is required. To my mind, the most strategic aspects of such a policy relate to the development of our human resource base, agriculture and infrastructure. Economic development in a balanced manner holds the key to our ability to meet with the challenges of globalization and accommodate the upsurge of identities.

7

Social Organisation

Society can be looked upon as a process; as a series of interactions between human beings; each person stimulating another person and responding to the stimuli from the other person. No social life is possible without such interactions. This is why communication is basic to social life. Communication is interaction in terms of a stimulus, a gesture, or a word which one person produces in response to another stimulus, gesture, or a word from the other person. The mother-child relationship is a typical example of the interaction process. The care of the child, the upbringing and socialization of the child is based on the interaction processes between the mother and the child. In fact, the personality of the child is largely determined by the socialization process in this early relationship with the parents and others at home and later on with the teacher and the peer group at school. But one should not imagine that the personality of the child is wholly or completely determined by this interaction process, in the sense that the child is a mere replica of the parents. Each child starts with his own needs and psychoneural bases for emotional experiences and cognitive orientations, and develops his own personality. The interactions with others may lead to cooperation as well as to conflict. While cooperation is the process of working together for commonly accepted ends, conflicts arise when there is a struggle between rivals for the same goods and services or for recognition. Besides, there is the process of competition between the two interacting persons or groups when they strive to attain the same goods or services or recognitions. Thus, interactions lead to uniformities as well as diversities, so that while there are many similarities between the individuals in a group, whether it is a family group or a neighbourhood group or a national group, there are also many diversities. In fact, as our experience makes it obvious, each member of the family and each member in the classroom or of a football team is a unique personality. In the same way each group is also unique. Just as no two individuals in a family are alike, no two families are alike. As we observe larger groups, these diversities and unique features become more obvious. Thus, the whole human society and each group in the society can be viewed as the manifestation of the social processes between the interacting members.

The concept of social process is closely tied up with the evolutionary thought that society is a developing organism, that society has passed through evolutionary changes in the sense in which Charles Darwin (1809-82), the British biologist showed that species of organisms have evolved. There is no doubt that the concept of evolution has been very helpful to understand the development of various kinds of organisms. In the biological field, the term evolution indicates the emergence of new structural organizations. There is certainly nothing analogical to this in the social field. While the structure of the tribal society in the north-eastern frontier of India is totally different from the structure of the society in a metropolis like Bombay, by no stretch of imagina-tion can this difference be equated with the differences, either anatomical or behavioural, between the fly and the rat or between the rat and the man. However, though the evolutionary theory of society may be discredited empirically as well as theoretically, there is no need to discredit the concept of social process.

The concept of structure indicates an ordered arrangement of parts. The parts may vary but the structure is persistent. The interactions or processes are accomplished with this persistent framework of the given social structure. The advantage of the concept of structure is that it helps in the analysis of social events at a given time. This is why short-term empirical studies can be more easily made using the concept of structure.

However, when a social system is considered over a period of time, it is necessary to look at the origin and growth of the system.

Though Parsons is a structuralist, he relies on the concept of social process in order to account for social change. The struc-ture itself may change through time. As Parsons writes, "A social structure is a natural persistent system. It maintains its continuity despite internal changes from moment to moment, year to year, just as a living organism remains the same living organism in spite of metabolic changes; it is dynamic"(Parsons, 1965).

It is generally argued that in studying 'structure', we study essentially the interrelation or arrangements of parts in some total entity. The components of social structure are the human beings; the structure here is the arrangement of persons in relationship which are institutionally defined and regulated (Rad-cliffe-Brown, 1957). Further, social structure also consists of ideas regarding the distribution of power between the persons or the groups at a given time. Thus, as Nadel puts it, "social structure is a conceptual tool; it is an abstraction indicating the network of relationship between the persons who have different roles to play" (Nadel, 1965). The basic social data consist of the interactions between persons. The term 'role' is used to refer to the regular repetition of interactions over a period of time. It is clear that in any social organization like an administrative office or factory producing goods, there is a social structure, in which various persons in various positions, from the head of the organization to the peon and the sweeper, play the roles assigned to each one. The persons playing the roles may change from time to time but the roles played will be fairly constant. As Smelser (1970) puts it, "Social structure can be defined as identifiable patterns of roles that are organized primarily around the fulfilment of some social function or activity." Another aspect of the problem is that all social behaviour is subject to certain kinds of social regulations, sanctions, norms and value orientations. Thus, the main ingredients of social life are the interactions between persons who are in role relations to one another and whose interactions are governed by sanctions, norms and values.

Changing Scenario

Towards the end of the 19th century and at the beginning of the 20th c , sociologists and anthropologists were preoccupied with the problem of how societies evolved, from their original primitive state. The concept of evolution formulated by Charles Darwin in the biological field was applied to the social field. Also the great progress made by the Western European nations in the field of colonialism in 17th and 18th centuries, in the field of political organization with the development of democratic institutions, and in the field of industrialization and economic organization in the 19th century, stimulated the social thinkers to account for the onset of these changes. But the great devastation which took place in Europe as a result of the First World War (1914-1918) and the tremendous communist revolution in Russia (1917) made the social scientists to concentrate more on the problems of social structure and maintenance of order. However after the Second World War (1939-1945) and with the emergence of new states since 1947 when India obtained independence, there is again a preoccupation with the problems of social change, and social development. When the United Nations Organization was formed in 1945 there were only 51 member states; by 1960 there were 100 member states and today there are 191 member states. The former colonies in Asia and Africa have now become independent states; they have accepted modern forms of political organization; their aim is to adopt the modern economic organi-zation by industrializing their economies so that the standard of living of the people is raised. These great changes have now induced the sociologists to be engaged in the study of social change.

The Indian sociologists are greatly interested in the problem of social change since the Indian society has now taken up the task of changing itself from an agricultural society to an industrial society, from a colonial society with emperors and monarchs to a republican society, from a society based on caste and class to a society which aims to be casteless and classless with equality of opportunity to every citizen guaranteed by the Indian Constitution adopted in 1950.

In other words, the urgent problem of contemporary social situation in India is the transformation of the individual from a member of a tribe or a village or a caste or a creed or a language group to a citizen of India. This transformation of man and society has been the central and quite dominant concern of sociology right from the time when it emerged as an independent branch of learning. One of the chief aims of sociology has been to study the conditions under which the disruption of the old traditional order of society occurred and the conditions which lead to the explosive emergence of a new individualism. During the nineteenth century, as noted above, the main aim of sociology was to understand this rapid revolutionary transformation of society. Comte (1798-1857). J.S.Mill (1806-1873), Spencer (1820-1903) and Marx (1818-1883), in their several ways provided an analysis of this transformation of society. Tonnies (1855-1936) in his book Community and Association constructed two clear 'types' of society, the living community (the gemeinschaft) in which all the members were bound together in a shared order of kinship and neighbourhood, living and working within a known and loved territory with clear and well-understood rules, values and social arrangements and the complex network of formally and rationally devised associations (the *Gesellschaft)* of which men were members only in a contractual sense, in which the relationship rested entirely on meansend calculations, in which both men and principles became impersonal.

This transformation of men and social relationship is necessitated by the new social, political and economic organizations. Political independence and the formation of one central government, urbanization on a vast scale with the development of the great metropolitan cities, the planned industrialization and the development of rapid modes of transportation and communication, the development of huge banking organizations with branches in most of the villages and all the towns and cities, the establishment of primary schools in practically all the villages, all these developments since independence have necessitated a transformation of the society. So it is the task of the social scientist to study how the transformation is taking place and analyse the nature of the resistances which are preventing or which are slowing down the speed of the transformation.

Social Process

However, as Becker (1957) pointed out, any social system may be viewed as occupying some position along a continuum varying from maximum reluctance to change to maximum readi-ness to change. He even goes to the extent asserting that a society may run the risk of extinguishing itself by preventing change or, on the contrary, may extinguish itself in pursuit of change. In other words, both maximum reluctance to change and maximum readiness to change are suicidal; no society can survive under either condition. Survival depends upon some flexible approach which takes into account the situation which arises when factors inducing or necessitating change are operating. Such change- inducing factors may arise from within or from without.

In a broad way it may be asserted on the basis of the anthropological and sociological data available, that the more primitive societies are more reluctant to change while the more modern societies are more ready to change. To put it in another way, the simpler societies are more reluctant to change while the more complex societies are more ready to change. In fact, the more modern and more complex societies have in-built mecha-nisms, as it were, to change. For example, the more modern societies encourage the growth of science and promote facilities for the application of such new knowledge by establishing special institutions for scientific research and technological progress. Similarly the political institutions in the democratic framework provide for periodical general elections and formation of new governments. The Parliament is empowered to repeal old laws or amend them or bring on down. Public administration provides the framework through which the controlling authorities are transferred from one section to another.

Similarly research in agriculture has been sponsored in the universities of agricultural sciences in various parts of the country, by the Indian Council of Agricultural Research, and the Indian Agricultural Research Institute, New Delhi; besides several special research institutes like Central Rice Research Institute, Cuttack; Indian Institute of Sugar Technology, Kanpur and others. The universities of agricultural sciences as well as the state departments of agriculture have their extension wings which make the knowledge of new methods and the facilities and equipment available to the farmer. High yielding varieties of foodgrains, increased use of chemical fertilizers and the maximum use of minor irrigation facilities were all introduced as a package deal in 1967-68. This led to a great spurt in agricultural production in what is called the "Green Revolution".

In the same way there is what is called R and D, the Research and Development Organization, in the Defence Services of India to promote and apply scientific research in the Army, Navy, Air Force and Communications. Several institutions are engaged in advancing knowledge as well as technology; training courses are conducted so that the personnel are not only equipped with but also trained to use the new techniques.

In this context, it may be recalled that Gandhiji formulated the principle of satyagraha as a form of protest against the unjust laws or the unjust government and developed the technique of non-cooperation to see that political, economic and social changes can be brought about in a social system by mobilizing public opinion and public action. One of the outstanding events of human, social and political history is the fact that the political struggle in India led to the intervention of the British Government to establish, through negotiation, the Constituent Assembly to frame the Indian Constitution and to the attainment of Independence in 1947, which set in motion the liquidation of the colonial form of government in the various countries of Asia and Africa.

One of the established facts of history is that the prediction of Karl Marx regarding the polarization of classes in an industrial society did not materialize since the state as well as the society in western European nations and in North America brought about changes in the working conditions through reform, legislation and economic reorganization and by legitimizing the trade union movement among the workers.

Thus, the more complex societies have built-in mechanisms in the various institutions to enable them to change themselves in response to the strains and stresses which arise and also in response to the new knowledge and techniques deliberately developed to overcome the strains and stresses:

Gradual Process

Long ago, the ancient Indian thinkers tried to discuss the problem of persistence and change. The Upanishads; nearly three thousand years ago, looked upon the *Brahman* as the ultimate reality and asserted that the *atman,* great sayings *(mahavakyas)* of the Upanishads like *tattvamasi* (thou art that), *aham brahma asmi* (I am Brahman). The self as well as the universe are real and permanent, *nitya.*

On the other hand, Buddha (2500 B.C.) developed the doctrine of momentariness *(Kshana-bhanga vada)* and impermanence *(anityatva)* and asserted that nothing that is, lasts for longer than one instant. While it was commonly assumed that the self not only persists as long as the organism persists, but also that the self survives the body, Buddha declared that this was an error. The self, Buddha said, is not permanent; it is undergoing change almost constantly. Thus, Buddha postulated a changing self, as a protest against a static, permanent self postulated in Upanishads.

But the problem arises as to what is changing; something must exist and persist to change. Buddha explained that what exists is the aggregate, the, *samghata;* he even accepted the doctrine of *karma* and *samsara,* that one has to go through a series of births to perfect oneself to attain *nirvana* the state of non-being. Thus the Buddhists believed both in the doctrine of unenduring self and in the doctrines of rebirth *(punarjanma)* based on the fruits of *karma*. However as Hiriyanna (1932) puts it "The belief in the karma doctrine really presents no new difficulty to Buddhism; for if there can be action without an agent, there can well be transmigration without a transmigrating agent. Further, we have to remember that according to Buddhism there is trans-migration or, more precisely, rebirth, not only at the end of this life as in other Indian beliefs, but at every instant. It is not merely when one lamp is lit from another that there is a transmission of light and heat. They are transmitted every moment; only in the former case a new series of flames is started."

The same problems of permanence *(sanatana)* and change *(parinama)* was discussed by the ancient writers on social problems. For example, Manu is aware of the social changes which had taken place nearly two thousand years ago when he wrote his code of laws. He asserted many customs practised by the ancients had to be discarded because of *yuga dharma*. He recognized that each period of time had its own norms of behaviour and judgement and its own set of values. This is why Bhishma explains in Shantiparva (78:32) "Righteousness becomes unrighteousness, and unrighteousness becomes righteousness, according to place *(desha)* and time *(kala)*. Such is the power of place and time (in determining the character of human acts)." As Prabhu (1963) writes, the recognition of the role of time and region in the forma-tion of *dharma* is an indication of an awareness that the concept of *dharma* was no rigid concept but a flexible, modifiable and dynamic principle related to the exigencies of time, place and human needs. "And, moreover to speak of *dharma* itself becoming *adharma* and vice versa according to the times and the locale is really to speak of much more than just allowing the possibility of modifications in *dharma;* it is to ask man to be prepared for such complete and radical changes in *dharma* which may even be contradictory to the generally sanctioned *dharma* practices in order to suit the exigencies of the time and the conditions, if the latter necessitate such changes. It is in view of the impossibility of visualizing the emergencies of the locale and the times that the *sastrakaras* have not attempted to dwell on the *dharmas* of desa and kala."

Thus, the ancient Indians, nearly three thousand years ago, were aware of the general problem of permanence *vs* change and the specific problem of social change. But the general belief, throughout the millenia, has been that the social system is something god-given and that it was the duty of the political authority to preserve and enforce the *sanatana varnasrama dharma,* the permanent, unchangeable, social structure based on the four *varnas* (castes) and the four *ashramas* (the stages of life) (Ghosal, 1966).

Cohen (1968) has discussed this problem of continuity. He asserts that it is obvious that one cannot conceive of a social structure or social system unless one assumes that social life has continuity. Even when one assumes that all societies are constantly undergoing change, it is important to recognize that what changes is the social structure. As he puts it, this is "another way of saying that the study of social change is the study of the disruption of social persistence and the study of social persistence is the study of social processes which inhibit or fail to produce change". As he puts it elsewhere "No society is persistent without change, nor changing without being persistent". Discussing the problem of partial change and total change in social structure he points out that when the whole system changes, there is no way of identifying it is as the same system. It is clear that even when there is 'total' change as in a revolution, something persists, something has not changed so that it is possible to say that a change has taken place in the given social system.

The conundrum can be clarified by a few illustrations from recent social history. There is no doubt that the Russian Revolution of 1917 was a great revolution in the total structure of the Russian society. But it is clear that the Russian society has endured in spite of the drastic change in the social structure. There is a continuity.

Even the big change in the post-Stalin era in 1964 did not "completely" alter the Russian Government or the Russian people any more than the 1917 events. Many aspects of Russian culture and many aspects of Russian personality structure have endured in spite of the drastic changes in the Russian social structure. The same thing can be said of the Chinese Revolution of 1948.

Another illustration can be given regarding some profound changes in culture, which have altered, but not 'completely' changed the Hindu culture. It is a familiar fact that the Vedic Hindus (1950-1000 B.C.) were completely dominated by ceremonials, the *yogas* and the *yajnas* involving animal sacrifice. With the complexity of the sacrificial ritualism, the doctrine of the four *varnas* and four *asramas* began to take shape.

The *Upanishads* (800-700 B.C.) represents a spirit different from and even hostile to ritualism. The Upanishadic theory of universe is quite distinct from the theory of universe of the Brahmanas. In fact, one of the clearest onslaughts against sacrificial ceremonial is to be found in the Mundaka Upanishad (I.II.7) which asserts that one who hopes for real good to accrue from these rites is a fool. In the age of Upanishad *jnana* took the place of *yajna*. Further not only the beliefs in gods and the sacrifices but also the practice of caste system was condemned.

After the Upanishadic age (600-400 B.C.) the sacrificial rites became prominent once again and there was a greater rigorous insistence on the *varna* doctrine. Thus, the orthodoxy of the priests remained practically unaffected by the Upanishadic philosophy. It is in this period (560-200 B.C.) that Buddhism and Jainism became powerful emphasising the ethical ideals of the Upanishadic age but condemning the authority of the Vedas, the ascendancy of the priests, the supremacy of sacrificial ritualism and the practice of caste system. It was also in this period that non-violence, *ahimsa,* became most influential and the worship of images in temples started. As Sarma (1956) writes "The cult of the worship of images seems to have arisen spontaneously when the Vedic sacrifices became too elaborate and complicated and the various *Upasanas* recommended in the Upanishads came to be substituted in their place" (p. 10) (see also Sen 1961).

In the Epic Age (200 B.C. to A.D. 300) with the fall of the Mauryan empire, the prestige of Buddhism suffered and there was a revival of Hinduism. The Ashvamedha sacrifice was perfor-med by Pushyamitra, the Brahmin general, who killed the last Mauryan emperor and founded the Sunga dynasty. It was in this period that the great epics, Mahabharata and Ramayana took their final shape as didactic books. It was also in this period that the codes of Manu and Yajnavalkya were composed. All these developments brought about a great change in the outlook of the priest class in particular and the people in general. The movement set afoot by Buddha modified the Hindu beliefs and doctrines. As Sarma (1957) writes "The gates of the temple were at last thrown open to the classes. The knowledge which had remained the exclusive possession of a small class was made available for all. Not only that, there was a fusion of the Aryan culture with the Dravidian culture. The gods and goddesses worshiped by the common people were given honoured places in the Hindu Pantheon" (p. 22). The organized sects of Vishna-nism, Sivism and Saktaism (the worship of Durga) came into prominence. In this age the sacrificial altar gave place to the temple and image worship. Both the *Yajna* of the early Vedic age and *Jnana* of the Upanishadic age gave place to *Puja* and *Bhakti.* The Hindu scheme of life as expressed in the formula *Dharma-artha-kama-moksha* was fixed and widely taught.

All these new developments in Hinduism are expressed in the Gita. The traditional concepts of *Yajna, Karma, Varna* and *Dharma* are given new interpretation. According to the Gita, *Yajna* does not mean animal sacrifice; it means the pursuit of all activities of life in the spirit of sacrifice. Similarly *karma* in the Gita does not mean ritualistic actions but all human actions having moral or spiritual value. *Varna* is not based on birth but on *guna* (character) and *karma* (moral activities). *Dharma,* according to the Gita, is not simply the caste-duty of popular ethics, but the duty imposed on man by his own ideal of life *(swadharma).* Another outstanding feature of the Gita is the formulation of *Bhakti,* devotion to God. "Thus the Gita everywhere follows the old tradition, but every-where extends it in such a way as to recreate it. It retains the old Upanishadic ideal of *jnama,* but balances it with *nishkama karma and bhakti"* (Sarma).

This short description of the various phases in the Hindu religion from the Vedic period (2000 B.C. to the Epic period A.D. 300) clearly shows how profound changes in the concepts, beliefs as well as practices did not affect the continuity of Hindu religion. As it is well known, the Gita is one of the most important books in the Hinduism of the 20th century and has led to various commentaries by the leaders of thought and action from Tilak to Gandhi. This shows how changes do not lead to disruption in social and cultural life, however, profound and drastic they may be. The social system persists with all the changes incorporated.

It is like the profound changes, physiological, psychological and social which take place in each individual. When the child is born, he is small and helpless. As he grows up he is highly egocentric. With the further growth, profound changes take place in his body, mind and social behaviour during adolescence. Further changes take place in adulthood when he takes up an occupation, marries and settles down to rear his own family. Finally, further profound changes take place when he retires from his occupation and also from his family life. But throughout he is the same individual, having bodily, mental and social identity. The ancient Indians recognized this and formulated what they called the *asrama dharma*.

New Setup

From the foregoing it is clear that the distinction between persistence and change is more a matter of approach rather than something substantive.

There are two well-established types of social inquiry — the *synchronic* and the *diachronic*. The former is concerned with static or simultaneous study of an array of facts in a social system, while the latter is a study of the phases separated in time, a study of the successive changes in a society. It is clear, however, that the two terms should not be understood in a rigid manner since nothing in the sphere of social facts is literally static. The subject-matter of sociology consists of regular, repetitive social behaviour. It is obvious that such a regularity in behaviour is only visible over a period of time. From this point of view, the synchronic approach limits itself to the study of simultaneous as well as continuous states of affairs in a society over a short period of time. By contrast, the diachronic approach is concerned with broadly separated time phases in a society. It is this approach which helps the study of social change, namely, the change in social structure (Radcliffe-Brown, 1957).

Those who are interested in the problems of social stability and who consider that the main task of sociology is to explain social stability adopt the synchronic approach. They look upon social situations as though they were static or endlessly repetitive; as a result they study the problem of social structure as it exists at the given time and the social forces which are conducive to the maintenance of the system. They show that human acts, groups, rules of conduct and goals or values are interrelated. As Moore (1961) puts it "The inter-relationship constitute the major data for meaningful description or analysis of social systems. By their predictability, their persistence, they constitute a major source of order, of reliability in social affairs...." He then proceeds to observe "Besides the orderly persistence of interrelated patterns of action, there are also ample sources of disorder in social systems, of tensions and conflicts, of intrinsic sources and paths of change.... If an equilibrium model is taken at all seriously, these circumstances are downright embarrassing." This is the main difficulty of the synchronic approach to the study of social systems. With emphasis on social order and social stability, every conflict and tension is looked upon as a source of disturbance, a source of disorder and confusion. Cultural and social change is looked upon as a separate field of inquiry involving separate methods of study and separate models.

But there are others who seek out situations furnishing evidence of development or other forms of change. As Nadel (1951) puts it, "In describing social phenomena we can choose whether to consider some roughly contemporaneous phase or several such phases stretching back in time; in the latter case, we might well be describing also processes, developments, that is, phenomena of change. But in explaining social phenomena we have only one method at our disposal, namely, that of examining their interdependence; and this, in turn, is visible most clearly when change sets in, that is when some variable in one pheno-menon can be seen to promote concomitant variation in others." It is obvious that diachronic approach is more helpful to study the social system from this point of view. Nadel also makes the point noted above that at one end there are societies which are rapidly changing and interdependent and at the other end there are the societies which are self-contained. But it must be acknowledged that with the rapid growth in the means of trans-portation and the means of communication and with their immense spread, it is hardly possible for any social system to be so self-contained, at any rate in India.

Next, there is the other problem of planned social change; in all contemporary states and certainly in the states which have emerged recently, five-year plans have been launched. With political independence, the people in these new states are eager to have higher standards of living and greater access to modern developments. It is necessary to study the extent to which such planned changes have been effective why there are resistances to them.

The very idea of human society presupposes order. The interactions among the actors in the system are reciprocal and interdependent. When these interactions are repeated and persist over a period of time there is an order in the social relations. The term social order refers to the existence of *restraint,* the inhibition of impulse, or more specifically, to the control of violence in social life. Secondly, as noted above, social order refers to an element of *reciprocity* or mutuality in social life. Next, it refers to an element of predictability in social life; that is, there are certain expectations in interactions. The fulfilments of these expectations is possible when there is some *consistency* in the interactions. Finally, social order implies *persistence.* As Cohen (1968) puts it, all these meanings of the term social order are logically and empirically related. Thus, any society is the organization of human relation-ships. This constitutes the social structure.

The ordering of human lives in terms of a matrix of social expectations comprises part, or perhaps all, of the distinctively human qualities of behaviour (Moore, 1967). Social order is based on learning; individuals learn to internalize the restraints during the process of socialization in early childhood. This implies the existence of rules or norms. This is how the society patterns and regulates individual behaviour (Kuppuswamy, 1973). The ancient Indians identified these norms which hold together the individuals in the society as the *dharma.* Literally *dharma* is that which holds a thing together, makes it what it is and prevents it from breaking up and changing into something else. The term *dharma* is derived from the root *dhri* which means to sustain, uphold, to hold together.

It is obvious that without norms, social relations would be

haphazard, chaotic and dangerous. It is the norms which give order, stability and predictability to social life. Norms are at the basis of social structure. As Durkheim pointed out, a situation of complete normlessness or *anomie* would be intolerable. No normless or anomie society could endure. As anarchy is the contradiction of government, so anomy is the contradiction of society. No society can exist when there are no norms to govern the social relations of the members. This is why norms constitute one source and locus of the order that society exhibits. In a total absence of norms men would be unable to get together for any purpose whatever; no civil society would ever be possible.

According to Durkheim, the social solidarity of mankind in the past was merely *mechanical* based on kinship, friendship etc., while in the modern world social solidarity is increasingly *organic* based on division of labour. However, he showed that division of labour sometimes creates the very negation of solidarity. He wrote "If the division of labour does not produce solidarity ... it is because the relations of the organism are not regulated, because they are in a state of *anomie.* Since a body of rules in the definite form which spontaneously established relations between social functions have taken in the course of time, we can say, *a priori,* that the state of *anomie* is impossible wherever solidary organs are in contact or sufficiently prolonged". Thus *anomie* is the product of urbanization and industrialization.

It is the compliance with the social norm which promotes social order. Sumner (1907) showed the distinctions between the various type of restraint exercised by the society on individuals; *folkways* imply that one is normally "expected" to comply with the norms; *mores* imply that one "ought" to behave in compliance with the norms; *laws* require that one "must" comply with them. But compliance with social norms is not always or necessarily based on external restraints. In a properly socialized individual who has developed his own ideals of behaviour, compliance is due to internal restraints which may be based on guilt feelings or on a spontaneity which arises from the free and voluntary acceptance of certain ideals and rules of conduct.

Merton (1957) has analysed the various sources of social deviation. He has shown that conforming behaviour requires the acceptance of both the norms (institutional means) and the values or the cultural goals. Deviant behaviour may arise from adhering to goals while departing from approved means as in *innovation;* or from rejecting values while complying with standard rules, as in *ritualism;* or from rejecting both values and norms as in what he calls *retreatism;* he adds *rebellion* which rejects the extant values and norms and the espousal of others.

According to Merton *conformity,* represents the adaptation in which both the cultural goals and the norms (the institutional means) are accepted. Most people in a given society, occupying any position, are conformists. Their commitment both to ends and to norms constitute the chief components of the stable society. As Merton puts it, "It is, in fact, only because behaviour is typically oriented toward the basic values of the society that what may speak of a human aggregate as comprising a society."

Innovation is the rejection of institutional norms while accepting the culturally prescribed goals. He gives the illustration of those who accept accumulation of wealth as a success goal but use various means unapproved as institutional means to reach that goal. He also gives as illustrations the "white collar" crimes among the members of the upper classes and various forms of delinquency, crime and racketeering among the members of the lower classes; crime and delinquency, thus, are illustrations of the substitution of "proscribed" norms in the place of "prescribed" norms.

Ritualism is a mode of adaptation by which the cultural goals are rejected while the institutional norms are accepted. He looks upon, such deviation as "a *private* escape from the dangers and frustrations which seem to them (the lower-middle class) inherent in the competition for major cultural goals by abandoning these goals and clinging all the more closely to the safe routines and institutionalized norms." The ritualist slavishly follows the rules not because of over-identification with them but "from a lack of security in important social relationships in the organization". He is a conformist to the institutional norms though he rejects the culturally prescribed goals and replaces them by goals more possible for him to achieve. In passing, it may be mentioned that many social problems arise in contemporary Indian situation because of this ritualism among the higher caste persons, particularly in the rural areas, often even in the urban areas.

Retreatism, according to Merton, is a "privatized rather than collective mode of adaptation" of the socially disinherited. They reject the cultural goals as well as the social norms, the institutional means. In this category of deviants Merton includes the vagrants, the tramps, the vagabonds, the chronic drunkards and the drug addicts. He also includes in this category the persons who have suffered an abrupt break in the familiar normative framework and established social relations in their lives like the woman who is overwhelmed by sudden widowhood, or the man who withdraws from all social relations because of some disastrous experience. In such deviants there is a failure to look upon any-thing as valuable, anything as worthy of effort; they are cynical; they are disenchanted with the cultural goals; they do not care to observe the norms.

Rebellion is the rejection of the prevailing goals and substituting them with new goals and also the rejection of prevailing norms and substituting in their place new norms. This presupposes alienation from the generally accepted goals and standards and an attempt to bring about a new social structure. This rebellion "involves a genuine transvaluation, where the direct or vicarious experience of frustration leads to full denunciation of previously prized values". According to Merton there are two factors which contribute to adaptation by rebellion. One is the pressure for achievement coupled with a realization of the existing restriction of opportunity. The other is ambivalent or conflicting norms resulting from an admittance of open class and casteless norms in the society.

Innovation, ritualism, retreatism and rebellion are individual valuation of various aspects of the goal-norm complex. Merton looks upon them as a typical to the society as a whole, though occurring with sufficient frequency in significant numbers of individuals. This categorization and analysis, according to Merton, also helps to understand the phenomenon of *anomie* as noted by Durkheim. He further notes that these non-conforming adap-tations are not "rationally calculated and utilitarian"; on the contrary, since they arise out of pressure and frustration, a degree of irrationality might be expected.

While crime as part of innovation, ritualism and retreatism and even rebellion of some kinds lead to social disorganization it cannot be said that all deviation, particularly innovation in technical and organizational field and rebellion against social injustice and exploitation can be looked upon as leading to social disorganization.

Three terms are in usage, namely social order, social stability and persistence. It is true that the opposite of the first two terms are social disorder and social instability. This is why in general all societies are against innovation and rebellion because they envisage such movements to lead to social disorder and social instability and all the consequences of normlessness and violence associated with them. As an illustration of this fear may be given the instance of resentment against the Hindu Code Bill in early fifties among the Hindus. It was widely believed that the right to marry another wife when one wife is living was sanctioned by religion. There is a similar resentment now among the Muslims to bring about uniform personal law as required by Art. 44 of the Indian Constitution.

However, the opposite of persistence is change and even the most radical changes, as noted earlier, do not lead to social disorganization, though they may lead temporarily to social instability: the successful radicalist is as eager to preserve social order and stability as the most conservative person. The radicalist is actively and fervently interested in social order and social stability since it is in such a social situation that he can work out the radical programmes of his ideology as exemplified by the Russian revolution.

Social change takes place when there is a structural change in society. With technological and institutional innovations there are changes in economy as well as in the aspirations of the people. When cultural changes as well as changes in social norms take place in response to the new situation, social change may take place smoothly. Otherwise there may be rebellion and social disorder.

As Talcott Parsons has said social systems have to be conceived as *open systems* engaged in complicated processes of interchange with the environing systems. Internally, the social system has to be conceived as differentiated and segmented into a plurality of subsystems, each of which must be treated analytically as an open system interchanging with the environing subsystems within the larger system. Thus there is a "strain" within the system. If the strain becomes too intense, the mechanisms of control and restraint will not be able to ensure conformity; as a result there may be the breakdown of the structure. As Parsons puts it, the strain may be relieved either by restoring full conformity with the normative expectations or by a change in the structure itself. He defines structural change "as alteration in the normative culture defining the expectations governing that relation". As regards the problem of identity of the changing social system he asserts "It follows that the crucial focus of the problem of change lies in the stability of the value system. A change in structure of a social system is a change in its normative culture." The most important factors favouring structural change are adequate mechanisms to overcome the vested interests which generate resistances of institutionalized structural patterns (Parsons, 1961).

The only opposite of social order is not disorder; similarly the only opposite of social stability is not instability; change is the opposite of persistence. Social change may take place with the least disorder and instability or after considerable disorder and instability. But change can only take place in something persisting; further with change, order will be restored and stability will be established to implement the change programme even after a violent revolution. Social change involves an alteration in social structure, certainly with new social norms being established, probably also with new social values. Analysis of the various cultural systems show, however, that the new elite can trace elements of the new social order to the values cherished in the old order. In general, it may be stated that there are greater possibilities of generating new social norms and new social institutions than of generating new social values. This, at any rate, is true of Indian culture in which the new social value enshrined in the Indian Constitution can be traced to the Upanishadic age and to the epic age of the ancient times, particularly to the Gita, Shantiparva, etc.

Continued Changes

A social structure is a nexus of present relationships. It endures because it is maintained by the members of the social system in the present. As MacIver and Page (1952) put it, social structure is a web that exists only as it is newly spun. It appears to persist because the attitudes and interests of the members persist. It is the members who maintain its continuous existence. "The most sacrosanct and seeming permanent institutions exist by no other right and in no other strength than that which they derive from the social beings who feel and think and act in accord with them," Social stability and social change are both the features of any social system. It is generally assumed that the tribal society and the village society are stationary. This is because we know hardly anything of their past it is also because there are hardly any technological changes; the tools as well as the techniques used are practically unchanged, transmitted as they are from father to son; they live in relative isolation; the various sub-groups within the small group, accept the social structure as something perma-nent and unchangeable; probably it is looked upon as sacred and it will be a sin even to think of any change. But changes do take place as the anthropologists who have revisited these groups have shown, though the members do not perceive any change whatever probably because they do not look upon them as per-ceptibly significant. As noted above a close study of Indian cultural, religious and social institutions clearly show profound changes which have taken place from time to time though the members of the group feel honestly that nothing has really changed. As Buddha pointed out long ago, persistence and change are both characteristic of not only objects but of individuals and social systems. Both persistence and change are problems for study in sociology. The social system changes in response to changing conditions within and without, internal as well as external.

8

Social Transformation

Significantly, the study of social mobility is an indispensable part of the study of social stratification. In all societies there is a hierarchy of positions, or groups of positions, called strata, that are set off from each other by the amount of property, power, and honour they command. To that condition, where societies arranged into hierarchies of positions or strata that command unequal amounts of property, power, and honour, we give the term stratification. Mobility tell us how much movement or change there has been going on between and among various positions on the ladders of stratification. How many people are moving upward? How many downward? The answer to those questions tell us about the amount of opportunity or openness there is in a society. An open society is one in which it is possible for young people to rise higher on the socio-economic ladders than their parents did or to fall down to position lower than their parents occupied. A society in which such rising and falling goes-on over generational time is a open society, and people acquire their status by achievement. By contrast a society in which most children end up just where their parents were considered a rigid or closed society. The traditional Indian society was based on caste system in which there was no possibility of an individual moving up or going down in the hierarchy since, he belonged to the group in which he was born. Any social mobility was only possible in terms of the group as a whole in one area. But actually by social mobility we understand the process by which individuals or groups move from one social status to another in the social hierarchy. Caste system has been considered to be a closed system of stratification, but in reality no systems can be absolutely closed. Thus, social mobility has always been present within caste system. Caste mobility as a process of social and cultural change has been explained by Srinivas, in his concept of a Sanskritization. According to Bailey, the changed political atmosphere under the British disturbed the traditional caste hierarchy. However, he maintains that although there was an internal reshuffle of positions, the caste system continued to order political relations between the group concerned and to reflect their economic status. A system of social stratification such as caste, rests upon the unequal distribution of power between status groups having definite position in the prestige hierarchy. The British rule set the castes free from the territorial limitations inherent in the pre-British political system. Caste as a dynamic reality in Indian society has accompanied changes and in the process has continued to survive the onslaught of time. In spite of the varied forces of change, caste has continued to adapt itself to the new circumstances and remain a significant part of Indian society. Indian society has moved from a relatively closed system to an open system. A closed system is one in which elements like caste, class and power are combined together, whereas, an open system is one in which inequalities of caste, class and power are dispersed. In an open system a person can be of lower caste but belong to upper class. In Pre-British period education was a virtual monopoly of the Brahmins, but at present, educational system is far more open, both in principle and in practice. Because of this education, the non-Brahmins can compete on more equal terms with the Brahmins for white-collar jobs. The new opportunities, like educational, economic, political during British period were in theory caste free, that is they were open to all. No one was banned from having access to them by reason of birth in a particular caste, or sect. Social stratification may be closed and open. Closed stratification is characterized by lack of social mobility and open stratification allows easy mobility of individuals and groups. There are two forms of mobility — horizontal and vertical.

Horizontal mobility refers to movement which does not bring about change in the social position of the individual or group that has moved. For example movement from one territory to another, from one occupation to another of equivalent rank and status. On the other hand, vertical mobility refers to the movement of unequal status. Thus, people who share a common horizontal position may be vertically occupying different positions in society. There are two types of vertical mobility — ascending and descending mobility, also called upward and downward mobility. Ascending mobility takes place when an individual or a group moves from a lower position into a higher position. Descending mobility takes place when there is a movement from a higher position to a lower position. Upward and downward mobility takes place due to political, economic, religious, occupational and other factors. A distinction also needs to be made between inter-generational and intragenerational mobility. The former refers to changes in the occupants of positions from father's generation to son's generation. By contract intragenerational mobility refers to changes in the occupation held by people during the course of their life times or working carriers. Every society is characterized by some degree of vertical mobility. There are several means which permit individuals and group to move upwards or downwards and this function is performed by a number of institutions in society. In India, several religious institutions are providing an important means of social mobility, to the lower castes and the untouchable. Education acts as an instrument of upward mobility. Educational attainment has been the most important factor in achieving upward mobility. Similarly political institutions such as government, political parties, etc. present important channel for social mobility. Besides, economic activity has always been an important channel of vertical mobility. The most important criteria that influences mobility is the possession and accumulation of wealth. Marriage is a very effective mechanism of upward or downward social mobility. A woman of low caste could marry a man of high caste on which she assumed the status of his (Man's) caste. This is known as hypergamy.

The problem of social mobility is directly linked with the system of social stratification. Social stratification reflects social hierarchy present in the society and marks the rights and privileges of each stratum from the others. In Indian society caste offers an example of a stratified system based on the Hindu principle of purity and pollution. Social stratification may either be open or closed. In open stratification individuals can freely pass from one stratum into another, but in closed stratification social mobility is restricted. In the open stratification social position is determined by achieved criteria like wealth, power etc., which could be acquired by everybody. But in the closed stratification it is based on ascribed factors such race, caste etc. which are determined by birth, Race, caste, gender, property, occupation, power are some of the important variables which determine social stratification.

The tradition-modernity dichotomy in the studies of social mobility has often led to a confusion of perspective. It led to the contention that mobility was absent in the social system of traditional India, which was said to have a closed system of social stratification. This view is based upon classical literature and its ideology overemphasizes the element of continuity. Besides, for the Western scholars, the most striking feature in Indian system has been the contrast it offered to their own society. On top of all this has probably been the ideological bias, a moral sense of superiority felt by most Western scholars over the Indian society and culture which considered to have fallen under their colonial rule because of its own limitations. While traditional Indian society was; stationary in character, it did not preclude the mobility, upward as well as downward, of individual castes in the local hierarchy. Many tribals ascended to the position of royalty in India by establishing claim to kshatriya-hood by conquest and accumulation of power. Panikkar states that most Kshatriya royal houses after the time of Mahapadma Nanda were established by non-kshatriya castes. Various castes after being defeated, migrated to new areas where they established themselves, as rulers and also claimed higher-caste status. The political system of traditional India was quite fluid, especially at the lower levels. Due to large size of kingdoms, it became necessary for the kings to delegate their authority to subordinates. But the death of the king often resulted in efforts by chiefs to declare independence and stop payment of tribute. The king also had the power of raising ranks of castes as a reward or lowering their rank as a punishment. Availability of land along with scarcity of labour, excessive tributes, and natural calamities encouraged geographical movement or migration. This spatial mobility brought on social mobility. Each village had a local hierarchy and by moving to a new locality, it was possibly change one's position in the new local hierarchy. However, the units of mobility were generally individual families, not entire caste groups. Besides, hypergamy was another source of caste mobility in traditional India. There were mainly four avenues of caste mobility in the traditional India which were political, economical, ritual, and social respectively in nature. But, mobility in traditional India resulted only in positional changes, and it did not bring about structural changes.

Pre-British India may be regarded as on the whole a religious society. On the other hand, modern India has experienced steadily increasing secularization since her conquest by Britain. The British refusal to enforce the ban on sanskritization made it accessible in theory to everyone, though everywhere the locally dominant castes often used the sanctions at their disposal to prevent lower castes from rising. In modern societies, rate of urbanization becomes quite fast. There is migration from rural areas to towns and cities. An increase in occupational opportunities in urban areas pulls out the people from the rural areas. Above all, sanskri-tization carne to be seen by the lower castes as adjunct to other and more important things, such as educational and political power. Formal education can be regarded as a basic input in rapid socials change and economic development. Education has been a time tested means in social development in several countries. Formal education and training are very important in the determination of position of people in social structure. Education serves as a means of social mobility and as a determinant of social status. Education and mobility are closely related to one another.

Social mobility refers to a situation, in which new cultural goals, values and traits are adopted as desirable aspects for enhancement of social status. Vertical serial mobility can exert earth-shacking impact on social life. Stratification is marked by a hierarchical arrangement of various areas. Vertical mobility disturbs this ordering. Through education some people acquire competence for rare positions. This is how a vertical order emerges in a given society. Mobility makes the social structure quite elastic. In modern societies, forces generating social change work very fast. Since, diversification occurs generally in proportion to the growth of industries and use of technology, the faster the development, of industries and technology, the greater is the occupational diversification and modernization. One of the most important aspects of social mobility is the shift in the whole society from its traditional frame of reference to a modern one. There are no traditional or legal restrictions on upward or downward mobility. Such a mobility amongst members of a society is found both within their life time and between different generations of people. Social mobility is more in an open society, yet, some elements of closed systems of social stratification persists even in the relatively modernized society. Societies characterized by caste, race, ethnicity and these are relatively closed systems of social stratification. There is less social mobility in a caste society. In the traditional Indian society, the educational institutions were monopolized by the people from the upper castes. There is no doubt that lion's share of educational opportunities was availed by the dominant sections. With the advent of colonial rule in India the traditional system of education was replaced by the British formal education. The new system of education was secular and open. The new educational institutions were opened to all, irrespective of caste, religion, race, or sex. Though, the colonial system of education proved more beneficial for the privileged section, yet, people from the backward sections had the option to get entry into various institutions of formal education. Changes in the systems of education have resulted into change and mobility in large scale.

During the colonial rule, the nature of class hierarchy changed with changes in traditional class hierarchy. The new opportunities created in economy, administration and profession facilitated mobility. The traditional privileged class became modern privileged class. The new opportunities, at least at the higher level, were usually taken advantage of by the high castes, resulting in considerable overlap between the traditional and new cities. The British only succeeded in altering the nature of class circulation in India, and not its social base. The middle class that emerged, maintained the structural continuity in terms of recruitment and social background with the previous class structure. However, upward mobility of some individuals and certain groups of people belonging to the traditionally deprived section of the population occurred on a very limited scale.

Both horizontal and vertical social mobility have been possible as a result of increasing urbanization, industrialization and modernization. Occupational diversification through creating new avenues and opportunities of employment has facilitated this process. Social mobility of individual is more intragenerational in nature. Small social groups have also able to attain mobility across class lines. Particularistic ties of caste, community, village, neighbourhood, family, religion have played an important role in the process of social mobility. "However, on the whole, the rate of social mobility is very low. In fact, degree of social mobility across class lines is very low both in rural and urban areas. At the same time processes of social mobility have been at work due to indigenous and external factors. In the cultural domain, the processes of mobility are seen in sanskritization, Westernization, modernization, and conversions. In the sphere of social structure, they are witnessed in role differentiations, migration, political innovations, circulation of elites, bureaucratization. As a result of these process, changes have been observed in the system of social stratification in India. Increasing occupational diversification and politicization have provided opportunity of social mobility.

However, social mobility as a process has become more active in recent times. It has resulted from sets of indigenous and exogenous factors that have loosened the summation of status (denotes congruence of social, economic and political status) principles which the traditional caste stratification represented. The congruence of ritual status, economic status and power status as in the traditional caste stratification is withering away under the impact of social legislation, education, democratization, urbanization. These processes have created many alternative resources for supplementing one's social status and have broken the exclusiveness of the traditional principles of social status determination as a consequences of increase social mobility. Whether it is family, caste, or occupational mobility, there is one constant factor observed in their process towards change, that of structural adaptation. Social change in processes even through structurally similar, being generated by universal forces, such as population growth, diversification of occupational structures, industrialization and growth of technology and science, assume historically different shapes and propositions in each society due to its pre-existing systems of social institutions and ideologies.

Caste-based Movements

Caste is a unique system, it pervades the whole Hindu society in India and it is an all-encompassing system. Hereditary specialization, hierarchical organization and reciprocal repulsion make caste as a specific particularistic system. In India, caste has permeated the entire social life. Caste and class are different forms of social stratification. Caste groups are ranked in the caste system, whereas position is ranked in social stratification. Caste and class are two different notions in the study of Hindu society. Social stratification is a generalized aspect of human society. It means that a society distribute its resources unequally among its members, hence groups are formed known as strata, classes and castes. These strata are considered unequal and generally ranked in a graded manner one above another. Caste system is charac-terized by a hierarchical gradation, endogamy, occupation, rituals status, restriction on food, drink, restriction on social intercourse among different castes, privileges and disabilities etc. In the traditional society all these features of the caste systems were interwoven. Now-a-days, a lot of changes has occurred. Some features like hereditary occupation, Jajmani system have been changing a bit fast in comparison to other features. A variety of factors ranging from the monetized economy to the modern polity have brought about changes in the caste system.

Traditional Indian society though stationary in character, did not preclude the mobility, upward as well as downward, of individual castes in the local hierarchy. Gains in political power have usually opened the ways for economic advantages and eventual rise in Jati rank. Historically, the Kshatriya varna was recruited from a wide variety of castes all of which had one attribute in common, that is the possession of political power. According to Mandelbaum, in medieval India, rulers of low social origins were commonly accorded Kshatriya status after they seized power..." Arbind Shah has written the patidar were the principal local supporter of the Gaekwards (Maratha rulers of Central Gujarat). Some patidar had taken to arms and a couple of them had established petty principalities. All this had led the patidars to claim the status of the

Kshatriya varna and to adopt many kingly customs and manners. During medieval age, the open agrarian system was another important source of mobility.

Sanskritization as a process underlining social change in India was first of all introduced by M.N. Srinivas in his famous book "Religion and society among the coorgs" published in 1952. Srinivas defined Sanskritization in following terms:

> "Sanskritisation is the process by which a low Hindu caste, or tribal or other group, changes its customs, ritual, ideology and ways of life in the direction of a high, and frequently, twice-born/ caste. Generally, such changes are followed by a claim to a higher position in the caste hierarchy than that traditionally conceded to the claimant caste by the local community. The claim is usually made over a period of time, in fact, a generation or two, before the arrival is conceded."

By means of these changes in customs and rituals, the low caste people claim a higher position in the caste hierarchy. A low caste was able to rise to a higher position in the hierarchy by adopting vegetarianism and teetotalism, and by sanskritizing its ritual and pantheon. However, the mobility associated with Sanskritization results only in positional changes in the system and does not lead to any structural change. That is, a caste moves up, above its neighbours, and another come down, but all this takes place in an essentially stable hierarchical order. The system itself does not change. He also notes how the tribal groups such as Bhils of Western India, the Gonds of Central India claim to be a caste through Sanskritization and thus claim a place in caste hierarchy. According to Srinivas:

> "The best way of staking a claim to a higher position is to adopt the customs and way of life of a higher caste.... Through over a long period of time, Brahminical rites and customs spread among the lower castes, in the short run the locally dominant caste was initiated by the rest, even it was not Brahmin."

According to Singer, Sanskritization`was not only Brahmanization, but it could be based on other castes, like kshatriya, vaisya or shudra. Sanskritization is only a type of illustration of how the reference groups process operates. However, the dominant caste factor influenced the process of Sanskritization to a great extent. At times, the group enjoying the political patronage and power may be mediated. In the traditional society, the sanskritization may have been considered to cause dilution of the accepted religious and social sanctions. In the context of caste system which is a closed system based on birth, membership in the reference group is impossible, sanskritization reinforces and consolidates the immutable varna hierarchy. According to Srinivas, the ordering of the different varna is clearly intended to support the theory of Brahminical supremacy. As a result, the slight improvement in social position through sanskritization is severely limited, since the Jati as a hereditary endogamous group, continues to occupy the same position in the varna hierarchy.

The establishment of British rule resulted in radical and lasting changes in Indian society. During the 19th century, the British laid the foundations of a modern state by surveying land, setting the revenue, creating a modern bureaucracy, instituting law courts, developing communications, railways, post & telegraph and establishing schools and colleges, and so on. They set forces in motion which altered fundamentally the overall character of society. Indian society ceased to be stationary and the quantum of mobility increased as the years went by. The increase in status and prestige of high castes as a result of new education, made lower castes more determined to obtained Western education and the fruits only it could yield. Mobility in modern India has been characterized by B.Stein as corporate as distinct from medieval mobility which was familiar. The motive force for corpo-rateness comes from prospect of obtaining political power and using that power to benefit caste fellows. Srinivas has used the term Westernization to indicate the changes which took place in India during the British rule. Emphasis on humanitarianism and rationalism is a part of Westernization which led to a series of institutional and social reform in India. Westernization started having its impact on the elite because they studied secular subjects with English as the medium of instruction. Western education resulted in a big a change in the outlook of those educated. Western education had a great impact on the style of living.

The humanitarian outlook among the Westernised elite led to socials reform movement. The nationalist movement was dominated by the leaders coming from the Westernized elite section of Indian community. Besides, British rule brought in its train a process of secularization of Indian social life. The theory of pollution and purity was seriously affected. The way of eating food became more Westernizes and less sacred. People believe in cleanliness in living rather than casteism. Further, one of the results of prolonged contact with the West is the rise of an elite-class whose attitude to the west is ambivalent. Max Weber, calls modernization as a change from personal bonds to impersonal relations with bureaucracy. Modernization also implies social mobility. Because a mobile society has to encourage rationality for the cultures of choice, shapes individual behaviour and conditioned its rewards. Modernization has been termed as a process involving the rationalization of ends. It is necessary here to show the relationship between the two processes of sanskritization and Westernization identified by M.N. Srinivas. Sanskritization process promoted sacred outlook, while the secularism was the ideology of under the process Westernization. While sanskritization puts a taboo on meat eating, Westernization promoted meat eating. Similarly, there is conflict between the two processes with respect to marriage and divorce. Among the lower castes there is no taboo against widowhood, divorce and remarriage. These customs are in line with Westernization but were all tabooed by the Brahmins. The lower castes realized that mere sanskritization was not enough, since this process only helped them to improve their status within the immutable varna system. On the other hand, they adopted the Westernizes process which helped them to move up in the social scale without the limitation of Jati and Varna. They were determined to obtain Western education. High caste dominance in education and in the new occupation provided the raison dieter for the backward class movement. It is no accident that the movement was strongest in India where only one caste, the Brahmins, enjoyed a preponderance in higher education, the professions, and government employment. Thus the lower castes choose Westernization, rather than sanskritization.

Change of Faith

The backward classes do not constitute one single whole

but a multitude of social groups with varying positions and socio-economic standing in the social hierarchy of Indian society. They suffer from disadvantages mainly from the caste system. Low status, poverty, illiteracy are social problems which they have inherited due to their ascribed status of being born in a low caste or tribe. The problems of the backward classes came to be more sharply focused during the British rule. The scheduled castes constitute the most deprived and oppressed section of Indian society. The term scheduled caste was coined by the Simon commission. The expression depressed classes, exterior castes and untouchables were commonly used for the scheduled castes during the colonial period. The establishment of British rule brought about deep and far-reaching changes in the economic, political, educational and cultural spheres in India. It offered some new avenues of social mobility to the scheduled castes, e.g. new economic opportunities, education, Westernization, conversion and politicization. And the traditional process of mobility through sanskritization also gained more momentum during this period. Further, though the scheduled castes who become highly educated, got white-collar jobs and earned wealth were integrated in to the Christians fold, the backward ones could not remove their stigma of untouchability even after conversion. Their economic, social and ritual status continues to be depressed, although there are certain indications of change. On the other hand, the tribal people were ecologically isolated. They had developed their own traditions, customs, habits. Despite this, social forces were at work leading to transmission of cultural elements from the more dominant and better off sections of society to the more backward viz. the tribals. Two of the most important such forces at work were sanskritization and Westernization. One of the most important effects of sanskritisation of tribal communities is that it leads to the integration of segments of tribal society in to the wider caste of structure and its assimilation in the wider Hindu fold. Besides, the Christian missions play an important part among tribal communities in India. They operate as agent of social change. The spread of education and conversion to a new religion (Christianity) have led to rapid Westernization among the tribal communities. No doubt, other backward classes occupied a low position in the traditional society but they were above the line of untouchability.

These backward classes were the first to seize the new opportunities offered during the British rule in comparison to the scheduled castes and scheduled tribes. Yet, they experienced considerable gaps between themselves and the upper castes. Western education increased the cultural, social and economic distance between the upper castes and other backward classes. The other backward classes realized that mere sanskritization did not provide them the avenues to obtain well paid jobs in the administrative services. In fact, the demand for educational concessions was the major objectives of the backward class movement which started in the early part of 20th century. A characteristic feature of this movement was that it was caste based.

Since long efforts have been made to eradicate the social evils like untouchability. The first effort in this direction was the bhakti movement, and it was followed by other strong protests and movements to uplift the backward classes. During the early part of the 20th century, there developed a movement among the backward classes, on the part of the groups which lagged behind the upper castes in modernization. They demanded educational opportunities, employment in the government, and participation in the new political process which they felt to be essential for better social mobility. It led to widespread rivalry between the castes, eager to move up. Besides, the existence of a wide economic, culture and structural gulf between the higher and lower castes made the latter to work for their speedier mobilization. They wanted to share the opportunities, when they saw that these were being monopolized by the traditional elites. The desire for social mobility was encouraged through the caste groups as well. The increase in horizontal solidarity which thus occurred enabled the allied Jatis to be drawn into the mobility process. The caste associations came into existence in different parts of the country and each such association had, as its aim, the improve-ment of social and economic standing of its caste members.

The institutionalized inequality of caste stratification manifests its extreme form in the growth of completely segregated set of untouchable castes in each region. The scheduled caste who comprise the bulk of the untouchables are, technically, outside four fold varna scheme of caste hierarchy. For social stratification, the scheduled castes did not constitute a homogenous stratum. Before being scheduled, these castes were classified as exterior or depressed, if it was found subject to a set of social restrictions. In the 1931 census the listed restrictions were inability to be served by clean Brahmins,... inability to serve water to caste Hindus, inability to enter Hindu temples... and inability to dissociate oneself from despised occupation. However, occasionally, there used to be reform movements or even short-term rebellious upsurges but these did not alter the entrenched status or power of the upper castes. An indication of the widespread desire for mobility among the backward castes comes from an unusual source, namely the census operations. According to Ghurey:

> "Various ambitious castes quickly perceived the chances of raising their status. They invited conferences of their members and formed councils to take steps to see that their status was recorded in the way they thought was honourable to them ... The leaders of all but the highest castes frankly looked upon the census as an opportunity for pressing and perhaps obtaining some recognition of social claims which were denied by persons of castes higher than their own."

O'Malley has recorded that at the time of the 1911 census operation:

> "There was a general idea in Bengal that the object of the census is not to show the number of persons belonging to each caste, but to fix the relative position of different castes and to deal with the questions of social superiority...Many castes were aggrieved at the position assigned to them and complained that it lowered them in public estimation."

In the beginning the demand for being recorded in the census as a high caste emanated from leaders of the caste groups concerned. The attempt to use the census to freeze the rank of castes had the opposite effect of stimulating mobility and also increased inter caste rivalry.

The backward class movement started in the early part of the 20th century, when the schools and colleges were giving courses in secular subjects through the medium of English. Only the castes and classes with the tradition of education utilized the opportunity to educate themselves. The backward classes wanted a share in the new opportunities. According to Srinivas, the lower castes realized that mere sanskritisation was not enough. So they desired to get themselves educated through the English medium in order to qualify themselves for the new jobs. The main feature of this movement is that it is caste based. Even the qualified youth from the backward classes could not get admission in the professional courses as admission was based on marks in the school and college examination. Here they were at a handicap, since the boys from the upper castes were able to score high marks. Further, the examiners were also from the upper castes. A similar situation arose when they competed for jobs in the government services. Here also the appointing authorities at the lower levels were mostly Brahmins. With not very high marks and with the prevalence of nepotism, the young men from the lower castes found themselves at a disadvantage. This led to the anti-Brahmin feelings among the lower castes peoples.

The opposition to Brahmin dominance did not come from the low and oppressed castes but from the leaders of the powerful rural dominant castes. The backward classes movement from its earliest days developed a mythology of its own. Contemporary speculations identifying the Brahmins with Aryans, and Tamil with the original Dravidian language, were eagerly seized on by the leaders of the non-Brahmin castes to manufacture an elaborate theory of Brahmin Machiavellianism throughout the centuries. The Brahmin invader had brought the evil institution of caste into India, and had used his great prestige and power to strengthen his hold on the society by making laws in his own favour. For centuries, the Brahmins had exploited the others and this had enabled them to obtain their lead in education and the new employment opportunities. Present day Brahmins should pay for their ancestor's sins. Another important strand in the ideology of the non-Brahmin movement is self-respect. Although it was founded by N.V.R. Naicker in 1925, it seems to go back to the Satya Sodhak Samaj founded by Jyotiba Phule. The samaj aimed at stressing the work of the human individual irrespective of caste. Naicker started the self-respect movement, which was anti-Brahmin, anti-North, anti-Hindi and anti-God.

The first decade of the 20th century saw a sharp increase in nationalism as well as caste consciousness all over India. The Morley-Minto reforms of 1909 conceded separate electorate to Muslims. Sikhs, Indian Christians, Anglo-Indians. During the world war, I, the expectations of transfer of more power to Indians after the war made the non-Brahmin leaders of the Madras presidency to fear that Brahmins will become more powerful. So they wanted that there should be communal representation. In 1916 the non-Brahmin leaders of Madras formed the South Indian liberal federation (later on known as the Justice party) to protect the interests of the non-Brahmins. During the decade 1910-20 a section of the British in India made the Brahmins out to be their arch enemy. Chirol's Indian unrest, the Rowlatt report of 1918 justified that Brahmanism constituted a serious threat to continuance of British rule in India. One of the chief beneficiaries of the identification of Brahmin with nationalism was the justice party, which was able to obtain communal representation for non-Brahmins. The justice party had a clear conception that Western education, government jobs and political power were the important means to mobility. The Arya Samaja's Suddhi movement did have an appeal to Harijan castes in Western Uttar Pradesh, Bihar, Orissa. Sikhism also provided a channel of mobility for several low castes.

In 1920, an all India conference of the untouchables was arranged at Nagpur. At the end of the conference Ambedkar made attempt to consolidate the forces of the depressed classes, by arranging an inter-caste dinner. The growth of communal politics in India made the scheduled caste leaders, led by Ambedkar, actually conscious of their separate identity. It encouraged the process of horizontal mobilization among them. In early thirties, Ambedkar opted for communal electorate for the Harijans. Both integrative and alienative orientations in the scheduled caste movement have been in existence from the very early times. Traditionally, the scheduled castes were integrated into the economic system of the upper castes in an extremely asymmetrical manner so that the high degree of integration also meant a higher measure of economic dependence and exploitation. The ritual and social disabilities were a backwash effect of this economic dependence and servitude. Under these circumstances the urge for mobility, whenever pressing could not ventilate itself by frontal confrontation with the upper castes but only through imitative behaviours or sanskritization. But the scheduled castes always faced trouble as even sanskritization met with the wrath of the upper castes, and they could succeed in sanskritization either on the sly or through collective mobilization. The change in the strategy of the scheduled caste movements from sanskritization to consolidation of their own positive identity as a caste group through fusion of their sub-caste identities contributes to their freedom from the political dependence upon the upper caste Hindus.

Ambedkar established the depressed class mission society to articulate the demands of the scheduled castes. He led satyagraha to gain Harijan entry in the temple at Poona. His insistence on separate electorate resulted in big increase in the number of reserved seats for the scheduled castes in legislature under the Poona-Pact with Gandhiji. He also set up the scheduled caste federation for securing political rights for the scheduled castes through acquisition of power. The ground on which reservation of posts can be supported are two. First, that the Brahmins and other castes, which have a very strong majority in the personnel of the services, can and do harass the populace simply because they are non-Brahmins. Second, that in the selection for fresh vacancies the dominant castes make it impossible for the non-Brahmins to get the posts. V.R. Shinde and A.V.Thakkar have done much not only to rouse the feeling of the caste Hindus against the unjust doctrine of untouchability but also to prepare the depressed classes for better treatment by spreading education amongst them. Further, the old hierarchy of caste is no longer acquiesed in. Many are the castes that employ priests of their own caste. It is the lower castes that starts the movement in order to raise its own status. So, social and religious privileges and disabilities born of caste are no longer recognized in law and only partially in custom. Caste, no longer determines as individuals occupation, but continues to prescribe almost in its old rigour the circle into which one has to marry. The rule of endogamy is in a way the fundamental factor of contemporary caste.

At the same time there was the great movement started by Mahatma Gandhi not only against untouchability but also against caste system itself. The famous fast undertaken by Gandhi to prevent the establishment of separate electorate for untouchables is a great landmark in the history of the caste system in India.

Above all, the backward classes movement is fundamentally a movement to achieve mobility on the part of groups which lagged behind the upper castes in Westernization, Education, employment in the government, and participation in the new political processes were essential for mobility. No doubt, the scope for individual and familiar mobility has increased, but castes continues as an institution because it provides for a sense of identity. Though, social life in India has been revolutionized, but one cannot say that caste is not with us. Neither modern education, nor modern politics appear to have the strength to destroy it. It is a social institutions, so it caters to the needs of a people who are not yet politically integrated. But at about the end of the British rule in India, caste society presented the spectacle of self-centred groups more or less in conflict with one another.

9

Role of Casteism

The Greek, the Chinese, the Persian and other observers right from the days of Alexander have left their memoirs which describe the caste system in India. There is also internal evidence which traces the origin of the caste system to the hymns of the *Rigveda* itself,

The entire Hindu social organization is based on two fundamental notions, one regarding the natural endowment of man and other regarding his nurture and upbringing. These two are called the *Varna Ashrama Vyavastha,* the organization based on differences in caste and difference in stages of life. According to the Ashrama *dharma,* a man has to go through four stages of life—the *Brahmacharya* or student stage, when he acquires knowledge and prepares himself for his future duties; *Grihastha Ashrama* or householder stage in which he marries and brings up his family and takes up an occupation in order to fulfil his economic obligations to his family as well as to the society; the *Vanaprastha Ashrama,* when he gives up his household duties and occupations and retires into a forest hermitage to devote his time for the development of his personality, and finally the *Sanyasa Ashrama,* when he renounces the world and devotes himself fully to the achievement of the final aim of his existence—*moksha* or liberation.

Various Angles

The other aspect of social organization consists of the concept of natural endowment that fixes the position of man in society, namely, the *VarnadJiarma*. According to this view, there are some people who devote themselves to the performance of sacrificial rites, study and teaching. They are the Brahmins who constitute the intellectual elite. Secondly, there are the Kshatriyas whose duty is to protect the people. These are the rulers and warriors of olden days and the statesmen and politicians of modern days. Their duty is to maintain social order. Next, we have the third group of people who have a peculiar endowment to produce wealth and to engage themselves in trade, commerce, banking, etc. Right from the agriculturists up to the industrialists and the bankers all the people who are engaged in the task of production and distribution of wealth constitute the third group, the Vaisyas. Finally, all the rest of the members of the society who are the workers constitute the Sudra group. Thus, the first three groups are the elite groups—the intellectual, the political and the production groups—and the fourth group comprises the working class.

It is recognized that the *Varna Ashrama Vyavastha* is the cornerstone of the Indian social organization. These beliefs and practices are by no means peculiar to those practising Hinduism. Studies have shown that they also constitute the unique feature of the other groups in India like the Muslims, the Christians, etc. Broadly, this is true of any society in the world.

However, the peculiar feature of Indian system is the linkage of the innate endowment with birth and this is at the basis of the Indian caste system. A man is Vaisya, not because he has the aptitude to produce wealth and engage himself in occupations connected with this, but because he is born into a particular family. Secondly, all the various occupations become endogamous caste groups, the members of an occupation who marry only from the other families who are pursuing the same occupation and who belong to the same caste. Thus, it is birth and marriage that have given the unique feature to the Indian caste system.

Before we proceed further it will be useful to define the concepts of *varna* and *jati* because the two are often misunder-stood. The concept of *varna* differentiates between those who are within the *varna* scheme and those which are outside it. The traditional four groups—the Brahmin, the Kshatriya, the Vaisya, and the Sudra—belong to the *varna* scheme. But the untouch-ables who form one-fifth of the Indian population as well as the tribal people are outside the scheme. Within the *varna* system itself there are two special groups. The first three groups, namely, the Brahmin, the Kshatriya, and the Vaisya are the *Dvijas,* the twice born. They are so called because of the initiation ceremony or Upanayanam which permits them to assume the sacred thread. This is the second birth. They are now ceremonially reborn and are entitled to go through the sacred books. But the fourth group, the Sudras, are not entitled to the donning of the sacred thread and the study of the great literature.

The term *"jati"* or caste refers, however, to the occupational groups as well as the assimilated national and tribal groups. As Srinivas writes: "The *Varna* scheme refers at the best only to the particular categories of the society and not to its real and effective units."

The caste system is hierarchical determining the social status in the group. Broadly, we can classify these castes into four groups—the highest castes, the upper castes, the lower castes, and the lowest castes. The highest castes are the Brahmins and the Kshatriyas and among the lowest castes are the Harijans. Each of these groups has its own innumerable sub-castes. The status of an individual is determined by the social status of the group in which he is born. Nothing could alter this, neither education nor wealth, neither success nor failure, nor disaster. A man is born into a caste and he dies in it. His individual efforts do not alter his position, because it is fixed by the group to which he belongs. Any mobility, as we shall see presently, is of the group as a whole and not of any given individual.

As noted above, the caste is an endogamous group. The person of a particular caste has to marry only within that caste. He cannot be married either above *(pratiloma)* or below *(anu-loma)* except by breaking the caste rules. A man of higher caste could marry a woman of the lower caste according to Manu. But a man of the lower caste could never marry a woman of the higher caste. However, the *anuloma* marriages were also held to be against *dharma* by later Smritikars. The membership of the caste also determines what he eats and with whom he eats or drinks. In fact, one of the important features of the highest caste is that they are strict vegetarians, though among the other middle groups also there are many vegetarians. Caste membership also determines the customs and the rituals regarding birth, marriage, death, etc. Generally, caste also determines one's occupation, particularly among the lower castes and the lowest castes.

Thus, each caste is a social unit. It is autonomous. Each caste has its own panchayat which enforces conduct appropriate to that caste; if there is an infringement of the caste rules the individual or even the group is punished by fine or in extreme cases by ex-communication *(bahishkara).* Of course, rituals are also provided for the re-entry of those punished individuals back into the groups.

Even a change of religion does not destroy one's caste. There are castes among the Muslims, among the Jews and the Christians. On the other hand, whenever a new sect is born within Hinduism all the adherents of that sect are looked upon as belonging to that caste as, for example, the Lingayats of the South or the Sikhs of the North. Thus, the caste system is at once very rigid and very flexible.

It is this flexibility which has made it possible for the Indian Society to be a "plural society". In it are assimilated people of different races, tribes, occupations, religions, etc. The caste system enables the people in each group to retain their own autonomy.

Though, as has been noted above, there is no mobility possible for the individual, there is some scope for mobility of the group as a whole. But generally this mobility is in *varna* terms rather than in terms of the local caste. They are found as, for instance, in a local caste which calls itself a Vaisya caste or a Kshatriya caste or a Brahmin caste; in other words, in terms of *varna* rather than *jati.* As Hutton writes, "A member of such a caste who claims to be some special sort of Kshatriya or Vaisya at the 1921 census claims to be some peculiar kind of Brahmin in 1931." It may be stated that to alter one's caste in local terms is impossible because all the individuals or families would be known to all the people in that area. As Srinivas writes, "Bedas of Mysore would find it impossible to call themselves Vokkaligas (peasants) or Kurubas (shepherd) but would not have difficulty in calling themselves as Valmiki Brahmins." The smiths of South India, under pre-British times, changed their names to Visvakarma Brahmins. Under the British rule this tendency received special encourage-ment during the periodical census enumerations when the low castes changed their names in order to move up in the hierarchy.

Thus the caste system made it possible for the Indian society to be stable through these peaceful means of assimilation of the various groups with different customs, religious beliefs, social habits, etc. Even when political systems changed, the social system continued without being affected.

Practical Aspects

The caste system provided for various functions necessary to the social life from priesthood to scavenging. Each group has not only its social status but also its particular occupation. The sanction of religion has been used in order to keep the members of the various castes to conform to their own caste rules. The belief in the doctrine of *Karma* rendered this inequitable distribu-tion of functions acceptable as being part of the divine order of the universe. The caste order has been preserved by two methods. On the one hand, each member of the caste is enjoined to observe his caste rules because that is the only way in which he could obtain perfection. As the *Gita* puts it, "One's own duty, though defective, is better than another's duty well performed." According to Manu, a man could hope for birth in a higher caste in his next life by carefully fulfilling the duties of his caste in this life. Any breach of caste discipline is looked upon as a sin. On the other hand, there is a barrier for inter-caste marriage. The social rules are so strict that a man cannot marry outside his caste. Such a marriage was looked upon as invalid. This is one of the reasons why there is the system of arranged marriages in India. Thus from times immemorial each caste has retained its own unique feature, though from time to time according to historical evidence new castes have come into being with the assimilation of national groups like Huns or the Gujars or the tribal groups like Koli in the West, Chuhra in the Punjab, the Paliyan in Madras and so forth.

Though Dull refrained from defining caste, he gave the following description of its features:

> "The members of the different castes cannot have matrimonial connections with any but persons of their own caste; that there are restrictions, though not so rigid as in the matter of marriage, about a member of one caste eating and drinking with that of a different caste; that in many cases there arc fixed occupations for different castes; that there is some hierarchical gradation among the castes; the most recognized position being that of the Brahmins at the top; that birth alone decides a man's connection with his caste for life, unless expelled for violation of his caste rules, and that transition from one caste to another, high or low is not possible. The prestige of the Brahmin caste is the cornerstone of the whole organization."

However, in recent years Srinivas has defined caste "as a hereditary en-dogamous, usually localized group, having a traditional association with an occupation and particular position in the local hierarchy of castes. Relations between castes arc governed, among other things, by concepts of pollution and purity and generally maximum commensability occurs within the caste."

We may now proceed to a consideration of the changes in the caste system. But this is a very difficult problem. It is certainly not a modern problem. Just as the caste system has been in India from times immemorial, attempts to abolish caste system have also been there from times immemorial. Swami Vivekananda wrote, "The caste system is opposed to the religion of the Vedanta. Caste is a social custom and all our great preachers have tried to break it down. From Buddhism downwards every sect has preached against caste and every time it has only riveted the chains." Thus, right from the times of Upanishads, if not earlier, thinkers have spoken against the caste system. Buddha preached against the caste system 2,500 years back. Still the caste system has persisted, showing that it has tremendous vitality and resilience. During the twelfth century, Basavesvara developed a new sect which did not admit the caste system. At about the same period, Ramanuja brought a great reform in Vaishnavism. Right through there have been attempts by great reformers like Kabir and Chaitanya to uplift the people belonging to the lower castes and to the untouchable castes. In the nineteenth century, there were four great movements with the main aim, among other things, to abolish the caste system. Ram Mohun Roy established the Brahmo Samaj so that people of all castes could gather together and hear discourses from the Upanishads. As Sitanath puts it, "Though Ram Mohun Roy was in favour of social reform and spoke against caste system his writing shows that he desired anything more than the removal of the evil customs connected with caste." It was KeshabChandra Sen who along with his friends took practical steps in 1862 of celebrating, though privately, an intercaste marriage. "It was only from 1864 onwards," as Shivanath Sastri writes, "that missionaries were appointed by the Brahmo Samaj who were enjoined to 'discard idolatory and caste for they are abomination'." The second great movement is the Arya Samaj movement. As Lala Lajpat Rai writes, "The Arya Samaj repudiates caste by birth. It condemns numerous sub-divisions into which Hindu society has been split up by reason of castes and sub-castes. In considers the artificial barrier which caste in India has created to divide men from their fellowmen as pernicious and harmful." Thirdly, there was the Ramakrishna movement; Swami Vivekananda wrote about the degeneration in the religion which discusses whether we should drink a glass of water with the right hand or left and the number of times the hand should be washed to overcome the pollution; he looked upon Hindus as "don't-touchists" and Hinduism as the "religion of the kitchen and of the cooking pot." The Theosophical movement which established its headquarters at Adyar, Madras, in 1882 was another movement which worked for the abolition of the caste system, particularly since 1893, when Annie Besant became the President of the Society.

The British brought about a revolution by instituting a new principle of justice, namely, that all men are equal before law and that the nature of the wrong is not affected by the caste, the person committing it, or against whom it was committed, by the introduction of the Indian Penal Code in 1860.

No Hindrances

One significant feature in the twentieth century has been the weakening of the barriers between the sub-caste and the barriers arising out of pollution. Higher education, government employment, and urbanization have led to the crumbling of the sub-caste barriers. The endogamous circle widened and educated people tended to look upon the barriers of the sub-caste as not insurmountable when it came to finding suitable brides and bridegrooms for their children. This was also due to the new movement of the All-India Caste Conferences which fought for the consolidation of caste in the country as a whole and the breaking down of the sub-caste barriers. It may be mentioned that the caste system, as it was practised, restricted the choice of marriage not only to the caste and the sub-caste but also to the sub-caste within the linguistic zone and even there practically within the district or the neighbouring districts. The All-India Caste Conferences worked against these regional, linguistic, and sub-caste barriers. A third movement responsible for the weakening of the barriers was the nationalist movement which launched mass campaigns under the leadership of Gandhi. His campaign against un-touchability led to the weakening of the notions of pollution.

One of the problems which has engaged the attention of historians and sociologists is the lack of any organized movement on the part of the lower castes and the Harijans against the upper caste for the removal of their social disabilities. Narmadeshvar Prasad puts forth the familiar argument that there has been no revolution because of the myth of holiness and infallibility of the Brahmin and the indoctrination of the myth among the lower castes which made them accept the status of the Brahmin without questioning it. Srinivas takes up a more or less similar position by asserting that the belief of the people in the law *of Karma* and the doctrine of *punarjanma,* namely, transmigration of the soul, were responsible for the acquiescence of the lower castes to the whole system. These doctrines not only make one accept his position in the society but also look upon inequality as something for which he, as an individual, is responsible by his own acts in the past lives. Srinivas also puts forward some secular arguments to explain this phenomenon. Apart from the indoctrination of the lower castes with these notions, the upper castes also maintain their position of authority by the ownership of land in the olden days and by taking advantage of modern education in recent times. As against the above views, Bose argues that there was no revolt of the lower castes because the caste system involved a network of mutual inter-dependence and because it gave security to the individual in his own group. He also asserts that the polarization between the two groups was prevented by the custom of "conspicuous expenditure" at the time of marriage, funeral ceremonies, etc., in which all the poor people of the village partook in the feast and the ceremonies. While all these views are important, the most important is the lack of organization among the people of the lower castes. Because of the fragmentation into small sub-castes, each individual or even the group felt the humiliation of social discrimination as a private and personal experience. In fact, one of the characteristic features of the Indian society, at all levels, is the lack of organization. Even after independence one observes the lack of organized effort on the part of the various groups in tackling the various problems.

Before proceeding further, reference may be made to three important social forces in the nineteenth century which led to some organized attempts of the lower castes to fight for their privileges. As seen above, in 1860 the British introduced the rule of law by enacting the Indian Penal Code. Even earlier in 1833, the British declared that no person on account of "his religion, place of birth, descent, colour" would be disabled from holding any office or employment. The same principle of equality before law and for office in government formed part of Queen Victoria's proclamation of 1858. Thus, as far as employment in government and cases in courts of law were concerned, there was no disability for an individual on the ground of his caste. However, right up to the beginning of the present century, the educational opportunities that were provided by the British were largely taken advantage of only by the members of the upper castes, though education was open to people of all castes and creeds. The third important trend, besides the legal and educational reform, was the introduction of the new large-scale industries which threw open employment opportunities to people of all castes. It may be said that these trends of the nineteenth century were to a large extent responsible for the emergence of some organized movement among the lower castes in the latter part of the nineteenth century and in the beginning of the twentieth century.

One of the earliest organized protest movements among the lower castes was due to the efforts of Joyti Rao Phule (1827-1890) of Poona. He had started primary schools for boys and girls of the non-Brahmin castes as early as 1848. In 1851, he started a primary school for the untouchable children in Poona. In 1873, he started an association called the Satya Shodhak Samaj in order to assert the worth of man irrespective of caste. He exhorted the non-Brahmin castes not to engage any Brahmin priest to conduct their marriage ritual. He tried to simplify these procedures.

Another very important attempt of the non-Brahmins was in Madras. The South Indian Liberal Federation was formed in 1916 to advance, safeguard, and protect the interests of the non-Brahmin communities. The Federation, later known as the Justice Party, also started newspapers in English and Tamil. Actually this was an elite conflict and there was no mass movement behind it. The non-Brahmin elite found that the Brahmin elite, because of their education, were able to capture office of power in the govern-ment and so started this movement in order to capture the power from the hands of the Brahmin elite.

Both the Maharashtrian movement and the Madras move-ment were eager to get communal representation at the political level, and at the schools and colleges in the educational level, and, finally, the representation in the recruitment to the govern-ment office. In this fight these two movements were similar to the All-India Muslim Movement which fought for communal represen-tation on the basis of religion.

We may take note of two other important movements which arose among the Harijans against the caste system. Sri Narayana Guru (1854-1928) a leader of the Izhavas, an untouchable group of Kerala, led a revolt against the caste system. The Izhavas were the first people to give up the practice of untouchability with respect to the castes below them. They defied the restriction on free movement in the streets of the towns and villages based on the practice of untouchability. The upper caste Hindus found that there was no remedy in the court of law against this defiance because the law was clearly in favour of the unrestricted use of public thoroughfares. They also started temple entry agitation. While Christians and Muslims were allowed to go up to the outer gateway of the temples, the Izhavas had to offer their prayer 50 yards of more from the gateway. Sri Narayana Guru, Sanskritized and Westernized the Izhavas so that they could be classified as a backward caste rather than as an exterior caste or scheduled caste. This is one of the modern instances of the way in which the members of the castes by altering their style of living could move up in the hierarchy of castes. Agitation was also set-up by Ambedkar to remove untouchability.

Finally, there was the great movement started by Mahatma Gandhi not only against the removal of untouchability but also against the caste system itself. The famous fast undertaken by Gandhi in 1932 to prevent the introduction of separate electorate for untouchables is a great landmark in the history of the caste system in India. In many universities the students took a vow not to observe the hierarchy of castes in their social dealing with others.

All these movements culminated in the temple entry proclamation in the Travancore State in 1936, according to which "none of our Hindu subjects, who, by reason of birth or caste, or community be denied entry into temples of Travancore."

Finally, the Indian Constitution, adopted in 1950, proclaimed the principle of equality to all citizens irrespective of caste differences and made discrimination on the basis of caste justiciable in a court of law. The Constitution also abolished the practice of untouchability which was made a punishable offence in 1955. Finally, the Hindu Marriage Act of 1956 removed the legal obstacles for inter-caste marriage.

As Panikkar puts it, "The two other important changes, the effects of which are equally far-reaching and revolutionary, relate to the marriage and succession làws which the Indian Parliament enforced in 1956." According to the Hindu Law, "The very possibility of a lower caste man marrying a higher caste woman was ruled out. It was something horrible to contemplate. Such a relationship was altogether void and illegal." According to the 1956 law, marriage between Hindus of all castes has been made legal. As Panikkar puts it, "This provision it particularly important. The strength of the system of exclusive castes lay in the prohibition of inter-marriage. By permitting marriage between different castes without reference to their superiority or inferiority, the new law has struck at the root of the caste system itself." Much earlier in 1935 Gandhi wrote a strong article entitled "Caste Must Go".

Louis Dumont (1970) is one of the outstanding French students of Caste System in India. His book "Homo Hierarchicus" has been recently translated from French to English. He shows that the caste system is based on the fundamental social principle of hierarchy. Both the principles of equality and of hierarchy are facts of modern, social and political life. However, caste system, like the other traditional social systems, emphasises the collective idea of man, in contrast to the modern social systems which look upon the individual as "the essence of humanity", as autonomous and that there is nothing over and above his legitimate demands; the two great ideals of modem life are the freedom of the individual and the equality of men. Both these ideals are negated by the three basic features of caste system, namely, heredity, hierarchy and endogamy. Hierarchy by itself is inescapable in any human society. The unique feature of the caste system is that the hierarchy is based on birth. An individual is knit with emotional ties with the group in which he is born. Secondly, hierarchy is based on the principle of purity and pollution; the pure is superior to the impure; the pure and the impure must be kept separate; thus arises the operation of the principle of endogamy. The system is further complicated by the territorial factor; even when the caste and sub-caste are the same' the different territorial groups do not intermarry. According to Dumont, caste endogamy is an expression of the principle of separation: marriage, commensality and contact with members outside the group are forbidden, with varying degrees of strictness in that order. All these rules are governed by the caste panchayat which has the power to excommunicate the family which violates the rules, the *dharma*.

Regional View

In the opinion of the present writer the operation of the factor of territorial-ity is based on *(a)* convenience; in general the marriages are arranged within a short radius so that the parents could visit the daughter with ease and as frequently as possible and *(b)* familiarity-cum-purity; the greater the distance, the greater the fear of impurity because the group is a strange group; it is safer to have a marriage alliance with a group that is well-known to one's own group, (c) third reason is the differences in customs; it is well-known that customs vary from group to group within the same caste or sub-caste; here again territory is an important factor; the farther the family the greater the variation in customs (Gupta, 1974). These appear to be the important reasons why generally marriage alliances are formed within the limits of one's district, except in the case of those who lived on the borders.

Thus the edogamy of territorial group is the basic feature of the operation of caste *(jati)* system. This is a clear indication of the survival of the tribal principle of endogamy. This is the Hindu method of tribal absorption, as Bose (1967) puts it. Manu (X, 20-23 and 43-44) has described a large number *of jatis* as being fallen as they did not conform to the conduct of the orthodox *varnas.* Many of the names given by Manu are either tribal groups in India or come from outside. Field studies have also shown that when tribes are assimilated within the caste fold they bring in the principle of endogamy like the Oraons and Mundas. It also accounts for hierarchy; the new tribe is placed at a lower status; all the other factors of food, marriage customs etc., also operate in the determination of the status. It also shows the operation of the principle of heredity. Admission to the caste system and transformation by Sanskritization, all these do not affect the principles of heredity, endogamy and hierarchy. Both the territorial jari and the tribe have the common feature of pronounced particularism.

The above analysis shows that the roots of the *jati* system lie in the tribal characteristic of endogamy prevalent in the Aryan and non-Aryan tribes. It is possible that the Vedic thinkers made use of varna classification to make it appear national. This probably gave rise to the myths regarding the origin of new jatis as developed by Manu and other Smriti writers in the ancient times.

Line of Thinking

The present writer studied the attitude of college students in the composite Madras state in 1949-50 (Kuppuswamy, 1956). Some of the items in that study have been used by Anant (1972) in his study on some adult groups in Agra, Delhi and Varansi regions. It may be noted that my study was made among college students in the South before the Constitution was adopted in 1949 and Anant's study was made in the North among adults of varying educational levels in 1968.

The results show clearly that the resentment against caste system is very much higher in the South than in the North. The results also show the significant effect of education on opinion. The whole group responses in 1968 study are more in favour of the caste system than the graduate group. It will be noticed that the college student responses are more radical than the graduate responses, while the whole group responses are the least radical.

It would be interesting to repeat the study in the South among the college students as well as among adults to determine changes in attitude.

Breaking the Chains

The *Mahabharata* describes a number of inter-caste marriages. Santanu, the progenitor of the Kuru-Pandavas first married Ganga and later Satyavati, a fisher-woman, both outside his caste. Manu has classified and named the offspring of *anuloma* (higher *varna* man marrying a lower *varna* woman) and *pratiloma* (lower *varna* man marrying a higher *varna* woman) marriages and all possible combinations of the marriages, indicating that during his time *inter-varna* marriages were prevalent. He was one of the social thinkers who forbade such marriages.

As Kannan writes, "During the first thirty years of the 20th century, inter-caste marriages were very rare because in an agricultural society following caste system and arranged marriages, it is very difficult for a man or a woman to marry outside the caste."

However, since the thirties, probably with the increase of women's education, there have been many inter-caste marriages. Kannan made a study of 200 inter-caste and 50 inter-community marria-ges in Maharashtra. Of the 200 inter-caste marriages, 74 couples were both Maharashtrian, 75 couples with one Maharashtrian and one non-Maharashtrian and the remaining 51 couples were non-Maharashtrian Hindus. Of these 200 marriages, 11 were arranged either by parents or by friends, 11 by social organizations like Jati Nirmulan Samstha and the remaining 178 marriages were love marriages of which 64 took place because the couples came together in educational institutions, 39 because they were working together, 41 because they were living in the same neighbourhood and 34 by coming together in picnics, social gatherings, cultural programmes, etc. A large majority said that they were not bothered about the caste of the person, when they discovered that they belonged to a different caste. Higher education and high age at marriage were the two conspicuous features. Only about 10 per cent were non-matrics and 20 per cent of the women and none among the men were below 20 years of age. More than 80 per cent of the men and women accepted the proposal spontaneously because they were confident that their parents would approve or would not object to the marriage. Of the 200 marriages, 79 were *pratiloma,* 76 *anuloma,* and the remaining were either between sub-castes or between same castes from different linguistic areas. In 129 cases the parents were favourable, in 34 they were against In the remaining the parents were not alive. Of the 400 persons, 162 were Brahmins (72 men and 90 women), 39 were Prabhus, 34 Marathas, 34 Nairs, and 20 Tiyas. Of the 162 Brahmins, 76 married within the caste (sub-castes) and 86 outside the caste. Half the parents of the men and more than two-third of the parents of the brides participated in the marriage function. One-fifth of the parents of the bridegrooms and one-quarter of the parents of the brides were against the marriage. The two important reasons for opposition were traditional outlook and the fear of the opinion of the relatives and caste people. It was also found that class factor operated to break down the resistance. When the spouse or the parents of the spouse were wealthy and persons of prestige, there was parental cooperation. Kannan reports that there were not significant differences either between the three linguistic groups (both Maharashtrians, one Maharashtrian, and both non-Maharashtrians) or between the three kinds of caste groups—different sub-castes, *anuloma* marriages and *pratiloma* marriages. One-half of the marriages were in traditional Hindu style and the other half were registered marriages; but there was no difference even here regarding the three caste-groups. It was also found that when there was opposition, it was the mother who reconciled herself more easily to the match than the father. About 75 per cent of the parents of the men and 50 per cent of the parents of the women were reconciled within one year. There was complete lack of reconciliation among the parents of one-tenth of the men and among 22 per cent of the parents of the women.

One of the interesting features of the study is that it was found that nearly 20 per cent of the couples stayed with the parental family of the man after inter-caste marriage. Three couples were with the parents of the women. In four cases the parents came to live with the couple after some lime. Thus inter-caste marriage did not mean a break with the joint family as a consequence. Deviation and tradition coexisted in 25 per cent of the cases. Even those who had set up independent households received cooperation from the parents of both the sides except in 34 cases where the parents were against it.

More recently, Deshpande submitted a study of inter-caste marriage, again in Maharashtra in 1969. He used a control group, matched in caste, education, age, etc. It was found that 23 per cent of the girls of the control group had married before the age of 15 years as against 5 per cent of the experimental group. Nearly 50 per cent of the control group and 63 per cent of the inter-caste group had married between 21 and 30 years and 3 per cent of the control group and 13 per cent of the other had married above 30 years. Of the 78 men who had married outside the caste, 24 were Brahmins and of 78 women, 20 women were Brahmins. Thirteen men and seventeen women were Harijans. There was parental opposition in 70 per cent of the cases of inter caste marriage; only 10 per cent gave their approval. The main basis for opposition was caste. While two-thirds of the group married after informing parents, relatives and friends, one-third eloped and married. While 60 per cent married according to Vedic rites, 40 per cent married by registration. Both the inter-caste group and the control group were well adjusted in their married life. One significant finding of this study is that when one marries a Harijan there is a rejection by the families on both sides. It was reported that even the society, in general, did not accept them; maid servants did not accept any food from those house-holds. A study was also made to find the attitude of students towards inter-caste marriage. It was found that two-thirds of the group were against inter-caste marriage—60 per cent among the boys and 67 per cent among the girls—because of the general "caste-mindedness" of the society, that the parents would feel miserable, that there would be differences in culture, customs, food, habits, etc., and that there would be difficulties with respect to the marriage of the children later on.

Thus, from the above two studies it may be inferred that there was opposition from the families as well as from the society, in general, when a man or a woman married a Harijan. When the person outside the caste was wealthy and had social prestige there was general approval. Persons with higher education and who are older marry outside the caste. In the two studies it was found that a considerable number of those who marry outside the caste are Brahmin men and Brahmin women. Finally, it was found that the mothers reconcile themselves to the deviation more easily than the fathers.

Of course, it must be borne in mind that all these conclusions are based on the two studies, both of them from Maharashtra. Further, even today the vast majority of the marriages are within the caste and are arranged by the parents. The only significant change is with respect to the taboo against sub-castes which has now been practically eliminated, at least in the urban areas among the educated persons, due to the formation of the All-India Caste Organizations which emphasize the identity of the caste group.

The Conflicts

We have seen above that in many parts of the country the lower castes became aware of their position and resented oppression and discrimination by higher castes. This change in the outlook of the lower castes led to inter-caste tensions.

Broadly, we can distinguish between two categories of these tensions *(a)* that between Brahmins and the non-Brahmins, and *(b)* that between so-called caste Hindus and the Harijans.

As we have noted above, in Maharashtra and in other parts of South India the non-Brahmin caste found themselves in a disadvantageous position because the Brahmins, on account of their education, had practically a monopoly of the government jobs. The non-Brahmin movement laid stress on two aspects: with respect to reservation in admission to the college courses and with respect to the recruitment to the government jobs. In both these they wanted that the reservation should be according to the population proportion. Both the demands created a good deal of resentment among the Brahmins who now found them-selves being discriminated on the ground of their caste. However, this resentment on the part of the Brahmins did not lead to any violent clashes with the non-Brahmins because everywhere they constitute a small minority, below five per cent of the population, and, even more, because they cherish the ideals of tolerance and *ahimsa*. Even when the members of the aggressive groups of Dravida Kazagham and Dravida Munnetra Kazagham in Tamil Nadu carried on a virulent campaign against Brahmins, there were hardly any violent outbursts. Generally, the Brahmins resorted to the law courts to fight against these discriminations, particularly after the adoption of the Constitution which embodied the fundamental Right of Equality.

In Northern India, many of the people had been classified as Sudra castes claimed a higher status. They Sansantized themselves and wanted to put on the sacred thread in order registered themselves in the census as members of the Vaisya or the Kshatriyas castes. This led to violent clashes between the Brahmins and Kshatriya on the one hand and the Sudra castes on the other. The census report of 1921 mentioned that there was violence when the Ahirs (cowherds) of Northern India decided to call themselves Kshatriyas and took steps to don the sacred thread.

We can now describe the caste tensions which arose when the Harijans put forth their claims to walk in the streets, to draw water from the common wells, to enter the temple for offering their prayers, and so on. In these cases the conflicts were between the non-Brahmins and the Harijans, the Brahmins being involved in a remote way. These conflicts led to violence, rioting, and arson. In many cases police had to intervene in order to restore order. By way of illustration of such tensions we can quote the case of the Kalians of the Ramnad district in Madras State as recently as 1930. The Kallars drew up a statement prohibiting Harijans from wearing gold and silver ornaments, good clothes, etc. They were also against Harijan women using flowers; they wanted to prohibit the Harijans from cooking their food in metal vessels. On the other hand, the Harijans, with a new awareness of their rights, would not put up with these demands of the caste Hindus.

We may now refer to the results of a recent study by Singh. He found that the main source of tension between the Thakurs of United Provinces and their traditional tenants and agricultural labourers who belong to the Ahir, Lohar and Chamar castes were land conflicts, fear of destruction of property, and mutual fear of domination by the other group. He also found a very interesting correlation of age with tension. The older Thakurs and the younger low castes showed higher tension than the younger Thakurs and the older low castes. According to this study, the older low castes were not bothered by the new situation as they had been brought up to respect the Thakurs, to accept the treatment meted out to them by the Thakurs. On the other hand, the younger persons of the low castes resented the authoritative attitude of the Thakurs. But the younger Thakurs, who have been brought up in the new society with democratic ideas, were probably looking upon the demands of the low castes as being just Thus, there was a great tension in the minds of the older Thakurs and the younger people of the low castes. The older Thakurs expected the younger people of the low castes also to behave in the same docile way in which older people were behaving. The author concludes, "Apparently in both the high and the low caste people, the younger generation does not feel committed to the perpetuation of the traditional and social arrangement between castes."

A survey has been made in this chapter of the essential principles on which the caste system rests in India and the attempts that have been made from times immemorial to abolish the evil effects of the caste system. We have seen how the social reformers and the Indian Nationalists broke down the barriers of caste, particularly with respect to inter-dining and inter-marriage. We have seen how education, industrialization and urbanization have removed the connection between caste and occupation. We have further seen how the equal opportunity of education has provided a number of individuals of all castes to rise up in the social scale and how the Indian Constitution as well as the Untouchability

Offences Act of 1955 and the Hindu Marriage Act of 1956 have completely removed all legal disabilities with respect to untouchability and with respect to inter-marriage.

We may now consider the net effect of all these drastic social changes on the life of the Hindus. It must be said that as far as the Hindu is concerned whether in the village or in the city, he has accepted all these changes, though not in a docile way. But he continues his life as a member of his caste group little bothered by the removal of the various legal disabilities.

Whether he is a Brahmin or a non-Brahmin or a Harijan, caste endogamy is a living institution because the Indians as a whole, whether they are Hindus or Muslims or Christians, accept the principle of arranged marriages. It is true that there are several instances of inter-caste marriages—sometimes in defiance of the family, but often with the concurrence and approval of the members of the family. Mere inter-caste marriage by itself does not alter the caste affiliations. Similarly, though the Hindus as a whole, with very few exceptions among the orthodox people, now practice inter-dining, this does not affect the practice of the caste system. As we have seen above, caste continues as an institu-tion because it provides for a sense of identity with a larger group and a sense of security. The kinship relation, as noted above, is a very strong factor in the life of an Indian. His attachment to his relatives is so strong that neither affiliation with a political group nor living a thousand or more miles away from the home town or home village affects the strength of his kin affiliation.

Describing the changes which have taken place in the Hindu society in the last 30 years, Santhanam writes, "I may state my own personal experience. Coming from an orthodox Brahmin family in South India, I have a full experience of caste and un touch ability as they were in the first decade of this century and as they are now. During my boyhood days, the Vaishnavaite Brahmins of South India would not dine even with Samrta Brahmins. There was no question of their eating or associating with non-Brahmins. Today, excepting the remote villages, the taboo against inter-dining or other forms of association has almost disappeared. My sons have been living in hostels with members of all castes and in fact they do not know the caste of their hostel mates. I have attended innumerable Congress Conferences during these 20 years and have not found in them any distinctions of caste or untoucliability ever observed. Whatever may be the politi-cal value of the great Civil Disobedience Movements of 1920-23, 1930-33 and 1940-45, there can be no doubt that the intimate social contact of thousands of national workers in jails as equals and comrades in utter disregard of all rules of caste has brought the day much nearer when the caste system will have disappeared altogether. It goes without saying dial with the disappearance of the caste system itself, the social incidence of untouchability also will vanish."

Thus, though social life in India has been revolutionized, still one cannot say with any confidence that caste is not with us. It is there and probably will continue to be there in the foreseeable future. The only net result of these agitations and upheavals and legislative action is that no caste council can condemn a man for having broken a caste rule. Though caste may continue to operate in the field of social relations within the homes and the principle of endogamy persists, the Hindu as a citizen is not hampered by these limitations. At home as well as in his work place, the Hindu behaves like a citizen of the world. However, the caste taboos and discrimination do operate to a considerable extent in the rural areas. Further, it must be recognized, as Bhaskaran points out, the caste system appears to persist in spite of all the changes in it and in the social system. Neither modern education, nor modern economics, nor modern politics appear to have the strength to destroy it. Caste is a social institution which is an extension of the family and so it caters to the needs of a people who are not yet politically integrated. It provides the sense of security and fulfilment which the individual requires to bear the burdens of life and its responsibilities.

Since caste is really a kinship organization it is impossible to foresee a change in it. It looks as if it may be possible to strike at the roots of its hierarchic basis by emphasising *SadharanaDharma*. The practice *of Sadharana Dharma* will promote the social values of equality of man and human dignity.

10

Caste-based Setup

Indian society was based on a sort of realistic idealism. The practice of life was made to agree with its philosophy, there was no partition wall in the Indian mind between the secular and the spiritual, which were peculiarly blended into a harmonious whole. In his relation to the rest of society, the individual, according to the Indian scheme, lays stress upon his duties—his dharma by which he is to secure his own advancement, and thus may be distinguished from the European, who emphasized his rights. The most salient feature of Indian social tradition is its long and unbroken continuity.

The Background

India has received peoples from outside for thousands of years, but this age long contact of varied cultures has never resulted in a conflict so severe that one culture attained survival by the complete annihilation of the others. A cultural compromise was always effected between the old and indigenous on the one hand, and the new and foreign on the other, so that elements of all the cultures have survived in the resulted tradition. This process was helped by an attitude of tolerance towards other Gods, creeds and customs. The peculiarities of the cultural process in India are responsible for the relative importance which different social institutions have for the life of the individuals. Due to infinite variety in the patterns of social institutions, the institutions of the family have been strengthened beyond all others, and the sentiments relating to family life have become all powerful. By the family is generally meant the extended family, where kinship is reckoned through the blood-bond and martial connection. The most striking peculiarities of Indian society are represented by the Hindu caste system and the Hindu joint family system. Other peculiarities of the Indian social system are the Hindu laws of inheritance, the Purdah system, the profoundly religious attitude towards the problem of marriage and of begetting children, the religious and spiritualists outlook, prejudice against female education and other social ceremonies. But the religious attitude, pervades every sphere of life, and tends to engender rigid traditionalism and conservatism. Many religions are represented in India, but Hinduism and Mohammedanism, together with several sects closely allied to Hinduism, which have given its peculiar characteristics to Indian social organization and have led to the overwhelming emphasis upon the spiritual side of life. Indian culture finds its foundation in religion i.e. Dharma. Dharma is the most important concept of Indian society. Dharma is a comprehensive doctrine of the duties and rights of an individual in an ideal society. Dharma binds the Indian way of life. Eighteenth century is an inglorious period in the history of India. Gradual disintegration and ultimate collapse of Mughal imperial authority and debased character of the mobility marred in that period all progressive forces and subjected the country to dreadful political turmon, social disorder.

In Indian social evolution the family has always meant the joint family made-up of many generations of collateral relatives living under one roof and sharing a common heritage. The typical joint family consists of father, his sons and grandsons, together with the corresponding women folk until some of them are married off and enter into other joint families. Jointness is the normal condition of Hindu society. In the words of I.P. Desai: "We call that house a joint family which has greater generation depth, than under family and the members of which are selected to one another by property, income and the mental rights and obligations": No separation or particularization of accommodation is unthinkable in the joint families. Sir Henry Maine opines that joint family is a group, constitutes of known ancestors and adopted sons and relatives related to these sons through marriage. The earning of all the members are put in a common pool out of which the needs of every member are met. The senior most member of the family controls and conducts affairs with the advice of others but his voice is final. The joint family is generally supposed to be a characteristic peculiar to the Hindus. As a matter of fact, it seems to be general in India, as it is found among, many communities, non-Hindu as well as Hindu. The joint family and caste as usually described as the basis on which social life among the Hindus, is organized. These two institutions, the caste and the joint family are in practise interlocked to an extend which makes them in effect a common institution. Thus, it seems that the joint family was a group of agnatically related males of several generations, their unmarried sisters, daughters. There was common worship and common kitchen. It was the duty and right of the eldest male member to fix individual responsibility for various tasks on all other members. The head rules the family laying more emphasis on love and persuasion. Besides, the members of the family jointly undertake production and consumption and are joint owners of the wealth of the family. Because of its joint ownership and presence of cooperation among the member it has been called a cooperative institution. Accumulated capital pays for contingent expenditure on such occasions as marriage, deaths and litigation. According to Kapadia "The whole history of the Hindu family unfolds one significant fact that even when the trends towards individualism were recognized and attempts were being made to harmonize them with the interest of the joint family, the family constitution was unequivocally declared to be, and maintained as joint and agnatic". The trend towards individualism became strengthened with the passage of time. Specific decisions by British courts may be cited to show how their administration of Hindu family law dealt serious blows to the joint family. The joint family system guarantees economic security to all. The joint family system acts as a social insurance company for the old, and the sick. It promotes the spirit of cooperation and unselfish service. It avoids fragmentation of holdings and evils inherent there in. At the same time, the main defects of the system are as follows. Namely it encourages litigation, beads to quarrels, loss of privacy and not favourable for capital accumulation. But the joint family system Is disintegrating rapidly due to the increase of population and the spread of Western culture. As a consequence of economic changes and legislative measures, the Hindu joint family has suffered in size, and internal cohesion and solidarity. Further, due to industrialization, extension of communications and transport, decline of agricultural and village trade and impact of the West are solely responsible for the disintegration of the Hindu joint family. Yet, the Indian people still keep intact the family attachment and live their traditional morality. The joint family is a cooperative institution where every member does his duty under the guidance of the eldest member.

One of the oldest institutions in Indian society is caste system. The caste system was the steel frame of Hinduism. A caste or sub-caste is an endogamous social group. One has to view the caste as an extension of the family, the principle of grouping appears to be the blood-bond and relationship through marriage. Birth determines irrevocably the whole course of a man's social and domestic relations and he must throughout life eat, drink, dress, marry and give in marriage in accordance with the usages into which he was born. Ghurye list the following features as characteristic of Hindu caste system, segmental division of society, hierarchical arrangement of castes, restrictions on feeding and social intercourse, civil and religious disabilities and privileges of the different castes, lock of unrestricted choice of occupation and restrictions on marriage.

According to M.N. Srinivas:

> "Caste is undoubtedly an all-India phenomenon in the sense that there are everywhere hereditary, endogamous groups which forms a hierarchy and that each of these groups has a traditional association with one or two occupations. Everywhere there are Brahmins, untouchables, and peasants, artisans, trading, and service castes,... certain Hindu theological ideas such as Karma and Dharma are woven into the caste system, but it is not known whether awareness of these concepts is universal or confined only to certain sections of hierarchy. This depends on the degree to which an area is sanskritized.
>
> But the existence of some universal features should not lead us to ignore the significant regional differen-ces... All the Brahmins in India do not form a single

> endogamous group. There may be a dozen endoga-mous groups among them.... There are hundreds of Jatis or endogamous groups in each of the linguistic area of modern India. The four or five varnas represent only broad all-India categories into which the innume-rable jatis can be grouped for some limited purposes. According to a varna model, the Harijans or untouch-able are outside the caste system and contact with Harijans pollutes members of the other four varnas".

Liche writes "Caste, in my view, denotes a particular species of structural organization indissolubly linked with what... is a Pan India civilization." Risley has defined caste as a collection of families or group of families bearing a common name, claiming a common descent from a mythical ancestor... In the words of Rapson the caste system now divides the great majority of the inhabitants of Northern and Southern India into hundreds of self-contained groups. A man is obliged to marry outside his family, but within the caste. A family consists of persons reputed to be descended from a common ancestor, and between whom marriage is prohibited. The cardinal principle which underlies this system of caste is the preservation of purity of descent, and purity of religious belief and ceremonial usage, Ghurye writes caste is a Brahmanic child of Indo-Aryan culture cradled in the land of the Ganges and thence transferred to other parts of India by Brahmin prospectors. James Mill believes that caste system developed as a result of the need for division of labour. Many mentioned four caste functions as teaching and preaching, administration and protection, agriculture and commerce, and service and manual labour. Their corresponding names are the Brahman, the Kshtriya, the Vaisya, and the Shudras. In the beginning, movement from one to the other was possible, but gradually the caste system became rigid and hereditary. The institution of caste is essentially Brahmanical, and has spread with the spread of Brahmanism. The uniqueness of caste system did not consist in that it was based on differences of Functions. Its specifications lay in the fact that it made birth the basis of social grouping. It implies not only the negation of equality but the organization of inequality exclusively on the basis of inheritance. Differences there will be in any imaginable society, differences of function at all events. It is not in recognizing their inevitability that caste is peculiar, it is in the method it adopts to systematize and control them. Further, the caste system was sanctified by the sanction of religion. Its very genesis was attributed to Brahman. Religion forfeited the hold of the caste over its members. The caste system thrived for many centuries primarily because of the low level of economic existence of the Indian people. The precapitalist economy on which it rested was primarily because of the low level of economic existence of the Indian people. The hierarchic construction of the caste gave rise to inequalities among the peoples. Even in matter of residence, the lower castes were segregated from the higher ones. Even the untouchables were forbidden from using the public wells and tanks. Their mere sight contaminated and an unapproachable who, wittingly or unwittingly, happened to come within the ocular vision of the holy Brahmin, was often meted out most brutal punishment. The caste system is based on two main principles, i.e. the doctrine of Karma, and religious unity of the family. The doctrine of Karma lays it down that a man is born into that position which he has earned in a former incarnation. The principle of religious unity of the family is largely responsible for the emphasis laid on community feeling, as opposed to individualism. It also accounts for the joint Hindu family system, many features of the marriage system, and the position of women in the society.

The Mohammedan invasion and rule were to leave village life fundamentally unaffected and simply to increase the insecurity of life and property. The day when the government attempts to interfere with any of the more important religious and civil usages of the Hindus will be the last of its existence as a political power. The main principles of the government remained unchanged throughout the ages. The Mughal rule did not succeed in welding the population into a unified whole. Rather, the presence of foreign rulers caused the Hindus to tighten up their social organization in self-defence. Of course, the Hindu adopted the Purdah system of the conquerors. The caste system was not at all weakened by the foreign invasion rather it influenced the foreigners (Muslims) to such an extent that they themselves have tended to form exclusive classes, and the resulting fabric of society has thus become far more resistant to external influences, and consistently conservative. There was perfect freedom of worship in the Hindu society. It was the freedom of worship which had sustained the power of assimilation, and also maintain the continuity in the society. The Mohammedans themselves tended to become a caste, instead of helping to break-up the caste system, and the very contact which might have been expected to induce social progress became a factor helping to crystallize the status quo. Thus, the peoples of India are divided into a number of religious and social sects, classes and castes, each of which keeps itself to, maintained purity of descent and its own social ideals and customs and belief of its fellow members. Thus social stratification has become an apparently irremovable fetter on material progress. But on account of the economic and administrative changes in India since the middle of the 18th century, there was some laxity in professional specialization on caste basis. All proper Hindus regret that in these days no caste adheres to its proper duties, but many persons, in order to procure a subsistence, be take themselves to professions for which they were not ordinarily intended. The rigid rule of caste forcing its every member to follow the hereditary occupation. The caste system was one of the root causes which obstructed social reform in other fields of social life also. Later on in the 19th and 20th century the social reformers attacked heredity as the basis of distinctions, and the law of Karma which supplied the religio-philosophic defence of the undemocratic authoritarian caste institution. However, endogamy, the formidable pillar which sustained the caste structure, remained almost unshaken. In a society which lacked central or political organization, social security dependent very largely in the first instance on the prosperity of the joint family, and on the strength and solidarity of the caste group. The scattering of cultural entities, the lack of a strong central power, and the resulting isolation and stagnation have preserved the Hindu social organization in spite of the powerful attacks of Christianity and Mohammedanism. Muslims were no less divided by considerations of caste, race, tribe and status, even though there religion enjoined social equality. The Shia and Sunni nobles were sometimes at loggerheads on account of their religious differences. A large number of Hindus converted to Islam carried their caste into the new religion and observed its distinctions, though not as rigidly as before. Moreover, the sharif Muslims consisting of nobles, scholars, priests, looked down upon the ajlaf Muslims or the lower class Muslims in a manner similar to that adopted by the higher caste Hindus towards the lower caste Hindus.

Family system was mainly patriarchal in character, except in Malabar and among some primitive communities in backward areas. The senior most member of a family was its head. In case of a joint family the mistress of the house had a dignified position. It is true to say that the Hindu marriage is not a contract but a religious sacrament and spiritual bond. Hindu marriage binds the wife and husband to undertake the dharma, to procreate and to discharge other duties concerning physical, social and spiritual requirements. According to Hindu beliefs male offspring are necessary for the performance of the religious ceremonies that will secure salvation. Caste rules, make marriage obligatory. Although marriage is usually contracted at a very early age amongst Hindus, as a rule marital relations do not begin until puberty is attained to quote Mandelbaum:

> "Two kinds of rules are followed in marriage negotiations, explicit structural rules such as those of endogamy and exogamy, and the implicit rules of the game of maneuvring for family advantage. The structural rules require that the couple belong to the same endogamous group, the jati, and also that each spouse come from a different exogamous category within the jati. Each jati defines these categories in its own way and there are myriad elaborations on these rules, but in funda-mental outline they are quite similar throughout land. Exogamy means that husband and wife may not be related to each other before marriage in ways that are prohibited... The tabooed relationships are those of kin, position of kin grouping, and in some of the Northern regions of locality two people in certain specific kin position are forbidden to marry, as for example, a man and his mother's sister. Prohibited also are the unions within kin groupings, such as between two who are paternally descended from the same real or mythical ancestors. In jati which follow Sanskritic usage, the prohibited kin positions are collectively known as Sapinda relations are traced through both father and mother". Amongst

Mohammedans, marriage usually occurs at adolescence, but although the evils of pre-puberty marriage are thus avoided. The universality and early age of marriage, together with the intense desire for male offspring, tends to increase the birth-rate. Frequent, motherhood saps the vitality of Indian women, and tends to increase both maternal and infant mortality. The physical strain on the young wives is aggravated by excessive sexual indulgence. These evils are accentuated by the frequent disparity in age between husband and wife. Considering the physical immaturity and ignorance of the young mothers, the insanitary surroundings, the lack of care for female infants, and malnutrition which necessarily are found in large families belonging to the poorer classes, it is little wonder that a large proportion of the babies born die in infancy. But society in general had feelings of reverence for its womenfolk. A Hindu woman can go anywhere alone, even in the most crowded places .... A house inhabited solely by women is a sanctuary which the most shameless libertine would not dream of violating. Purdah or seclusion of women in houses was observed in Hindu and Muslim families. In Indian village life, Purdah is the hall mark of the lady. The Rajput women cannot even draw water from the well, and being a lady must have servants to help her in her domestic tasks. The purdah system and pride of caste withdraw many women from productive employment, and prevent them from assisting their men-folk even at busy seasons.

Succession among Hindus is governed by the Mitakshara and Dayabhaga school of law. Under the Mitakshara system the ancestral property is owned and enjoyed by all members of the family as a body. The head of the family is only a manager for the time being. He has no right to dispose of any property without the consent of the male members. In case of a member's death there is no succession to his share. The family remains joint till there is a partition of ancestral property. On the other hand in case of Dayabhaga the head of the family is an absolute owner of the entire property during his life time and he can dispose of the property as and when he likes. Under this law there is no succession even in joint property and a dead members share goes to his heir. Under both systems of law, woman have no right to ancestral property. On the other hand, Islamic law gives a share of the property to both males as well as females though not on an equal basis. But in actual practice, customary Hindu law is followed by Muslims. 17th and 18th centuries law of succession leads to a number of evils. Land gets subdivided into smaller pieces, till it is uneconomic to cultivate. The laws encourage litigation which wastes time and money and it also discourage large-scale enterprise.

Untouchability was prevalent in society. The untouchables were the outcastes of the Hindu society. For centuries, untouchability persisted in the Hindu society. Historically, untouchability was the social fruit of the Aryan conquest of India. Hallowed with tradition and sanctified by religion, it continued to exist in all its barbarous vigour for centuries. In the Hindu society, the hereditary untouchables were assigned such low functions as those of scavengers, of removers of dead cattle, and others. History has known hierarchically graded societies were based on social privileges and inequalities. The mere physical touch of an untouchable was a sin. The Hindu state enacted draconic laws to punish those untouchables who rebelled against their intolerable conditions. They had to reside in a separate area in the village or town and had no freedom to use public wells and tanks which the caste Hindus used. The social oppression of the untouchables had religious sanction. The outraging of human reached its high watermark under it. But the extent of untouchability varied from place to place. The depressed classes were demarcated from the upper caste Hindus by certain fundamental social oppression and disabilities common to them. Above all, untouchability had basically economic foundation and the untouchables were the most poverty stricken section of the Indian people. Their low social position accentuated their economic exploitation and their economic conditions tended to stabilize their low status.

Among the upper classes, the evil customs of incurring heavy expenses on marriages and of giving dowry to the bride prevailed. Ordinarily dowry is the property which a man receives when he marries, either from his wife or his family. Dowry is the amount received by the grooms party and the chief evil of this system lies in the compulsion that is employed to extract these things from brides party, much against to their capacity, willingness and desire. Besides, ordinarily there was no polygamy. Dubios note significantly "polygamy is tolerated amongst persons of high rank. None-the less plurality of wives amongst the great is looked upon as an infraction of law and custom, in fact, as an abuse.. I know only of one case in which a man can legally marry a second wife, his first wife being still alive, and that is when, after he has lived for a long time with his wife, she is certified to be barren, or if she has borne only female children.." But polygamy had become a regular and notorious practice among those who were regarded as kulins in Bengal. Among the kulins family pedigree was like a marketable commodity. At the same time polyandry was exceptionally practised in Indian society. Buchanan writes that polyandry prevailed among the Tiyahs in Malabar. Similarly as early as in 200 A.D. widow remarriage was prohibited for being a sin against the departed soul of husband. But widow remarriage was widely prevalent among the non-Brahmins of Maharashtra. Even the Peshwa collected a tax called patdam on the remarriage of widow. In the 19th century many social reformers fought for widow remarriage notable among them was Iswar Chandra Vidyasagar with whose efforts saw the enactment of Hindu widow remarriage act in 1856. To quote Altekar in this context, for nearly 2,000 years from 200 B.C. to 1800 A.D. the position of women steadily deteriorated. The prohibition of remarriage, the spread of purdah and the greater prevalence of polygamy made her position very bad." The great social changes which took place after 300 B.C. led to a degradation in the status of women. One shocking practice rampant in certain parts of India was sati, that is women burning themselves on the funeral pyre of their husband. It was mostly prevalent in Rajputana, Bengal and other parts of Northern India. In the 18th century it was widely prevalent. The lot of the Hindu widow was pitiable, and there were all sorts of restriction on her diet, clothing and movement. Such is the influence of customs and sense of shame that women of highest birth will undergo, this awful sacrifice with as much compassion as ever were exhibited by any philosopher of antiquity. Ideologically women were considered a completely inferior species, having no significance, no personality, socially, she was kept in a state of utter subjection, denied by polygamy, the Purdah, early marriage, self-immolation of widows or a state of permanent widowhood, all these contribute to the smoothening of the free development of women.

Slavery prevailed in the country during the 18th century. There were two types of slavery in India, domestic slaves and slaves tied to the land. The serfs attached to lands were considered to be property of their masters, and when lands were transferred from one master to another they had also to change masters. A poor man sold himself under perpetual bondage to a rich man and he even sold his children as slaves or servants in lieu of money. Of course slaves are treated by the Hindus with great indulgence, and if they conduct themselves well are considered rather as hereditary servants of the family than as menials. However, the foreign companies carried on traffic in slaves and even there was a slave market in Calcutta.

Friendly relations between Hindu and Muslims were a very healthy feature of the 18th century. In fact there was little religious intolerance in the country. The evolution of a composite Hindu-Muslim culture continued unchecked. In religious sphere, the mutual influence and respect that had been developing in the last few centuries as a result of the Bhakti movement among Hindus and Sufism among Muslims, continued to grow. The development of Urdu language and literature provided a new meeting ground between Hindus and Muslims.

Role of Religions

Hinduism was characterized by an attitude of toleration towards other faiths and adaptation to new environments. The general body of the Hindu population were followers of the old forms and practices of religious worship. Religious performance filled the days of the Hindu. In the words of Forbes:

> "In its simplicity, Hinduism taught that was one supreme ruler of the universe who was styled Brahma, the great one, this supreme intelligence consisted of a triple divinity expressed by the mystic word OM, and distinguished by the name Brahma, Vishnu and Mahesh.. Images of these attributes were placed in temples and worshipped daily."

In course of time, this sublime religion had been, supplanted by a system of polytheism and idolatry. There were many followers of the cult of Shiva and Vishnu and their sub-cults which appeared in course of time and spread in different parts of the country. Besides the old religious sects, new ones appeared during the 18th century. A few of the latter were either of an eclectic or monotheistic nature, and the rest were Vaishnava sects. The founders of these sects were mostly non-Brahminical castes, and Guru worship was a common feature of all of them. The founders of these sects directed their energy against rituals, ceremonies, Brahminical supremacy, religious persecution etc. The birth of these sects were simply a protest movement.

The Bhakti movement of the middle ages was a protest against the ritual of Brahmanism and the superstition of the masses. The supremacy of one God was the first creed with everyone of the saints. But in spite of the existence of numerous reformist sects, the majority of the Hindus followed the traditional ways of performing religious rites and ceremonies. Idol worship was very common. Along with idol worship many irrational practices had crept into the Hindu religion in the form of ceremo-nies and sacrifices. By giving much importance to the observance of rituals and ceremonies, they promoted the priesthood in society. But some new religious sects appeared during the 18th century, and the founder of these sects raised voices of protest against certain prevailing abuses which had crept into the religious system in course of centuries. Ghasi Das the founder of the Satnami sect of Chhatisgarh was a chamar, Balarama, the founder of Balarami sect, was a Hari whose social position is about the same as that of a chamara, Ramasarana Pala, the real founder of the Kartabhaja sect was a Sadgopa. They have been influenced by a desire for social betterment for which orthodox Hinduism holds out no prospect, is evident from the fact that they nearly all abrogate caste if not altogether, at least in their religious houses and at their festivals. Whether the sects profess vaishnavism, monotheism, or eclecticism, there is one feature common to nearly all of them - viz. Guru worship. Amongst Hindus, the Guru or spiritual guide from the remotest antiquity has been held in the highest respect. But the guru of the sects is something more than a spiritual guide. The founders of several sects like the Kabirpanthis and the Satnamis taught the unity of the God head, and abjured idolatory.

The Charan Dasis Sect was founded by Charan Das about the year 1758. He preached the worship of Krishna and Radha. Like most other Vaishnavas, the Charandasis regard their guru as divine. According to Wilson:

> "They affirm that originally they differed from other sects of Vaishnavas in worshipping no sensible representations of the deity, and in excluding even the Tulsi plant and Salagrama stone from their devotion, they have, however, recently adopted them, in order to maintain a friendly intercourse with the followers of Ramananda... Their moral code, which they seem to have borrowed from the Madhwas, consists of ten prohibitions. They are not to tell lie, not to revile, not to speak harshly, not to discourse idly, not to steal, not to commit adultery, not to offer violence to any living being, not to imagine evil, not to cherish hatred, and not to indulge in pride."

The Bhagavata Purana and Bhagavat Gita are the recognized scriptures of the sect.

Sahajananda Swami, who became famous as Swami Narayan, was the founder of Swami Narayan Sect. He was born near Oudh in 1780-81 A.D. His guru was one Ramananda and when he settled down at Ahmedabad, the orthodox Brahmana made his stay there so uncomfortable that he had to retire to Wartal. He erected there a temple of Lakshmi-Narayan. He preached the worship of Krishna and Radha, and directed his effort to the abolition of bloody sacrifices, Sati, infanticide. In fact this sect arose as a protest against the voluptuousness of the Vallabhacharis. He held the tenth book of the Bhagavata Purana as the supreme authority.

The Paltu Dasi sect came into existence during the last part of the 18th century. Paltu Das after whom the sect is called was a disciple of an ascetic called Gobind Sahab. Paltu gadi is still in existence in Oudh, where a great annual fair is held on the Ram Navami day. The Paltu Dasis salute each other by saying Satya Rama (Rama is true). They worship Rama and mostly found in Oudh and Nepal.

There are two distinct sects bearing the same name Satnami, one in Northern India and the other in Central province. During the last part of 18th century an inhabitant of Oudh named Jagajiban Das was the founder of Satnami sect in Northern India. He was the author of several works in the Hindi language. The creed of the Satnamis is a form of Pantheism. They address God as the true name (Satnam). Caste distinctions are observed by the Grihastha members of this sect, but not by the ascetics. On the other hand, the Chamars form the largest caste in Chhatisgarh. They mostly belonged to the Satnami sect. They are agriculturists, rather tenacious of their rights, and as they are untied, quite capable of holding their own against the Hindus who look down upon them with great contempt. They also call themselves Rai Dasas after Rai Das, a chamar reformer and disciple of Ramanand who lived in the 15th century A.D. The modem Satnami creed is a revival of the doctrines of Raidas Preached by Ghasi Das. Ghasi Das an unlettered but thoughtful charms was deeply impressed with the degraded condition of his community, who were deeply addicted to drink and other bad habits. He gradually acquired considerable influence by his wisdom and high moral character. He spread the message that there is only one true God, the Satnam, that all man are equal, that the idols of the Hindus are false, and that meat, intoxicating liquors and smoking are interdicted. Ghasi Das became the Guru of the Chamars. The dissemination of the Satnami doctrines infused new life into the Chamars, and they rose to positions of comparative influence and respectability, which apparently made them an eyesore to their Hindu neighbours, to whom the veiy name of chamars is a byword for all that is degraded.

The lower strata of the Hindu society in Bengal, Bihar and Orissa worshipped strange creatures like Kallo Rai, the patron saint of tigers, Rama Thakur, a ghost, the cult of Baro Bhaiya, twelve demons, the son of Vana Durga, a tree goddess, came into vogue in the 18th century. This village cult was affiliated to tantricism and Sanskrit mantras came to be used in its worship. There arose a number of saintly reformers amongst the depressed classes. Garib Das, a Jat by birth founded a small sect, the followers of which worship God in the name of Rama, Hari and Allah. He advised his followers to adhere to the path of love and devotion. Sadhu Shanti Das founded the Ramasanehi sect. He asked his followers to avoid image worship. He prescribed the offering of prayers in the morning, noon and in the evening. He enjoined strict moral discipline. His followers do not observe Hindu festivals. Madhavgar, a Kanbi farmer of Nadiad in Gujrat founded a sect and raised his voice against the worship of images, condemned caste distinction and did away with the practice of untouchability.

The Kartabhajas sect was founded by an ascetic named Aulechand. Tradition has it, that he was picked up in a field by one Mahadeva of the Barui caste, in the village of Ula in the district of Nadiya. After leaving for Mahadev's house for sometime, he left it to travel and preach in various parts of Bengal. He had some disciples and all belonging to low castes. Among these disciples was Ramsaran Pal of the Sadgopa caste an inhabitant of Ghosphara near Naihati. This sect acknowledge the authority of Gurus from the non-Brahman community. They were far in advance of the orthodox community in matters relating to social reform. The Kartabhafes disregard caste distinctions, at least in religious celebrations. They encouraged the remarriage of widows. The majority of the sect belonged to the Sudra order. A sect known as Spastadayaka is said to have been founded by Rupram Kaviraj. The date of its foundation in unknown. The Vaishnavas belonging to it do not recognize the divinity of the Guru. The members of the sect sing and dance together, overpowered by love for Chaitanya and Krishna. The female of this sect shave their heads and keeping only a slender tress. Admission into the sect is made without distinction of caste. Siva Narayan, a Rajput of the Uttar Pradesh founded a sect in the first half of the 18th century. He was a pure monist and he did not admit the validity of Image worship. The followers of this sect are forbidden to use any animal food or intoxicant. Baldeva Vidyabhusana, a leader of the Vaishnav community in Orissa wrote a commentary on the Brahmasutra. He undertook the task because the followers of Ramanuja, Nimbarka tauntingly said that while each of the older Vaishnav sects had their special Bhashyas on Venta, the followers of Chaitanya had none. He thus made a significant departure from the philosophical tent; preached by the earlier teachers of the sect. The founder of the Balarami sect was Balarama Hari, an inhabitant of the village Meherpur in the district of Nadia. He was a man of great natural parts and succeed in gathering round him a few disciple. The Balarami ridicule idolatry, and recognize no distinction of caste. The Bouls were another sub-sect of Vaishnavism. The Boul sect was born out of the fusion of the Buddhist, Sahajiya, Sufis. A Boul did not abide by any social or moral injunction. The Hindu Bauls followed many of the Vaishnav practices. The Bauls philosophy was based on naturalism. Through their songs, they contributed much to bring about religious harmony among different religions. The Apapanthi sect came into existence during the 18th century and its founder was Munna Das, a goldsmith by caste. His gaddi existed at Madava, West of Awadh. Dariya Saheb, who was a worshipper of Satyanama (true name) was another religious preacher who flourished in the 18th century. He was born in Sahbad district. His father was Piran Saha, a Sufi thinker. He was greatly influenced by Sufi thought and the teachings of Kabir. He did not recognize the external formalities of religion, such as, worship of idols or caste distinction.

Caste Structure

The most striking feature of the Indian society is represented by the caste system. This system is of very ancient origin and through the passage of time it has undergone profound changes, but it is still a very powerful institution in our present day socio economic organization. The Indian caste system is perhaps the most unique pattern of social organization in the world. The first literary traces of the caste system are to be found in the Rig Veda, and the Purusa-Sukta hymn. In the Bhagavad Gita, the caste system is sought to be justified on the basis of the ideas of Guna, Karma (deeds), and Dharma (Religion). The features of caste prevailing through the past centuries may be described under nine heads hierarchy, endogamy and hypergamy, occupational association, restriction on food, drink, distinction in custom, dress, pollution, rituals and other privileges and disabilities, caste organization and caste mobility. Hutton mentions the following features as characteristic of the Hindu caste system: endogamy, hierarchical basis with the Brahman at the top, caste distance based on the notion of pollution, traditional caste occupations, and the fixity of caste status. Ghurye put forth the following features segmental division of society, hierarchical arrangement of castes, restriction on social intercourse..., lack of unrestricted choice of occupation and restriction on marriage. Ketkar says, "A caste is a group having two characteristics, membership is confined to those who are born of members and includes all persons so born, and the members are forbidden by an inerroble social law to many outside the group. According to Davis the hereditary basis of membership, fixity of status, caste endogamy and restrictions on social contact are certain common features of Indian caste. Nesfield writes, function and function alone is responsible for the origin of caste structure in India.

In theory the caste system is interlinked with the varna model which divides the Hindu society into four orders — Brahmana, Kshatriya, Vaishya and Sudras. The first three caste are twice-born or dvija since the men from these caste are entitled to use the sacred thread at the vedic rite of upanayana, which the Sudras were not allowed to perform. The untouchable caste are outside the varna system. The term varna literally means colour and it was originally used to refer to the distinction between Arya and Dasa, in ancient India. According to the Rig Veda it was not applied to any classes, such as Brahmana, Kshatriya etc. The caste system is an all India [phenomenon] of which the Varna model provides an all India] macro-structural scheme.

Emile senert is of the opinion that the two terms (Varna and Caste) are confused in the literary tradition, which is less concerned with the faithful record of facts than with their arrangements in systems conforming to the tendencies of a strongly raised group. According to K. M. Panikkar, this four fold division is only ideological and is not in any social system. It is what Hindu sociologists wanted their society to be a theory of caste idealism unrelated to actual practise. The people of each endogamous group follow certain characteristic patterns of behaviour and have certain assigned attitudes—among them a specialized occu-pation according to which a group is remarked in local hierarchy. The criteria for ranking have to do, village responds declare, with the ritual polluting and purity that are inherent in group practices. Every member of the endogamous group shares in the rank position of the group and his relations with members of other groups. The term Jati is used here for this endogamous group. The word is common to a number of languages in Northern India being derived from the Sanskrit root meaning to be born. This word and equivalent terms in other Indian languages carry the connotation of social birth right as well as one's inherited group. The Varna model provides a framework within which the innumerable variations of castes throughout India are found. The Varna scheme is a hierarchy in the literal sense of the term because the criteria of ritual purity and pollution are at the basis of differentiation. According to Varna scheme there are only four castes, and it excludes the untouchables. But this is not true in reality since even during the Vedic period, occupational groups existed which, were not subsumed by Varna, although one cannot be sure whether these groups can be called caste or not. According to Srinivas:

> "Varna scheme has certainly distorted the picture of caste but it has also enabled ordinary men and women to understand and asses the general place of a caste within this framework throughout India. It has provided a common social language which holds good in all parts of India. This sense of familiarity, even when not based on real facts leads to a sense of unity amongst the people".

One of the common misconceptions about the Hindu social institutions is that they are unchanging. Hindu caste has been against the background frame of the Varna hierarchy. It is the Varna frame which remains more or less constant while caste vary from region to region. All modern scholars are agreed that caste (Jati) is not same thing as varna complex than the four fold division of the society. The Vedic varna divisions were not as rigid as caste divisions. The term caste or Jati refers to the occupational groups. As Srinivas writes, the varna scheme refers only to the particular categories of the society and not to its real and effective units.

Caste structure is a pattern of social behaviour in which groups and individuals are guided by prescribed set of values and norms. Hierarchic gradation, social and other inequalities, endogamy, restrictions on dining, and the lack of freedom regarding the choice of vocation, were the principal features of the caste system. The caste structure of the society is hierarchy or system of subordination held together by the relations of superiority and inferiority at the apex of which are Brahmins and at the lowest rung are the Sudras. In the social hierarchy the lowest rung of the caste society is composed of the untouchables who are ritually the most impure. The concept of hierarchy forms the crux of the caste society. The highest caste is that from whom a Brahmins will accept food. As a consequence of this hierarchy the Brahmins enjoy a number of social and religious privileges while they suffer a series of disabilities.

Endogamy is the most important element of caste system. Marriage within one's own caste or sub-caste group is an essential feature of caste system. The system has become so rigid that inter-caste marriage have become too difficult. It is one of the main reasons for the persistence of caste system. Caste is innate. A man dies in the same caste in which he is born and it is the caste that determines his station in life. Every caste regards some occupation as its own hereditary and exclusive calling and tries to debar the others from exercising it. Jajmani system, (the person receiving the services from a particular functionary is called Jajman), found in rural Indian enabled each caste to have a near monopoly over their hereditary occupation. The original and exclusive occupation of Brahmins was to perform priestly duties. Each caste was also ranked higher or lower on the basis of the ritual purity. In course of time many adjustments and changes have been made in these rigid pursuits of occupation. Besides, each caste has its own caste council where the grievances of the caste members were heard. The caste panchayat usually exercises such authority and it is traditionally concerned with all matters belonging to the code and discipline of the caste. It acts as a court of law and apply the penalty in the cases of the violation of the caste practices.

According to Ghurye:

> "In each linguistic area, there were about two hundred groups called castes with distinct names, usually birth on one of which determined the status in society of a given individual, which were divided into about two thousand smaller units generally known as sub-castes-fixing the limits of marriage and effective social life and making for specific cultural tradition. These major groups were held together by the possession with, few exceptions, of a common priesthood....complete acceptance of the system in its broadest outlines by the groups making up that system and their social and economic interdependence in the village not only prevented the exclusivist organization of the groups from splitting up the system into independent units, but created a harmony was not the harmony of parts that are equally valued, but of units which are rigorously subordinated to one another".

Caste structure is intimately related to the kinship system amongst the Hindus, this happens due to endogamous nature of caste system. An individual becomes a member of a caste in which he or she is born. Even if there is social mobility in the caste system through the process of sanskritization, it is only a positional change. Groups placed low in the social hierarchy seek to achieve such standards of conduct as bestow higher status within the system. The objective scale of values behind caste stratification itself induces people to violate the main principle of caste. No doubt individual members of caste have not been able to change their caste and status, yet castes, or sub-castes as a whole have succeeded in rising their status. The process by which the objective has been achieved has been described by Srinivas, he call it Sanskritization. According to Srinivas:

> "Sanskritization is the process by which a low Hindu caste, or tribal or other groups, changes its customs, ritual, ideology and way of life in the direction of a high, and frequently twice-born caste. Generally such changes are followed by a claim to a higher position in the caste hierarchy than that traditionally conceded to the claimant caste by the local community. The claim is made over a period of time in fact, a generation or two, before the arrival is conceded".

However, the mobility associated with Sanskritization results only in positional changes in system and does not lead to any structural change. Sanskritization process promoted the sacred outlook, whereas westernization promoted the secular outlook. Lower caste peoples realized that mere sanskritization was not enough, which only helped them to improve their status within the immutable varna system. They realized that the adoption of the westernization process which helped them to move up in the social scale without the limitation of jati or varna. In pre-British India, the self-sufficiency of the village community was one of the most important features of rural society. But after the British conquest of India village autarchy withered away. The establishment of private property in land brought about a change in property relations between castes. The growth of industry gave rise to new social conditions.

Kinship is a method by which individuals as members of society relate themselves with other individuals of that society. Kinship is an analysis of the internal structure of the sub-caste. Due to the practise of endogamy a person marries within the sub-caste group. In North India Hypergamy is practised according to which a man takes a wife from a clan which is lower in status to his own clan. In central India, there is general practice of caste endogamy. But the Southern region follow the patrilineal family. The hereditary associations of caste with an occupation used to be a very striking feature of the caste system. A caste is considered to be high, if its characteristic way of life is high and pure. The term way of life mean whether its traditional occupation is ritually pure or polluting. There markable aspect of caste system is that the presumed hierarchy of way of life, which includes diet, occupation does not often correlate with the observed order of caste ranking found in several parts of India. The traditional association of a caste with an occupation determines its rank in the local caste hierarchy. In the association of caste structure with a hereditary occupation the Jajmani system forms the framework. The Jajmani system is a system of economic, social and ritual ties between different caste groups in the villages. The person receiving the services from a particular functionary is called Jajman and the men rendering the services is called kameen of the Jajman. Though barter transactions have been a integral part of the Indian rural life, yet the traditional Jajmani relations are more conspicuous in the village life because they entail ritual matters and social support as well as economic success. Jajmani system is an integral part of the Indian rural life. The advantages of Jajmani system for economic stability and security are still sufficiently great that many villages want to continue with at least some arrangements. The cultivators gain from them in that he gets better credit and a more certain labour supply than he usually can through caste transactions. Artisans and service families work for him through out the year without much pay and then are given a large payment at the time when the farmer can best afford to do so at harvest. The patron castes differ from one region to another depending on the socio-economic and political status of the castes.

The tendency of land ownership by the high castes serves to maintain and reimpose the caste hierarchy. At the top of occupational hierarchy stands a group of families which control and own most land rights in the village. However with the changing times, the general association of higher caste with higher class (in terms of wealth and power) has been disturbed. Land Ownership is a crucial factor in establishing dominance. The pattern of land ownership in India is such that the bulk of the arable land is concentrated in the hands of a relatively small number of big owners as a large number, who either own very little land or no land at all. The big land owners are patron of the bulk of the poor villagers. Each household from serving and artisan castes provides goods and services to a certain number of land owning households, traditionally these ties have been stable, continuing from generation to generation. In Orissa, in Bisipara, an Oriya hill village, the warrior castes owned most of the land and combined soldiering with farm management. The out-castes, referred as Proja, were their servants. The other castes, including the Brahmin were in a position of economic dependence and political subordination to them. In the district of Tanjore, there is a clear-cut hierarchy existing in the caste system with Brahmins as land owners. In case of Punjab and Haryana, the dominance of a single agricultural caste referred to as Jats. According to Srinivas, a caste is said to be dominant when it is numerically the strongest in the village and economically and politically exercises a preponderating influence. But in regions where religious groups and tribals are inter-mixed and no single caste possess enough land, in such a condition, there is bound to be multiple domination in a region. The order of dominance among castes, parallels the order of caste rank. The nature of high ranking castes is further reinforced by ritual notions of purity and pollution. High ranking Brahmin castes not only possess landed wealth, power, but also the traditional right to perform rituals and right to worship at temples. Other castes are obliged to worship as per their ritual prescriptions. Their economic and political subordination further enhances the dominant position of high ranking castes.

The mobility characteristic of caste in the traditional period resulted only in positional changes for particular castes or sections of castes and did not lead to a structural change. So, while individual castes moved up or down, the structure remained the same. A potent source of social mobility in pre-British India was the fluidly of the political power, however, a caste had to have a marital tradition, numerical strength, and preferably also ownership of a large quantity of arable land. Once it had captured political power it had to sanskritize ritual and style of life and lay claim to being kshatriya. Sanskritization has been a major process of cultural change in Indian history.

The consolidation of British rule involved, the abolition of feudalism. In the process territorial limitations on caste loyalties were lifted. Castes were able to organize themselves as political association on regional and country wide bases. The consequences of British rule on the economic aspect of caste have been even more pronounced. The growth of industry gave rise to new social conditions, occupational opportunities and social classes. Many traditional occupations associated with inferior social status are being abandoned. New occupations have led to the formation of groups like trade union which cut across caste barriers. But the occupational aspect of caste is not at all an important factor. Caste as a ritual division of society is losing its importance. Caste continues to be preserved and protected in villages, towns by endogamy, caste has not as yet gone out, it has only changed its tactics.

11

Problems Ahead

The study of contemporary social changes in the Indian society cannot be dissociated from the initial social conditions of the society. Its historical roots provide a base for its evaluation. The social and economic distortions created by colonialism, emergence of the ideology of freedom movement, its crystallization in the form of the Indian Constitution, and the planning process for social transformation, are some of the historical factors which have set the direction and patterns of social changes in contemporary India. These historical forces and the social and political conditions generated by them define the shape of these social change processes. These are organically related to the 'model' that India adopted for social change.

Social Mobility

The objectives of social transformation in India as envisaged ideologically could be characterized as revolutionary in content and evolutionary in strategy or methods. There is structurally an intimate though ideologically discriminant relationship between revolution and evolution. This was realized by the leaders of Indian freedom movement. They had also envisioned how social structure, history and tradition, which form the initial conditions of a society, set a limit to the strategies, goals and methods of social transformation. Gandhiji was foremost in hit thinking in this regard. Jawaharlal Nehru completed this process by evolving a model for Indian path to social transformation. It recognized that revolutionary changes in institutions, social structures and values of the Indian society were essential if social change was to be brought about through democratic participation. One had also to employ non-violent means. This was essential part of the ideology inherited from the leaders of national movement. Much debate in India has taken place on the class character of this movement and its orientations. Indeed, the model of social transformation that India gave to itself is contained in the Constitution. It lays down the normative principles which are the overriding elements in the entire strategy for social change. Its emphasis on parliamentary democracy, justice, freedom and equality comprise the fundamental values to which all other processes of social change, the economic, social and cultural should be subordinated.

Democracy, equality and freedom are revolutionary ideas. These are indeed difficult to realize through a single leap forward. To realize these ideals human resources need to be generated which take time being essentially evolutionary in nature. It shows how revolution and evolution as social processes have an intercontingent relationship. One cannot be realized in totality without the other. When we talk of revolution, we do so either in a limited sense or imply a partial aspect of revolutionary transfor-mation. The Indian path to social transformation seeks to achieve these objectives through a series of institutional changes initiated through democratic participation. The Constitution enunciates them as establishment of a socialist democratic republic, which guarantees freedom of expression, occupation, religion and social justice to all citizens irrespective of their birth, sex and religion. It provides for measures for protective discrimination in favour of the deprived castes, classes, tribes and minorities. These objectives call for establishment of new institutions, abolition of outmoded ones and modernisation of economy, technology, education and cultural life.

The industrial policy resolution of the 1950's defined that social purpose must be the guiding principle of industrial production and ownership in society. That is why a mixed economy comprising both the private sector and the public sector has been envisaged; it is also envisaged that the latter must always have a commanding position and set norms for the former. The agrarian policy envisaged abolition of all feudal institutions in ownership and production relations in agriculture. It aimed at evolving a modernized peasant proprietary agrarian structure. Both in the industrial and agrarian sector of the economy, an equitable and socially viable labour policy forms an integral element. It lays down standards of wages,' conditions of service and union rights. A set of institutional measures ensure civic, participation right from the village to the block, district, state and the national level in electoral decision making which are revolutionary in content and radical in practice. A variety of institutions have been provided to reinforce this process.

The social transformation envisaged through the Indian Constitution is thus pluralistic and voluntaristic with state having the crucial role of setting norms and evolving the policies. This is evident in the distribution of powers between the federal government and the states, the pattern of decentralization of authority and the nature of the political institutions. This model also inheres a mix of the capitalistic and socialistic policies and institutions to bring about social change and Modernisation. In operational terms, it does not envisage violent class struggle for the achieve-ment of objectives. On the contrary emphasis is on persuing goals through legal constitutional means and through civic protests and political mobilization. The freedom of association and expression ensure these rights. All this implies that voluntary associations, people's movements, and political parties have to play a crucial role in ensuring that the objectives of social change as envisaged in the Constitution are realized.

The dynamic movements by the government and the state on the one hand, and by the people and their organized bodies (either as voluntary associations or as political parties or interest-group movements) on the other, form the strategy and the dialectics of this social transformation. The more effective it is, the more it ensures that those in authority or power are responsive to the needs of the people, especially the weaker sections of society. To make this model successful it assumes that the dominant classes and powerful sections of society reconcile themselves to accepting the rational and reasonable demands made by the not so well-off sections of society for the improvement in their social, economic and cultural conditions. In other words, the democratic process of social transformation has to be *consensual* and *reconci-liatory* in nature. This alone ensures social mobility, diffusion of economic and cultural privileges and resources in society contri-buting ultimately to the emergence of a socialist, democratic and just society. If the '*reconciliatory*' process is blocked either due to political short-sightedness or sheer force of class authoritarianism, this model of social transformation breaks down resulting into authoritarian decadence or violent civil strife.

Collective Mobility

Processes revolutionary in potential were set into motion in India soon after Independence. These comprised a series of institutional innovations. At the national scene, the electoral rights based on adult suffrage was introduced. It meant a great qualitative change in the social psychology of people and their social, cultural and political self awareness. Social scientists have rightly called the elections in India as a measure of 'silent revolution'. It activated new social solidarities, structuration of people's aspirations. It also gave a new shape to people's social and political consciousness. It forms the single most powerful measure of regulating consensus and reconciliation in the system through operation of political processes and political mobilization. It also subordinates the administrative and professional authority to the authority of people's representatives making the system more responsive to needs.

Institutions based on electoral participation were introduced all along the social system. In villages, the traditional, panchayats based on caste, landlordism and administrative nominations were abolished. These were replaced by village panchayats based on elections open to all adult citizens in the village. This was further reinforced by establishment of councils or panchayats at levels of the block and the district. These institutions assumed great significance as they were reinforced by land reforms. The land reforms included abolition of zamindari, intermediary fights in land, tenurial reforms and ceiling on land holdings. Development Council was provided at block level comprising elected village presidents. They elected the Head of the block to look after the implementation of development policies. The power of administration was further decentralized and democratized at the district level too. Not the district collector, an administrator introduced during the colonial time, but the elected 'Zila pramukh' or chief was now put in position to guide the development activities. Community Development Schemes were not only introduced for the village social and economic reconstruction. In cities and towns, they were expected to supplement the development activities of other urban agencies.

At the national level major institutional innovations included establishment of the Planning Commission and Development Council, the creation of a chain of scientific and educational institutions such as the Council for Scientific and Industrial Research, university Grants Commission, Councils for growth of research in social, historical and philosophical sciences, the Indian Councils of Medical Research etc. These institutions were to serve as agents of modernisation and development in India to create a demo-cratic, socialist republic. Special institutions and offices were created for the development of the scheduled castes, scheduled tribes, weaker sections, women, children, minorities and the backward classes. A chain of agricultural universities, scientific laboratories, institutes of technology, management and business administration were established to generate skill and human resources to accelerate industrial and agricultural growth in the country. New institutions were established to promote cultural and artistic heritage of India to safeguard against one-sided modernisation. Massive economic investment was made to modernize both industry and agriculture.

New Setup

Four decades after Independence these institutional changes brought about major social transformation in the Indian society. The life expectancy has risen from 32 to 56 years. The number of people who have crossed the poverty line is more than sixty percent. The domestic consumption of electricity has risen by twenty times. India has solved the problem of food shortages and ranks tenth in the world as an industrialized country. These changes have set into motion a process of social re-structuration which creates larger domains of social mobility, emergence of new caste class alliances, new forces of social mobilization on the principles of status, class and value system. It also generates new arenas of social conflict having both beneficial and harmful consequences for social, economic, and political development of the society.

Institutional innovations and measures for social and economic reforms set into motion basic and irreversible changes in the rural society in India which comprises the largest social segment. During 1950's and 1960's the impact of these changes was more in the realms of values and consciousness than in the social structure. Its impact was more on people's aspirations and outlook than on their material conditions. In some parts of the country, the new electoral and political rights initiated important changes in the power structure, especially in the rural panchayats and district and state level Councils. In South India, the Brahmins and other upper caste landlords lost their power base in villages, and soon thereafter in the state political power structure. In north India, however, a ding-dong competition for power between the middle castes-classes who were formerly the tenant-cultivators of landlords and the upper caste landlords ensued in which due to better manipulative ability and demographic factors the upper caste landlords barely maintained their power and influence. The Community Development Programmes also favoured the upper caste-class groups since they had the resources to absorb technology, government aids, and they were also better educated and had good connections with the administration. The landless workers coming largely from the lower castes, were least bene-fited. They neither had the resources to participate in development programmes nor were they organized to bargain for a share in the new opportunities. There were as yet fewer new employment opportunities. They, therefore, maintained their bonded relation-ship with the upper and middle caste-classes to survive in a state of future anticipation.

The measures of decentralization of power, land reforms and continual electoral participation, however, set into motion a process of social, economic and cultural restructuration. The patterns of feudal relationship came increasingly under pressure of challenges from different quarters. The electoral participation gave impetus to caste groups, especially those in the middle and lower ranks to form larger caste associations. The associations altered the traditional ritual-based kin-oriented nature of caste. It led to fusion and fission amongst caste groups in persuit of modern goals, such as political power, economic mobility and cultural and educational privileges. Even though anchored in traditional caste structures, these associations had a modern outlook, organization and programme of activities. This movement started during the 1950's and 1960's and was stronger in south and western India though championed by some political parties in the north. Among the lower castes, political consciousness led to neo-Buddhist movement in western and northern India. This movement, though religious in idiom was entirely social and economic in its goals. These changes in the social structure coincided with changes in agricultural technology, educational opportunities and processes of urbanization.

By early 1970's, the process of restructuration in both rural and urban India began to take a more concrete social shape. The investment in agriculture, development institutions and technology in villages had brought about a 'green revolution' in several parts of the country. This created sharp social cleavages and led to new class formations. An important result was the rise of the 'middle caste-class' peasantry into power often supplementing the traditional upper-caste-class landlords. Not the twice-born castes such as the Brahmins, Rajputs, Bhumihars and others but the middle-caste peasantry such as the Jats, Yadavas, Kurmis, Koeris etc. in the north, Kunbis, Patels and Marathas in the West, and Kammas, Reddis and Okkaligas in the south were in the leadership of green revolution. This development had several sociological consequences, some positive some negative in nature. On the positive side, green revolution contributed to food self sufficiency adding economic stability to the system. It led to multiple cropping, improvement in technology, new building and construction activities, increasing employment for the working classes. It widened the scope and level of participation in development administration in villages. It led to the establishment of banking and marketing institutions, proliferation of schools and welfare activities. More importantly, green revolution reinforced a value system that was oriented to entrepreneurial initiative, emphasis on savings and austere living and stronger family and kinship bonds. The green revolution was largely carried out through a family mode of production.

These developments though beneficial to the system in the most crucial sense also generated several negative consequences. The relationship between these peasants and the landless workers became more pugnacious and exploitative with the rise in their economic and political influence and power. This is reflected in increased incidence of conflict between the landless workers and farmers in different parts of the country. It led to increased caste-class tensions in villages generating potential for violence. Increase in the income level of peasantry contributed to imitation of evils of the former landlords such as demands for dowry in marriages, conspicuous waste in ceremonies, traditional customs and beliefs. Ironically, despite economic and technological modernisation in agriculture and industries in villages a comparable degree of cultural modernisation did not take place. On the contrary, conservative ideology such as casteism, communalism, masculinism, and obscurantism have increased. This is so despite the fact that the youth now play an influential role in the peasant household, especially those who have some education and can successfully negotiate with institutions such as banks, marketing societies, police and revenue administration etc.

If the middle caste-class peasantry has shown upward social mobility and greater political influence due to betterment in economic status, the position of the upper caste-class landlords in villages presents an uneven picture of social change. This group is going through both upward and downward social mobility. They have suffered a significant degree of prolitarianization, especially in the northern states, such as Uttar Pradesh, Rajasthan and Bihar. Mostly, these comprise families which did not adjust with changed times, did not alter their style of living and work or did not move ahead through higher education and employment in non-agricultural occupations. Among such families not only the agricultural productivity is low but the increase in the size of their family over a period of time has led to fragmentation of their landholdings reducing them to the status of marginal cultiva-tors. Often this causes a conflict between their psychological, social and cultural self-image and their objective economic condition leading to their lumpanization or even criminalization. Sometimes, this process is also repeated among other caste-class groups. Much social unrest in many northern states of India results from conflicts generated by a large section of the alienated youth from such classes. The alienation of a segment of such caste-class groups coincides with upward social mobility of its other segments which have successfully adapted to changes and reforms. The agrarian structure as demonstrated by changing size the operational holdings reveals that marginal, small as well as large size holdings have declined between 1970-71 and 1980-81, whereas the number of the medium size holdings has increased during the same period. It supports the sociological observation on alienation of land both from the marginal and large landowners in favour of the medium size landowners who presumably represent the middle caste-class agrarian strata in the rural society.

This re-structuration of the upper and middle caste-class strata in villages also coincides with major social changes in its working class population which mostly comprises the scheduled castes, or other deprived lower castes. The policy of protective discrimination in their favour in operation during the past four decades has brought about a substantial change in their self-image, class consciousness and their social and economic conditions. In some regions, such as the Western Uttar Pradesh, Punjab, Haryana, Maharashtra and most of the peninsular India there has been a noticeable upward social mobility among this group with improvement in their social and economic condition. Their educational level has also gone up. Interestingly, these are also the regions where the green revolution first started. As the lower castes constitute a substantial number in these regions they tend to be better organized, have some political influence, can keep a more successful watch on the implementation of the welfare policies of the government for their benefit and can bargain better with the dominant rich and middle class peasantry. In other regions, especially the eastern Uttar Pradesh And Bihar, the-condition of these classes has not yet improved. They are subject of exploitation, repression and violence. Occasionally there is eruption of violent protest, as also active mobilization of political groups which support violence. The state of Bihar is a case of this kind in India. Here, the process of green revolution as also restructuration in social system has not yet taken place since the agrarian reform policies were subverted by feudal landlords and politicians.

The process of social restructuration is product of social and economic development. It has, however, generated social conflict in society. On the one hand, the middle caste class peasantry clamours for more privileges and power as revealed by the 'back-ward class movement' in northern India, on the other, the working classes and the scheduled castes lead organized protests and demand betterment of their social and economic conditions. The upper caste-class groups, which traditionally held power have except in some regions, a marginal role in these processes, as their success depends largely on coalition and cooptation in search of power. This is particularly true for northern India where upper caste-classes do not have a substantial rural population.

Role of Industries

Modernisation in India is symbolized by green revolution in villages. It is also organically linked with the process of urbanization and industrialization. During the past four decade there has been massive growth in urban centres and industrial units. The urban population which in 1901 stood at 25.9 millions, in 1951 at 62.4 millions rose to 156.2 millions in 1981. It comprised 17.3 percent of the total population in 1951; in 1981 it had risen to 23.3 percent of the total population. More importantly, the composi-tion of older cities has radically changed with pressure of migrant population. Between 1951-1981, about 355 new towns emerged in India and the percentage of class-I towns roughly trebled. Similarly, substantial industrial expansion has taken place. The figures of joint-stock companies both public and private show that their number in 1971 was to the tune of 30,461, and it rose to 118,305 in 1985 (December). The growth in private companies has been more rapid in terms of numbers than in the public companies. The number of labourers working in organized sector roughly doubled during 1961 and 1984 rising from 12-09 millions to 24.2 millions.

Sociologically, these changes have had major implications for social restructuration not only in these sectors of activity but also in the society in general. Expansion in industrial activities enlarged the social base of industrial workers. More important than this, it created a large number of industrial-urban middle class in India. The rank of traditional industrial capitalist classes was joined by a new breed of mercantile capitalists and industrial entrepreneurs. Their number runs in thousands. The impetus given by government's industrial policy led to the rise of a new class of capitalist entrepreneurs in the corporate sector. This trend coincided with swelling of the ranks of professional classes in the domains of technology, education, science, law, medicine, civil services, army and police services, journalism and architecture etc.. The urban middle class comprises these upward mobile groups which represent the process of modernisation in India today.

The rise of these classes is a result of investment in development and modernisation since Independence. It is indicative of social mobility and restructuration going on in society. It contri-butes to and represents the outcome of the processes of social change. Let us understand the social base of this new professional and industrial middle class. It comes largely from the upper caste- class strata of the traditional Indian society. Its outlook and ideology is highly utilitarian which makes it ready to absorb modern techno-logy and use all opportunities for upward social mobility. Its social outlook and-belief systems are, however, traditional, rooted in religiosity and tend to be conservative. Its growth does not repre-sent only change but also continuity, a continuity which symbolizes social resilience but is often anchored in disvalues. Opportunism, obscurantism and corrupt practices have penetrated a segment of this class because of the nebulous nature of the ideological anchorage it has in the value system of a modern society. The new urban middle class, therefore, is a measure of both India's development as well as its underdevelopment. The underdevelop-ment can be witnessed in the fast expansion of slum population in most cities, specially in the Indian metropolises. It can be seen in the rise in the number of alienated youth, and social crimes.

Role of Culture

The contradictions of social development are also reflected in the cultural changes that are taking place in India today. Both in the rural and urban social systems the quest for economic and social modernisation has activated cultural forces which legitimize values like acquisitiveness, opportunistic utilitarianism, revivalism, communalism and primordialism. These have resulted from social restructuration in society during the past fifty years. The rural development symbolized by green revolution, and urban development reflected in entrepreneurialism and professionalism have ironically generated a sense of narrow utilitarianism instead of liberal and cosmopolitan values of modernisation. This has probably resulted due to the lack of clear ideological orientation in the processes of economic and social development. It may also be attributed to the inevitable pangs of capitalist development in a society professing the goals of a socialist democratic transformation.

The cultural changes in India today mirror both forces of resilience and transformation. The resilience can be seen in the expanding role of religion and its expressions in people's life. Religion gets equal patronage from political leaders, corporate executives, professionals and capitalists. Education of science and technology does not seem to displace religion from people's private and public life. Instead, a unique mode of dualistic coexistence of scientific rationality in instrumental roles with religious values in fundamental domains of life has been worked out by most professionals in India who occupy scientific and technological offices. The same is true in social life, such as family, caste and kinship organizations. The traditional cultural values of instrumental nature such as those related to health, food, nutrition, transport and communication are, however, being fast replaced by new, 'rational instrumental values of science and technology. One finds this reflected in high degree of acceptance by people of modem medical science, new varieties of food and food technology, material culture, and their acceptance of new modes of information and communication. The commitment to modern values is also reflected in electoral politics, new management structures and scientific and technological institutions of society. It is indicative of the resilience of the traditional values and institutions which accommodate and adopt new values of social and cultural, modernisation. The basic pluralism of Indian social structure and its inter-structural autonomy facilitated the initial process of cultural modernisation when India was exposed to the West through colonization. After Independence, cultural modernisation became more participatory and less exclusive with mass participation in institutions of social, economic and cultural development. This has enlarged the base of people's participation in modern ways of life and sharpened their political consciousness and sense of identity. It has also set into motion new values as well as disvalues as the process of social restructuration takes place in society on a meaningful scale. Revivalism, casteism, communalism and regionalism are some of the disvalues which have emerged as a result of this development.

Communalism is a particularly powerful social disvalue which has continually been active in the Indian process of social and cultural modernisation. Its historical roots go far back to British colonialism which gave birth to this ideology in order to divide and rule over the Indian people. Their geopolitical interests later led them to strengthen communalism in India and divide the country on religious lines before departing from the subcontinent. Indian leadership never accepted the ideology of two nation theory based on religion and its surrogate ideology of communalism. It was historically refuted when Bangladesh came into existence. Communalism, however, once implanted in the mind of the people has continued to torment and thwart the process of cultural modernisation in the society. It has during the past four decades taken a complex social and ideological form. In the first instance, it gets mixed up ideologically with the process of social restructuration in society. In this form, it serves as a disguise for class and interest group ideology. The new middle classes of various religious communities exploit the communal identities of the poorer sections of their coreligionists. The deprivations of these communities in social and economic fields are attributed to religious minority status in contravention, of the objective situations. In this sense communalism does often function as false consciousness. In other situations, communalism is simply engineered by opportunistic political and economic interests of contending groups and factions within a political party or by political parties. Communalism emerges in India as most important threat to cultural modernisation. It is a complex process but its causes generally subsist in the contradictions generated by the forces of social restructuration. The uneven pace of social mobility and a sense of deprivation by groups and communities which perceive the chances of their status mobility blocked is probably an important contingent factor which fuels communal prejudices and makes it possible for opportunistic elements in society to exploit it. This coincides with new assertiveness of socially mobile sections from among the minority communities which contend for higher social and economic position and treat communalism as a tool for social mobilization. This breeds communal strife, sometimes communal violence.

Another form of communalism which is of recent origin is that of religious fundamentalism. It has both national and international dimensions. It comprises propagation of a worldview of religion to which according to its belief all other aspects of life must be subordinated, be they political, economic, social or cultural. It is in complete contradiction to the scientific rational world-view of secularism, a cultural policy, to which India is committed. In India, since the past few decades there has been a rise in fundamentalist movements, but these too have links with political and economic issues. Whether it is Sikh fundamentalism in Punjab or Muslim fundamentalism in parts of the country, these movements have arisen only after the communities concerned have gone through a certain level of social mobility, economic development and rise in aspirations. This process, therefore, indirectly confirms the view that like other forms of communalism religious fundamentalism too has its roots in the social and economic restructuration of the contemporary Indian society. The measures to overcome this too will have to be linked with policies of economic and social development in furtherance of a secular cultural policy.

Wave of Reconstruction

The pattern of social change that one witnesses in India today reflects elements of continuity with modernisation. The continuities can be discerned in areas of social structure and belief systems which show resilience. It can be seen in the adaptive mode of modernisation through the medium of traditional institutions. The role of joint family system in maintaining and promoting entrepreneurial activities both in industry and agriculture, the uses of religious and ritualistic symbols in modern modes of communication of highly political and educational messages, the use of caste and kinship in the mobilization of people for political, developmental and other forms of associative and professional persuits, etc. are its examples. There is no linear change in India from tradition to modernity, instead we find a process of modernisation of tradition.

After seventies, however, we witness social movements in

India which out-cross caste and kinship ties. More associations and professional bodies of scientists and experts, have emerged which do not mirror in their organization and activities elements of caste, kinship or regional identities as the caste associations did in the 1960's. Social movements of professionals', youths and women which cut across caste, region and religion have emerged. Several popular people's movements in various parts of the country have sprung up which have as their objective popularization of modern scientific outlook, concern for social ecology, social justice and equality. This has activated in India a process of social change where not *community* but *category* becomes an important nodal point of social mobilization, interest articulation and Organization. The significance of communatarian social structures such as family, caste, tribe and kingroup is still predominant, but increasingly new social arenas are being mobilized for econo-mic, organizational, professional and technological achievements whose-membership is not by primordial identity but on the basis of class, professional skill, economic interests, gender and age or other civic principles. This has resulted as the pace of economic, technological and scientific development has become stronger in the country.

It is in this context that the role of class formation can be examined in the analysis of social change in the contemporary India. There is massive data and theoretical material on class structure and the process of social change in India. The rural, corporate and professional sectors of Indian society have been studied using the class model for the analysis of social change. Obviously, the significance of class as a structural concept for understanding the continuity and change in society increases more, when it is viewed as a Process, a reality in a state of flux and formation rather than as a finished product. The notions of modes of production offer advantages for the analysis of processes of social change to the extent that the conceptual packages and operational tools employed in this model view social reality in a state of *becoming* rather than *being,* a feature from which only a few studies using this model do not suffer. The Indian social transformation is not such that can be adequately explained by a linear model of transition from one mode of production such as 'feudalistic' to another such as the 'capitalist'. It is mote complex, and at each stage of social existence one may witness more than a single mode of production. A 'feudal' mode of production might inhere 'capitalist' elements. The 'ancient' mode of production such as bondage and collectivism on the principle of kinship or *biradari* might coexist with capitalist mode of rational allocation of technological resources for production. For similar reasons, some social scientists have even ventured to speak of a *jati* or caste mode of production. Conceptually, therefore, in the analysis of contemporary processes of social change in India what is important is to fully grasp the process of continuity and change in society. The more social scientists are faithful to this task the better models of understanding social transformation they may be able to evolve. Analysis of social change through mode of production can be treated only as the first step towards greater challenges that might be encountered in its operationalization.

The Indian persuit for social development and social change is orientated to socialist transformation within the framework of a parliamentary democracy. This itself puts limits on the policies and strategies for social change. These policies consciously inhere elements which are both capitalistic and socialistic in persuits. In many sectors of social life and economy such as agriculture, the policy of peasant proprietorship on capitalist lines was followed by land reforms such as ceiling on land holdings in persuit of socialist goals. This has strengthened middle class capitalism as also created dominant caste and kingroups akin to feudalistic social formations. The concepts of feudalism and capitalism are, therefore, in the Indian context of social change more sensitizing than definitive or explanatory in character.

12

Women and Society

The Gandhian era and the decades after independence have seen tremendous changes in the status and the position of the women in Indian society. The Constitution has laid down as a fundamental right the equality of the sexes, but the change from a position of utter degradation of women in the nineteenth century to a position of equality in the middle of the twentieth century is not a simple case of the progress of women in the modern era. The position of women in the Indian society has been a very complicated one. In feet, it would not be an exaggeration to say that the recent changes in the status of women in India is not a sign of progress but is really a recapturing of the position that they held in the early Vedic period.

Historical Backdrop

Literary and historical researches have now established beyond doubt that the women held aposition of equality with men during the Vedic period. The girls as well as the boys were required to undergo *Upanyanam* ceremonies in order to be initiated to the Vedic studies. In fact, the education of women was looked upon as so important thai the *Atharva Veda* asserted that "the success of women in her married life depends upon her proper training during the Brahmacharya." According to *Sarvanukra-manika,* there are as many as twenty women who composed the hymns of the *Rig Veda*. Some of the renowned Vedic women are Lopamudra, Viswavara, Sikata, Nivavari, and Ghosha. *Aswalayana Gruhyai,stra* required posterity to read every day the names of great women like Sulabha, Maitreye, Gargyachafcnave. Unfortunately, there is no record of their work.

It is well known that in the; Upanishadic period there were great Brahmavadinis, who were lifelong students of philosophy. In the *Bhrihadaranyak Upanishad one* of the greet challengers of the eminent sage Yagnavalkya is Gargi, who asked many subtle and intricate questions. One of the most celebrated Upanishadic passages is the conversation between Maitreye and her husband Yagnavalkya. Yagnavalkya decided to divide his property between his two wives and renounce the world. Maitreye preferred to get initiation to the knowledge of Brahmavidya rather than choose to inherit her husband's property. Even in the Buddhist time there were great women scholars. Some of them like Sanghamitra, the sister of the great emperor Ashoka, went to Ceylon to spread Buddhism. Among the authors of Ttieraegatha are 42 women, 32 of whom were unmarried. According to the Jaina tradition, Yayant, a princess, remained unmarried and received ordination from Mahavira himself. On the basis of these facts from literature Altekar writes, "We may therefore conclude that many girls in well-to-do families used to be given a fair amount of education down to about 300 B.C."

While marriage was looked upon as a religious and social duty, and while it was held that an unmarried, person was not eligible to participate in Vedic sacrifices, it was not looked upon as compulsory for every girl. The women who remained unmarried and grew old in the house of their parents were called "Amajur". As Shakuntala Rao Sastri writes, "The extent of the word "Amajur", which means a girl who grew old at her father's house, and the reference to the attendance of maidens, young women at the 'Sumana' festival as well as the unmarried female rishis as Apala-atreya, suggests that matrimony was not compulsory for a woman and that no limitation had been placed on the age of marriage."

The Vedic women being grown up and educated had a voice in the selection of their husbands. Often there were also love marriages—*Gandharva Vivaha*.

The reference in the *Rig Veda* to the life of a widow are very few but it was not characterized by restrictions and austerities as in the post-Vedic days. Re-marriage of widows was allowed. There are a number of references to the custom of Niyoga where a brother of the deceased husband could marry the widow with the permission of the elders. Other versions show that she could marry any person, not necesssrily the brother of the deceased husband. The earlier Dharmashastra writers allowed divorce. In fact, Kautilya gives detailed rules of divorce. As regards *Sati,* burning of the widow, Shakuntala Rao Sastri writes, "*The Rig Veda* does not mention anywhere the practice of the burning or burial of widows with their dead husbands."

As regards property rights, according to the Vedic hymns, both husband and wife were joint owners of the property. As noted earlier, the *Brihadaranyaka Upanishad* refers to the division of Yagnavalkya's property between his two wives. As Romesh-chandra Dutt (1848-1909) wrote: "Hindu women held an honoured place... They inherited and possessed property; they took share in sacrifices and religious duties; they attended great assemblies and state occasions; they also distinguished themselves in science and learning at their times.... Considered as intellectual companions of their husbands, as the friends and loving helpers in the journey of life of their partners, in their religious duties, and the centre of their domestic bliss, Hindu wives were honoured and respected in ancient times."

Thus, the position of the Hindu woman in the early Vedic times was very different from the lower status to which they were degraded after about 300 B.C. As Altekar writes, "The reasons why daughters were not unpopular in ancient India during the early centuries are not difficult to understand. They could be initiated in Vedic studies and were entitled to offer sacrifice to God. The son was not absolutely necessary for this purpose. Further, the marriage of the daughter was not a difficult problem; it was often solved by the daughter herself. Further, there was no dread of widowhood, because levirate and remarriage were allowed by society and even fairly common." The description of the position, of women before 300 B.C. shows that they enjoyed a high status. It appears as if several drastic social changes took place in the Indian society from about 300 B.C. to the beginning of the Christian era which led to the curtailment of the freedom of women. Students of Indian social history have tried to find the reasons for the changes which took place in the status of women after 300 B.C. One of the reasons advanced is that the sons were valued more than daughters because the Aryans encountered various tribal people who inhabited the Gangetic plains when they moved East from the Punjab. This movement led to a desire for sons who would participate in the wars against the people of the area. Another hypothesis is that greater importance was placed on ancestral worship than in the Rig-Vedic days. Consequently, sons were more valued than the daughters. Yet another reason advanced by scholars is the reaction to the Upanishadic, Buddhistic and Jaina influence of asceticism. As the *Brihadaranyaka Upani-shad* stated, "Seeking the self alone monks relinquish all rites and renounce their homes. Ancient knowers of the self did not desire progeny as also rites and meditation of conditioned brahmin, the three means respectively to the three external worlds.. . . They renounce their desire for sons, for wealth and for the worlds and wandered about as mendicants."

Many young women renounced their homes and joined the Buddhistic and the Jaina monasteries. The life which some of these monks and nuns led gave rise to a revulsion to the ascetic way of life and the monasteries. It is also presumed that one of the reasons for practice of early marriage of girls is to prevent them from entering monastic life. Whatever the reasons, there is no doubt that the great social changes which took place after 300 B.C. led to a degradation in the status of women.

With the consolidation of the Aryan power a vast majority of the subjects were non-Aryan people. The Aryans married the non-Aryan women. Vishnu and other early *Dharmashastra* writers did not object to these marriages but prohibited the non-Aryan women from participating in the religious rituals. The non-Aryan wife could not participate in the religious sacrifice as she did not know Sanskrit and as she had no education. Gradually, all women, Aryan as well as non-Aryan, became ineligible for Vedic studies and religious duties. There is also the problem of increased complexity of the Vedic sacrifices which rendered the wife's association a more formal affair. The complex rituals needed a long training of over ten to twelve years which even the Aryan wife could not obtain. Gradually, Upanayanam for girls became a mere formality. Since girls were not educated early marriages became common; girls were married soon after puberty. By about A.D. 205 some of the *Dharmashastras* declared that marriage was a substitute for Upanayanam for girls. Since Upanayanam was performed at about the age of eight or nine, marriages came to be performed at an early age. As Altekar writes, "The discontinuance of Upanayanam, the neglect of education and the lowering of the marriage age produced disastrous consequences upon the position and status of women." Gradually, Niyoga and widow remarriage were prohibited. Marriage became an irrevocable union as far as the wife was concerned. The *Smriti* writers preached that the wife should look upon her husband as a God. Some of them went to the extent of asserting that she should worship him even if he was a rake.

When the kingdoms became large, the kings maintained large harems. This inevitably led to the seclusion of women among the kings, and among the nobles who imitated them. The purdah system also came into the royal families.

The political conditions also appear to have had their impact on the status of women. The period between 300 B.C. and A.D. 300 saw the invasion of the Greeks, the Scythians and the Parthians, then the Kushans. The political reverses, the atrocities due to the war and the decline of prosperity produced a wave of despondency in society. Once again the ideals of renouncement and Sannyasa preached earlier by the Upanishads, Buddhism and Jainism began to spread. These new developments affected the status of the widow. Those who opposed the Niyoga and remarriage of widows were strengthened in their position. The widow was asked to devote herself to an ascetic life at home. All this led to the increase of the childless widows. The tonsure of the widow also came into vogue by about the eighth century A.D. The purdah custom was practised more widely among the middle classes. To quote Altekar, "Thus for nearly 2,000 years from 200 B.C. to A.D. 1800 the position of woman steadily deteriorated though she was fondled by the parents, loved by the husband, and revered by her children. The revival of *sail** the prohibition of remarriage, the spread of purdah and the greater prevalence of polygamy made her position very bad." Thus, there was a vast gulf between the status of the woman in the early Vedic period and that in the nineteenth century. The dual standards of morality set up by Manu prevailed right up to 1950.

As Neera Desai puts it, "Ideologically woman was considered a completely inferior species, inferior to the male, having no significance, no personality; socially, she was kept in a state of utter subjection, denied any right, suppressed and oppressed; she was further branded as basically lacking the ethical fibre. The patriarchal joint family, the customs of polygamy, the purdah, the property structure, early marriage, *sati* (self-immolation of the widows) or a state of permanent widowhood, all these contributed to the smothening of the free development of women."

Thus, it appears as if the neglect of the education of women, which was coupled with child marriage on the one hand, and the customs of polygamy, seclusion, and purdah on the other, brought about a tremendous degradation in the status of the women.

Reforms Movement

The wave of reformist thought in the nineteenth century initiated by Rammohan Rai (1774-1833), and followed up by Iswarchandra Vidyasagar (1820-1871), Dayananda Saraswati (1827-1883), Keshab Chandra Sen (1838-1884), and others, led to very significant legislative, social and educational changes. Finally, Mahatma Gandhi and the Indian National Movement led to the great emancipation of the Indian women in the twentieth century.

Before proceeding to describe the efforts of the enlightened men and women in the nineteenth century and the first half of the twentieth century, it must be emphasized that most of the disabilities regarding purdah, seclusion, lack of divorce and remarriage of the widows were confined to the upper castes and to those living in the urban areas. It must be remembered that upper caste people and the urban people hardly constituted ten per cent of the population. Rural women, though uneducated, had the freedom to divorce the husband and remarry. The widow could remarry, though even in the rural areas, the divorce and the remarried women were looked upon as inauspicious. (The *Sudhrakamalaakara* written in the 17th century expressly permits divorce to the Sudras and other lower castes.) Further, the rural women took full part in agriculture and the craft-work of the husband. They also had the freedom to sell milk, vegetables and other produce in the neighbouring towns. In fact, early in the morning even now one can see hundreds of women coming from their villages with headloads of all kinds of merchandise to sell in the towns. Women could move about freely and could participate in the religious festivals, fairs, etc. Thus, more than 90 per cent of women had considerable freedom in society and a large share of equality with men, though child marriage and polygamy existed in the villages and thus curtailed their freedom.

We may now briefly enquire into the changes in the outlook regarding the status of women among the enlightened Indians of the nineteenth century. One of the important reasons for this change in outlook is the acceptance of the tenets of liberal philosophy from the West which emphasized the principle of contract rather than status, a rational outlook of life and its problems, freedom of speech, criticism of authority, questioning of accepted dogmas, and, finally, the recognition of the value of the individual and insistence on the *rights* of man as opposed to his *duties*. The other great impetus to the changed outlook is the study of the *Upanishads* by the reformers like Ram-mohan Rai and the Brahmos on the one hand, and study of the ancient Vedic society by the revivalists like Dayananda Saraswati and the Aryasamajists on the other. Next there was the realization among the Indian liberals like Dadabhai Naoroji, Gopalkrishna Gokhale, Badruddeen Tayabjee, and others who were convinced that national uplift and national progress was impossible without the education of women and their emancipation. Finally, there was the firm faith in Mahatma Gandhi and the leaders of the national movement that the liberation of the country from the bondage of imperialism was impossible without the active participation of women who constituted half the population of the country.

The nineteenth century saw for the first time in India, social legislation enacted by the Government. It was Rammohan Rai who showed for the first time that the ancient Hindu scriptures did not prescribe *sati*. This strengthened the hands of Lord William Bentinck, the Governor-General of India at that time, and in 1829 he abolished *sati* and made it a crime.

The Bramosamaj established by Rammohan Rai stood for the principle of freedom of women and equality of sexes. So it campaigned for widow"remarriage. It was the untiring efforts of Iswarchandra Vidyasagar that led to the promulgation of the Widow Remarriage Act of 1856, which made widow remarriage legal. Thus between them, these great Indian leaders of the nineteenth century enabled the Hindu widow to attain a status in society by removing the legal obstacles in her way. But it took another century before there was a real social change in India, a change in the outlook of the people, particularly in the higher castes, towards the widows. The great leaders of the nineteenth century were shocked that so many thousands were child widows because of the practice of child marriage that was prevalent throughout the society. Another great landmark of the nineteenth century was the Civil Marriage Act of 1872, which was passed on account of the courage and perseverance of Keshab Chandra Sen. This Act made marriage a secular ceremony. It provided for the registration of the marriage. It raised the age of marriage of girls to 14 years and permitted widow remarriage and inter-caste marriage which were illegal up to that time. But the most significant feature of the Act was the enforcement of monogamy. Here again it took another three-quarters of a century before the Hindu society accepted these great social changes of inter-caste marriage and monogamy in 1956.

The basic aim of the ancient Hindu law-givers was to preserve the property of the joint family. So a woman could not inherit the property because she would take the property out of the family to her husband's family. The only redeeming feature was the recognition of *streedhana*— movable property which was given to the woman by her parents or her husband. So a revolutionary change was implied in the Married Women's Property Act of 1874 which widened the scope of *streedhana* to include earnings by a woman and the money she acquired through her artistic and literary skills. This legislation provided the incentive to the woman to engage herself in remunerative work and acquire property on the basis of her own earnings.

As noted above, for more than 2,000 years, girls below eight were given in marriage. This led to the horror of "child widow". Children of six to eight years were looked upon as "widows" when their "husbands" passed away. It must be remembered that even in 1930, the longevity of an Indian was only 25 years. It was the efforts of another great social leader, Behramji Malabari which led to the Age of Consent Act of 1881, which raised the age of consent to 12 years. This abolished at least by law, though not in practice, marriage of girls below 12 years.

Thus through their efforts, the great social leaders of India of the nineteenth century were able to get many legislations passed which removed the obstacles in the way of the progress of women. It must be realized that there were no elected legislatures at this time. The Government, due to the Indian War of Independence of 1857, were reluctant to interfere with social matters.

Another significant feature of the nineteenth century India is the attempt made by these social leaders to educate Indian girls. For more than 2,000 years, from about 300 B.C., there was practically no education for women. Only a few women of the upper castes and upper classes were given some education at home. But even here there was tremendous social resistance because at that time only dancing girls could read and write and so literacy of woman was looked upon as a disgrace. Of course, it must be realized that hardly five per cent of Indians as a whole were literate in the country throughout the history. So it is inevitable that women should be illiterate but the important change that we have to bear in mind is the view of the later Dharmashastra writers, who asserted that women, like the Sudras, were ineligible for Vedic studies. Thus, according to them, only a "handful" of men in the country were eligible for education.

It was the American mission which first started a school for girls in Bombay in 1824. According to the figures available, by 1829, within five years, as many as 400 girls were enrolled in this school It was only in 1851 that an Indian society was formed to start girls' schools. In Madras, Munroe reported in 1822 that more than 5,000 girls attended the indigenous primary schools as against nearly 200,000 boys. On the other hand, in Bengal, Adam wrote, "The notion of providing the means of instruction for female children never enters into the minds of parents. A superstitious feeling is alleged to exist in the majority of the Hindu families, principally cherished by the women and not discouraged by men, that a girl taught to write and read will soon, after marriage, become a widow." According to the report of the National Committee on Women's Education of 1959, "It cannot be denied that the general picture of the education of women was the most unsatisfactory and women received practically no formal instruction whatever, except for the little domestic instruction that was available to the daughters of the upper class families."

According to the Charter Act of 1813, the East India Com-pany was entrusted with the responsibility for the education of the Indian people. But its efforts were restricted to the education of boys since the policy of the Company was one of strict social and religious neutrality;they were afraid of promoting education of girls since it was believed that the Hindu religion at that time prohibited it. The famous Woods Despatch of 1854 reported that there were 65 girls schools in Bombay Presidency with 3400 pupils, 256 girls schools in Madras Presidency, attended by over 8,000 girls, and 288 girls school in Bengal Presidency attended by over 7,000 pupils. But in the rest of the country mere were very few schools. Thus, due to the efforts of the Christian missions and the voluntary Indian bodies. Significant progress had been made in the enrolment of girls in primary schools by the middle of the nineteenth century in comparison with hardly any education at the beginning of that century, except in some parts of the South.

Education for Women

While in the first half of the nineteenth century, the missionary efforts as well as the efforts of the Indian voluntary organizations led to the starting of girls primary schools, particularly in Bombay, Bengal and Madras States, four events in the second half of that century led to the great increase of girls schools and enrolment of girls. The Woods Despatch of 1854 on education is one of the most significant features in the history of Indian education, since it accepted the responsibility of the Government to promote primary education in general and that of the girls in particular. However,

Government efforts could not go a long way due to the upheavals that took place in 1857 as a result of the Indian War of Independence. The Government became very hesitant after this and pursued not only the path of religious neutrality but also that of social neutrality. For example, the 1859 Despatch on education was very cautious and referred to "bom the difficulties and the importance of female education" and looked for "safe and proper methods" to permit extension of schools for females. But soon there was a change in the outlook of the Government which led to the establishment of the municipalities and Local Fund Committees in 1870. The local governments were enabled to help in the development of primary education in India. As a result of this, facilities were provided for the starting of special schools for the girls. Further, in the same year 1870, training colleges for women were established for the first time and women were trained to become teachers in the girls' schools. Finally, the Education Commission in 1882 discussed the problems of women's education with great insight; it made several recommendations not only to open more schools for girls but also to attract girls above twelve to the schools. It also recommended the employment of women teachers in the schools and the appointment of women as inspectors of the girls schools so that the teachers as well as pupils could be comfortable. Another important recommendation that it made was that special stipends should be given to widows who came for teacher training.

As a result of all these efforts, great progress was made in girls education in the last quarter of the 19th century. The census report of 1881 gave tables not only regarding the position of girls education but also regarding literacy among the women. The report of the National Committee on Women Education 1959 observes, "If these statistics are compared with those of 1854 given earlier, it will be readily seen that the number of girls under instruction had considerably increased. In spite of these advances, however, this table will show that the gap between the education of men and women was still wide; that for every 1,000 boys at schools, the number of girls under instruction was only 46." While in 1854, only about 25,000 girls had been enrolled in schools, the enrol-ment went beyond 117,000 in 1881 and increased to 127,000 in 1892. For the first time two women from Bethune School graduated from the Calcutta University in 1883. By 1902 there were over 256,000 girls in various institutions and as many as 169 in the liberal arts colleges, and 87 in the professional colleges.

Another significant feature of the last decades of the nineteenth century is the entry of women into the professions. As noted above, due to the opening of the women training colleges and the special facilities recommended by the Education Commission of 1882, a large number of women became teachers. Secondly, many women entered the newly opened schools and colleges to qualify themselves as nurses and doctors. Thus, women were attracted to the two professions of teaching and medicine by the end of 19th century.

An increase in enrolment of girls on the one hand and entry of women into the professions on the other indicate the marked change that took place in the outlook of men and women in the latter part of the nineteenth century. When one realizes that at the beginning of that century there was hardly any literate woman in the country excepting a few in the aristocratic houses, it is astoni-shing that by the end of the century hundreds and thousands of girls were enrolled in the newly opened institutions all over the country and that they were eager to graduate from the universities that were established in the middle of the century. There is no doubt that the changed outlook towards women advocated by Rammohan Rai at the beginning of the nineteenth century had tremendous impact not only with respect to social legislation, which removed some of the disabilities suffered by Indian women for more than 2,000 years and helped in raising the age of marriage, but also led to the establishment of several thousand institutions for the education of girls. When one considers that at the beginning of that century sati was prevalent and thousands of women were burnt at the funeral pyres of their husbands and that hundreds of thousands of girls were killed as soon as they were born, it is astonishing that the Indian society could change so drastically that by the end of the century girls were not only sent by the parents to attend schools and colleges but also to go and work as teachers, doctors and nurses.

Probably, Rani Laxmi Bai of Jhansi (1835-1858) inspired women as well as men of India regarding the potentialities of women by the way in which she participated in 1857 war of Indian Independence and died fighting valiantly on the battlefield. She has become a legendary figure since then.

There were also several Indian women leaders who worked for the emancipation of women in the nineteenth century. Among them the work of some women may be briefly recounted here.

The foremost among them was Pandita Rama Bai (1858-1922). She came from a learned Brahmin family. She was a great scholar of Sanskrit and addressed many learned groups in different parts of the, country and was given the title of "Pandita" and "Sarasvathi" for her deep knowledge of Sanskrit. After the death of her parents, she and her brother travelled in different parts of the country. She spoke about social injustice done to women in the society. They went to Calcutta in 1878. Two years later her brother also died. A little later in 1880 she married a Bengali pleader of a lower caste. Thus, even at that time she was bold enoagh to many a man of different caste and different language. After the death of her husband two years later she returned to Poona and started the Arya Mahila Samaj with the help of leaders like Ranade and Bhandarkar. In 1882, she gave evidence before the Hunter Commission who were very happy to see 300 women being educated in the Samaj. She pleaded for facilities for women to qualify themselves in medicine. In 1883, she went to England and was baptised as a Christian. She went to America in 1886. On her return to Bombay in 1889, she started the Sharada Sadan to provide a home for the destitute high caste widows, again with the help of Ranade, Bhandarkar and others. However, because the Hindu widows were converted to Christianity there was a strong protest against the institution by Tilak and other Hindu leaders, as a result of which even liberal leaders like Ranade and Bhandarkar had to give up their connection with the Sadan. After this, she shifted to Khedgoan near Poona and established the Mukti Sadan. The institute soon prospered and had on its rolls nearly 2,000 children and women training sections enrolled in the different sections from the kindergarten to the teacher and the industrial section. In spite of the criticism against her, she was able to give general educational and vocational training to several thousand women who were able to become self-dependent.

Another outstanding woman who contributed to the emancipation of women in the nineteenth century was Rama Bai Ranade (1862-1922). She married the great economist and social reformer Justice Mahadev Govind Ranade when she was just eleven. Ranade educated her and helped her in her various activities. She started the Hindu Ladies Club in her house in 1884 and later opened classes for illiterate women and widows. She also started the Poona Seva Sadan with branches in different parts of Maharashtra. Finally, she started a Nursing Medical Association and trained nurses.

Another woman of outstanding merit was the great revolutionary Madam Cama (1861-1936). She was a pioneer in the struggle for freedom. She left India in 1902 and settled down in England and joined the Indian revolutionary movement there.

Toru Dull (1856-1877) of Bengal was a great literary celebrity of the nineteenth century. Another great writer was Svamakumari Devi (1855-1932) of the famous Tagore family. She wrote historical and social novels in Bengali. Para, a talented painter of the Kangra school of Rajput painting, was a woman artist of great repute.

In the last decade of the century, Swami Vivekananda (1863-1902) gave a tremendous impetus to the emancipation of women from seclusion and bondage. He said, "That country and that nation which did not respect women have never become great nor will ever be in the future." He took a stand for the liberation of women and equality of treatment on the basis of the Vedantic ideals that "one and the same self is present in all beings." He attributed the helplessness and dependence of woman on man to the training given to her and asserted "however, when she is no longer oppressed she will become a lion." He emphasized the ideal that through education, women should be enabled to solve their own problems by thinking independently.

Another great Indian figure who lived to be a centenarian was Karve who started the Hingne Women's Education Institution in Poona in 18% in which he imparted training not only in academic subjects bat also in domestic economy, to unmarried, married, widowed and deserted women with branches in other parts of Maharashtra. Ultimately, he was responsible for starting the S.N.D.T. Women's University in 1916, adopting the mother tongue as the medium of instruction. It was recognized as a university in 1938. It has a number of high schools and colleges affiliated to it. Thus, it was a great step in the advance of women's education, particularly in Maharashtra.

The year 1917 is of great significance in the history of the progress of Indian women. It was in 1917 that Annie Besant (1847-1933), an enlightened British woman who settled down in India since 1893, launched the Home Rule agitation. When she was interned by the British, the Indian women led processions to temples to offer their prayers for her release. In the same year she was elected the President of the Calcutta Session of the Indian National Congress. In her Presidential address she said, "The strength of Home Rule movement was rendered tenfold greater by the adhesion to it of a large number of women who brought to its helping the uncalculating heroism, the endurance, the self-sacrifice of the feminine nature. Our league's best recruits and recruiters are amongst the women of India."

The Calcutta Session also expressed the opinion that "the same tests be applied to women as to men in regard to franchise and the eligibility to all elective bodies concerned with the local Government and Education."

Thus, the Congress recognized officially the equality of the sexes by inviting a woman to be the president and by expressing that the same tests should be applied to men and women regarding franchise and election as early as 1917. It was in the end of that year that a deputation of Indian women represented to the British Parliament and demanded the enfranchisement of women on a basis of equality with men.

After the Jallianwalabagh massacre in 1919, when hundreds of men, women and children were killed, a large contingent of women delegates, nearly 200, attended the Congress Session at Nagpur. This was a striking evidence of the political awakening of the Indian women.

Mahatma Gandhi rendered signal service to the advancement of the women's movement by making thousands of them, of all classes, to come out of their homes and participate in the political movement. As Amrit Kaur wrote, "A passionate lover of humanity, an implacable foe of injustice in whatever form or sphere, it is small wonder that Gandhiji early espoused the women's cause. Gandhi's fundamental faith in the equality of women was based on the doctrine of non-violence. He wrote, "In a plan of life based on non-violence, woman has as much right to establish her own destiny as man has to establish his."

From the very beginning Gandhi preached against wrongs done to women in the name of *Dharmashastras,* law and tradition. He wrote, "It is sad to think that the *Smritis* contain texts which could command no respect from men who cherish the liberty of women as their own and who regard her as the mother of the race. Of course, there are the *Smriti* texts, which gave women her due place and regard her with deep veneration. The question arises as to what to do with the *Smritis* that contain texts that are repugnant to the moral sense, all that is printed in the name of scriptures need not be taken as the word of God or the inspired word."

On another occasion he was even stronger in expression, "I have defended *varanshrama dharma.* But Brahminism that could tolerate untouchability, virgin widowhood and spoliation of virgins, stinks in my nostrils. There is no knowledge of Brahman therein. There is no true interpretation of scriptures. It is undiluted animalism.

Thus, Gandhi was very clear in his mind that ancient Indian scriptures do not advocate social inequality and social injustice. As seen above, he is wholly correct in his standpoint as far as the most ancient texts are concerned; but later texts, particularly those written after 300 B.C. have directly advocated social inequality, not only regarding the education of women but also by promoting child marriage and widowhood till death. With respect to these passages he declared that they should not be followed. In other words, according to Gandhi, the important criterion to judge the *Dharmashastras* is whether they advocate social equality and social justice, between man and man and between man and woman.

This is why he was always a fighter for the equality of human beings and freedom for individuals. Consequently, he unequivocally stood for the emancipation of women as he stood for the emancipation of the untouchables. He wrote, "I passionately desire utmost freedom of our women." He asserted continuously that woman has the same right of freedom and liberty as man. He wrote, "I am uncompromising in the matter of woman's rights. In my opinion she should labour under no legal disabilities not suffered by man," As a barister, he desired the rule of law which is against all kinds of discrimination; so he was a champion for the equality of women and for their rights as human beings.

Though he himself was a victim of child marriage, he condemned child marriage in unequivocal terms. He has described in detail in his autobiography the sufferings he and his wife had to undergo because they were married as children. He writes, "The so-called marriage rite ought no longer confer legality upon an immoral and inhuman act, which consummation even at the age of 14 in my humble opinion undoubtedly is." Though the social reformers at the end of the last century campaigned against child marriage, probably no person condemned it as vehemently as Gandhi did as something immoral and inhuman.

With equal vehemence he condemned widowhood of children and strongly recommended widow remarriage. He was shocked at the condition of little girls who were called widows because they went through the ritual of marriage and lost their so-called husbands. He wrote, "...forced widowhood upon little girls is a brutal crime for which we Hindus are daily paying dearly. There is no warrant in any *Sashtra* for such widowhood; voluntary widowhood, consciously adopted by a woman who has felt the affection of a partner adds grace and dignity to life, sanctifies the home and uplifts religion itself. Widowhood imposed by religion or custom is an unbearable yoke." Thus, as a person who passio-nately believed in the freedom of the individual, he was unequi-vocally against the imposition of widowhood on a girl, because of custom. In fact, he went to the extent of advising the students "to make a sacred resolve that you are not going to marry a girl who is not a widow, that you will seek out a widow girl and that if you cannot get a widow girl you are not going to marry at all." Thus, he wanted to carry on two campaigns at the same time; he wanted to see that little girls are not married, and he also wanted to see that young men marry the widows girl so that such a widowhood is wiped out.

We can thus understand how the whole society was transformed because of this campaign adopted by Gandhi so that after freedom, there was drastic change in the legal status of the women.

Continuously, he urged the women to think independently by themselves and arrive at decisions on the basis of their own judgement instead of depending on man or blindly following the custom. In order to enable the illiterate women in the rural areas to develop these capacities and to think independently, he wanted the enlightened women from the cities to "enroll women as voters, impart or have imparted to them practical education, teach them to think independently, release them from the chains of caste that bind them so as to bring about a change in them which will compel man to realize woman's strength and capacity for sacrifice and give her a place of honour."

The most important thing he did, right from the years in South Africa, was to make women participate in social movements and public work. As a great campaigner and leader of social and political movements he could see and realize the importance of the participation of the women who constitute 50 per cent of the population. It is obvious that no movement could be popular, no movement could be a mass movement unless women participated in it. The most astonishing thing is that right from the beginning women responded to his call in large numbers. The very first non-cooperation movement that he launched in 1920 brought a large number of women throughout the country to participate in the movement. Of course, as noted above, the new outlook among women was gradually coming in towards the end of the nineteenth century and in the beginning of the twentieth century. We have seen that when Annie Besant was in jail in 1917, women went in procession protesting against it. So by 1920 when Gandhi gave the call for non-cooperation to liberate the country, women came out of their homes in large numbers. In August 1921, Gandhi acknowledged the services rendered by the women. He wrote in his *Young India*, "The women of India have during the past 12 months worked wonders on behalf of the motherland.. .you have parted with your cash and with your fine jewellery, you have wandered from house to house to make collections. Some of you have even assisted in picketing. Some of you who are used to fine dress of variegated colours and had numbers of changes during the day have now adopted the white and spotless lot heavy khadi saree. . .yours is the purest sacrifice untainted by anger or hate. Let me confess to you that your spontaneous and loving response all over the country has convinced me that God is with us. No other proof of our struggle being one of self-purification is needed than that lakhs of Indian women are actively helping it." He wanted that the women should have the same share as man in winning independence. Even in 1921, when he was asked whether the participation of women in public work would not lead to the neglect of home and children, Gandhi replied, "More often than not a woman's time is taken up not by the performance of essential domestic duties but in catering to the egoistic pleasure of her lord and master and for her own vanities. To me this domestic slavery of women is a sample of our barbarism. It is high time that our womanhood was freed from the incubus. Domestic work ought not to take the whole of a woman's time."

He wanted the women to participate in what he regarded as the vital tasks of constructive work, namely, picketing liquor shops and the shops which sold foreign cloth. He was convinced that it is only a group of women who could make an effective appeal to those engaged in the sale of liquor and foreign cloth; he was also convinced that even illiterate women could take part in this work of conversion. As a matter of fact, thousands of women, educated as well as illiterate, took part in this picketing throughout the country.

Even as early as 1921, he advocated the enfranchisement of women. He wrote, "Women must have votes and equal legal status. But the problem does not end there; it only commences as the point whether, women began to affect the political deliberation of the nation." As we will see presently, he lived to see women participating in the State Governments in 1937 and in the Central Government in 1947.

Thus the ground prepared by the nineteenth century leaders and the untiring work of Gandhi led to the emancipation of women and helped them to take their rightful place in society in the way in which women of Vedic age participated in the ancient times. We may now briefly describe the way in which, side by side with their participation in the national movement, women also started a separate movement to fight for their rights.

While Pandita Rama Bai, Rama Bai Ranade, Karve and others started great institutions in Maharashtra to educate women and to help them to understand their rights in society in the latter part of the nineteenth century, it was really in the beginning of the twentieth century that new ideas swept across the country and a strong women's movement took shape. In this work three Western women played an important part. They are Margaret Nobel, later known as Sister Nivedita, Annie Besant, and Margaret, Cousins. These three women were, as Hanna Sen wrote, "frish in origin, suffragette in sympathy and former participants in the Irish home Rule agitation."

The Organisation

In 1917, some Indian ladies of the South established the Indian Women's Association in Madras and organized its branches in different parts of the country. Margaret Cousins started *Streedharma* in order to mould public opinion in favour of women and to educate the women about their rights. As noted above, it was in December 1917 that a deputation of women, under the leadership of Sarojini Naidu (1879-1949), presented a memorandum to Montague, the British Secretary of State for India, demanding votes for women and also for increased educational and health facilities. This was a significant event which marked a new awakening of Indian women of their political and social rights. In their address they said, "We have asked for a portion of your valuable time because the women of India have awakened to their responsibilities in public life and have their own independent opinion about the reforms that are necessary for the progress of India." They further said, "We pray that when such a franchise has been drawn up, women may be recognized as 'people' and it may be worded in such terms as will not disqualify our sex to allow our women the same opportunity of representation as our men."

The British Parliament appointed the Southborough Committee in 1918 to make recommendations regarding franchise, the women of India met this Committee when it toured round India. In 1918 also, the Indian National Congress as well as the Muslim League endorsed the demand of women for enfranchisement. But the Committee ignored the claims of the women in its report published in 1919. It was understood that the Committee felt that franchise for women was premature on account of the social customs prevailing in India. However, the women held several protest meetings in various parts of the country and sent resolutions to the Secretary of State for India in London, requesting him to carry out the expressed wishes of the Indian men and women and to enfranchise women. The British Parliament appointed a Joint Select Committee to take evidence of the representative Indians on the suggested reforms when the India Bill was introduced in July 1919. After the Indian deputations which went to London to give evidence supported women's franchise. Viewing this overwhelming public opinion, the Joint Select Committee decided to leave the question of women's franchise to be settled by the Legislative Councils of India in each province. So the women next issued appeals to the members of the Slate Legislative Councils. In March 1921, Krishna Nair, a prominent member of the Madras Legislative Council, introduced a resolution that women should be enfranchised on the same basis as the men. The resolution was adopted by a large majority. In August, the same year, a similar resolution was adopted by the Bombay Legislative Council and in 1925 in the Bengal Council.

In the meantime, the princely States of Cochin and Travancore of South enfranchised women and also nominated them to the State Legislative Council in 1920 itself.

In 1926, Kamla Devi Chattopadhyaya stood for election to the Madras Legislature and secured over 4,000 votes, but she was defeated by a narrow margin. Immediately afterwards, the Women's Indian Association campaingred for the nomination of at least four ladies to the Legislative Council.The Government of Madras nominated Muthu Lakshmi Ammal. She was elected by the Legislature as Deputy President.

Thus, within a period of ten years from 1917, the agitation of the women of India to obtain enfranchisement in the whole country on an equal status with men bore fruit. This is one of the most outstanding social changes that took place in India fifty years ago.

In the middle of 1926, Margaret Cousins, the secretary of the Women's Indian Association, sent out an appeal to the various states in the country requesting the women leaders to hold constituent conferences in each state. During the last quarter of 1926 conferences were held in as many as 22 places. As a result of these local conferences the All-India Women's Conference was established and it held the first session in January 1927 in Poona with representatives from all over the country. Thus the women established an all-India organization to help them in their struggle for their rights. It laid down that reforms in the field of women's education was its primary objective. In its annual conference it had not only been fighting for the expansion of educational opportunities for girls and women but also established a National Education Fund and in 1932 it set up the Lady Irwin College at New Delhi to give advanced education in Home Science for women. In its 13th session, the conference spelt out its aims and objectives in a clear and comprehensive manner. In the field of social reforms it carried on a propaganda against early marriage, polygamy, excessive expenditure at the time of marriage, etc. It fought for equality in matters of property. The conference made studies about the condition of women in the factories and mines and drew the attention of the Government to the low wages and unhealthy working conditions. As early as 1932 it demanded universal adult franchise. Very early it conducted a campaign in the field of family planning to prevent overpopulation.

The All-India Women's Conference is today a huge organization with nearly 500 sub-branches and a membership of 3.25 million. It conducts magazines and issues news letters. Another important field in which it has been active is the starting of hostels for working women in the urban areas.

The Conference has played a very important part in supporting social legislation in India. It gave full support to Haribilas Sarada and mobilized public opinion so that the Act of 1929 raising the age of marriage of girls to 14 was passed. Because of its campaign the problem of the codification of Law was taken up and important legislations were passed giving for the sexes during the fifties.

Thus, the close association of Indian women with the political movement enabled them to bring about radical changes in their status with the least resistance from men.

As noted earlier, the Constitution of India laid down equality between sexes. It also provided for special steps to be taken by the Government to improve the condition of women by establi-shing separate institutions. By 1956, many laws were passed removing the inequalities between sexes. There was considerable divergence between social norms and the legal norms in the first half of the twentieth century. As Panikkar had noted, Hindu religion had never looked upon women as inferior. In fact, woman was looked upon as the symbol of "Shakti", power and energy in the cosmos. "It is the law of the Hindus and not the religion which depied women property rights, used to compel girls to marry before puberty and deny the rights to remarriage of widows. Now all these three have been changed without in the least affecting Hindu religion." A radical change has been brought about in the Hindu social system by these new laws. The raising of the age of marriage by legislation may lead to the problem of unmarried daughters which was an impossibility for more than 2,000 years. Similarly, the recognition of the claim of the daughters to inherit their share in the family property has denied the very basis of the Hindu joint family. In the same way the claim of the widow to an independent share in her husband's property. "It will be clear from the above discussion that the claim of the daughter, the wife and the widow, to share in the property of the family involves a revolution unseen but fundamental in the Hindu life." Further, the educated woman would get the ability and confidence to form her own judgement and may not subscribe to the old ideal of looking upon the husband as a god, *patidevata*.

It is now nearly twenty years since Panikkar made this observation and since the legal changes were made. But one does not see any sign of social tension as a consequence of these radical changes. The whole change has been achieved and accepted so smoothly that there has been no occasion for any conflict. This is a further proof of the ability of the Indian society to assimilate radical social changes without upsetting the social balance.

A reference may be made to the problem of the purdah by way of illustration. As noted earlier, even in the pre-Muslim days, the monarchs and the nobles practised seclusion of women particularly because they indulged in polygamy. Many of the ruling princes have had, even in recent decades, large harems. With the advent of the Muslim rule in India, the social norm of purdah and the seclusion of women spread even to the middle classes, particularly in the northern parts of country. Towards the end of the nineteenth century and in the first decades of the twentieth century, enlightened Hindus as well as Muslims campaigned for the abolition of the purdah. Apart from the social injustices involved in this practice there was the shining example of the freedom of movement among women in the whole of peninsular India from Maharashtra to Kerala. In spite of this campaigning neither the Muslims nor the Hindus in the North were prepared to give it up. Here also, Gandhi was a great force to bring about a radical change.

Early in 1927 he wrote, "Whenever I have gone to Bengal, Bihar or United Provinces, I have observed the purdah system more strictly followed than in other provinces. At Darbhanga ... I was called upon to address the ladies behind the purdah. The sight of the screen behind which my audience, whose numbers I did not know, was seated, made me sad. It pained and humiliated me deeply. I thought of the wrong being done by men to the women of India by clinging to barbarous custom which, whatever use it might have had when it was first introduced, has now become totally useless and was doing incalculable harm to the country .Purdah is being retained even in educated household, not because the educated men believe in it themselves, but because they will not manfully resist the brutal custom and sweep it away at a stroke. A few months after this many influential women of Bihar signed an appeal for the total abolition of the purdah. The appeal stated, "We want that the women of our province should be as free to move about and take their legitimate part in the life of the community in all particulars as their sisters in Karnataka, Maharashtra, and Madras, and in an essentially Indian way, avoiding all attempts at Europeanization, for while we hold that a change from enforced eclusion to a complete anglicization would be like dropping from the frying pan into the fire, we feel that the purdah must go, if we want our women to develop along the Indian ideals," In July 1928, there was an organized demonstration against purdah in many places in Bihar State. At one of their meetings they passed the resolution, "We men and women of Patna assembled, hereby declare that we have, today abolished the pernicious practice of the purdah, which has done and is doing incalculable harm to the country, and particularly to the women, and we appeal to the other women of the province who are still wavering, to banish this system as early as they can and thereby advance their education and health." The demonstration, the resolution and the "funeral of the purdah" in Patna in 1928, were given wide publicity in the country. The campaign against purdah was intensified in all the other regions. Finally, the civil disobedience campaign of the thirties liberated the women from the oppresive custom of the purdah. Thus, there is clear evidence of the way in which the influence of Gandhi was able to bear fruit within a few months and enabled the men as well as the women in the Bihar State to throw away a custom which persisted through centuries. However, it must be realized that even now some of the lower class illiterate Muslim women continue to observe purdah, though the Hindu women have completely given it up. As noted above, this is another illustration of radical social change taking place in a smooth manner in the Indian society

As regards education, while in 1901 only 12 girls were enrolled in the primary schools for every 100 boys, in 1950-51 the enrolment went up to 39, in 1965-66 it was around 55 girls and in 1989-90 it was around 74 girls for every 100 boys. Though there is an enormous increase in the enrolment of girls in the primary schools in the class I to V, which went up to 5.4 million in 1950-51 to about 18 million in 1965-66, 24 million in 1973-74 and is nearly 40.96 million in 1989-90, there is a big gap even now between enrolment of girls and that of boys. Thus the parents even today are not as enthusiastic in sending their girls to primary schools as they are with respect to their boys. It is now clear the main obstacle to Universalisation of Primary Education in the country is the resistance of the parents to send their daughters to schools. The following reasons have been identified as the major obstacles towards UPE for girls:

1. Poverty, particularly in rural areas. As long as rural incomes are low, children will be forced to work to supplement family income.
2. Girls, who, even if they do not work outside, play a supportive role in the household, providing child care and household labour as surrogate mothers.
3. The low value given to female education, and socio-cultural biases and practices which prevent parents from 'investing' in girl's education.
4. Accessibility of schools. When this matter was last surveyed (1978), it was estimated that there are 1,91,000 habitations without primary schools, of which 11,370 have populations of 500 or more. Even where schools are available, distance from place of residence is an inhibiting factor.
5. Lack of female teachers who could help overcome the bias of sending girls to co-ed schools, especially if they are first generation learners.
6. The unattractive environment of schools, particularly those which lack even the basic facilities such as toilets, drinking water, building, blackboards etc. The 1978 survey showed that 53 per cent of schools do not have permanent buildings, 59 per cent lack safe drinking water, 40 per cent lack blackboards and 71 per cent do not have libraries.
7. Single-teacher schools where teachers are often absent or unable to cope with the responsibility of organising consistent and meaningful educational activity.
8. Lack of community or parental involvement in educational processes which would encourage a sense of accountability on the part of teachers and officials.

Educational Level

% age	***Males Total (lakhs) (lakhs)***	***% age % age***	***Females Literates (lakhs) as percent age of the total population excluding the age group 0-4***
Literate with Educational level 66.6	1,139 1.670	70.6 69.3	531 28.7
Primary 34.0	489 760	30.3 31.5	271 13.1
Middle 16.8	290 424	18.0 17.6	134 7.3
Matriculation / Higher secondary 12.5	279 379	17.3 15.7	100 6.5
Non-Technical Diploma of 1 certificate not equal to degree	 0.1	2 3	0.1 0.1
Technical diploma or certificate 0.3 not equal to degree	8 10	0.5 0.4	2 0.2
Literate, without educational level 33.4	474 740	29.4 30.7	266 12.7
 100.0	16.13 2410	100.0 100	793 41.4

We get a similar picture regarding enrolment of girls at the secondary level. While in 1901 only four girls were enrolled at the secondary level for every 100 boys, in 1950-51 it went up to 15 and in 1965-66 it was around 26, it further went upto 36 girls in 1980-81. But the greatest change has occurred in the enrolment of girls at the university stage. In 1901 there were altogether only 177 girls studying in the colleges. In 1950-51 there were forty thousand girls at the college level and was around two lakhs seventy thousand in 1965-66. This further went upto 23 lakhs in 1980-81. Though the achievement is very spectacular, yet in comparison with the enrolment of the boys at this level there were only 14 girls for every 100 boys in 1950-51 and it went up to 25 girls in 1965-66 and to 32 girls in 1980-81.

Educational Level

(Enrolment in '000)

Educational Level	*Boys*	*Girls*	*Sex Ratio*
Primary	51732	34733	671
Middle	18132	9992	551
Higher Secondary	10427	4070	390
Pre- University/Intermediate Pre-degree	1382	482	349
Teachers Training School	47	51	1085
Technical and Industrial Arts and Craft School	217	66	304
Polytechnic	112	12	107
B.Ed./B.T.	48	37	771
MBBS	56	24	429
B.Ed., B.Sc.(Engg.), B.Arch.	135	9	66
B.Com.	598	158	264
B.Sc.	452	192	425
B.A.	799	488	611
MCom.	54	12	222
M.Sc.	53	26	491
M.A.	113	70	619
Ph.D./D.Sc/D.Phil.	20	9	450

There were about 53.1 million girls in schools and colleges in 1980-81, 27.1 million in class I to V, 13.4 million in Class VI-VIII and 10 million in matriculation or higher secondary classes. The progress in the field of professional education is even more spectacular. As against merely 87 girls in 1901, there were 5,000 girls in 1950-51 and around 50,000 in 1965-66, and this increased to 56,701 in 1981-82.

The Department of Women and Child Development in the Ministry of Human Resource Development, Government of India prepared a National Perspective Plan for Women (1980-2000 A.D.). Recognising that education is the most important instrument for human resource development, education of women was given top priority. The National Policy of Education (NPE-1986) attempted for the first time to address itself to the basic issues to women's equality. In the section titled "Education for Women's Equality", the policy states:

> "Education will be used as an agent of basic change in the status of women. In order to neutralize the accumulated distortions of the past, there will be a well conceived edge in favour of women. The National Education System will play a positive, interventionist role in the empowerment of women. It will foster the development of new values through redesigned curricula, text books, training and orientation of teachers, decision makers and administrators."

It gives overriding priority to the removal of women's illiteracy and obstacles inhibiting their access to and retention in elementary education. Emphasis has been laid on women's participation in vocational, technical and professional education at different levels as also to promote women's participation in non-traditional occupations and existing and emergent technologies.

The Programme of Action for implementation of NPE(POA) spells out the meaning of women's empowerment:

Women become empowered through collective reflection and decision making. The parameters of empowerment are:

— Building a positive self-image and self-confidence
— Developing ability to think critically

— Building up group cohesion and fostering decision making and action
— Ensuring equal participation in the process of bringing about social change
— Encouraging group action in order to bring about change in the society
— Providing the wherewithal for economic independence...

The programme entails the following:

(i) A phased time bound programme of elementary education for girls, particularly upto primary stage by 1990 and upto the elementary stage by 1995.
(ii) A phased time bound programme of adult education for women in the age group 15-35 by 1995.
(iii) Increased women's access to vocational, technical, professional education and existing and emergent technologies, and
(iv) Review and reorganization of educational activities to ensure that they make a substantial contribution towards women's equality, and creation of appropriate cells/units therefor.

A number of measures have been suggested to achieve the stated objectives of the National Policy on Education. The Action Plan enunciates that every educational institution should take up by 1995 active programmes for the development of women. All teachers and non-formal education/adult education instructors should be trained as agents of women's development special programmes should be developed by research institutions to promote general awareness and positive self-image amongst women through programmes like discussions, street plays, wall papers, puppet shows, etc. Preference in recruitment of teachers upto school level should be for women.

National Literacy Mission (NLM) which aims at eradication of illiteracy in 15-35 age-group by 1995 concretises what is envisaged in NPE as regards literacy and adult education. The Mission document emphasises the importance of imbibing the values of national integration, conservation of environment, women's equality, observance of small family norm etc. and goes on to say that "the focus of NLM would be on rural areas, particularly women and persons belonging to the Scheduled Castes and Scheduled Tribes,"

For universalization of elementary and adult education, the present programme of non-formal centres for girls needs to be extended to all education- ally backward pockets of the country. Increased assistance should be given to voluntary organizations to run non-formal education centres for girls. In rural areas, special support services should be provided to relieve the girls from sibling care and other household work like fetching water, fuel, etc. Skill development linked to employment opportunities in the villages is required to be given priority so that there is an incentive on the part of the parents to educate girls. It is necessary to develop adult education programmes for women linked with upgradation of their skills and income generating activities. Skill development for girls should be a continuous process of learning and should be supported by programmes administered by other agencies such as polytechnics, Industrial Training Institutes (ITIs), Women's Centres in Agricultural and Home Science Colleges, etc. Conti-nuing Education Centres should be set up in a phased manner to organize vocational training, provide opportunities for retention of literacy skills, and application of this learning for improving their living conditions. There are 104 ITIs functioning exclusively for women and 97 wings in general ITIs reserved for women. These would need to be revamped during 1988-90 in terms of diversification of trades and courses, keeping in view the job potential, and facilities for vocational counselling, imparting information about credit, banking, entrepreneurial development and women's access to technical education, etc.

Women's studies programmes would also have four dimen-sions, viz. teaching, research, training and extension. Women's issues would be incorporated in courses undo various disciplines. Research would be encouraged on identified areas/subjects. Seminars/ workshops would be organized on the need for women's studies, and for dissemination of information and interaction. Educational institutions would be encouraged to take up progra-mmes like adult education, awareness building, legal literacy, infor-mation and training support for socio-economic programmes of women's development, instructional programmes through media, etc., which directly benefit the community and bring about the empowerment of women.

Modern Education

The programmes for women's education will have to be implemented as a priority so that women attain a comparable level of education by 2010 A.D. The strategy to be adopted for raising literacy levels and education among women has to keep in view the vast cultural, geographical and ecological variations as also the problems relating to poverty and ignorance. The cultural and geographical variations call for decentralization of educational planning. Within the national perspective, planning, implementation and monitoring of educational programmes has to be done at district and block levels, keeping in view the socio-economic and geographic parameters of the area. The vocational and occupational components have to be designed in accordance with the availability of resources and job opportunities in the regions. Voluntary organizations and women's groups active in the area should be involved in the task.

In view of the social and cultural handicaps that have operated against women's education and taking account of the multiple roles that women are required to play, the need for adopting a set of objectives specific to women's education is imperative. The objectives to be achieved by 2000 A.D. in regard to women's education are:

1. Elimination of illiteracy, universalization of elementary education and minimization of the drop-out rate in the age group 6-14 years and stagnation to negligible proportions.
2. Ensuring opportunities to all women for access to appropriate level, nature and quality of education and also the wherewithal for success comparable with men.
3. Substantial vocationalization and diversification of secondary education so as to provide a wide scope for employment and economic independence of women.
4. Making education an effective means for women's equality by (a) Addressing ourselves to the constraints that prevent women from participating in the educa-

tional process; (b) Eliminating the existing sexist bias in the system; (c) Making necessary intervention in the content and processes of education to inculcate positive and egalitarian attitudes; and (d) Ensuring that teacher's perceive this as one of their essential roles.

5. Providing non-formal and part-time courses to women to enable them to acquire knowledge and skills for their social, cultural and economic advancement.
6. Impetus to enrol in various professional degree courses so as to increase their number in medicine, teaching, engineering and other fields substantially.
7. Creating a new system of accountability, particularly in respect of the basic educational services, to the local community, interalia, by active involvement of women.

It is hoped that the goals and strategies spelt out in the National Policy on Education, POA and the National Literacy Mission will ensure a much larger access for women to education.

Thus the most important problem from the national standpoint as well as from the standpoint of women, is the need to take special efforts by the state and the society to make the parents of the girls in the age group of 6 to 11 to send the girls to the primary school. As the Education Commission (1964-66) puts it, "For full development of our human resources, the improvement of homes and for moulding the character of children during most impressionable years of infancy, the education of women is of even greater importance than that of men. . . .In the modern world the role of women goes much beyond the home. .. .She is now adopting a career of her own and sharing equally with man the responsibility for the development of society in all its aspects. This is the direction in which we shall have to move."

When we compare this statement with the actual condition of women in the nineteenth century, when widows were burnt on the funeral pyre of their husbands and infant girls were put to death as soon as they were born, the great change in outlook is something tremendous. With respect to the occupational picture also we find a radical change as far as the women in the middle classes are concerned.

Job Opportunities

The rural women, as noted above, have always been working in the fields and farms from time immemorial. They constitute about 80 per cent of the womanhood in India. They have worked because that is the way of life. Similarly, women have been working to help their husbands in the cottage industries. Thus, as far as the rural women are concerned, they have been working and they now continue to work.

The great change, however, took place when the machines were introduced for manufacture. According to the 1991 Census, out of a total of 285.4 million main workers and 29.5 million marginal workers, the share of female main workers was 23.2 per cent (66.2 million) and of marginal workers was 85.5 per cent (25.2 million). Thus female workers constituted about 29 per cent of the total work force in the economy. The Work Force Participation Rate (WFPR) for females (main marginal workers) works out to be 22.7 per cent In 1981 out of a total of 222.5 million main workers and 22.1 million marginal workers, the share of female main workers was 20.2 per cent (45.0 million) and of marginal workers as 84.0 per cent (18.6 million). Female workers constituted about one fourth of total work force in the economy. The work force participation rate (WFPR) for females (main marginal workers) works out to be 20.3 per cent

But the most spectacular increase has been in the employment among the women of the middle classes who are working in secretarial, and administrative capacities or as stenographers, clerks, telephone girls, sales-women and receptionists to mention but a few new careers. In the educational field about 30 per cent of the teachers at the primary and at the secondary level are women. At the university level it is around 15 per cent in 1986.

According to the ELO report, in the world as a whole, 27 out of every 100 women are active and women constitute about one-third of the world's labour force. The significant thing is the new opportunities for women in the non-agricultural sector.

Population, Total Workers, Main Workers and Marginal Workers in States and Union Territories by Residence and Sex, 1991

Total	***Persons***	***Total***	***Total***
Main	***Marginal***		
Rural	***Males***	***Population***	***Workers***
Workers	***Workers***		
Urban	***Females***		
Total	Persons	836,605,522	
314,903,642	285,422,913	29,480,729	
	Male	433,791,705	
223,506,153	219,233,479	4,272,674	
	Females	402,813,817	
91,397,489	66,189,434	25,208,055	
Rural	Persons	621,267,297	
249,330,072	221,590,657	27,739,415	
	Males	320,06940	
167,822,985	164,159,136	3,663,849	
	Females	301,204,357	
81,507,087	57,43,1321	24,075,566	
Urban	Persons	215,338,225	
65,573,570	63,832,256	1,741,314	
	Males	113,728,765	
55,683,168	55,074,343	608,825	
	Females	101,609,460	9,890,402
8,757,913	1,132,489		

The total number of working women was around 40 million from 1901 to 1951. There was a sudden increase between 1951 and 1961 and there were as many as 59 million women workers. However, as the total population of women had increased from 118 million in 1901 to 264 million in 1971, we observe that actually the percentage of women working has gone down from 32 per cent to 11.9 per cent. However, this went up to 22.7 per cent in 1991. We also observe that there is an actual increase in the proportion of women workers in the agricultural sector from 75 per cent to 82 per cent and a decrease in the secondary and tertiary sectors from about 13 per cent each to about 8 per cent to 9.5 per cent each. Generally, it may be said that workers in the primary sector involving agriculture, are illiterate women, while the educated women tend to go into the tertiary sector, of trade, commerce, transport, communication, teaching, higher professions, etc.

There has been a great increase in the recruitment of women in the services. In 1981, there were 44.97 million female workers in different occupations as compared to 31.02 million female workers in 1971— an increase of 45 per cent This may be due to large numbers of educated women in the urban areas entering the employment field. In the public sector, including the Government as well as local bodies, the total number of women employed increased from 3,42,000 in 1951 to 4,53,000 in 1961 and to 18,63,000 in 1985.

It is also gratifying to note that a number of women are entering the All India Services and other Established Civil Services, The following table will indicate the number of women recruited to the Civil Services through UPSC during the last 11 years.

On an average about 12.6 per cent of the total recruitees are women. It is also gratifying to note that during 1990-91, the Indian Navy and the Indian Army have announced recruitment of women as "officers" to the Armed Forces, though the Indian Army has been recruiting women to the Military Nursing Service as 'officers' for a number of years. This is the first time the Army and the Navy have thrown open its doors to the women in all its branches.

In the Arena

It was earlier noted that in 1917 the Indian women represented that they should be enfranchised to the same extent as the men, and that immediately the Congress in its Calcutta Session expressed the opinion that the same tests should be applied to women as to men in regard to franchise.

When the elections were held in 1946 for the Constituent Assembly, many prominent women of India like Sarojini Naidu, Hansa Mehta, Durga Bai, Renuka Rai and others were elected. Sarojini Naidu was the first woman to be appointed in 1947 as the Governor of the United Provinces, the biggest state in India, and Rajkumari Amrit Kaur was the first woman in the Union Cabinet to be the Minister for Health.

In the first general elections held in 1952, several women stood for the Lok Sabha, the Central Parliament, as well as the State Legislatures. As many as 23 women were elected to the Lok Sabha and 19 woman were elected or nominated to the Rajya Sabha or the Upper House. In the 1957 elections there were 27 women in the Lok Sabha and 23 women in the Rajya Sabha. As many as 342 women stood for the State Assemblies and 195 were elected. Thus, there were altogether 245 members in the legislatures in 1957. In the 1962 elections there were 36 women in the Lok Sabha and 18 in Rajya Sabha. In the 1967 elections, 31 women were returned to the Lok Sabha and there were 21 women in the Rajya Sabha. As on 15th of July 1981 there were 26 women in the Lok Sabha and 27 in the Rajya Sabha (as on 10th August 1981). In the 1991 General Elections 36 women were elected to the Lok Sabha and there were 22 women members in the Rajya Sabha, out of a total strength of 545 in the Lok Sabha and 245 in the Rajya Sabha. However, in the 8th Lok Sabha there were a total of 75 women members of Parliament in both the Houses (of 790 members) almost reaching 10 per cent of the total strength. As a result of 1991 elections much more women were sitting in the State Legislatures in the country, as against 78 women sitting in State Legislatures in 1952. As Frank Moraes wrote, "In the two Houses for the next four years women members proceeded to master the parliamentary procedures, contributing important work not only in the field of social legisla-tion, which is always uppermost in the minds of the legislators, but in a varied range of subjects from defence to finance."

One wonders whether in the coming decades, the proportion of women legislators would increase significantly, more than in 1991, in the Central and the State Legislatures. However, the most impressive fact is that a woman was elected as the leader of the majority party in 1966 and Mrs. Indira Gandhi became the Prime Minister of India. We have a women Vice-Chairman of the Rajya

Sabha today and quite a few State Legislatures in the country have Dy. Speakers or Presiding Officers who are women.

Thus with the removal of legal disabilities and by availing themselves of the opportunities in the field of education, women are now taking their rightful place as citizens in a free democracy. It must, however, be noted that most women in the rural as well as in the urban areas are not fully participating in the economic, political and social fields since they are not being educated and since the old social values are continuing to operate, inhibiting them.

13

Role of Law

The interaction between law and society can be seen at several levels: the judicial process and its socio-cultural linkages; law as an indicator of the nature of societal complexity, and its attendant problems of integration; and finally, law as an agent of modernization and social change. A sociology of law would have to deal with all the above levels of interaction between law and society. In our analysis, however, we shall focus on the relationship between law and social change and modernization in the context of the Indian Society. Using a sociological perspective, we shall treat law in its institutional and historical contexts and analyze its dialectics with society in its broader social structural setting.

Legal Provisions

The dialectic of law and society in India has been determined by historical experiences during the passage from colonialism to nationalism. In the course of this passage, the paradigms both of the social and legal systems have evolved. This process bears an acute imprint of historicity; yet in the light of our observations of similar interactions between law and society in the industrially advanced western countries, some convergence of experiences at a universalistic level cannot be denied. The processes of law and social change in India, while in large measure unique, do share some commonalties with industrially advanced nations particularly the crisis and contradiction of the paradigms of law and society.

The primary components of legal systems and the paradigms

of modernization of the industrially advanced countries are based on the ideology of rational utilitarianism. Their Gesellschaft mode of society implies movement from the status to contract; from community to individual, from participation to administration, from guild to state, and from empathy to selectivity. It was the product of the Laissez-Faire ethos of a market-oriented, non-personalized legal system. Bentham, Weber and Schumpeter, the mentors of this "rational legal order" created bridges between the legal system and the social structure. The crisis of the late 1960's early 1970's in the industrial societies gave impetus to the awakening of interest in the Frankfurt School of sociology, of neo-Marxism and phenomenological existentialism. These new interests tended to shift the pendulum, in ideological if not structural terms, towards the search for alternative models of both modernization and the legal system. This development is largely a product of the structural contradictions of the post-industrial society; it surpasses the ideological confines of the capitalist and socialist states. Kamenko and Tay have written:

> In the communist world, the tension is between revolutionary transformation and the desire for social stability, between mass campaigns and the provision of social and psychological security for individuals, social spheres and activities, between utopian spontaneity and technical administrative realism. In the west, the crisis is a crisis in the individualistic view of society, in a legal model attuned to the need of the individual house or property holder, the entrepreneur, the settled citizen living on terms of equality with those around him, secure and confident as an individual in his bearing vis-a-vis the state and the rest of society. Against this, the new demands elevate the interests of "require-ments" of the comparatively poor or underprivileged as contrasted with those who are "at home" with law: they pit the interest of "society"' or of "humanity" against "excessive" respect for individual fights and powers, especially proprietarial fights and powers; they tend to see men as social products and not as free moral agents, as people to be cured or helped rather than judged. The new demands are suspicious of lawyers as a profession

> in the common law world because they see them as a privileged caste with guild traditions and powers; in Continental Europe they see them as characterless servants of state. (Eugene Kamenka and Alice Erh-Soon Tay, 1978:50-1)

This new perception of the legal system and its paradigm obviously inheres the contradictions of an industrial society: its increasing unidimensionality, its failure in the liberation of human personality, and its de-humanizing abstractness resulting in the alienation of man. This process represents a legal order which, in the course of the structural and normative changes that it brought about, also introduced seeds of disenchantment and mystification. This challenge necessarily brings sociological jurisprudence into full play as the social dialectic tends to deeply influence the legal system. It spurs the shift from

> Private law, concerned with the security of the individual, to public law, concerned with welfare and social utility. Even in the heart of the private law, in the law of tort or torts, and in contract, they have discerned similar developments. In torts there is the movement from the legal-individualistic principle of fault liability to the social, actuarial cost-benefit analysis that leads to the principle of loss distribution; in contract, the concept of a bargain struck between ideally equal and freely contracting parties is increasingly infringed upon by the courts recog-nition of social and economic inequalities and of, the one by the sided restriction of the power to bargain, existence of standard contract." (Kamendo and Tay, 1978:48-9).

In addition to the above, new areas of law in the fields of industry, environment, consumer protection and social services have come into being. These fields are beyond the nineteenth, century conception of the common law and its judicial processes. The deeper implications of the changes in the industrial society are responsible for these legal innovations as the, response to the demand for basic alterations of the paradigm of industrial society. Thus, the crisis of the legal system is also simultaneously a crisis of the industrial society. The transition from an industrial to a post-industrial stage of development ushers in social demands on the one hand, and structural changes in the society on the other. These structural changes especially in the society's modes of production and patterns of leisure time, necessitate redefinition of the legal order of society at the inter-personal, inter-group, and inter-societal or international levels. New meanings of "responsibility," "freedom," civic culture," and "rationality" emerge. The structural changes which occur at the post-industrial stage of development tend to contribute to not only formal "differentiation" in roles and relationships, but also their "de-differentiation," "personalization," and possible revitalization of the principle of "status" in "contract." These changes may be made possible by the giant leaps in both technology and culture; they are already evident in the current electronic and computer revolutions.

We have thus far discussed the challenges faced by the industrial societies at a higher stage of development. The dialectic of law and social change in the industrially developed nations has a historically endogamous character. The new challenges and contradictions that legal systems face in these societies are generally different from the ones faced by the developing societies. In the nations such as India, where a colonial interlude fundamentally transformed the indigenous evolution of the legal system, the early legal structures were characterized by the dualism of the indigenous hierarchical and colonial utilitarian traditions. The universalistic element in the contradictions, of the Indian legal system is confined to the utilitarian-Bentharnite legal administration and philosophy which the British imposed on India. The British system is itself faced with contradictions in the light of the waning impact of utilitarian liberalism and the increasing demands of welfarism and socialism.

The dialectic of the legal system in India, with its entrenched "multiplex of social structures" on the one hand, and its multiplicity of indigenous, colonial, and developmental traditions on the other, is tremendously complex. The significant element in the interaction between law and society in India rests on the heavy burden of these multiple traditions and the social concerns and orientations of each. The convergence between the dialectic of legal systems in the industrialized nations and the legal system in India points to the developmental phase of legal system in India following independence. The contradictions inherent in the administration of justice, exemplified by the conflict between abstract individual property rights, the pursuit of profit, and the protection of the weaker and more vulnerable groups, represents a crisis in the paradigms of both society in general and the legal system in particular in India. The situation in the West is similar, but probably less complex.

Effect on Society

The relationship between law and society in India could generally be studied in three phases: the traditional or indigenous, the colonial, and the developmental. The indigenous legal system in India did not have a homogeneous character. It reflected the basic features of the Indian social organisations, it was based on the principle of "inter-structural autonomy" (Singh Y:1973). The three basic components of the social system in India, the polity, the system of stratification, and the cultural norms, were relatively autonomous and unique. Under this system, the king or his administrative and judicial authorities constituted the top of the hierarchy; they were centers of redressal or appeal and they intervened in few cases. The custom prohibited the king from intervening in disputes related to local customs, norms, and practices of castes, subcastes, or tribes. These groups had their own judicial processes throuh Panchayats, community leadership of elders, or the intervention of the chief of the dominant local caste. The normative structures of the legal system were not totally integrated in the Dharmashashtras, the often quoted sources of the Hindu legal traditions. The system represented at best the principle of interpretation at times of dispute. Depending upon the exigency of circumstances, local priests and community leaders always had the fight to new interpretation of the legal codes. And yet, there was a system in this judicial administration. The system was based upon the hierarchical order of authorities from the local caste, community and tribal panchayat, to the council of the dominant or ruling clans, to the court of the king. This linkage of judicial administration was also in consonance with the economic and cultural organization of the traditional society. The three territorial units the village, the small town and the capital cities were the focal points of social and cultural mobility on the one hand, and of nodes of commerce, administration, and political intercourse on the other.

In the studies of many scholars who have commented upon the indigenous legal system in India (see Cohn, B.S.: 1961 and 1965, Gallanter, M.: 1972, 1968, and Kane, P.N.: 1950), one finds the focus on the diversity, and not the integrative principle, of the system. It may well be, as Bernard S. Cohn suggests, that in the eighteenth century, Indian social relations operated in a "multiplex" manner, "a relationship in which a person, tends to occupy the same position relative to the same set of other persons in all networks of purposive ties-economic, political, procreative, religious, and educational." (Cohn: 1961:617). If, however, one considers the unit of interaction as caste or subcaste, the fluctuations of fortunes within each such unit of individual families would always cut across the matrix of multiplex relationships. This is the pehnomenon which still remains valid in India. The important feature in the indigenous legal system was, therefore, its sub systemic autonomy. Despite the ups and downs in the polity in traditional India, the highly enduring and innovative subsystemic autonomy persisted.

The main attributes of this legal system and its "judicial processes" were: large-scale participation, paternalism, flexibility, and innovative emphasis on compromise and hierarchy. Because community living in the Biradari or kinship group was the essential social matrix within which justice was sought, the resultant legal process was oriented more to "adjustment" than "judgement." This judicial process was as informal as it was in-expensive. It acted in harmony with the cultural ethos of hierarchy, continuity and community ties. The role of dominant castes, families and kinship groups did occasionally vitiate the process of justice; this however, occurred more frequently in the settlement of property and heredity disputes. Greater catholicity in the commitment to norms was observed in the larger towns where the mahajana supervised the justice of contractual obligations, trade and commerce.

The British who introduced the colonial legal system could never have a fuller appreciation of the traditional Indian legal system and its judicial process. It could not be understood in, dissonance with the traditional Indian polity, economy and social structure. Their colonial interests were basically at variance with these institutions and their linkages. They overemphasized the elements of discontinuity and normative multiplicity because these elements worked well with the objectives of colonial appropriation and profit.

The interests of both the British government and the East India Company coincided in these objectives. The need for "order", nevertheless led, to the imposition of a new legal system. The only legal system which the British administrators could consider viable was an improvisation of the Benthamite utilitarian tradition. There was, for a while, a debate between the modes presented by Cornwallis and Munro. Cornwallis opted for an embodiment of the commands of the government in formal legislative acts. He advocated administration by independent judicial administration in order to both secure private property and control the abuse of executive power. Munro, on the other hand, based his model on "paternalistic ideology" and assumed the role of personal authority to reign supreme in the Indian culture. Hence, his emphasis was on the evolution of a judicial system anchored in village panchayats, local customary tribunals of elders, and native judges. There was to be no complete separation between the judicial and executive functions. Though this debate continued for some time, and though Munro experi-mented with some elements of his system in Madras, the Cornwallis model of a legal system and judicial administration patterned after the British constitution and common law eventually triumphed (see Stokes, E.: 1959).

The judicial administration which Cornwallis imparted to India had come to stay. Its main features include: the establishment of a British-controlled court in every district to administer law and order, the administration of personal law in accordance with the customs of each religious group, and the settlement of revenue matters according to the principles of the pre-existing Muslim law of usage. In addition, judicial procedure was to be modelled after the British practice, judges of the district court were to be either British or British-covenanted civil servants (Indians could be recruited at lower levels), and the district courts were to be assisted in personal matters by, Hindu and Muslim priests. A legal profession was to be established; land revenue was to be permanently fixed; individuals or corporate groups were to be recognized as owners of land for revenue payment; revenue and judicial functions of the administration were to be separated; and ownership were to be settled in district, civil and appeals courts (see Cohn, S.: 1961:614).

Codification accompanied this structure of legal administration. Macauley, president of the first Law Commission set up in 1834, produced the draft of the Indian Penal Code which became law in 1860. Between 1853 and 1870, the Law Commission contributed to the civil and criminal Codes of Procedure which were enacted in 1859 and 1861 respectively. At about the same time, India was given a uniform judicial structure as a result of the unification of the Supreme and Sadar courts into High Courts. The Law Commission's efforts also led to the enactment of the Succession Act (1856), the Limitations Act (1871), the Evidence Act (1882) and the Contract Act (1882). Under the direction of the government of India, there came a Specific Relief Act (1877), the Negotiable Instruments Act (1881), the Trust Act (1882), the Transfer of Property Act (1882), and the Easement Act (1882) (see Singh, Y.: 1073:98).

This spurt of legislation impelled the emergence of a radically different legal order and impinged directly and deeply upon the normative and cultural system of the Indian society. It was not only a measure of formalization, but also a mode of modernization through westernization.

The significance of the imposition of the colonial legal system in India was marked. It created a new class of professional legal experts, the lawyers, judges, court administrators, and bureaucrats. These are the basic 'components of a civic society. The introduction of the colonial legal system led to the arousal of aspirations and demands for positive rights by the deprived classes and and communities. In course of time, it led to the growth of educated classes and to the creation of the substructure of a new middle class of capitalists, entrepreneurs, and civil servants. These and other sorts of professionals led the nation's movement towards independence. It is this movement which shaped the post-independence Indian Constitution and provided the legal boundaries for social change which exist today. The colonial process of modernization brought forth the sub-structural and subcultural character of social change which has remained an important feature of the Indian administration.

The inter-structural autonomy mentioned above enabled the new middle classes in the legal professions to emerge from the specific castes, communities and groups which already enjoyed a privileged position in the society. This made it possible to introduce social and cultural innovations without coming into conflict with the core of the structural and cultural foundations of the society, its caste structure and cultural ethos. The new forces of change thus could be absorbed and filtered through the middle classes to the rest of the society in gradual stages. The thirty years of the nationalist movement in India served to forge these forces and aspirations for change into a national ideology. The contradic-tions now faced by the independent Indian state with regard to its legal framework for social change are anchored in the levels of incongruities between its social and cultural ideology and the structure of its legal profession. A social ideology which is based on secular, civic and egalitarian features naturally comes into conflict with a legal profession which is based on individual rights and class structure and is, at least in the abstract sense, uncon-cerned with collective responsibility.

Thus, the colonial legal system introduced new challenges and possibilities for social change in India. It did, however, also create legal institutions which were, in terms of pedagogy and procedure, alien to the general population's experience and reach. The new system did away with the traditional participant mode of justice which had operated via the courts of the panchayats, chiefs, and kings. It introduced systematic codification on laws which were rooted in the alien cultural and philosophical soil. These new codes replaced the traditional customs and conventions of the dharmashastra, karan, and haidth. It also rendered justice remote and expensive and clouded its functioning in an atmosphere of mystification and suspicion. The result was the emergence of two cultures in the legal profession as it is organized in India today; these cultures are referred to by Marc Gallanter and B.S. Cohn as the "lawyer's law" and the "local law." The cultural hiatus that this dualism created in the realm of law and the legal profession is not specific to India alone, but is a general problem which occurs in the modernization of a traditional society which is characterized by a high level of historical and cultural depth. The crisis in cultural terms is a crisis of reconciliation between traditionalization and modernization.

New Era

The national movement in India which culminated the independence of the country failed to create an indigenous legal system. Mahatma Gandhi did voice his suspicion of the British sponsored courts and the lawyers in his many exhortations of the civil disobedience movements, but when India gained her freedom and the framing of the Constitution began, the Gandhian empha-sis on an indigenous legal system and judicial administration was not accepted by most members of the Constituent Assembly. The Constitution as it emerged contained elements of the Gandhian ideology, including village panchayats and democratic decentralization, in the Directive Principles of the new 'state policy. As late as the establishment of the Ashok Mehta Committee on panchayati raj in the late 1970's, the Gandhian ideologues who advocated the complete decentralization and autonomy of the village panchayat system did not find full support. While evaluating the need for indigenization of the legal system, the Law Commission of 1958 did not see any major contradictions between the present legal system and the "genius" of the people (Government of India: Ministry of Law: 1958). It noted that, "It is true that in the opinion of the Law Commission, the Indian legal system had, in the course of its functioning, undergone modifications adequate to render the imprint of the alien system more suitable to modern Indian conditions. Moreover, they agreed that, had the indigenous system been allowed to evolve independent of colonial intervention, it would have grown along a path similar to that of the present legal system. Such ideas lend perspective to the dilemma of the Indian middle class with regard to the challenges of modern nation building on the one hand and the rhetoric of indigenization on the other. Studies have shown that the dualism of the two traditions has been functionally well adapted in the Indian legal system (see Khare. R.S.: 1972 and Gallanter, M: 1972).

One important innovation since independence is the introduction of the panchayat raj system in villages. Together with the community development activities, the panchayat raj also incorporates the system of nyaya panchaynts for lower level judicial administration. Two national committees investigated the administrative and functional nature of these systems and decided to accord these panchayats the judicial power relevant to the day-to-day administration of justice. This decision was based primarily on the ideology of the village community, the role of participation, and the relatively informal judicial procedures which occurred without the intervention of lawyers. The introduction of these new systems rendered some levels of justice more freely available to the rural folk at a lower cost. They became more free from the legal substructure of the abstract rules and impersonal procedures. Subsequent evaluative studies carried out by state committees and research teams have, however, found that these nyaya panchayats are largely non functioning and are, for the most part, ridden with factious interests. Due to the system of elections which is used to select panchas or court members, the nyaya panchayats have become highly politicised. The states of Maharashtra and Rajasthan, whose committees reviewed the functioning of these village courts, have received recommenda-tions for disbanding them. This coincides with the Law Commi-ssion's insistence that judicial and electoral processes be kept separate. Findings such as these again enmesh the state and the rural politics together and expose the structural contradictions and the alienation of the masses. As Upendra Baxi rightly suggests, this institution of otherwise great significance has not made an impact. He correctly attributes this to the ambiguity of ideology and the marginality of the institutional linkages which act as an additional constraint in their functioning (see Baxi, U.: 1982:323-7).

Changed Scenario

The ideology of social change which has been adopted by India after independence is enshrined in the Constitution. It incorporates the elements of both the liberal democratic values and the Gandhian values of social change. This can be discerned in the dualism found in the fundamental rights and the directive principles of the state policy. The former is rational, liberal and individualistic in ethos; the latter asserts the principles of communal welfare, decentralisation of power, amelioration of the condition of the weak, and commitment to the abolition of the "unhealthy" social practices recognised by the Gandhian tradition (i.e. liquor consumption, etc.). Whereas the Constitution recognised the individual as the unit for interaction in matters concerning legal rights, voting, state administration, it also recognised the legitimacy of specific castes and communities for special treatment. Examples of such groups include Scheduled Castes, Scheduled Tribes, religious minorities, and backward classes. The instrument of social change in this model is social legislation. Social justice, equality, secularism, and democracy are its fundamental normative goals.

The Constitution thus brings out two apparently confirming principles: it presents universalism and particularism in the same ideological package of social change. Is this irrational? Is this a product-of ad hocism or a quirk of history or the colonial legacy? Or, is this an eclectic effort to synthesize modern with traditional values in the ideology of change? Sociologically, the answer to these questions lies in the fundamental commitment that the nation has made through the Constitution to introduce changes in a peaceful manner (the Gandhian or later the Congress ideology) so that India could become a modern, secular, demo-cratic and socialist state. Egalitarianism and freedom are difficult values to reconcile in the statecraft of a nascent democracy following its liberation from the colonial exploitation. Conditions arise which call for judicious and selective use of legislation for bringing about social changes commensurate with the objectives of the Constitution.

The civic model of change, as derived from the Constitution, could not logically recognize primordiality, caste, religion, and ethnicity. It could not leave the most exploited, the weak and vulnerable groups in the society at the mercy of the market forces of social change which always structurally favour the rich and the strong. Hence, reservations, protective discrimination, and special favour to religious minorities and the weaker groups emerged. With the aid of legislative reforms, the strategy of change implicit in this model relies on the application of the pressure of social change through structural changes in the social, economic, and cultural systems. For this purpose, the Constitution enjoins upon the executive, legislative, and judiciary special responsibilities. justice Krishna Iyre has very aptly analyzed this relationship:

> A collective consciousness which makes India great is that collective consciousness that makes every Indian feel elevated. Now, so I plead that the Constitution's code, its fighting creed, as has been put in the title of this talk, is not elitist. It is democratic. It is proletarian. It is people-oriented. Now, this people orientation must be manifest in the operation of the three instrumen-talities

which I called the Constitutional troika. The executive, when it operates, must function as if it has raised itself to the consciousness of the Constitution. In that event there would be no unimplemented laws which were enacted long ago. Likewise our legislature has to pass many laws. Mahatma Gandhi, in a publication "The Harijan" has-said, "I visualise Independent India to be again engaged only in making legislation after legislation to save the poor." There is so much to be done to save the poor. And all this must be by legislation because the executive has the authority only when the legislature passes a law. So, legislation must be made. Continuous stream of legislation, all welfare-oriented legislation. And then we come to the interpretation of these laws by the judiciary. No country can have a civilisation safe if it does not have a competent and independent judiciary. I emphasise competent judiciary as an important ingredient. An incompetent judiciary, a fraudulent judiciary, an absolutist judiciary, a judiciary given to judicial excesses, can be as dangerous as an executive given to excess. An absolutist executive, and absolutist judiciary and an absolutist parliament cannot be persona grate in a democracy. What we want is a judiciary which is accountable, a judiciary which is responsible, and with these parameters, a judiciary which is absolutely free, fearless and independent. If you seek to pressurise the judiciary, then the poor will suffer. Because who has the ability to pressurise? It is the rich man who has got the ability to pressurise (Iyre, V.K. 1982:9-13).

The above interpretation of the intent of the Constitution is the most empathic. The Marxist interpretation, in comparison, treats the Constitution as a bourgeois document intended to perpetuate the capitalist state. The liberal interpretation claims that the Constitution is elitist and charges it with neglect of the egalitarian pursuits that pervade its corpus, from the Preamble through the Directive Principles. The question of interpretation apart, there is a logical principle and strategy behind the Constitu-tion. One jurist has termed it "civic revolution." This differs from socialist revolution which is based on the open legitimacy of class struggle and its attendant socio-economic and political implications. India has deliberately chosen a path of development and social change which promotes social mobility, opportunity, and well- being of the deprived sections of society in a nation which is no doubt dominated by the rich and the elite. It does, however, employ a method of legal consensus which is based on a reconciliation model. In such a model, the responsibility of the dominant classes becomes acute because reconciliation implies, almost in a Gandhian style, the voluntary accommodation of the demands of the poor, the weak and the deprived, and the underprivileged. Its logical compulsion is more pragmatic than ethical; the privileged should know that such accommodation is also in their self-interest. In Marxist terminology, it is the tactics of the intelligent national bourgeoisie's who forewarned of revolu-tionary potential, attempts to contain it. One the contrary, the specificities of the Indian social structure and its historicity would show imperfections both logical and historical in the nature of alternative paths of development and modernization,

Indeed, the contradictions of the relationship between law and social change in India rest not so much in the inadequacy of the models as in the processes of implementation and execution of these models as such. During the three and a half decades of functioning as a democratic nation with planned development, India has succeeded on many frontiers of social change. The landed aristocracy stands abolished as a class; the power structure in the villages has passed almost completely from the traditional rural elites to a new rural middle class. A new class structure has emerged in the villages and a peasant middle class, which is aggressively entrepreneurial, has quickly adopted scientific methods and techniques of agriculture and is the leader of the green revolution. The monopoly in higher education, previously a privilege of the upper caste and classes, has now slowly started percolating to the middle classes in the villages. These changes are a result of legislation and other reform measures. The reserva-tions which the Constitution accorded in the legislatures, govern-ment services, and schools for the underprivileged have now successfully spawned a new generation of educated youth. New voices have been added to the demands for change and have contributed to the increasing mobilisation in the social structure.

The demonstration effect of these has been so acute that, in some pockets of the country, it has led to retroactive protests. In the field of land reform legislation, the ceiling level on land holdings which was enforced during the 1950's and 1960's has been further reduced in most Indian states. This is an indicator of the consciousness of reconciliation. The impact of land reforms, though uneven from state to state, has spurred agricultural growth and green revolution in several parts of India. This in turn has created a new phenomenon of labour migration from poorer states such as Bihar and Eastern Uttar Pradesh to states such as Haryana and Punjab. It has had far reaching social consequences in the liberation of the working classes in their home states from the clutches of the dominant classes or castes. It has provided new capital and savings for investment in land, houses, and cattle and it has opened up new possibilities for social mobilization and the independent political functioning of the working classes as a group. This has been especially true of the lower castes such as the Harijans and the Girijans. The recent increase in inter-caste tensions in rural areas is indeed a result of the trends of mobility in the rural social arena.

Another important area where "civic revolution" seems to have made a successful impact in India is in the area of electoral behaviour. Electoral awareness has increased throughout the country as the election procedure has spread through the village panchayats, the nyaya, panchayats, the assembly, and the parliamentary elections. Direct elections now dominate the selection process. In addition, there are electoral procedures for representation for several bodies of voluntary associations and cooperatives. The system of electoral politics and its concomitant consciousness have created a new sense of power and self-esteem in various segments of the rural and urban population. No doubt it has also activated factional politics and kindled a narrow breed of "casteism" and ethnicity. Sometimes, these identities emerge into communal principles in voting. If however, we use voter participation as a measure, rural and urban participation in India is significant and comparable to voter participation in many developed democracies. This new electoral politics and participation rate has indirectly reinforced a vital component of the civic culture, the legal consciousness.

Another positive social change which has taken place following independence is in the field of industrialisation and growth of the entrepreneurial classes. The commanding height of economic power continues to vest in public sector industries. However, during the past three decades, a sizable middle class of small entrepreneurs, commercial classes, and professional groups has emerged in the urban centres. Together with the rural middle classes, these groups comprise roughly one-fifth of the population. The rise of this middle class is a stabilising and critical element in India's process of social change today. This class adds stability to the system, contributes to economic growth and mobility, offers employment opportunities, and makes use of public and private resources for development. On the other hand, this class suffers from the cultural gauchery of the new rich and is less scrupulous about conformity to legal norms and established middle class values, The middle class's demonstration effect on the social structure is both acute and deviant. Its approach to the weaker sections is more cynical and indifferent rather than cosmopolitan; it has, therefore, increasingly tended to flout the norms of "reconciliation" and "consensus." This is indicative of what is known as the "underdevelopment of development" process in India.

The positive direction of social changes has also taken place in the fields of science, technology and manpower. The population of scientific manpower in India is said to be the third largest in the world. Managerial skills and innovation, the credibility in science and scientific ways, has become deeply rooted in India, even down to the level of the remote villages. The traditional thought patterns have not, however, declined. There is a precarious and often dialectical coexistence of the two in the Indian society. The same holds for the nature of the legal profession. Related studies by sociologists demonstrate the persistence of a large body of traditional and non rational practices both in the structure and the functioning of the legal professions and its organisation (see Gandhi, J.S.: 1982, Sharma, K.L.: 1982 and Oommen, T.K.: 1983). The problem now confronting the legal system is the product of the process of "under development", of certain sections of our society in the wake of overall development and social change.

The Other View

The positive aspects of social change in India, as we have discussed above, have generated a substantial number of contradictions in the social system. The rise of the middle class in villages and cities has led to hostile attitudes toward the weaker sections and the poor. In villages, the tensions between the Harijans and the Hindu upper castes have increased and necessitated the passage of the Civil Rights and Disabilities Act. The act makes derogatory reference to the Scheduled Caste status as a cognizable offence. The exploitation of the labourers, by rich peasants held under bondage through the extension of loans has been held legally void, but there is evidence of its perpetuation. Minimum wages for labourers in the unorganised agriculture sector stands as one piece of evidence of failure and the lack of uniformity in the introduction of small scale enterprises and shops is another. Similarly, effective legal norms with respect to the vulnerable sections of society, the children, the prisoners, the women, the prostitutes, the slum and pavement dwellers do not exist; or, their existence is rendered feeble by the resourceful, powerful, and influential vested interests in society

The development aspects of social change in India have given birth to a new awakening among the SC, the ST, the poor, and the working classes. Evaluation studies show that social and economic reform measures undertaken by the state for the benefit of these groups are not successfully reaching them. In areas where these groups are sizable or organised, these changes often culminate in protest movements. Although these movements are effective for the redressal of grievances, but they are isolated and scattered events. Unfortunately, the intervention of social workers is inadequate and rare.

In the wake of increasing social awareness of the asymmetry of the development process, the gaps between the rich and the poor, the agricultural labourers and the rich peasants, the basic contradiction facing the Indian legal system is met in the efforts to make the instruments of legal protection, legal bargaining, and legal redressal available to all. Greater emphasis has been given to this field over the course of the past decade. A movement for "legal aid" for the poor and destitute has begun. A government appointed committee has made a report on the implications and modalities of the legal aid movement. There has, in addition, been a significant resposnse from the bar and from the bench. The Supreme Court has recently allowed third party petitions by voluntary social workers and associations on matters of social concern. It has instituted investigations into several matters on the basis of legal aid and legal rights to all citizens. Until a few years ago, this would not have been possible.

Nandita Haksar writes:

> Now a public spirited citizen, concerned lawyer, or journalist, or a democratic fights organisation can move the court on behalf of an oppressed or exploited person or group of persons. The court will recognise their locus standi (legal standing). This right was first recognised in the famous transfer of judges case and later elaborated in the Asiad case. This was in conformity with the trend in other parts of the world. (Hindustan Times, New Delhi, May 22, 1983) Supreme Court judgements are binding for all courts of the land; therefore, the initiative of the court with regard to its decision to allow third parties to be represented in matters of social justice and social concern has tended to set in motion a new democratisation process in India. It is reported that hundreds of requests for legal aid are now pouring into the courts. These letters are addressed directly to the judges of the Supreme Court. The cases of the bonded workers in Haryana, of the prisoners (undertrials) in Bihar, of the inmates of the women's rescue home in Delhi, of the children in juvenile institutions, and of the torture of ordinary citizens by the Army in Nagaland, just to name a few, demonstrate the wide spectrum of the new movement for legal aid. A new area of what is called "public interest litigation" has come into being. It is being run by public spirited jurists, social workers, journalists and politicians. Several organisations which are working for the protection of the democratic rights in India have been established. Considering the vastness of the country and magnitude of the population in need of such legal protection, this new development has touched only the fringe of the problem. The movement has, however, by

selectively addressing the most critical issues of legal aid, already made a very significant impact.

The impediments of this movement toward social change may be observed in the indifference, or even hostility, of the executive and the political functionaries. There are many feudal impediments in the Indian political and civil service systems which make it necessary that some aspect of the legal aid movement be institutionalised by the government. As we have mentioned, the democratic development in India is bound to create an upsurge among the rural and urban poor, and their protest movements are bound to grow (see Desai, A.R.: 1983). The "civic revolution" as a model of social transformation would make it a logical necessity that law as an instrument of social change is held under constant review. More importantly, the judicial processes and legal administration, and the role of the executive in the proper implementation of the legal norms, should be rendered more effective. Finally, the efforts of the Indian government and the efforts of the public organisations and enterprises working to advance the movement of democratic law and social change must be linked.

Legal Factor

The general function of law is to influence the sub-groups and persons belonging to a society to conform to the group expectation. Thus, the law is a means of social control. If all the sub-groups and persons conform to the law of the society, it is assumed that solidarity will be facilitated.

In ancient India, social conformity was attained by means of two social mechanisms—*Dharma and Acnara* or custom. Manu asserted that *Dharma* is "that which is observed by the learned who are virtuous and who are always without hate or passion and that which is approved by one's own heart". Thus for Manu, there are two criteria to judge whether an act conforms to the *Dharma* or not. First, whether a given action is in conformity with the way of life of persons who are learned and who are free from passion and aversion, and second, whether one's action is acceptable to and approved by oneself. Ancient Indians also believed that *Dharma* has four sources, namely, Veda or Shruti, Smriti, Sadachara and what is satisfying to oneself—*Swasya Cha Priyamaatmanaha*.

Manu also said, "Immemorial custom is transcendent law".

In India, custom or the way of life of the group is a very important binding force. Any deviation from custom provokes the wrath of the group. The judges have always taken into account the custom of the group while giving their decisions. The essentials of a valid custom have been laid down by the various courts in India and have been incorporated in Hindu Marriage Act of 1955.

All these criteria show that the law *or Dharma* contains different elements which give a continuity to social behaviour on the one hand and leave enough scope for the operation of change on the other. The enlightened persons could bring about social change which in due course becomes the custom of the group. Behaviour which satisfies one's conscience is another element which could bring about a change in social custom.

The importance given to custom in ancient India is a clear indication that each group could develop in its own way or it could continue to maintain its old ways. This is a manifestation of the value of tolerance in Indian society.

These are the elements which have promoted a pluralistic society in India. Different groups with their own ways of life could live in harmony with other groups with other ways of life because of the outlook of tolerance. These elements also gave scope for variation in social behaviour leading to variation in custom and ultimately in law.

But, these very elements also give rise to enormous diversity among the various social sub-groups living in the country, thus preventing the building up of a national outlook and social solidarity. They also helped in the perpetuation of irrational, inhuman and even barbarous customs. We may give two illustrations with respect to diversity in social behaviour and in the law governing them. Right from ancient times, there have been two kinds of outlook in India regarding widowhood. The elite group was against the remarriage of widows. In fact, elite groups were even in favour of burning the widow on the funeral pyre of the husband, namely Soli. Even among the more human section of the elite the widow was exposed to several indignities and was bound by several restrictions. The hair on her head was shaven off; she was prevented from wearing jewellery, attractive clothes, etc. On the other hand, among the masses, widow remarriage was permitted by custom, though even among the masses the widow is looked upon as an inauspicious person and the remarried woman was not looked upon with the same respect as the first-married woman. Still, the masses were in favour of both divorce and the remarriage of widows and divorcees. Both these outlooks regarding divorce and widowhood have gone on side by side for thousands of years in Indian society. Another illustration may be given regarding differences among the creeds. Till recently, the Hindus as well as the Muslims practised polygamy. But the Hindu law has been changed in the recent years because of social agitation in favour of monogamy and equal rights for men and women. But the Muslims continue to be governed by their personal law, though the directive principles of the Constitution enjoin that there should be a common code for every citizen in India. Still the legislature has not made it binding on all citizens of India to be monogamous. Particularly in the recent years with the awareness of the people regarding family planning and population control, many feel that this discrimination may have far-reaching effects in the composition of the population. Even if a Muslim citizen adopts family planning, the ends of the family planning will not be met because he can have four wives. In fact, the great changes brought in law since independence have aimed at two objectives, namely, to eliminate diversities among the various sub-groups in the society and to bring the law in line with the changing outlook.

Traditional View

In ancient and in medieval times the state never issued any edicts or statutes. The king had no power to promulgate a law. The duty of the king was to administer justice according to the *Dharamashastraṣ. Dharma* was looked upon as being "above the King and as the king of kings". The problem arises as to the agency which brought about changes in law according to changes in social norms. As Setalvad writes, "The powerful impact of social and cultural values on law is acknowledged by the *Smritikars* who did not claim to be law-makers but only the exponents of percepts laid down by divine authority and compilers of tradition handed down from generation to generation". Thus, it is the *Smritikars* and the commentators who modified the law "so as to make it accord with the changing conditions of society and altered social values". However, since the advent of the British the Hindu law became stagnant because the British courts looked upon the *Dharamashastras* as a final authority. Still, enlightened leaders like Ram Mohun Roy and Iswarchandra Vidyasagar wanted the British Government to intervene and bring about changes in law to suit the new social values and social outlook.

Legal Support

There are two views about the functions of law. According to one view, the essential function of law is to reinforce the existing modes and to provide a uniform procedure for the evaluation and punishment of deviance from the existing rules. In other words, the function of law according to this view is social control and the major problem of law is to design the legal sanctions to minimize deviances and to maintain social stability. According to the other view, law could be more dynamic. It has not only the function of social control but it has also to bring about social change by influencing behaviour, beliefs and values. Often in the dynamic societies the social norms will be ahead of the legal codes. In such societies, it is necessary to bring the legal code into conformity with the prevalent social values. There is also another aspect; a dominant minority may have social values far ahead of the local code on the one side and the social practices of the masses on the other. Such minorities will endeavour to change the legal code as a means to persuade the rest of the group to adopt new social values.

As an instrument of social change, law involves two interrelated processes. By means of new enactments there will be institutionalization of new pattern of behaviour manifesting new social values. When this new pattern is incorporated in the legal code, any deviance from this new pattern could be punished according to law. However, as further discussion will show, mere institutionalization by itself is not enough. It may become a letter of the law but not a social force. In order that law could become an active social force, there should be a correlated cultural process, namely, the internalization of this new pattern of behaviour in the individual. These two are closely related; if the institutionali-zation is successful, it facilitates the institutionalization of the new value by bringing about a change in the attitudes and beliefs of the individual through social upbringing in the individual families. If such internalization does not take place then the mere legal codification and the institutionalization will not have any social value; on the other hand, it may bring law itself into contempt; people may lose respect for law.

We can take three concrete examples from the current Indian situation to exemplify the relationship between codification and internalization.

(a) According to the Hindu law, till 1955 polygamy was allowed. However, there was informal social control against a man marrying a second wife when the first wife was alive. He had to get the permission from his wife as well as from his relatives to marry again. This permission he could get if the first wife happened to be a chronic patient or was childless or was giving birth to only daughters. The parents and other relatives might give their consent if they did not like the first wife or the family from which she came. In other words, though law permitted him to marry, the social custom was against it.

From a long time social reformers were agitating that Hindu marriage should be monogamous. The Hindu women have always resented the second marriage by a man when the first wife was alive. This became more intense during the independence struggle when women realized that the law does not provide for equality between the sexes. The educated women were strongly against this.

But there was opposition from the orthodox section because monogamy entails divorce and facilitates the remarriage of the divorced women. So they were afraid that the whole social fabric would be affected by this change in law. But they were also conscious that polygamy means discrimination against women.

Finally, the Hindu Marriage Act was passed in 1955 enforcing monogamy and permitting judicial separation and divorce. After this Act was passed the opposition gradually died down. Probably, it is only in the remote villages that the new law may be violated out of ignorance.

Thus, this is a case where the social norms had changed ahead of legal provision. Most of the Hindus were monogamous; in fact, very few married a second wife when the first wife was living, though the law permitted them to marry. When the social reformers sought to bring about a change there was opposition from the orthodox section but when the Act was passed there was acquiescence because there was really no change in the social norm; the fear of the orthodox section that women would seek permission of the Court for judicial separation or divorce did not materialize since the prevailing social norm is against the wife seeking divorce. Secondly, though according to the 1955 Act, marriage is only a contract and it could be registered as a civil action, actually, the religious customs associated with marriage have not been given us. So, the wife looks upon her marriage as a sacrament. She would not like to annul the marriage unless her relatives gave their consent but the relatives would be reluctant to give such consent because the prevailing social norm is against separation and divorce.

(b) As a second illustration, we may take the Untouchability (Offences) Act, 1955. From times immemorial the Harijans in India have been made to live outside the village and outside the town, though their services were essential in all religious functions either in the home or in the village as a whole. They were looked down upon because they were illiterate and dirty.

However, enlightened citizens have been against this barbarous custom. Right from the times of the Buddha there have been attempts to condemn this practice and to integrate the Harijans with the bigger society. However, the large majority of the rural as well as the urban people were against this. As a matter of fact, even Muslims as well as Christians in India followed this practice.

Gandhi made the removal of untouchability an important element in his endeavour to reconstruct the Indian society. When the Constitution was drawn up, it not only declared that according to Articles 14 and 15, the equality before law was a fundamental right, it also abolished untouchability by Article 17, and made this practice punishable according to law. The Act was passed in 1955 providing for punishment against this practice.

Today, Harijan boys and girls are given full facilities for education up to the highest standards in the universities. The rules also provide for the reservation of jobs in the Government. As a result of this, many Harijan men and women have now entered the highest professions of law, medicine, etc. Those who have entered politics have become national leaders and have been ministers in the State as well as in the Central Cabinets.

Thus, in the urban areas, the Harijan today does not suffer from any severe disability. Like other citizens, he goes to hotels, restaurants and other places of entertainment. However, in the villages there is still considerable hostility towards them. They are not permitted to draw water from the village well, nor are their children permitted to go to the village school with freedom.

Thus, here we have a case of law which is ahead of the social norm, particularly in the villages. Though they have the fundamental right of equality and can seek protection of the court, the practice of untouchability has not been given up in the rural areas. In other words, as far as the village people are concerned, this institutionalization of a new social norm has not affected their way of life, i.e. the majority of the village people have not yet internalized this norm. Though the practice is illegal and the person practising could be punished by the court of law, there is a social approval in the rural society for this practice, and consequently many Harijans living in the villages are suffering hardship in spite of the changes in the law. This clearly shows that mere institutionalization does not meet the ends of justice. Passing an Act is not enough to alter the social practice. There should be a movement against this practice on the lines on which Gandhiji had organized it in the thirties and forties. Thus, the new law could be effective only when there is a new social movement educating the public through propaganda.

(c) As a third illustration we could take the case of law relating to prohibition. Here again we find the influence of Gandhi. When he was alive he carried on a vigorous propaganda against the consumption of alcohol and against collection of excise revenue from this source by the Government. Picketing toddy shops was one of the important items in his programme of constructive work. He was convinced that Indian society could be regenerated only by the prohibition. Consequently, the constitution-makers put this as Article 47 among the directive principles of slate policy.

Long before this, when the Congress Party was able to form a government in several states in 1937, they enacted laws to prohibit the sale and consumption of liquor. Particularly Madras and Bombay States enforced prohibition throughout the respective states. It was at this time that Rajagopalachari introduced sales tax to help the government to raise the revenues that were lost on account of prohibition.

However, right from 1937 there has been a strong opposition against prohibition from various classes. After independence, it became a standing joke that the only "cottage industry" that was thriving in India was that of illicit distillation.

As we have seen earlier, from times immemorial the tribal groups have been brewing their own liquor and one of their great hardships in the recent decades has been the imposition of excise duty on their drinks and later on the law of prohibition making it a crime. In the same way many village people in many parts of the country have also been accustomed to brew their own liquor and to drink toddy from the palmyra tree. While in the tribal groups alcoholic drink was part of their religious ritual, among the village people there was social approval for drinking.

During the British period the educated Indians who formed the middle class moved with the Westerners and cultivated the habit of drinking, particularly in the larger cities of India. It became fashionable to drink alcohol though the social norm in their group was against it. Gradually, the upper middle class built up a new social norm approving alcoholic drinks. In the fashionable clubs and lodges ii was normal to have a drink. It also became the practice among the upper classes to drink at home when they invited their friends for a dinner party.

Though prohibition was introduced by some of the state governments where the Congress Party was in a majority, there has been opposition from the upper middle class as well as from the lower class, This was the reason why illicit distillation became quite common even before independence.

It is true that studies have shown that prohibition has helped the urban labour families but there has not been any strong public opinion in favour of prohibition, nor was there any organisational effort to influence public opinion. The Congress Party which was in favour of prohibition felt satisfied that since legislation had made drinking a crime and was punishable by law they had nothing more to do. This was the difference between the Gandhian approach and the approach of the Congress Party. Gandhi was a social reformer. But the Congress Party is not a reformist party. Its aim has been to capture power and to exercise it like any political pa.:ty.

In the recent years there has been a difference of opinion among the Congress leaders. Those who are in administration realize that prohibition is a costly experience draining away the resources from developmental work. So there has been a move in some states in the last few years to relax the rules regarding prohibition.

Thus, the case of prohibition clearly shows how mere legislation without the support of public opinion is futile.

The above three cases show how important social values and social attitudes are to make social legislation a success. Law could be a powerful force for social change only if a large majority of the people are in favour of the new social norms and when the majority of the people have been actually following the new social norm though it was not a part of law, as, for instance, monogamy. In the case of untouchability, though some people are quite in favour of its abolition, the large masses in the rural areas and the big minorities in the urban areas do not want to give up their custom and consequently social legislation has been ineffective to bring about a change particularly in rural areas. Practically, the entire lower class and the upper middle class are actively against prohibition and so the social legislation has not only been ineffective but it has also become a target for ridicule.

Sati or the burning of the widow on the funeral pyre of the husband was the custom practised extensively in Rajasthan, among Rajput princes, and also among the Brahmins in Bengal, and to some extent in U.P. and other northern states.

Ram Mohun Roy began the active campaign against *Sati*. He studied the *Dharmashastra* and showed that they did not enjoin *Sati*. He pointed out that Manu never mentioned *Sati*. This led to a bitter controversy between the orthodox section which argued that this custom was required by the Vedas and the reformers who said that it was a barbarous custom which was not enjoined by the Vedas and Dharmashastras. Probably, this cam-paign by Ram Mohun Roy might have been responsible for the reduction in the number of cases of Sati from 839 in 1818 to 463 in 1828. It was at this time that Lord William Bentinck studied the matter, obtained the opinion of the military as well as civil authorities, and finally, in 1829 passed an Act prohibiting *Sati* and making it an offence.

Yet another revolutionary social legislation of this period is the Hindu Widow Remarriage Act of 1856. Though Sati had stopped, other customs continued to make the life of a widow miserable. Some of these customs are prevalent even now but in the middle of the last century enlightened Indians like Iswar-chandra Vidyasagar, Behramji Malabaree, and others denounced these customs and wrote to the government to make widow remarriage valid by legislation. The government passed this Act which is only to enable the widow to get married. The first widow remarriage according to this Act was performed in Calcutta in the very same year 1856. Iswarchandra Vidyasagar himself set an example by getting his son married to a widow. As a result of this Act, the social reformers started widow's homes and widow remarriage associations in different parts of the country. They gave education to the young women who became widows and enabled them to remarry.

Yet another illustration of social legislation is the Female Infanticide Prevention Act of 1870. Manmohan Kaur has given details of this barbarous custom of killing the female infants as soon as they were born. Because of the difficulty in getting a bridegroom in the same sub-caste and because of the heavy dowry and marriage expenses the new born female children were put to death. In 1870 legislation was passed prohibiting this custom and enforcing registration of births and deaths.

The next significant social legislation was the Special Marriage Act of 1872 which provided for marriage irrespective of differences in religion. This Act is the first Act providing for civil marriage and registration of marriage as against the general custom of looking upon marriage as a sacrament and involving religious ceremonies. But this Act did not provide for intercaste marriages. The Act was amended in 1923 in order to permit the intercaste marriage.

Another important social legislation in pre-Independent India was against child marriage. Little children of 5 to 10 years were being married. The leaders of Brahmo Samaj and Arya Samaj protested against this custom. In 1860, at the instance of Iswarchandra Vidyasagar, the Indian Penal Code prohibited the consummation when the girl was less than 10 years old. Keshabchandra Sen carried on a vigorous propaganda against child marriage and the marriageable age was fixed at 14 for the girls and 18 for the boys according to the Brahm Act of 1872. In 1891, the Age of Consent Bill was passed by the Government prohibiting cohabitation with a wife under the age of 12. With further agitation the Child Marriage Restraint Act was passed in 1929 raising the marriageable age of girls to 14 and of boys to 18. But this Act remained practically a dead letter because it never reached the village people for lack of publicity. Even the census of 1941 showed that there were marriages of infants of one year. Nineteen per cent of children between 5 to 10 and 38 per cent between 10 to 15 years were recorded as having been married. But, with the change in the social norms and with the belief that girls should be educated, gradually the custom of child marriage is now practically given up. This social legislation clearly shows that legislation by itself is ineffective when the people, particularly those living in villages, know nothing about it.

Another important Act of the pre-Independence era is the Hindu Gains of Learning Act of 1930. The law of inheritance was interpreted by the Court so that the earnings of a member of the Hindu joint family were his own if his education was a general education, but that such earnings would belong to the family if he had been specially trained to a profession. To remove this difference between general education and professional education and to enable a man to have full right over his earnings from his profession, Bhashyam Iyenger moved a bill as early as 1891 in the Madras Legislature. While the social reformers contended that the provisions of the bill would promote professional education, the opponents declared that the bill would hinder education since the joint family would not support professional education if all the earnings by profession were to be personal and not become a part of the family property. After many years, Jayakar was able to get this bill passed in the Central legislature in 1930.

In the precedings paragraphs we have traced the course of social legislation regarding marriage, joint family, etc. Now we may review briefly the social legislation regarding children, vagrants and beggars. While the laws noted above were passed by the Central Government, the laws regarding children and beggars belong to the provincial field.

The Madras Children's Act of 1920 provided that no child under 14 could be imprisoned. Its aim was to provide custody, trial and punishment of youthful offenders (those between ages of 14 and 18) and protection of children (those below 14). Within the next few years, many of the other Indian states passed similar legislation and established juvenile courts and certified schools.

These enactments reveal the change in the outlook of the people regarding juvenile delinquency. It shows a new awareness of the people that the children should be given proper education rather than punishment for their crimes.

Hyderabad State passed the Beggary Act in 1940 and Bengal followed in 1943. This Act gave power to the police officers to take a person before a Sub-Magistrate if he was wandering about asking for alms. Other states passed similar legislation and established beggar homes in the following years.

Finally, we may briefly refer to the labour laws passed in the pre-Independence era. According to Pant, "The first such law relates to the regulation of the recruitment and employment of Indians who were sent out to the colonies or to the plantations within the country as indentured labourers." The Workmen's Breach of Contract Act 1859 helped the planters of Assam tea gardens to prosecute labourers who wanted to run away from the plantations. The Employers and Workmen (Disputes) Act, 1860 made the worker liable to pay penalty for breaches of contract. The Indian Penal Code of 1860 also contains this provision. All these Acts, including the Penal Code protected employer and not the worker. The 1908 amendment abolished the system of penal contracts and the right of planters to arrest the workers. The 1915 amendment finally abolished the indenture system in Assam.

The Factory Act of 1881 prohibited employment of children below seven years in the cotton textile mills. It also fixed the hours of work for children between seven and twelve, at nine hours a day with a rest of one hour and four holidays a month.

The 1922 Act defined a child as a person under 15 and prevented employment of children below 12. It limited the hours of work of adults to 60 hours per week with one hour rest per day. The 1931 Act limited hours of work to 54 hours per week and the 1946 amendment reduced the work per week to 48 hours.

The Employment of Children Act of 1938 regulates the employment of children in certain industrial employments. Under this law, children below 15 years, in some cases are prohibited to take up certain types of employment keeping in mind the deleterious effect, working in such places, may have on the health of such children like bidi making, carpet weaving, cement manufacture and packing, cloth printing, dyeing and weaving, matches, explosives and fireworks, mica cutting and spliting, shellac, soap, tanning and wood cleaning.

The Children (Pledging of Labour) Act 1933 was passed to prohibit the pledging of the labour of children. In spite of this enactment in a number of villages in India, many parents continue to pledge children as bonded labour, against the advances they take from landlords and moneylenders.

Thus we see a constant effort on the part of legislation to prevent child labour and reduce the burden of children and also gradually to reduce the hours of work per week of the adults.

Besides the above Acts, there were four other significant labour legislations which are of a more general nature. These were all passed after the World War I because of the increase in the complexity of the industrial situation and the increase in the awareness of their rights among the labourers. The general public opinion was also in favour of the recognition of the rights of the workers.

The Workmen's Compensation Act of 1923 required the employer to give compensation for accident, disease, disablement, and death when these are due to the working conditions. Thus, this was the first measure of social security in India.

The Trade Union movement in India started even in the 19th century. The earliest recorded strike in India took place in Nagpur in 1877. In 1886, Lakhande convened a meeting of the factory workers in Bombay and drew up a memorandum deman-ding "limitation of hours of work, a weekly rest day, known time recess and compensation for injuries." After World War I, Trade Unions were formed; but there was no legal recognition for them. The Trade Union Act, 1926 provided for the registration of Trade Unions. Thus, the Trade Union became a legal body.

After World War I, industrial strikes became frequent. So, in 1929, the Industrial Disputes Act was passed which provided the machinery for the investigation and settlement of disputes. The Act also prevented strikes without notice.

With respect to wages, there was great variation from factory to factory and from State to State. There were also arbitrary deductions from the wages. To remedy the situation, the Payment of

Wages Act of 1936 provided for regular and prompt payment of wages and prevented arbitrary deduction from wages.

Thus, in the pre-Independence era, because of public opi-nion among the people at large as well as among the British and Indian administrators, a series of acts were promulgated to bring about a change in the social conditions with respect to marriage, the position of women, juvenile delinquency, beggary, child labour and women labour, and the condition of labour in general.

Development of Legal System

The Constitution of India provides for equality of status and the principle of social, economic and political justice to all citizens irrespective of caste, creed, sex, etc. In fact, this is put as an Article in the fundamental rights which are justiciable. Untouchability was abolished by Article 17 and Article 24 asserts that no child below 14 is to be employed in any factory. The directive principles of state policy have provided for legislation on various social matters. Thus, after 1950, it has been the policy of the government to bring legislation in line with the fundamental rights enunciated in the constitution. As a consequence of this, there has been considerable social legislation since independence.

The Hindu Marriage Act of 1955 abolished all caste restrictions as a necessary requirement for a valid marriage. Thus, for the first time the Hindus of all castes have the same rights with respect to marriage; intercaste marriages are now valid. Secondly, by not prescribing any specific form of ceremony for the solemni-zation of a marriage; this Act, while giving authority to the various customs prevailing in various groups, also provides for a secular outlook with respect to marriage and enables the registration of marriage. Thirdly, this Act enforces monogamy and thus brings an equality between the two sexes. It also provides for judicial separation and divorce or dissolution of marriage, so that the rights of men and women are the same. Finally, this Act defines the term "Hindu" in the widest possible manner to include the ancient protestant groups like the Buddhists, the Jains, the medieval protestant groups like the Veera Saivas and the Sikhs and the modern protestant groups like Brahmosamajists and Aryasamajists; it also includes the Harijans (the Scheduled Castes) and the Girijans (the Scheduled Tribes). Thus, for the first time, all these various groups are treated as Hindus. It only remains for the next step to be taken according to Article 44 of the directive principles of state policy, which enjoins the state to secure for all citizens a uniform civil code so that the people of other creeds like the Parsis, Muslims, Christians, Jews, and others could also come into operation of one secular marriage Act.

The Hindu Succession Act of 1956 confers for the first time absolute rights over the property possessed by a Hindu woman. Secondly, both the sons and daughters get the right of inheritance from the property of an intestate Hindu. Thus, this Act overcomes the prejudice against women getting the property of the father.

The Hindu Adoption and Maintenance Act, 1956, is also a significant departure regarding the status of women. It permits the adoption of a son or a daughter and makes adoption more a secular act than a religious one. Further, it makes the consent of the wife necessary. Finally, the widow has got the right to adopt.

Since a long time, many slates had passed legislation against dowry. The government passed the Dowry Phohibitions Act, 1961, making the giver as well as receiver of the dowry punishable. But this is another piece of social legislation which is absolutely ineffective. One sees hardly any change in the situation as a consequence of this Act. The social norm, in other words, has not been affected by this law, and the society follows the social norm rather than legal norm in this field.

The Children Act 1960 was passed to provide for the care, protection, maintenance, welfare, training, education and rehabilitation of neglected or delinquent children. The Minimum Wages Act 1948 was passed to provide for minimum rates of wages in certain employments.

The Family Courts Act was passed in 1984 to provide for the establishment of Family Courts with a view to promote conciliation and secure speedy settlement of disputes relating to marriage and family affairs. This Act provides for the parties to the dispute to plead their respective cases themselves and discourages the appearance of lawyers on behalf of the contesting parties. However, due to a variety of reasons including pressures from the various Bar Associations, Lawyers and Advocates are being permitted to appear on behalf of the contesting parties.

Another very significant Act is the Untouchability (Offence)

Act, 1955. This is in accordance with the Article 17 of the Constitution and it replaces all the State Laws in this regard which were passed earlier. This Act holds throughout the country. Offences against this Act are cognizable and compoundable. But, as we have seen earlier, the status of the Harijans in the villages has hardly improved because the upper castes continue to practise untouchability.

Even with respect to labour laws there has been marked change since independence because of the enunciation of the directive principles in the Constitution. The Factory Act of 1948, passed after independence, raises the minimum age of worker to 14 and made provision for annual medical examination of the workers between 14 and 18. The Motor Transport Workers Act of 1961 provides for eight hours of work per day and 48 hours per week.

The Employment Exchange Act of 1959 provides for registration of the unemployed people and for training programmes. Thus, the state has taken upon itself the responsibility of helping the unemployed individuals to get jobs; but with the increase in population, this Act is also of hardly any significance. Each Five-Year Plan sees a larger backlog of the unemployed people.

The Employees State Insurance Act 1948 was passed to provide for certain benefits to employees in case of sickness, maternity and employment injury and to make provisions for certain other related matters. This was followed by the Employees Provident Funds and Miscellaneous Provisions Act of 1952 to provide for the institution of Provident Funds including Family Pension Fund and Deposit Link Insurance Fund for employees working in factories and other establishments. Under this enactment, the Employees Provident Fund Scheme and the Employees Family Pension Scheme was introduced in 1971. The Deposit Link Insurance Scheme was introduced in 1976. To further improve the lot of labour employed in different industries, Parliament enacted a series of Social Welfare Legislations like the Bidi and Cigar Workers (Condition of Employment Act 1966). This Act provides for the welfare of the workers in the Bidi and Cigar establishments and regulates the conditions of their work and employment. Contract Labour (Regulation and Abolition) Act 1970 was passed to regulate the employment of contract labour in certain establishments and to provide for its abolition in certain circumstances. The Bonded Labour System (Abolition Act) was passed in 1976 to provide for the abolition of the bonded labour system with a view to preventing the economic and physical exploitation of the weaker sections of the people.

In order to help cine-workers, the Cine-workers Welfare Cess Act and the Cine-workers Welfare Fund Act was passed in 1981. These enactments provide for the levy and collection of cess on feature films for the financing of activities to promote the welfare of certain cine-workers. Similarly, the cine-workers and Cinema Theatre Workers (Regulation of Employment) Act 1981 was passed to provide for the regulation of the condition of employ-ment of certain cine-workers and cinema theatre workers.

The above survey of social legislation in India before independence as well as after independence clearly shows the efforts of the state and the society to bring the legal norms in line with the existing social norms on the one hand and to improve the social norms on the basis of new legal norms on the other. In the former case as in social legislation regarding monogamy, etc., there is considerable effectiveness, but with respect to the latter, the law has hardly any social force, because the change in the legal norms which are far ahead of the social norms involves an educational task. Mere threat of punishment will not be effective. Such a situation produces what Festinger calls "forced compliance"; there will be a discrepancy between public behaviour and private belief. So long as behaviour involves forced complia-nce, there is no internalization of the new values and so there will be disobedience of the law. There must be effort by voluntary organizations which have a faith in the new law as, for example, the prohibition law or untouchability removal law, to convert forced compliance or even non-compliance into voluntary compliance.

Social legislation can be an effective means of social change only when the prevailing social norm is given a legal sanction. No legislation can ever bring about a change in social norms. This is because the process by which social norms arise is not formal; nor is it imposed from above and from outside. Social norms arise within the group and are implanted in the child in the process of socialization within the first five years of its life. By way of illustration, it can be shown that the 1955 Act regarding Hindu marriage has succeeded with respect to monogamy which was already a social norm; while the provisions regarding age of marriage has not been effective because the prevailing social norm is contrary to legislation.

Thus, social legislation can be effective only when it follows an existing social norm and formalises it; it cannot initiate a change in social norm and thus a change in social behaviour.

Thus, social change could never be brought about by unaided social legislation. Social legislation could become effective only when there is organized voluntary effort to help the people understand the new values embodied in the new law. Even more important is the task of the parents in every individual home to help the child to internalize the new legal norm as a social norm.

14

Conclusion

The quest for relevance has been pervasive in the social sciences from their very inception. These sciences originated with the emergence of a kind of societal self-awareness under which indifference by social scientists to social problems could not have been possible. It is not mere chance that long ago August Comte, who gave sociology its name, linked sociologists' roles to that of 'priests' for creating a new social order, and again late in the seventies, Alvin Gouldner is struck by the fact that most American sociologists entering this profession had at some stage thought of taking to priestly calling. This recurrent pull towards acting as saviours of men in society undergoing industrial transformation is one manifestation of the quest for relevance. No doubt, its form and context vary with the nature of each social science, and its historicity.

A significant feature of social sciences is their intrinsic double dialectics: first, epistemological, as a social scientist endeavours to formulate (use) categories to replicate societal realities of which he himself is a part; and secondly, ethical, where a social scientist bears responsibility towards society for the uses of his knowledge which is a social product, a historical product, where the tensions of contemporaneity bear heavily upon him. The meaning of relevance in the social sciences is deeply entangled with and arises out of this double dialectics.

At the first level, relevance is defined cognitively. It refers to formulation of concepts and methods in social sciences which satisfy the principles of *adequacy* and *validity* in the understanding or explanation of social reality. Questions asked here are: To what extent are the social science concepts and methods or their operationalization adequate or valid? Is there a universal social science language equally applicable to societies and cultures historically distinct? Does the advocacy for a universal model in a social science contain ideological packages to perpetuate dependency relationship between the social sciences in the developed 'metropolitan' nations and the developing nations of the 'periphery'? It is obvious how matters apparently conceptual or theoretical in nature tend also to involve ideological and politico-economic issues defining the scope of relevance. Never-theless, the primacy of the context of relevance at this level is grounded in the nature of *explanation* or *understanding* of the social reality that is offered by social sciences.

At the second level, the notion of relevance is posited in the social responsibility of the social scientist. Caught as he is in the tensions of contemporaneity of which he is a social product, and sharp as is his self-consciousness to transcend the bondages of partisan loyalties, which he attempts to overcome through an epistemological leap towards objectivity in his craft, he seeks a way out of this dilemma in the notion of policy *science*. Most widely acknowledged meaning of relevance in the social sciences is associated with this connotation. Policy science implies an interdisciplinary social approach to resolve social problems. At the level of individual social sciences, however, it involves policy researches. In defining the relevance of social sciences in this context several questions arise: Are the values which define the goals of social engineering or social policy consensual or partisan? What is the nature of the relationship between the social scientists who conduct policy researches and the state apparatuses or the agencies, which sponsor such researches? Is this relationship autonomous, advisory or dependent? How consensual is the character of the ruling elites of the state apparatus itself which defines the goals of policy planning?

A distinction should be drawn between the role of the social scientist as policy planner working within the framework of the ideology of the ruling elite, and his role as 'organic intellectual' as postulated by Gramsci where he aims at basic transformation in the entire social system, including the elite structure of the society. Relevance is defined here not as an elite-sponsored programme for social construction which tends merely to replicate the patterns of domination (Bottomore, 1971: 51). It implies attempts to expose the truly 'partisan' character of the projects of social reform or developments (based on class, ethnicity and nationality, etc.) which mark the constraints of the structure of inequalities behind a facade of surface consensuality.

Indeed, several models of relevance can be formulated depending upon the manner in which the ideological bases of social planning are defined. A study of the models of relevance in American sociology postulates five such types. These range from *'no net-effect model'*, which postulates societal processes to be so powerful as to be beyond manipulative control to *'direct and positive-effect model'* which assumes a degree of consensuality in social systems and social policies on the basis of which social scientists could attempt the betterment of man's life in society. In between are the positions of the *'special constituency'* models, where the relevance is defined with particular reference to the interests of (a) the *'proletariat'* (as in the Marxist sociology, (b) the *'un-co-opted'* categories as in the writings of C. Wright Mills (1956) and Gary Marx (1972), and (c) the *government officialdom'* (see Eule, 1978: 78-93). Evidently, neither the constituencies of the interest groups in whose favour relevance may be determined, nor the profession of the social sciences, which is concerned with both theoretical and applied potential of the sciences, offers a consensual perspective on the notion of relevance. The meaning of relevance under these circumstances tends to be structured in ideology.

Mysteries Solved

This brings us to the process of mystification in both the paradigmatic and ideological foundations of social science which plays a vital role in the understanding of the notion of relevance. This is so whether we locate the meaning of relevance within the theoretical structure of social sciences or whether we posit the same in the 'special constituencies'. Mystification is a process of rationalization of models of society or of ideology which either consciously or unconsciously encapsulate meanings or values to serve partisan interests. It is a historical product of the inherent structure of inequalities in society and the social scientist's place in it which contributes to his alienation from a consensual understanding of social reality.

All paradigms of social sciences, particularly of sociology, offer to construct a model of society. Each of these models abstracts from reality a certain notion of order which posits a quality of relationship among its parts based, depending upon the model, upon either truce or consensus, or conflict or contradiction in society which severally constitute the degree of mystification in the societal model, and define the meaning of relevance. The meaning of relevance is thus pre-structured in the paradigms of social science. Each model of society selectively reveals and hides elements of reality in the manner it constructs the structure of society. It is a logical requirement in the formulation of models of society on the known cannons of science or objectivity. However, in each attempt of this kind, the existential background, of which the social scientists are product, introduces value loads which determine the nature of inclusion and exclusion of parameters in the model (see Saberwal, 1979: 242). Thus, social sciences mystify reality as they attempt to demystify it. The dilemmas of mystification become acute when one counterpoises paradigms like functionalism and dialectics in sociology. The functionalist assumes a consensual nature of society through shared values by mechanisms of socialization, enculturation and institutionalization. The dialectical models (both Marxist and neo-Hegelian) treat these values as manifestations of *estrangement* of meanings and symbols from man's species-self through labour on which he has no command. To functionalists the value system of a society *reveals* the character of the society, its achievements and deficiencies which may help in identifying the character of relevance, whereas to Marxists, these values tend only to *mystify* the true nature of reality which is pregnant with crucial contradictions irreparable through tinkering by policy sciences. The notion of relevance assumes two far different connotations in the two models of society.

The problem of mystification in the models of sociology has been aptly summed up by Alain Touraine in his formulation:

> The sociologist does not study facts but documents. In order not to become the prisoner of a 'reality' that he believes himself to be looking in at from outside when

> he is in fact part of it, he needs to subject himself to an intellectual access that will lead him to the discovery, behind society's organization and discourse of its social relations, in other words of its conflicts and its domination, as well as what that domination keeps concealed in the shadows (1977:11).

There is a certain model of society in this formulation. For Touraine, society is "not just reproduction and adaptation; it is also creation and self-production". It has a "capacity to act on itself", a *historicity,* which creates its contradictions, e.g., its class relations and historical actions through social movements. This only illustrates how models of society might inhere a normative statement about the nature of society which in turn defines the models of relevance. This is how competing models of relevance of social sciences arise. Since each model is a product of historicity, of which the social scientist himself is a product, the notion of relevance also becomes a problem of sociology of knowledge (see Singh, 1976). For instance, the eurocentricity of most paradigms of social sciences is widely acknowledged (Gellner, 1969).

At the 'special constituency' level of the meaning of relevance, the dilemma of mystification is ideological, and it is much more clearly visible. All social science projects of social engineering do reflect the critical differences between the definition of the 'desirable' by the donor 'elite' and the 'recipient' masses of the society. Mystification of relevance in these contexts of social policy lies not only in the partisan manner in which the objectives of social well-being are formulated, but also in the manner in which the strategy for its realization is outlined as measures of reform. The ruling elite does, under certain constraints, such as popular protest which threatens its position, yield ground by enacting policy measures for distributive justice. The manner, however, in which such legislations are drafted and the mechanisms through which their objectives will be ensured, leave deliberated loopholes to render them ineffective for fuller implementation. Such gaps between profession and policy level execution are concrete illustrations of mystification in models of relevance. The terms like 'development', 'modernization' and 'social justice', which evoke various models of relevance, also inhere acts of mystification.

In Search of Meaningfulness

The context of relevance in the Indian social science has been deeply influenced by the historical situation in which it has developed: colonialism and movement for independence are two interlinked historical experiences which define both the theoretical orientations and policy relevance of Indian social science. We attempt to analyze these factors at the levels of (a) theoretical and conceptual models of Indian social science, (b) social science researches and social policy in India, and (c) the emerging models of relevance in the Indian social sciences, with particular reference to sociology. The significance of mystification in the process of formulation of social science paradigms and welfare policies would be examined at all the three levels mentioned above. It may also be useful to raise some questions regarding the sociological character of social science profession in India as it may offer useful insights to related issue of ideology, theory and practice of Indian social science.

The history of social sciences in India is embedded in the colonial and post-colonial contacts with the west, particularly with Britain. From the late 19th century to the first quarter of the 20th century, the tradition of humanistic rationalism of the British universities spurred on a series of attempts towards rationalization of these powerful ideas in terms of the Indian intellectual tradition. More than universities, the social reformers of the 19th century made solid contribution to this process. The question of relevance was one of the most important objectives in these debates. Question was how to imbibe the western philosophical and social scientific constructs into the traditional Indian constructs and in what measure. The Brahmo Samaj in Calcutta, the Prarthana Samaj in Bombay and the Veda Samaj in Madras were reform movements which sponsored vigorous drives for selective assimilation of the ethical and philosophical presuppositions of the western social sciences and humanities into the Indian intellectual stream. This assimilation was itself considered to be a measure of relevance at this time. The project for relevance was westernization.

The kind of response by Indian intellectuals was conditioned by the acceptance of the historical superiority of the western cultural models reinforced by western colonial conquests and their industrial and technological progress, and its rationalistic ideology of that time. At this stage of the evaluation of the east-west relationship, the facts of colonial expropriation and exploitation were secondary. This did, however, surface in Indian social science during the first and the second quarters of the 20th century with rising nationalism, when ideological differentiation among the Marxists, the rational-positivist and nationalist orientations in the social sciences began to sharpen. Attempts to analyze the naught of caste, and the economic institutions, the use of a Marxist framework to analyze the eastern social structure and its intellectual traditions, and the treatment of the phenomena of capitalism and colonialism in India created new cultural self-awareness. This development in India also echoed the contradictions within the European social sciences due to the challenges from Marxism and Freudianism. Historically, the aftermath of the First World War and the emergence of a socialist society in the USSR also spurred this orientation.

The theoretical orientations of early 20th century social sciences were products more of scholar politicians and literatures than of the university academics whose works continued to mirror the paradigms of the western social sciences. The challenges to this orientation began to emerge from outside the university system in the nationalist movement led by Gandhi. His emphasis on to 'swadeshi' was not only an economic challenge to the British colonialism but also a cultural response to encounter the tide of westernization. Attention may specially be drawn to a chain of educational institutions that were started under this inspiration on indigenous models. No systematic study of the content of curricula or the nature of social science paradigms taught in these institutions has been made from the viewpoint of inherent models of relevance. It would, however, appear that the quest for alternative paradigms of Indian social science did not succeed in this experiment as well.

These developments, nevertheless, had an impact on the university-level teaching and research in social sciences. Comparative institutional frameworks increased in social science teaching. The awareness of the impact of colonialism on the rise of Indian business classes, the nature of the relationship between Indian and European capitalism and the consequent processes of de-industrialization and de-urbanization in India began to emerge as the foci of teaching and research. Sociology was just beginning to establish itself as a university-level discipline during this period. Its substantive and intellectual concerns were deeply influenced by the national debates on the merits and demerits of western interpretation of the Indian society. The evolutionary social science approaches of the 19th century social anthropologists, and their formulation on the religion, caste and tribes in India, constituted the foci of such debate. The search for relevance in the paradigms of Indian social science at this stage was more meta-theoretical than theoretical. Questions were addressed more to the nature of presuppositions implicit in western theoretical treatment of Indian social realities, rather than to the theoretical models themselves.

The intellectual context of the social sciences underwent a basic change following independence. The reference model now shifted from the U.K. to U.S.A., which had emerged as the most dominant international power. This contact also coincided with the rapid erosion of colonialism in most part of the world. But, the fear of neo-colonialism and imperialism in the mind of the Third World social scientists remained equally sharp. The socialist revolution in China added a new dimension to this process. Academic colonialism and 'dependency' in the relationship between the social science of the developed capitalist nations and the nations of the Third World now began to be examined.

In the Indian social sciences, particularly sociology, a two-way development took place: first, there was a substantial increase in the policy-oriented social research with the help of tools and methods of American sociology; and secondly, there was unprecedented growth in an empirical study of social structures in the rural, urban and tribal settings using a functional theoretical approach. There was also much research conducted on Indian societal reality directly by American sociologists, political scientists and agricultural economists. The model of society implicit in the paradigms of these sociological studies was consensual and plural. At this stage, the questions were not raised as to how far in the historical and cultural settings of the Indian society these models were relevant for its understanding. The doubts about the American intentions in studying Indian society were expressed by a group of social scientists led by D.N. Majumdar and D.P Mukherji at the Lucknow University, in the early fifties. They highlighted the neo-colonialist design of American sociologists and social anthropologists in these studies and also challenged the relevance of the paradigms used in these studies as such.

Soon, however, a more systematic effort questioning the relevance of some Euro-American models in sociology for' the study of Indian society followed. 'Towards the end of the fifties D.P. Mukherji wrote extensively on the need to formulate basic concepts in Indian social sciences and sociology commensurate with its distinctive history and tradition. Radhakamal Mukherjee offered a model of studying society in general from a neo-dialectical approach in which one finds a mixture of the notion of Hegelian and Vedantic dialectics. This was followed by a seminar of Indian sociologists in the sixties on the possibility of an Indian model of sociology. This seminar was the Indian sociologists' response to issues raised by Dumont and Pocock in their essays in *Contri-butions to Indian Sociology.* These debates generated substantial reflective writings in the sixties on the possibility of conceptual and theoretical specificity in Indian sociology, and the relevance of the western sociological paradigms for understanding the Indian sociological reality (see Unnithan, et al, 1967; Singh, 1979). This concern was coupled with the awareness of the politico-economic dimension of the social science relationship between the developed and the developing nations and its distorting effects in its theory and practice (see *Seminar,* No. 112: 1968).

The concern for conceptual specificity and relevance grew into the general ethos of social sciences in India during the seventies. It is reflected in the continued dialogue among social scientists during this period on the role and relevance of social sciences in India and the tensions in their development. The publication in 1976 of *Social Sciences and Social Realities: Role of Social Sciences in Contemporary India* (ed. S.C. Dube), which is a report of the seminar organized by the Indian Institute of Advanced Study, Simla, in collaboration with the ICSSR, explicates this concern. Ramakrishna Mukherjee analyzed the trends in Indian sociology in terms of theory and methodology, reviewing its past, its present and the emerging future orientations in his *Main Trends in Indian* Sociology (see Mukherjee, 1977) which offers critical insight into successive paradigms of sociology and their ideological interface. In this work, and more systematically in a later work, Mukherjee deals with the question of relevance from a formal methodological perspective (see, Mukherjee, 1979). Using an inductive inferential approach he postulates that the question, "what will it be?", can be answered for each value load of a social science model using 'inductive inferential' methods. He suggests a set of statistical techniques through which social science propositions could be tested and generated irrespective of the value premises involved. Mukherjee deals with the question of specificity of paradigm of sociology only at the level of concept formation and operationalization. Otherwise, his approach is nomological and based on statistical abstractions. He does not deal with the phenomenology of relevance as such.

The seventies mark a distinctive change in the concerns about theory and method in sociology. There is a shift away from the 'abstracted empiricism' of the fifties; there is more intense awareness of the need to explore the nature of structures and their processes using historically founded type-concepts and categories, which may vaguely resemble the Marxian, Weberian or functionalist traditions; the influence of neo-Marxist conceptual schemes is visible in many researches. But, the emerging strong impress is that of concern with history in the understanding of the process as within structure such as social mobility, modes of production and their social structures and social movements. Emphasis is more on the deeper understanding of structures, their symbolic significance and interlinkages using the native categories rather than the conceptual packages from abroad (see Jain, 1977; Singh, 1974; Dhanagare, 1977; Mukherjee, 1977; Saberwal, 1979a, 1979b). The attempt here is not to postulate master theories couched in abstract principles but to offer analytic understanding of concrete social structures and processes at significant points of historical conjuncture.

Simultaneously, further exposure of the limitations of the western models of social science for the developing countries is made through notions of academic colonialism, dependency (in transfer of social science technology) and ideology (see Chossudovsky, 1977; Forrester, 1974; Saberwal, 1979; Momin, 1972; Uberoi, 1968). These arguments assume new significance in the light of the rethinking in the western social sciences on the question of unity of paradigms. Functionalism, structuralism and Marxism are no longer treated as unified paradigms, but as synthetic theoretical schemes. This reinforces the plea for orientating concepts and methods in the social sciences to the specificity of the socio-cultural reality of each society concerned.

This concern is reflected in recent efforts made by Indian economists, sociologists, social workers, political scientists and psychologists through a series of UGC workshops to modernize the syllabi. The question of relevance has been analyzed in most workshop reports both at the paradigmatic and policy levels. The report on economics states: "Standard economics is supposed to explain the *modus operandi* of an idealized capitalist economy. The Indian economy being anything but that, the orthodox paradigms must perforce collapse." It concludes: "Most of the theoretical concepts evolved in the context of the developed industrial societies of the west are mechanically doled out to unsuspecting batches of students in this country. Not unnaturally we find these rarefied tools of analysis to be of little avail in comprehending their own situation" (1977). The reports on sociology and political science have also recognized the need for the indigenization of paradigms and have suggested that such attempts should proceed in phases keeping in view the unevenness in the development of these sciences in the country. Indirectly, these reports reflect the tensions that exist in social science today about the indigenization of their paradigms in order to render them relevant for the understanding of the Indian reality (see Singh, 1979).

The proposition that social science paradigms do not have a universal scientific (explanatory) relevance and should, therefore, increasingly disaggregate their structure in accordance with the historically or culturally specific experiences has, in the seventies, gained firm support in most social sciences at the international level too with the possible exception of economics. Here too it appears that the Indian experience is at variance. The 25th Anniversary Round Table of the International Social Science Association, which was devoted to an assessment of a quarter century of international social science (1952-1977), had several papers that highlighted the inadequacy of universal theoretical models or methods in social sciences and argued for the indigenization of social sciences (see Lousber, 1977). Reporting on the state of geography during this period Jones writes:

> Models in geography today have all been derived from our own western culture. We are in danger of accepting them as if they were universally applicable. Dealing with every city in the world as if it were Chicago is bad

> enough. A vast computerized exercise on the social areas on Calcutta does not mean very much to studies of urbanization; it must mean less to 600,000 who sleep in the streets of Calcutta at night. The trend in geography is towards the incorporation of value systems as essential elements in any organized use of space. *Relevance means not only relevance to the existing problems but relevance to the existing cultural system.* We are reminded of Pahl's statement that "geography is the product of a sub-culture" (italics added, see Jones, 1977).

The above establishes how the tensions both within the national and international professions of the social sciences is slowly converging to reinforce the disenchantment with the quest for universal paradigms. The context for such awareness is clearly the demand for relevance from the social sciences as tools for social explanation and understanding, and as aids to the develop-ment process in societies. The notion of relevance, however, has varied significance at the two levels despite the apparent convergence of meanings.

Matter for Study

The most widely acknowledged level of social science relevance relates to the contributions that researches make in the formulation and implementation of policies of social welfare and development in societies. India has a long history of policy-oriented research. The British colonial administration found it indispensable to understand the nature of the Indian society, its system of stratification and the rituals and customs of the Indian people in order to rule over them. Immense ethnographic researches on tribe, caste, language and culture, rituals and belief systems were conducted by the missionaries and administrators. Their objectives broadly were to aid Christianization and colonization though in varying degrees of enthusiasm. The census operations, land settlement and codifications of penal and civil laws were all policy oriented to perpetuating a social order for colonial expropriation of surpluses. The British rule contributed in an unprecedented measure to the institutional, organizational and administrative innovations, establishing the legitimacy of policy-oriented research. The 19th century utilitarian rationality and colonial urge to exploit resources provided a spur to this process. This phase of policy research offers a pure case of the linkages between the modes of power structure, its interests and policy researches.

Independence led to further rationalization and proliferation of policy research in India. Both in terms of institutional set-up and funding, there was expansion. Universities and colleges, government-funded autonomous research agencies, aided research institutes with governmental and private control and research organizations of the government attached to various ministries offer a variety of institutional apparatuses through which researches were sponsored. During the fifties, most sociological researches were conducted in policy relevant areas in the form of urban surveys, demographic studies, village studies and evaluation of community development schemes and panchayati raj systems, etc. Similar policy-related researches were also conducted in other social sciences, particularly economics and political science. Researches by professionals in the institutes and agencies contributed a large proportion of the total output.

In order to examine the relevance of these researches a few questions arise; these are of the value loads in terms of which relevance of policy research is determined, the relationship between the state, its ideology and its definition of relevance, the extent to which the ideology of the state is consensual or partisan. Added to these questions are the problems of the conceptual and theoretical structures of social sciences, and the extent to which the sciences are autonomous or dependent in the matter of the technology of research and personnel.

Moreover, the policy researches have a heterogeneous character. There are researches which simply generate data on a periodic basis for purposes of social and economic monitoring and planning. The census operations, the national sample surveys and other surveys and descriptive researches conducted by numerous public agencies belong to this category. The question of value load is not directly involved in such researches, except in the definition of concepts, their operationalization and the inclusion or exclusion of items from observation. A second category of policy researches is where the goals of social or economic development are normatively built into the objective of research, the problem is defined as to how to achieve such an objective most efficiently. Researches of this kind are in the very heartland of the dominant ideology defining relevance. The third type of policy research may be of an evaluative nature, a follow-up study of the consequences of measures of social engineering or planning. The urgent problems in such researches are not of ideology or sponsorship but of technology of research, its designing and operationalization. Finally, one may also include in policy researches studies which attempt to examine the value loads of social policy measures and their impact on society; such researches by implication also suggest alternative strategies of planning for development by exposing the contradictions inherent in the social forces which contribute to the various types of policy researches.

On a rough estimate it would appear that policy researches of the above three kinds in India have been in most cases conducted outside the university and college systems, mainly through public or private institutional facilities. There researches of the fourth kind, the 'critical' policy researches have originated more from the university systems. This pattern of orientation in research is logical, because the manner in which research is socially organized to a large extent conditions its orientation, cognitive boundaries and responsibility.

To our mind, the assessment of Myron Weiner in regard to the relatively inadequate role of the universities in policy researches (see Weiner, 1979: 1581) does not take into consideration the differentiated nature of the policy researches as such. His inventory of general attributes of policy researches, however, indirectly supports our thesis. Weiner finds that most policy researches in India are "not social science studies, but are intended to provide a data base for policy". Secondly, "a large number of the research studies, conducted in these institutions centre on individual development projects" and thirdly, "none of the studies (cited above) are comparative". These characteristics of policy researches, if true, put them in a very unenviable light. These also seriously damage the many assumptions with which Weiner argues his case for internationalization of policy researches in India.

Considering the types of policy researches in India it is not necessary to expect that all of them should be 'social science'.

Similarly, it is also not legitimate to characterize all varieties of basic researches as non-policy oriented researches, since the role of criticism, demystification and alternative modes of social construction of reality is helpful in correcting the premises on which policy researches are based. For instance, the class character of Indian society, especially the existential and structural conditions to which most poorer sections of our society are shackled, offers a more viable explanation of why several developmental measures do not appeal to them, and why to some others they are violently apathetic. A huge bulk of funds and efforts in policy researches in family planning and community development during the fifties and sixties went near-waste in the absence of the appreciation of such basic sociological phenomena.

Policy researches are grounded in the most varied pre-suppositions about the model of development in a society. At any time, this ideal is represented by its ruling elite. Depending upon the character of this elite, and of the state, the ideal of development may be placed on a continuum of *consensuality* and *partisanship*. The credibility of the policy researches depends upon the extent of consensus that the policy under consideration evokes. Given our socio-political reality, relevance in the short run can be determined only through the degree to which the objectives of developments as set by the ruling elite are promoted by sponsored policy researches. Within the framework of policy researches the scope for formulating them can be only technical, not ideological. An ideological appraisal of policy researches implies structural changes in the character of the ruling elite. It implies alternative models of relevance.

If we take sociology as a case in point, we find various models of relevance in policy researches. The very notion of the relevance of sociology has been rejected by A.K. Saran in his numerous writings. To him, sociology is a symptom of the sickness of modern industrial society, it is a false ideology which modern man restates as a substitute to the disintegrating traditional worldview. Saran has few followers in sociology but many from other disciplines like philosophy and divinity. In the fifties, the dominant model of relevance in sociology was policy research for the government-a tendency which in the sixties and seventies has declined in professional circles of sociologists in the universities. The relevance model now in vogue tends to be more in favour of what Rule calls the constituency of the 'proletariat' or of the 'un-coopted' strata. Diagnostic and analytic sociological studies now use either class or interest groups as the framework for understanding the contradictions in the Indian social structure. Emphasis on the study of social movements, agrarian structures, social inequality and power structure is the new direction of research implying alternative models of relevance.

An interesting feature of the emergence or co-existence of these models of relevance is that they have remained independent of the influence of the funding agencies like the UGC or government ministries. The ICSSR sponsored a number of national level research projects in the priority areas of national concern. These have been mainly in the nature of fact-finding studies rather than structural or comparative in perspective. These also reflected the interests of the concerned ministries of the government of the time. It would be doubtful if these researches have generated any significant sociological ideas or propositions which could form the basis for significant debate in sociology. It is noteworthy that sociological contributions which have evoked relatively more interest in the profession have come from individual research scholars working as one-man team with limited funds at their disposal rather than from expensive sponsored projects.

The points raised in this paper may be summed up as follows: The notion of relevance in social sciences is a product of double dialectics: (i) social sciences as epistemological systems, and (ii) as ideologies. Relevance at the epistemological levels directs our efforts towards examination of the validity of concepts and methods in terms of their universality, historicity and cultural specificity. Increasingly, social sciences are tending to articulate that most concepts and theories of social sciences are historically and culturally grounded. Hence, one measure of relevance for Indian social science should be to search for autonomy and indigenization of paradigms and methods of social enquiry.

The second level of relevance, ideological, is associated with policy researches. Policies of social welfare and social development are based on normative projects of the ruling elite. These projects have hidden in their normative structure a model of society which is seldom made fully explicit to the people at large. This is true for all ideological systems. This is implicit in the existential teleology of functionalism as well as the historical teleology of Marxism. Its realization is a painful experience for those social scientists who are neither mystagogues or ideologues. To determine social scientist's responsibility in terms of relevance at this level is difficult indeed. He is apt to play the role of supporter of a ruling elite merely as a technician to oil the wheel of the state apparatus. Short of this, he may play the role of a critic of the dominant ideology by demystifying it, by objective and critical analysis of the structure of social reality and its processes.

The quest for relevance in the Indian social sciences has been mounting at both levels mentioned above, i.e., epistemo-logical and ideological. Within the domain of each social science, the awareness for autonomy and indigenization of concepts, paradigms and methods has increased. The social sciences have not arrived at any definitive solution of this problem on their agenda except through increasing use of the native categories and comparative Indian data for the understanding of the historicity of social processes. The attempt is bound to gain momentum with time.

The nature of policy researches in India is not uniform. These range from mere data-generating activities to preparation of cultural and social profiles of tribes and communities. The challenges that social sciences face in the context of the issue of relevance, therefore, do not equally apply to all types of policy researches. In most policy researches in India, the relevance signifies the attempt to use most objective and valid methods and concepts, commensurate with the specificity of the concerned social phenomena. The model of society implicit in any notion of social development does not operate here as a significant frame of reference. The problem of relevance in such researches is technical and operational. The challenges of indigenization of social science research at this level are in terms of devising appropriate categories and methods. The policy researches, where the objective is formulated in terms of a specific developmental target, are also those where a normative model is *ipso facto* implicit. To maintain relevance in researches of this kind, the quest for historical and cultural specificity of social realities should be combined with rationalization of the technology of research. Sociologist's role as social critic may not always be relevant in researches of this type. However, social sciences as social criticism, or as instruments of demystification also belong to the domain of relevance in a more fundamental sense. But their relevance at this level is caught up in the whirlpool of power structure to which the social scientist is not always a 'marginal'. He is a social and, a historical product, and his existentiality enters into the notion of relevance he postulates as a critic of society. Logically, social science as social criticism inheres a transcendence from such historicity defining the limits of relevance. But, the limits of this transcendence are also set by the historical nature of the social forces, of which the social scientist is a product. All social sciences have a truly historical character.

Bibliography

Aggarwal, Pratap C.: *Caste, Religion and Power: An Indian Case Study,* Shri Ram Centre for Industrial Relations, New Delhi, 1971.

Ahmed, I.: *Castes and Social Stratification among Muslims in India,* Manohar Pub. Delhi, 1978.

Bagchi, A.K.: *Europe and Indian Entrepreneurship in India,* OUP, London, 1970.

Bailey, F.G.: *Caste and Economic Frontier,* Oxford, 1884.

Balkrishna, R.: *Commercial Relations between India and England,* Madras, 1958.

Barnes,: *Social Thought from Lore to Science,* Dover Publications, Inc., New York, 1961.

Bell, D.: *The Coming of Post-industrial Society,* Heinneman Educational Books Ltd., London, 1974.

Berger, P. L.: and Luckmann, *The Social Construction of Reality,* Doubleday and Co., New York, 1966.

—*The Sacred Canopy,* Doubleday and Company, New York, 1969.

Berna, J.J.: 1960, *Industrial Entrepreneurship,* New York, 1960.

Beteille, A.: *Caste, Class and Power,* Barkeley, 1964.

Bettelheim, B.: *Dynamics of Prejudice: A Psychological and Sociological Study,* New York, 1950.

Bhatt, Anil: Caste, *Class and Politics: An Empirical Profile of Social Stratification* in *Modern India,* Manohar Book Service, New Delhi, 1975.

Bose, N.K.: *Culture and Society in India,* Bombay, 1967.

Buch, M.A.: *Rise and Growth of Indian Liberalism,* 1938.

Buchanan, D.H.: *The Development of Capitalist Enterprise in India,* New York, 1934.

Chopra, P.N.: *Social and Cultural History of India*, Sterling, 1979.

Chopra, Puri, Das: *A Social, Cultural and Economic History of India*, Macmillan, Delhi, 1974.

D'Souza, Alfred: *Women in Contemporary India*, Manohar Books Service, New Delhi, 1975.

Das, R.K.: *The Labour Movement in India*, Berlin, 1923.

Desai, I.T.: *Some Aspects of Family in Mahuva*, Asia Publishing House, Bombay, 1964.

Desai, N.: *Women's in Modern India*, Bombay, 1952.

Durkheim, E.: *The Division o f Labour in Society*, Macmillan Company, New York, 1933.

Dutt, N.K.: *Origin and Growth of Caste in India*, Calcutta, 1931.

Farquher J.N.: *Modern Religious Movement in India*, OUP, New Delhi, 1914.

Ghose, K.: *Agricultural Labourers in India*, Indian Pub., Calcutta, 1967.

Ghurye, G.S.: *Caste, Class in India*, Bombay, 1950.

Giri, V.V.: *Labour Problems in Indian Industries*, APH, Bombay, 1958.

Gough, Kathleen: *Class Developments in India*, McGill University Press, Montreal, 1975.

Hazlehurst, L.W.: *Entrepreneurship and Merchant Caste*, Duke University, City, 1966.

Heimsath, C.H.: *Indian Nationalism and Hindu Social Reform*, Princeton, 1964.

Homans, G.C.: *Social Behavior: Its Elementary Forms*, Harcourt, Brace and World, New York, 1961.

Hutton, J.H.: *Castes in India*, Oxford, 1961.

Imtiaz, A.: *Caste and Stratification among Muslim in India*, Monohar Book Service, Delhi, 2001.

Ishwaran, K.: *Tradition and Economy in Village India*, Allied Publishers, New Delhi, 1966.

Kapadia, K.M.: Marriage and Family in India, Bombay, 1958.

Karnik, V.B.: *Indian Trade Union*, Manaktalas, 1966.

Kothari, Rajni : *Caste in Indian Politics*, Orient Longman, Delhi, 1970.

Mannheim, Karl: *Man and Society,* Routledge and Kegan Paul Ltd., London, 1940.

Marriott, McKim: *Caste Ranking and Community Structures,* University of Chicago Press, Chicago, 1955.

Mead, G.: *Mind, Self and Society,* University of Chicago Press, Chicago, 1934.

Mehta, S.C.: *Caste in India*, New Delhi, 1965.

Merton, R.K.: *Social Theory and Social Structure,* The Free Press of Glencoe, 1968.

Mishra, B.B.: *The Indian Middle Class,* London, 1961.

O'Neill, John: *Sociology as a Skin Trade,* Harper and Row Publishers, New York, 1972.

Perkinson, C.N.: *The Evolution of Political Thought,* London, 1958.

Prasad, N.: *The Myth of Caste System*, Patna, 1957.

Revri, C.: *Indian Trade Union Movement*, Orient Longman, New Delhi, 1972.

Shah, A.M.: *The Household Dimension of the Family in India,* Orient Longman, New Delhi, 1973.

Sharma, S.R.: *Social Stratification and Change in India,* Manohar Publication, Delhi, 1989.

Singer, Milton: *Traditional India: Structure and Change*, Aldine Publishing Company, Chicago, 1968.

Singh, Karan, *Prophets of Indian Nationalism*, London, 1963.

Thapar, Romesh: *Tribe, Caste and Religion in India,* The Macmillan Company of India Ltd., New Delhi, 1977.

Thapar, Romila: *Past and Prejudice,* National Book Trust of India, Delhi, 1975.

Unnithan, T.K.N.: *Sociology for India,* Prentice-Hall of India, New Delhi, 1967.

Verba, S., and Ahmed, B.: *Caste, Race and Politics: A Comparative Study of India and the United States,* Sage Publications, Berkeley Hills, 1971.

Index

J

K

L

❑❑❑